Footprints
in Obscurity

FOOTPRINTS IN OBSCURITY

A LIVING STORY

PRAMUDITH D. RUPASINGHE

PARTRIDGE
A Penguin Random House Company

To order additional copies of this book, contact
Partridge India
000 800 10062 62
orders.india@partridgepublishing.com

www.partridgepublishing.com/india

CONTENTS

FOREWORD

My MAIDEN WRITING, THIS book is humbly dedicated to my father, the late Dhanapla Rupasinghe, who was the prime inspiration for my journey to Africa, and my dear mother, Irannganie Swarnalatha Perera, who encouraged me in every single fall of my life.

ACKNOWLEDGEMENTS

THIS BOOK IS THE final destination of a long journey of five years in Africa, supported by several wonderful human beings whom I'm surrounded by. Without them, this could have been just a dream. My beloved wife, Yuliia, who was my shadow till I finish this book, bearing and sharing the pressure and stress with me throughout the writing, being my helping hand for each stage, encouraging me, travelling with me, taking care of me in difficult times and currently doing the translation of this book into Russian; she deserves a greater part of this book. My dear mother, Irannganie Swarnalatha Perera, who demonstrated an enormous resilience in living all alone for the period of five years I was away from home and yet encouraging me constantly, whenever I fall during the lengthy and difficult time that I was away from home. My heartfelt gratitude and love to her more than just thanking. My dearest sister Praharshinie Rupasinghe, who is my partner in adventure since my childhood, supported me enormously, travelling with me especially in the southern part of Africa, to whom I'm grateful all the time. Ms Dominique-Eve Weil, my colleague, who served as the key for me to reach the continent of Africa, will always be remembered. My colleagues who provided me with information for my travels and who supported me in their countries, although it is hard to mention all the names, I'm thankful to all of them. I hereby convey my profound gratitude to all. Without the support and encouragement rendered to me from all of you, this would not have been a success.

INTRODUCTION

First, THIS BOOK TAKES the reader on a journey through the process of unlearning what one learns before having to experience something first-hand, breaking down the rock walls of prejudice, melting iron hard stereotypes that one would acquire from very childhood, how one would develop his own prejudices and stereotypes in one's own experience of individuals, societies, countries, and regions. A dynamic process of learning and unlearning enriches the life of one; probably the experience could be bitter but the learning is a wealth gained as a result of it.

Second, the conflicts of cultures imposed by cultural norms and dimensions influence one to judge others. What is bad and what is good for one would not be the same to another who is from another culture. Therefore, during the journey, a lot of relativism and comparisons were made from the standpoint of a Sri Lankan or most specifically from the culture in which he grew up, which could look more like an ethnocentric viewpoint to the rest of world. But it was not, as it has been used intentionally as the pre-existing viewpoint which is the 'raw' state against which the reader sees the transformation of the traveller, or the author, at the end of the book in the 'Journey of No Return', where the 'final product' of the story, 'footprints in obscurity', comprising two dozens of pages to unfold before the reader.

Third, the inspirations that the author has gotten from the 'free-time stories' of his father serve as the 'energy' that pushes him in the form of a 'dream' to determine when to take risks to live and research in abundance under high risk. The moral persuasion is the third point, that it is his unconscious obligation to his father to pay him back with unique real-life experiences of discovery following the paths of his stories. But the clarity of what and how to do it was a challenge that remained in 'obscurity' when the initial trip was being planned. The third chapter, 'Embracing Darkness', explains that it was a decision influenced by the urge of a 'dream' to walk into the perceived 'obscurity'. In the meantime, most of the stages, especially the trip to 'Uganda', 'Congo', and 'Sierra-Leone' were merely risky advances where he could have lost his life, which were 'footsteps in obscurity' in its real sense. In addition to everything mentioned above, the global perception, especially of those who live in other parts of world, on Africa is often associated with 'obscurity', which had not been neglected here but serves as an eye opener, not as a label. Finally, in terms of 'footprints of obscurity', in the context of this book's core interface for 'dreams' of 'childhood', it came into being, inspired by the 'free-time stories' to flow as 'dreams' that are 'real', unlike 'daydreams', which are seen in 'obscurity' and most often are 'realised' in 'obscurity' even though one has to steer with full consciousness.

Fourth, 'footprints in obscurity' does not have a face of merely a 'novel', not a fiction at all as the story is built on the author's real and first-hand experiences, a narration of an interconnected series of stories that are presented through true incidents and individuals despite the pseudonyms that are used to maintain the confidentiality of individuals who supported the story with information. The key element of the book is its simple language, which aims to offer clarity of the story at its maximum possibility, not only to native English speakers but also for whose mother tongue is not English. In brief, the style and the modality of the book are simple and nonfiction which is a human experience not a scientific study, that's where the reader would have a long and wide space for his or her opinions, to agree or to disagree, and to learn and to unlearn and have his or her own imaginary experience in the process of reading. Simultaneously, facts, mostly in liaise of certain events and individuals, are presented supplementary to the story not only to make it a leisure reading but also to add some educative aspects into it. Hence, 'footprints in obscurity' is an all-in-one type of writing which is pretty unconventional and unique.

Pushing the reader back and forth in the story, breaking the monotony of narration, sometimes changing the tone or the rhythm of the story, shifting from narration to presenting facts, or vice versa, the author makes diversity and enriches the experience of 'reading'. Use of easy-to-understand expressions and proverbs carefully picking subjects from different cultures, yet making them simple enough to be universally understood, 'footprints of obscurity' simply is an irresistible universal experience to the reader. The tone stored in words utilised maintains the vibration of emotions like a 'roller coaster', at a time intense fear, horror, or terror dominates the story, and the next moment, it is full of curiosity, then a transition to humour and calming sensations, the reader is allowed to experience a multitude of human feelings in one single story, which is quite endemic to 'footprints in obscurity'. Besides stimulating humanity not merely in the form of superficial sympathy, profound empathy is another element found in the book.

Then, three core beliefs dominate throughout the reading, 'Endurance' in terms of making one's 'dream' a reality, which is the first core belief that runs in the theme. 'Negatives' are the stepping stones for 'Positive' change, and 'Negatives' should be discussed and be brought to the surface to see the 'Positives' hidden underneath the 'Negatives', which are linked to the surface story of the book, and the reader is persuaded to use his/her 'critical thinking' to discover the 'Positives' which are latent. The third and final belief is a realisation at the very end of the author's stay in Sub-Saharan Africa and his travelling in all regions of the continent that 'inevitable transformation' that one would be subjected to through one's veritable experience, which is more individual and unique than collective or generic, which is the final product of conscious or unconscious 'learning' and 'unlearning'.

Reasonable effort has been taken in the book for highlighting the pit-holes, gaps, and challenges at the level of attitudes, lifestyle, and governance in Africa, although a sounding loud 'Negative' aimed at

'Positive' reflection (the logic of the author to first see the 'Negativity', 'Obscure side' of the continent to pave the way forward to the 'Positivity' of the story which is not found in pages but in the mind of the reader) gives some reality-based clues to novices who are inspired to work in Africa. However, the book does not cover every country in detail, but in a nutshell, key areas from North to South, East to West, have been touched, making the story a 'holistic experience' in Africa.

Finally, a boy, who was longing to discover the imaginary world he dreamt of while listening to his father's 'free-time stories', reaches the final destination of his childhood dreams, breaking frontiers and jumping over diverse hurdles, and makes it his own primary experience which he presents in its 'raw form' to the world. 'A dream comes true' demands a lot of 'tolerance' and 'effort', and along the path, there are a lot of 'snares', 'traps', and 'challenges' which often appear superior to one's 'courage' and 'coping', but 'mindfulness' and 'endurance' would suffice to defy them all and see the 'dream' realised. The final realisation is that when turned back, there is a rich life that has been lived along the way full of extraordinary experiences accumulated which stand like a line of candles, along the way to the future, giving light at each footstep that one takes. One has not to follow the 'footprints in obscurity' anymore, as the experience of walking in 'obscurity' has already lighted the pathway for the future. One needs to see the darkness of 'obscurity' to see the light of one's life.

Yuliia Yurevich.

Chapter 01

FREE-TIME STORIES

H E USED TO PASS most of his evenings with my sister and me, telling us diverse stories, singing and joking with us. Most of his stories are un-erasable from my adult memory yet. It was such a dramatic way of presentation, rich in information, educative, and funny. It's like my mom's dried fish curry that used to be in our main meal for decades, which still remains the most favourite of mine.

My father was a teacher in political science with a great interest in history and economics. Beyond everything, he was a great lover of reading. He had an unquenchable passion for reading, whatever is at his reach, irrespective of content, and he had an unbelievable memory retention of almost every detail he had read. When he returns home from school, we used to wait like rabbits trying to sense the surrounding before coming out of their den. Waiting with curiosity blended with excitement, we prepare ourselves for the next episode that is going to be revealed.

'Pigmies are the smallest among human kind,' he says. We start to imagine the voyages of Gulliver—small human beings, not taller than an index finger, running here and there with their tiny legs like toothpicks.

'They live in a forest called Congo in Africa,' he adds, expanding our imaginary pictures to a cluster of antlike creatures which cover their prey, drag it along the terrain, and exterminate the prey like piranhas

With perceived fear that they would come to our home, I raise my voice, 'Do they eat human beings?'

'No dear, they do not.' Only then was I able to ask other 'curious boy's' questions.

'Do they wear Sarongs?'

His reply made me laugh and shy, but it was one of the few conversations where I realised that everyone is not the same in this world.

'They stay naked.'

'Naked? Their parents? They do not tell anything?' It was out of the curiosity of a childish mind. Today, it reminds me of child developmental psychology lessons I took in college. How irrational it is to my adult mind today whereas it was a major concern to my child mind that was modelled to perceive the good and the bad based on the norms in my society which seemed to me universal.

'No, they do not tell anything as everyone is naked.'

It was hard for me to understand that people wear different clothes or wear simply nothing. Also, nudity is a taboo in Sri Lankan society and it's one of the first things in which a child is trained in his or her not-to-do list in public. On top of everything, I was lost in a world where children see their parents naked. I battled with the newly discovered human story for days and days and I was unable to accept me in living in such a society where I see the nudity of my parents, siblings, and neighbours every single minute of my life. These little things in his stories stimulated my reflection enormously, though they looked like illusions to me.

'Idi-Amin, Ugandan President, was found keeping human brains in his freezer' and 'He used to eat those brains of his enemies.'

His new story on Ugandan dictator General Idi-Amin became a chronic diarrhoea. I was unable to digest that human flesh is eaten by human beings.

'Why he eats human flesh?' Dozens of human parts on a dining table surrounded by cannibals appeared in my imagination. By that time I had not seen an African, but I had heard that they were black. I started seeing delusions of dark huge man licking a leg bone and a servant lady takes

2

a plate full of leg bones away. I felt a sudden current of fear and horror running all over my body.

'It depends, some people eat for anger and some do as rituals and based on some beliefs.' He kept on describing all sorts of causes of cannibalism, exemplifying several incidents in history in different countries across Africa.

'Several times, missionaries who came to Africa ended up being eaten by cannibals, and in some parts of Africa, they eat their loved ones when they pass away. It's a gesture of respect,' he added, with a deep sigh.

I felt that he was kind of touched by what he said, but I was not mature enough to understand why he felt it. When I reflect on that moment of silence warmed by a deep sigh, I think, he was hit with an inward scene that he is being eaten by me in the name of love and respect. It's merely beyond imagination for an individual who has grown up in South Asia.

There were soldiers with African origin deployed in Sri Lanka in the 1940s during the Second World War by the British colonial reign and the local perception on Africans is immensely influenced by the nature of the interaction of those soldiers with the local population. Their sexual aggression and ruthlessness, curly hair, big eyes, and heavy lips, an image which is pretty much closer to the Sri Lankan image of the devil, seem to have concreted the perceptual-set that my father's generation carried when it comes to Africa, which confirmed what they had heard that those are man-eaters.

Though it was only a few seconds, the silence between us was full of happenings in me and I was profoundly preoccupied with thoughts about family members eating their loved ones.

I'm a 7-year-old child, sleeping in my room; my grandmother feels terribly hungry, she comes slowly with her walking stick, *tik* . . . *tik* . . . *tik* and *tik*, the sound comes closer. She peeps though the door curtain. . .

Oh no!

I wake up screaming, with sweat all over. My heart is palpitating like a fish jumped out of a water tank.

No . . . I cannot even think of this. . .

I was unable to forget that dream. It was real to me, and I became so vigilant about my sister who was just 4 years old. When a stranger passes by, I always used to hide her in the room. At some instances, I tried to console myself that what I dreamt was not real and I try to suppress my immediate thoughts like a child who tries to play with sponge balls in the rainy waters.

'They eat their loved ones when they passed. It's a gesture of respect,' echoed in my ears day and night for some time and faded away But what I went through persuaded me to read more and more on ritualistic cannibalism and cannibalism in general in later years, which made me suffer from an unquenchable thirst for me to go and meet their descendants.

Every little story has left something exciting, memorable to discover. The end of a story is the beginning of another. My curiosity rises to the peaks of Mount Everest, and the next moment, I'm plunged into pensiveness deep down to the bottom of Mariana followed by an infinite curiosity to discover what I heard, by my own. My mind was like an old dusty filing rack of a civil court where there are thousands files with barely visible and almost unreadable writing of unresolved cases and obviously not going end without a final verdict where justice seems buried with the accused and the accuser. I was charmed by my father's stories, and every evening, after my school homework, I sat with him for his exciting stories that take my imagination beyond the line of horizon to disappear into infinity, and finally, I find myself as a fisherman's wife waiting by the beach, leaning her heavy hips to the neighbour's anchored boat, with a pensiveness laden with incertitude and hope.

'During wars, they consume some body parts believing that the consumption of an enemy's body parts makes them bulletproof, more audacious and powerful.'

'Father . . . what body parts do they like?' My curious question was unanswered, and he put an end to the stories of cannibals, leaving me in a world where human beings eat human beings and I was not in a position either to realise why or justify why they do, yet my little mind was haunted day and night by cannibals who have black and curly hair.

The year 1994 opened another African chapter in my dream book. The genocide in Rwanda was widely discussed in public media and that was the first time I showed interest in watching news in the television. I didn't have a clue about Hutus and Tutsis, but those were the words constantly repeated in almost every channel.

'Who are the Hutus? And Tutsis?'

'They are tribes in the Great Lakes area.'

'Tribes?' I questioned.

'Yeah they are groups of people who share same culture, speak same language, and most probably possess the similar ancestry.'

Though he was not an anthropologist, his explanation was detailed and simple enough for me to understand that there were different groups of people though they are generally called Africans.

'Tribes' became the latest addition to my diction and I spontaneously asked him whether cannibals are also tribes.

'Yeah. . . Some tribes practice cannibalism . . . some do not; not everyone eats human flesh.'

Hmm. . . My visualisation of Africa is a beehive where there are lots of chambers allocated for different people. That was my first lesson on cultural diversity in Africa.

'Why do they fight?'

'Why does no one stop them killing?'

It is complicated. Each group has its own demands and on top of that there are other invisible hands. There was Western interest in the Great Lakes area, especially French and Belgians. He kept on explaining how the countries of Africa have been formed, dividing the tribes causing so many confusions that lead to conflicts.

No African country has been formed at the interest of the people of those countries. The frontiers have been marked by the colonial masters as most of the other things in Africa.

My mind was inundated with hundreds of question and I was almost lost without knowing where to start.

'Tribes are fighting in Rwanda but the West had their interest in it? What do you mean?' Actually, I asked myself, but without my knowledge, words jumped out from my mouth as a shaken champagne bottle, I was unable to resist my urge to know.

Being a teacher of political science, his knowledge in world politics was wide and profound. He had a keen interest in history and economics. Yet, he tried to explain to me the situation, bringing forth very vivid examples simplifying the whole story into a very interesting historical episode which heightened my passion to go to Africa, giving me another direction to go and work for the affected populations. But I did not know how I would get there. It was an illusion, like a taxi driver who dreams to go to Mars; although I wanted to, I did not have the means or at least the silhouette of a clear path. I asked my father how can one go there and work.

'You first need to know the linguistic diversity Africa; it's not a single country where everyone speaks same language. It's a continent which is geographically, demographically, ecologically, linguistically, and culturally diversified. You should not only have the linguistic skills but also have to have the right attitude and adaptability to work with them in difficult environmental conditions and cultures different from yours.'

'Some groups do not wear clothes as you do and nudity doesn't offend anyone; most of the animals we do not eat here in Sri Lanka are consumed in that part of world, and family structure is different from ours. But if you work there, you need to be ready to accept them as normal and respect them.' He kept on explaining, glancing at me beneath frames of his eyeglasses.

He paused, removed his glasses, and bent towards me . . . without breaking his eye contact.

'Remember!' He touched my shoulder gently. 'The most difficult yet most important thing is to accept a culture which is different or totally opposite from one's culture and look at it as normal.'

Though it was a detailed advice, I took it as another universe to discover. 'Cultures that are different from mine.' What might be different, why do they do things differently, and how do they become different? I battled with myself endlessly in my imaginary world where I try to navigate in the stories, trying to see myself with people who might not understand my culture and yet I'm trying to work towards their well-being. In my mind, I tried to answer the questions popping up. Might they see me as normal? Be willing to accept a stranger? How am I going to cope with their food? All of a sudden, a piece of unspecified roasted meat appeared in front of my eyes and dragged my mind into a live scene of a cannibal waiting greedily till the meal reaches him.

The next couple of weeks of my vacation were fully focused on finding out more and more details about Africa although I did not know where to start and from whom I would ask. By that time, the Internet was not a part of ordinary life in Sri Lanka. The only way of searching information was to go to a public or school library where there were not many resources about foreign countries, especially about Africa. I have heard there were old-book shops in Maliban street in Colombo where there were used books sold by tourists coming from different parts of the world. My speculation was that it might be possible to buy some books about Africa from those old-book sellers. I waited till my parents go to work and left home to catch the train to Colombo without a clue of where Maliban street is. Finding a place in such a messy and overcrowded city is a nightmare. The only reliable information I had was that the bookshops are found in two different locations in down town of Colombo called 'Fort' where most of little retail shops of all kind of commodities stand attached to one another covered by cloth ropes of unauthorized cloth sellers on the pedestrian corridors who try to sell their fake haute-couturiers, pulling whoever passes, by whatever part of their body, and would not allow you to leave their dens till you buy something which they call only-for-today deal. When you pull out your wallet, dozens of eagle eyes of pickpockets start counting the notes faster than electronic money counters do, and then on you are followed till your wallet is removed from the back pocket of your trouser, without even giving you a chance to feel that there is a human being behind you. Top of all harassment one encounters in this part of Earth, under the burning sun and smelling dirt, the roaring screams of bus conductors, who drag anyone into hacked Leland-Vikings irrespective of where the passenger wants to go, blend with the sharp metal noise of Hindi film songs coming out from lottery huts where most clients scratch to become billionaires overnight out of ten rupees they made selling sweat the whole day.

Lost in the fear of losing my 300 rupees collected from my father, inhaling heavy air full of dust and smoke under the burning sun, I was pushed along the human river flows towards downtown. 'Malcolm street' I get disconnected from the large crowd pushed along the pedestrian way and turned to the cross street seeking someone to help me to find out the old-book shops. I walked forward along the cross street passing the small boutique where mountains of shoes, clothes, and electronic items are stored even without leaving a space for the seller, pretending it was not my first time in this area so that I would not be a prey of opportunistic robbers. It was getting to twelve mid-day, if the clock at the central railway station was accurate. I noticed an old man with an office bag and probably was going home after this morning's shift of work. I approached him and ask where Maliban street is, where you find old-book shops. He looked at me as if I'm an alien, took his time, and asked me, 'You came alone?'

'Hmm, yeah, no, my friend,' I felt that adrenaline has started to circulate in my bloodstream already. I felt I'm trapped for a moment and tried to find my ways out of it.

'Well,' the old man, said, 'you go straight and take your left and then again left. When you walk around fifty metres, you will see a line of old-book shops.'

I was relieved partially by old man's, reply but an inexplicable feeling of incertitude mixed with fear remained.

'Thank you,' I turned my back to go.

'Hey! Child!' the old man's calling turned me back with a slight panic. 'Not many children like to read these days, unlike in my days.'

He smiled at empty skies. I walked away, heading to the old-book shop areas.

Little shops filled with old papers, magazines, and books appeared before me, while my head was filled with an endless joy as if I discovered a treasure. 'Hey, boy, I got what you search for,' a voice rose hidden behind a mountain of old magazines inside of a little boutique where I was pushed by my instinct.

'What you like? Indian or white ones?'

I was lost for a while, and the man said, 'I have got Sri Lankan, too,' before I realize what he was referring to. It is not a secret that prohibited pornography magazines are sold to school children by old-book sellers.

'No no, I was searching for some books about Africa,' my reply diverted the conversation into another direction. The seller kept looking at me for a few seconds as if he was astonished by the area of interest and said, 'I have few books lying in the boxes that I brought in when I started the shop and no one wanted to buy those. It will take some time to find them out.'

He looked at me again as if he wanted to see whether I did still have the interest.

'It is alright, I will help you to take them out.'

I followed him to his storage along a corridor which is not more than two feet wide in thick darkness, and I started feeling suffocated with air full of dust and the smell of fungus. With the help of a torch, we pulled out a box covered with a thick layer of dust and cobwebs that gives an impression that the box might have been there for a couple of decades. Covering my nose with the T-shirt I was wearing, I started to help the seller pull the books out of the box, and it was another work of wiping the books to see what is written on the cover page. After a dirty dusty work of almost thirty minutes, I was able to find out one book called *States of Africa* among all the discarded papers and magazines rested in peace for decades in the dusty darkness.

'How much you need for this?'

After a moment of profound pensiveness, the seller said '300 rupees at least' without giving me eye contact.

I knew that it was always the higher price for the first time and I had to bargain.

'Give me your last price!'

I acted as if I know the area very well.

'Give me 250 rupees.' His price was still high, knowing that I need the book

'No' I objected and turned back pretending that I'm going to leave without buying the book.

'Okay, what is your offer?'

The moment I was waiting for came. Spontaneously I said '150 rupees'.

His face was apparently not showing a single mark of contentment but I knew it was still a good price for him and a win-win deal. Yet, his gestures showed his acceptance. I started wiping the book with a piece of cloth and put it in a brown paper bag. I paid the money and left the shop with full of joy and sense of accomplishment. It was a day of achievement, a ray of light to the path of darkness; I ran towards the central bus station of Colombo and stopped near a bus going to my town 'Gampaha'. I got into a bus, sat on a single seat so that I would not be interrupted by anyone, and started reading impatiently. That was the day I learnt that the continent of Africa is composed of more than fifty countries and I was able to familiarise myself with the names of some countries that I was able to recollect, came across in the stories of my father.

I came home late in the evening. When I entered home, I saw my father on his favourite teak chair with an evening newspaper in his hand. He used to read left wing newspapers as most of the other political science teachers and Sri Lanka Freedom Party activists. As there was no television in our home that time, it was his only source of information and he single-handedly loved to believe what is in them and he was preparing himself to endless arguments with his colleagues, on the following day, on current political issues. As a child, I used to listen to those endless yet peaceful discussions that echoed in the staff room of his school during tea break.

'Here it is. I found a book.'

My victorious voice was bit strange for him and he looked at me over the newspaper with astonishment, maybe because he had never seen me reading or buying books before.

'Let me see.'

I found his gestures were a bit indifferent and rigid, though it was not his most usual way of interaction with us, as if he was unable to believe what I said. Now, I can understand: it is natural as he never knew I was interested in discovering Africa to an extent that I had bought a book and was going to read, which was quite unnatural and beyond imagination of his son who cut classes and always became the centre of blame in the classroom, and he considered me as an insult to his career as a teacher. I remember once he told me that the only path I might find my living one day is becoming a garage worker, which is considered a low-class job in local context.

He went through the table of contents, and I heard he was telling 'Interesting,' then he looked at me in the eyes.

'What made you to chase after a book like this? Guess this is too heavy for you.'

I didn't reply. I took the book and ran to my room, telling myself that the era of bibliographical discovery of my dream continent is about to commence. Though the book was quite old and did not contain the most updated data, it gave me a general idea of the continent, which was detailed enough for me to clarify and understand most of the black spots I had in my imagination. I read about the slave trade in Africa for the first time; names of countries that I have never heard before such as Togo, Upper Volta, Benin, Gambia; kingdoms such as Ashanti; and about the gates of no return along the coasts of West Africa. I visualised, black people with curly hair, nude, manacled and chained, carried by the white colonial masters, dressed in prestigious outfits though the gates of no return to somewhere leading to nowhere beyond the horizons in the Atlantic.

The Great Ashanti Kingdom, Mali Empire, and Nubians in sooth were in an infinite combat in my inner self, with a perceptual set of South Asian kings and queens, such as Sajahan and Ashoka, well dressed in majestic royal attires, with their Annthappura (*pool of queens as most of the kings of South Asia were polygamous*) in sophisticated palaces equipped with traditional spas and pools. But I felt that there is a difficulty in connecting my imagination with what I was reading, which I identify as lack of cultural competency. It was a quasi-experience of getting lost in the diversity of man kind. I was trying to get away from my perceptual set as a little beetle caught in a cobweb, to understand what I read. The complexity of the content and context transformed me to a continuous reader of various subjects on Africa ranging from lifestyle to politics. At the end of each reading, I went to my farther and briefed the stories to him, which he listened to with so much attention and interest. Simultaneously, I clarify the obscure areas of my reading with him and he was able to simplify those for me to understand better.

My visits to the old-book shops became more frequent and my pocket money was almost spent on old books on different themes on Africa. Sometimes I skipped my snacks in school and saved money for my books. Every Friday afternoon, I used to cut my school sessions and ran to railway station to get in to the slow train to Colombo by 9.00 a.m. so that I'm able to come back unnoticed. But few times I was caught by the teachers, and they informed my father. One time, our section chief, Mr Dayaranjith, who was an unsympathetic fellow and a friend of my father, had seen me jumping out of the school wall and strongly insisted my father to get me out of the school as I was a useless student and undisciplined. That day, my father returned home with a very frustrated mood and asked me what happened in school. He always demonstrated trust, and even though he had enough reasons to believe what he heard from my section chief, he posed me an open question, giving me enough space to express myself, which I always loved and sometimes misused by taking advantage. I didn't deny that I left school early, but I told him I fell in the school toilets and returned home as all my clothes were dirty. I used to play cricket every morning with my friends, and I do not remember a day I returned home with clean uniform. I showed him the uniform which was already in the basin, soaked with water, still brown and muddy. 'Well,' he paused what he was going to say and left the room. I know for sure he was not convinced but I made sure that I slow down my activities for a while. However, I had accumulated enough literature for many months and most of my afternoons were spent referring the old papers with wonders of the continent of my dreams. Every page I read revealed new horizons to discover, beyond infinity, beyond my imagination, and I did not know from where and how to start as it always appeared endless.

Over the course of a few years, I had collected a considerable number of old *Geo-Magazine* and *National Geographic* magazines which provided me with some knowledge in the biological, ecological, and geographical diversity of Africa. With those old collections, I discovered great savannas like Masai Mara and Serengeti, Kruger; deserts such as Sahara, Kalahari, and Namib; mountains like Mt Kilimanjaro and Drakensberg; and great rivers such as Niger and Nile. The photos of iconic places facilitated me to have a panoramic imaginary view of Africa in diverse aspects that added real tropical colours to my dreams. Besides the literature I chased and hunted, I discovered another source of information. 'Discovery Channel', although I'm not a TV lover, I used to watch National Geographic Documentaries and programs of Discovery Channel on Wild Africa with an enormous enthusiasm. I imagined myself wandering in great savannas and catching the games of wild animals to my naked eye, seeing cheetahs sprinting behind escaping springboks, herd of lionesses trapping and killing a wild buffalo which doesn't want an easy death, ruthless hyenas enjoying an easy prey attacking an already wounded wildebeest, hungry vultures haunting the skies till the hyenas leave the prey and to clean up the hunting ground, and giraffe heads appearing among the high acacia trees as if there are radar centres in the wild to monitor the games. Heavy white Rhinos waddle across the savannah with their fleshy kids just like rolling rocks, a disturbed kudu is running aimlessly over the pale grass burnt by hot sun, a herd of elephants play in waters, and a group of baboons enjoy the seasonal fruits. As I have heard that dreams contribute immensely to one's directions in life, my drive to explore Africa grew like a giant shadow behind me, following me everywhere and every moment irrespective of what I was doing, what was my mood, or with whom I was.

My endless drive to go to Africa, in any means, one day slowly but steadily changed my educational path as well as professional path later on. I do not remember a time of my life, or a moment, I gave up my African dream. My first pragmatic initiative was taken in 1996 when I had the autonomy to decide upon my Advanced Level Subject Stream. I chose French and English as subjects along with Political Science and History as I have read about 'Scramble for Africa' and in most of the states either French or English is used as official languages, as a result of the division of continent between French and English colonial powers despite a few areas occupied by Portuguese, Dutch, and Italians and the northern areas where Arabic is spoken. As an ant that collects food to survive in the rainy season, I went on hunting necessary skills and knowledge to carve the way towards the realisation of my dream and to survive within it.

My father was known as a very good teacher in Political Science and he used to give tuition to the students in our home. I have been hearing his lectures since the day I know, and when I was about 11 years old, I had already learnt most of the lessons of advanced level curriculum in Political Science. When I selected Political Science as a subject, I almost had nothing to learn new but to refine and defragment what I already have accumulated abruptly over decades. He not only had me a dream to pursue but also provided a means to achieve it, but all that remained in the latent part of myself and I didn't realize it that time. I was lost in a dream as a bilingual professional in political affairs or diplomacy travelling in different states of Africa, discovering the continent and people in it. This visualisation reigned every single second of my life and it became my sole motivation to reboot myself whenever I felt that I was following a dream that would never come true.

Days, months, and years passed by, life was under the constant influence of nature, and it had been changing as it was meant, I didn't give up my attempts and efforts. In 2004, the month of May, I was undergoing an examination in the university as another step taken ahead towards my African Dream, my father was hospitalised on Monday 24 May 2004, suffering from flu and asthma. As we never expected, though the reality of life is mere uncertainty, he left us in the morning of Thursday, 27 May 2004, leaving a key role to me, being the only male member of the family whose mother was already an aging person and sister was still a student. Then life started mocking at me; the weight of responsibilities, day-to-day hardships added to the grieving I went through because of the sudden death of my father. I felt that all my dreams were fading away, lost in the clouds of dust and flew thousands of miles away in infinite skies, in thick darkness of moonless nights and killer clod in impenetrable poles. Nonetheless, dreams remained hibernated, covered by a thick layer of hopelessness and helplessness, like what alpine marmots do in harsh winters waiting for the maiden sunrays to penetrate the cold air bringing hope one day somehow. He who gave me the life, name, hope, direction, and a dream to pursue had closed his eyes for eternity, leaving me with a path to walk all alone in this name, but I'm left without hope and help yet with a dominant desire and a need along with a little determination brought by his free-time stories.

Chapter 02

MIDNIGHT SUN

It WAS DAWN OF Monday, 26 December 2004, seven months and one day after the death of my father. The sun was peeping through the cloudy horizon, bringing the usual light of the day to those who were sleeping tightly in post-Christmas and Poya holiday comfort, but an unknown yet the most destructive vague hit the coastal line of Sri Lanka, sending more than fifty thousand human lives in the hands of death, devouring almost every living thing through the jaws of the killer Diablo of waters. We didn't know what was that, it was 'sea flood' in our local terms and I have read in historical literature about the occurrence of such an incident 2500 years ago.

We sat before the television screens and watched news, which was already kind of depressive and scary. Death had reined the whole island, irrespective of age, gender, ethnicity, religion, class, cast, political affiliation, or any other differences or nuances. Thousands of people succumbed in the mass graves together leaving their loved ones, wealth gathered over decades, and egos behind. There was nothing but the mark of woe, death, destruction, and misery stretched till the horizon and the ocean had already dressed up in its innocent lambskin just a few minutes after the event as if nothing had happened, which reminded me the a character of a typical politician in Sri Lanka.

The tsunami left thousands of decomposing dead bodies among the debris as if there is no difference between a dead human being and a broken brick. Tens of thousands became widows and widowers in a few seconds. It robbed loving parents from their children, making them orphans on the dusk of same day. Hundreds of mothers and fathers were left without their loving kids who were with them a few minutes ago. It was a time like no other, when everyone felt the same, going through a process of grieving, leaving all the differences behind. Naturally, the enormity and the magnitude of the event and its impact on human life not only in Sri Lanka but also in all affected countries brought us to a point of realisation that death could come to you at any moment and it's part of life. I felt that my exposure to the impact of the tsunami mitigated the impact of the death of my father on me. It helped me in accepting my reactions that I felt were overwhelming and unique to me, as normal reactions to an abnormal event. Not only that even realising that death is an event that can be expected at any moment without prediction of its form or cause, the passing of my father was assimilated to my life as an event that belongs to the past, yet it transformed my grievances into energies towards supporting the communities affected by the tsunami.

As a result of continuous attempts to get an opportunity to contribute for affected populations by the tsunami, I was able to get a job in the Psychosocial Program of the American Red Cross, which was part of larger tsunami recovery program implemented in South and South East Asia. I enjoyed the work with the communities and schools and at the same time learned new areas of expertise such as disaster preparedness, water sanitation, and public health. Though I found enormous challenges in many areas, grace to my continuous efforts, attempts to maintain a positive attitude, as well as especially because of a high level of enthusiasm and motivation in involving not only areas of responsibility but also other areas, I gradually stepped up in the career ladder, expanding my wings not only in the country level but also in the South Asia regional level. With my professional growth, my dream to go to Africa appeared not impossible; a kind of a confidence in me grew in terms of finding a path to go to Africa. With my ambition to get my dream come true, I worked long hours, underwent almost all possible professional trainings at my reach, and always tried to do something more to qualify the deliverables in programs. Consequently, I was awarded best project officer of Sri Lanka Red Cross Society in 2006 and received Leadership Awards of Psychosocial Program in 2007 and many other rewards and awards from different partnering societies as well as from other local and regional entities. With each exciting event I went through, I felt as if I was pushed towards my dream, feet by feet, but it was as obscure as finding one's way back in a dessert at night under a cloudy sky. I knew that one day it would come, but I didn't know when exactly and how to get there soon.

In 2009, most of the programs under the tsunami operations had come to an end and I moved to the north of Sri Lanka as 'program manager' of a psycho-social program funded by Danish Red Cross. This time, my target population was the internally displaced families in north of Sri Lanka as a consequence of the so-called ethnic conflict. That assignment was far more challenging for me because of two major reasons, my ethnicity and the language barrier, plus the context was also different. It was a significant shift from one end of disasters to another, natural to man-made, as well as a passage for new learning that would help me to realise my dream one day. I moved to Vavuniya, the most proximate township in the Northern Province of Sri Lanka, once under LTTE, on 8 May 2009. When I reached the entry checkpoint to go to previously LTTE-controlled areas that were just captured by government forces, I had to undergo so many checks as well as questioning. The police officers repetitively told me not to go and raised their concerns in terms of security, especially as I was a Sinhalese. I remember one officer asked me what was my motivation to work there. I simply replied that it was high time to work there as the people were in need. He cracked in laughter. I was, however, intimidated because of the extreme level of informal authority enjoyed by the armed forces and the police in Sri Lanka under emergency law during the aftermath of the war. Again, one police constable reached me and asked my educational qualifications. I simply handed over a copy of my biodata that he pretended to have understood every single word and gave back to me. I smiled and asked him to take it if he wants. He looked quite happy and folded it into four and pushed into his wallet. After checking in my luggage, backpack, and documents, they allowed me to go yet insisting that the situation was not safe enough for a Sinhalese to work. I thanked all of them and walked along the narrow path fenced with barbed wires, till I got to the vehicle park where there was a person from Sri Lanka Red Cross Vavuniya district branch who had come to fetch me.

Suppressed feelings of uncertainty and unidentifiable fear started to dominate my mind while I was searching for a vehicle with a Red Cross and Crescent logo which was supposed to take me to Vavuniya where my new workstation is. A Land Cruiser covered with dust and with all windows open was parked under a huge turmeric tree, which added a mysterious look to the vehicle when the whole picture was partially swallowed by the mild darkness of the silent evening once agitated by firing guns and blasts of bombs and rockets leaving screams of fearful, dying humans. I started advancing towards the jeep, and a very skinny man, with only a few buttons on his white shirt, was chewing beetles leaves, leaning on the bonnet of the jeep. Once he noticed me coming towards him, he stood suddenly and showed his first sign of recognition with a very loyal smile showing his orange-coloured teeth with beetle leaves and started moving hurriedly towards me. I was trying to put words together to greet him in Tamil, and he reached to me and asked, 'Kohomada Sir, Gamana amaruda?' 'How are you sir, was it difficult, your trip?' in very well-articulated Singhalese. I almost got tears in my eyes, not because I was touched by hearing my native language but merely because of his attitude of choosing to talk to me in Singhalese. I felt a sudden bridge way between our two ethnicities. Before all, I told him, I can speak a little Tamil and I will try to use it, too. He was more than happy to hear that; I believe that in doing that, I take opportunity to respect his attitude towards me. I asked his name in Tamil. He said 'Sandaran'. We introduced each other and I chose to carry my own luggage though he pleaded me to give them to him. I added, 'Sandaran, I'm able to do that and if it's too heavy to lift while trying to put into the jeep, please give me a helping hand.'

Sandaran started the jeep after a few attempts and he slowly picked up his speed along the partially destroyed road creating a waste cloud of dust behind us. Passing many uninhabited, destroyed, and ruined houses lost among the palmira and mango trees that prestigiously standing in the torture land which is literally barren, we started moving towards Vavuniya. The extreme speed of the jeep, dilapidated condition of the road, and heavy presence of armed personnel along the road made me feel a bit vigilant although I was very much comfortable with Sandaran as an individual though we only met a while ago. We were stopped by more than a dozen of military checkpoints on the forty kilometres that we drove to reach Vavuniya and checked almost everything in my bags and my documents.

'Do you have clearance for your laptop?'

I was questioned at one checkpoint.

'What is this? Please open this to see!' one soldier asked indicating my external hard drive.

'This is a hard drive for the computer; this is how it is, if you open it, it will be out of use.'

I tried to be more diplomatic and tactical as much as possible to prevent provoking the ignorant soldier. His next question made me angry yet an inexplicable fear covered me from top to bottom.

'Tell me, what is then inside this?'

I intentionally avoided telling that it contained documents and other information required for the projects and so on, as that would have augmented his inquisitiveness to force open it or else ask me to show. Instead I replied, 'This contains the same structure like the computer and it helps the computer to work beyond its inbuilt capacity.'

The Captain was satisfied with the technical explanation, probably he might not have understood a thing but I was given the green signal to move towards my final destination.

We moved along the dusty roads, passing broken bridges and the small checkpoints where there were only a few police or else the village protectors were stationed, where we were not stopped. By nine in the evening, we reached Vavuniya town, which is almost haunted, and there were only a few shops that were open where there were a lot of people having their late night dinner after a long day of labour.

'Sandaran,' I awaked my voice.

'Yes Sir.'

His receptive and jumpy voice replied from the next end.

'I need to eat something'

'No problem, Sir. Kolikottu?'

His reply made me kind of lost among two languages. In Singhalese 'Kolikuttu' is a type of banana which is very common in the North and Mid-North areas of Sri Lanka, and again, 'Koli' in Tamil is chicken and 'Kottu' is a kind of a bread mixture with any kind of meat or fish curry.

Sandaran stopped the jeep near a night restaurant where the answer for my ambiguity was visible and evident. The noisy 'kottu' table and the drum beat of 'Kottu boy' convinced me that I was not going to end up eating banana for dinner. I got a hot pack of chicken kottu for dinner and we drove to the District Branch of Vavuniya, of Sri Lanka Red Cross Society, where the IDP operation centre was at work twenty-four hours seven days a week.

'Hi Pramudith.'

'Welcome to Vavuniya!'

'How are you?'

The welcoming and warm voice of the branch executive officer made me relieved from various negative distortions that I had since the time of commencement of my journey to Vavuniya.

'Have you had your dinner ?'

'If not, please come with me to my home.'

I did not expect such a welcoming treat at my arrival and I was really positively surprised though there are so many underlying fears and insecurities running inside my mind. However, I tried my best to stay positive and to have a receptive attitude to everyone as much as possible.

'Pramudith, the driver will take you to Red Cross guest house where you can stay next 3 months of your assignment.'

Ronald, the branch executive officer, took me to his driver and asked him to drive me to the guest house. We reached to a huge old, yet well-maintained, house where I was given a single nonshared room.

For the next three months, this will be my home. I told to myself, looking around checking the door locks and windows. Though everyone looks very friendly, a kind of vigilance and paranoia were reigning inside me. The first night in my life in a postwar area was about to be spent with millions of mixed feelings fighting with each other making me restless and sleepless. Whether I would like it or not, there will be ninety days ahead with the internally displaced populations by the ethnic conflict in Sri Lanka. Nearly 300,000 affected and displaced population in the restricted camps where each accommodates 40,000 in average. I'm here as the program manager for a psychosocial support program implemented by the Sri Lanka Red Cross Society and financially and technically assisted by the Red Cross National Society of Denmark. I read my field briefing notes and the sleepless night profiting the long hours without sleep.

As usual, I left the bed early and after a typical Hindu breakfast which is 100 per cent vegetarian, I left to office for starting my first day at my new job. Almost 35 degrees Celsius, dusty, and noisy because of crowds who had come for relief aid and I found my little office with old rickety chair and unstable table cosy and matching with my designation in the field. On the very first day, I got my logistics support at a quite satisfactory level. I was given an extended cable from one of the offices nearby for my Internet; I was given a desk telephone and a fan for the office although it's literary impossible to use a fan because the dust in the office room makes it create a mist of dust with zero visibility once it's on. However, I was contented with what was given to me and started my first day with positivity. The noises came from the neighbouring cubicle and the verbal battles of the volunteers for daily payments. After a battle of almost half a day, I cleaned my little cabinet (workstation) in order to make it operational and healthy enough to for me to stay in. However, I had already realised that I would be working from this office for the next three to four months and would be exposed to all these noises and the dust on an everyday basis.

The following day, after I assumed my duties in the new office, I went to the field, which is called 'Manik-Farm', a large cluster of internally displaced population which consisted of around five different camps where all the migrated populations from the war zone were fenced with barbed wires. The appearance of the camps from a distance was no different than any other refugee or IDP setups, whereas on a closer look it gives you an impression of concentration camps of the Nazi regime of Hitler. No communication devices were allowed in to the camps, no cameras were allowed in, no expatriate was allowed in, and whoever goes in will be screened carefully before the entrance. If you go in a car, the car is supposed to get an entry permit beforehand and it will be checked in and out even though there is a valid entry permit. The government armed personnel who were deployed at the entrances always made sure that whoever goes in is going in with an extreme level of fear and they are fully monitored and controlled irrespective of nationality, ethnicity, entity, where they work, and what they had come to do.

I gave my cellular phones, wallet with money, laptop, and some documents to the counter at the gate and proceeded through the gate in order to see my target communities. Dusty gravel roads and roadside bathing points full of stagnating water, lined up temporary shelter (tents) and the community centres made out of metal sheets, overcrowded temporary clinics, and child-friendly spaces where there are multiple nongovernmental organisations competing to have some activity for their visibility gave me a vivid image of a savannah full of vultures. It was visible that there were lot of entities and individuals such as government health workers, social workers, some local NGO members, and volunteers who were working with good faith for the affected populations and wanted to make a change but they also seemed terrified and horrified by the level of control and terror created within the camp environment by the armed personnel.

I used to visit IDP camps in the Manik Farm at least two days a week and every single visit ends with something unforgettable in either positive or negative poles adding a new lesson learnt for the rest of life.

'Vanakkam, Sir! Eppadi Sugam.'

One of the community members asked how I was doing and then he asked me to come along with him to his tent.

'Iringa Sir, Na dak ganne, Te thanni Kondu waran.' (Have a seat Sir! I will bring a cup of milk tea.)

I looked around the little 20 × 10 temporary tent that accommodates six members of his family including one infant, two little kids, and an old man who was not less than 80 years who was his father.

'By the way, what is your name?' I started.

'Prathap Sir.' We exchanged our names and started having a chat about the family.

'Sir,' a weak female voice broke our conversation. Probably that may be the only cup that they had in the tent to use for drinking water, feeding children, and to measure raw rice; however, the thought of respect, sharing, and caring was not hindered nor paralysed by the poverty or the remaining fires of ethnic tension hidden under the ashes of so-called imposed peaceful environment. I accepted the offer with respect though I had the immense fear of an ongoing epidemic of cholera. It tasted the same as the ones in the south, same mixture, same taste, but the tea was cold.

While having my tea, I had a long conversation with Prathap and discovered that he used to live in the heart of LTTE-controlled areas where most of the administrative offices of tigers were situated. When he started describing the beauty of the places and the regime of LTTE, I slowly slipped away as it was a time when even the flies and fleas could be spies or messengers and the massages are often misinterpreted and delivered in favour of the messenger. I left the camp with a mixed feeling that it was a pleasure that I was welcomed with such an unbelievable warmth and yet again with the uncertainty of whether I would be able to see him again in the camp tomorrow.

Each day, the IDP camps were filled with lots of news; whether they were good or bad, they always pushed me to think of new ways of initiating something to lift the lives of IDPs. Every afternoon, after my field visit, I used to take one hour of reflection. I locked my door of little cubicle, turned the door note 'out of office', tie my ear plugs so that I will not be disturbed by the fighting volunteers, and force myself to think of some new things that would help the affected people. As a result, I used to come up with few different activities to be implemented in the camps. As a next step I used to go to my staff and discuss, then go to the community for focus group discussions, and finally, we all come up with a creative invention to do in the camps of which the concept is community owned though it's initially a thought of mine. The next couple of days, we used to battle in convincing the bureaucrats in the district secretariat and the competent authority office to get projects passed.

With constant excitement blended with true passion to work, fear of uncertainty, and an inexplicable feeling of being in the north of Sri Lanka, especially among the people whom we considered as so-called enemies for last three decades, my days evaporated in a dry vent and flew across the slaughtered palmira grove.

Every evening after my work, I take my time of reflecting on my old hammock hung between two mango branches in the Red Cross guest house. Satheesh, who was the caretaker of the guest house, comes to me with a hot Nest-malt drink with milk and tea. Though his presence disturbed my sunset deep thinking, which goes way up to sky from the earth where I am, I enjoyed his company in the evening. Talking about his past war experiences, the difficulties he and his family went through, and the daily hassles of his life, but he doesn't forget to talk about the happy events of his little world, and his plans for the future. At the end of the conversation, he smiles with his yellowish set of teeth, coloured by beetle chewing. A true smile with humbleness along with his good night in Singhalese which is perfect makes me reflect on the vanity of the ethnic tensions retained about three decades devouring thousands of human lives.

On weekends, I go on visiting the nearby villages with one of my friends, Sathya, who is a volunteer for the Red Cross Society as well as a teacher in the government of Sri Lanka. We used to talk to village shopkeepers, farmers, teachers, and community leaders and discuss different daily matters of their lives as we walk along the rural roads. Every weekend, we hear a handful of different stories for evening discussions for the whole week. We add some intellectual aspects for the topics we picked from the people at the roadside and engage ourselves in never-ending discussions that usually become hot and aggressive after a couple of shots of locally brewed liquor. However, though the climate of the discussions rise up via different topics, though our little group consists of the two major ethnicities who are considered as so-called rivals since early 1980s, we never ever felt that we were different and usually everyone respected and loved each other as brothers.

The last day of assignment came over. The morning I got as usual and ran to the bathroom before anyone else usurps my fresh space for privacy but I was able to make just half of my way and there was a 'Human Shield' across the bathroom door. The term 'Human Shield' was a hot word by that time as it was repetitively used by government media in every news update referring to the fact that the LTTE was attempting to cover themselves, especially to guard their superior members using the civilian population left in their territory which was about to be captured by vigorously advancing government forces. So whatever which is not easy to penetrate was called 'Human Shield' whether there are humans or not.

I was blocked by a real barricade of humans, my friends, and their faces were not as cheerful as they used to be, one hardly spoke.

'Khalistan', who was the youngest among all, tried to tell me something and in a time of a flash, tears started running. The two staff who were my team members, who were fresh blood in the organisation, started crying like small kids. I was not able to resist for a long time. When the first word was properly uttered by Sathya, we had been looking at each other, still and in silence, for a couple of minutes. With wet tears on my cheeks and eyes, I crept in to the bathroom and the others headed back to the living area to wait for me to go to the farewell party. I cried over and over again in the bathroom like a child who just lost his favourite toy. I had accomplished my assignment better than expected ensuring a high level of sustainability with tangible results. I was happy to see the visible career development of my field officers and their increased level of competence and confidence, at the same time I was excited about my next assignment in Colombo, which is a country-level management position, and beyond everything, I was feeling an inexplicable feeling of discovering the wonderful group of people called 'Sri Lankan Tamils', their culture and simple lifestyle, and being able to live the rest of my life without 'imposed prejudice'.

The same evening, with overwhelming heart, I stepped out of the Sri Lanka Red Cross Vavuniya Branch. I was accompanied by 'Ronald', the branch executive officer, while being followed by the other friends and colleagues. I dared not look back; I feared my emotions more than ever before. 'Sandaran' was waiting, chewing a mouthful of beetles, in the same Land Cruiser which took me to Vavuniya, but its apparently repaired and painted. I got into the car, my hands were weak to say by bye to those who were waiting, and closed the newly tinted glasses. I knew that I would go with 'Sandaran' till the 'Old Tamarind Tree' but I was not sure whether It would be there in its prestigious stand as it used to be when I saw it first.

Chapter 03

EMBRACING DARKNESS

IT WAS A GLOOMY morning in December, in the year 2010, almost one year after my emergency psychosocial mission in the North of Sri Lanka. Usually, December is cold and gloomy in the west, whereas for the tropics, it's bright and dry. I opened my inbox as usual, 'availability check for Staff Counsellor in United Nations Mission in Democratic Republic of Congo'. I was startled with excitement and felt as if I have been awakened while seeing a dream.

Being deployed in The Democratic Republic of Congo as an aid worker was a dream to me. I was daydreaming and visualising working and helping the victims of sexual violence in eastern DRC. After having read miscellaneous literature and having watched hundreds of documentaries on DRC, I was able to brief about the country's history by heart. Despite that, I had learnt about the conflicts in the Great Lakes region and have gathered a waste knowledge on the demography, geography, and the political dynamics of the region. With all these preparations I had for my dream destination for work, I was feeling as if I was already hired. My level of confidence superseded the reality till I received the second availability check for Liberia, proving that the opening in DRC is no longer available. Termites fly high and die, high times come followed by the lows. While hopelessness was invading my life in those directions, I wrote back to Liberia saying that I was available at short notice. I started reading literature about Liberia, about the series of wars, preconflict history, demography, geography, and the society in general, sticking in to the belief that anyone can be hopeless in many things but no one can be totally hopeless in all spheres of life in all the time and nothing will come before the time and more than the luck.

In few days' time, I'm convinced that Africa is open for me, though what I exactly expected was not reachable for the moment as if the action is not as fast as the impulse.

'I had a dream to contribute for the peace and development of Africa.'

I replied with a high pitch when I was questioned why I wanted to come to Liberia. I was unconscious of the challenges that I might face and I was overtly fascinated by the news of being offered a position in Liberia with the United Nations Mission at a capacity of a staff counsellor. I was determined to deal with any difficult situation in Africa and made my mind that I'm finally on the verge of witnessing what I heard in the 'free-time stories' of my father.

After a long and extremely overwhelming bureaucratic process, everything was set for me to go to the dreamt continent but not to the country I dreamt so much to go. It was the third week of January 2011; I was busy with all necessary arrangements for my first deployment in Africa. I had merely a piece of paper that had barely described what to be brought when coming to Africa. I remember that there were two things that had been insisted many times: 'mosquito net' and 'yellow fever vaccination'. The curiousness and the fear mixed with excitement of a first missioner made me dig out more information about Liberia for preparing better for the mission. As an attempt of kayaking across great oceans, I was wandering among an infinite land of fantastic information on my next destination. The more I read, the more I needed to read, and that never ended. Starting from the first independent state in Africa, till the flesh-eating second Liberian civil war, the stories swing between good and bad, sweet and bitter, and bright and dark as history of rest of the world. Rather getting tired with contradictory and endless information,

I decided to go ahead shopping what I thought I need for my next year in Liberia. Some cotton clothes, one full suite, few shoes, few ties, socks, some sportswear, toiletries, a few books, and some emergency medicine were carefully packed into a travelling bag. The I packed my backpack with my netbook, copies of certificates, travelling documents, and with a few other stuff. Simply, I was ready for my journey to my dreamt continent. I felt I'm being awaited. A mild wave of happiness conquered me. An awaited moment is about to come over; I felt it in every nerve of me, in every drop of blood running in my veins, and in every cell.

In a few days I will be in Africa, where I dreamt to work, whose inhabitants I wanted to serve, the part of world that I visualised while I was a child listening to my father's free-time stories. Overriding all what the cyber media has to say about the piece of land called Liberia and its bloody war-tone recent history, a current of excitement was passing through all over me, as if I have been intoxicated with opium. A fantasy is going to be a reality, an illusion dream has almost come true. For a few days, I was wandering in a state of mind where I was visualising my coming days in Africa and trying to feel each imaginary scenario as if they are happening at present. A phase of positive disillusions and sensation seeking made me live in a virtual honeymoon despite the extreme busy schedule, getting ready for the departure.

A delightful departure, though overwhelming feelings of escaping from responsibilities, being selfish, being guilty, and yet again increasing fear of going to a place where life is uncertain, started capturing every single millimetre of space in my soul. After my father's passing, I was reluctant to move away from my family, as I was the only male child, and being the elder child, my physical presence was vital for the well-being of the family in many aspects. My mother was almost a 68-year-old pensioner and I knew the days ahead will not be easy for her. Even though she was very delighted that I had achieved what I ever wanted in my life and she was extremely helpful to me, I felt what she was trying to hide from me. As the face is the mirror of one's heart, the sorrow that comes out of fear of me leaving to wild Africa seems hindering her own fears about herself. Her failing attempts of hiding her emotions were like trying to hold a broken damn with her hands, her feelings like raging waters that were kept by force within the damn, floods destroying the land. Tears had left their traces, like fossils on hard rocks, though a smile with a lot of effort was trying to give some radiation to her pale face. Vicariously, I started feeling guilty, and sad, opening up a quasi-internal conflict within myself. My rational self with emotional self, my personal self with professional self entered into a quadruple battle to which there would never be a concrete answer. My mum, who is alone, widow, aging, and entering the time when she needs me around, standing at one corner, where as my dreams of decades have almost come true and it's visual and auditory, from the other corner. I was like a spring barely alive between the jaws of a lion and a hungry scavenger hyena. I didn't know who will grab me, but I knew whoever grab me, my fate would be the same. The end will be painful and then will be no more pain.

We lived in a three-bedroom, single-storey house with a basic kitchen and a toilet which is not annexed that was put up by my father in early 1970s where my whole life so far was spent. With basic facilities, we lived happily leaving hundred thousands of memories. My mother used to take loans from her working place and did some modifications in the house from time to time. I felt that as a woman she was longing to have some luxurious home according to her perceived level of life. I remember, one day, she took a small loan from the welfare association of teachers in her school and decided to get a pantry cupboard done. Once it was completed, she made us some typical Sri Lankan sweets, as if she wanted to celebrate a key achievement of her life. Those little things added some. Neighboured by distant relatives, descending from our ancestors, I dreamt to build my own creation in the same place one day. But I never verbalised it with anyone as it remained a dream that I thought would become a reality. If I were not wrong, it was when I was 15 that I found a piece of magazine left in the discarded section of the library. I used to read a lot, even though most of my preferred literature were irrelevant for my studies at that time. When I was rolling pages of that piece of magazine, I found an image of a house, all white, two storeys, with large windows and open balconies. Without my knowledge, I tore out the page and brought it home. The paper was lying on my study table for a few weeks and then I put it inside my 'Le Petit Robert' where it remained years and years being taken out from time to time. Looking at the image of the house, I used to have my private time of self-talks. That satisfied my inner self, taking me to heavenly and infinite horizon of dreams from which I, after few minutes, fall down to the black hole where I see only utter obscurity when I realise that I do not have means to reach what I want to have. When I was reading the offer letter of my job in Africa, each one of the characters appeared as blocks of my dream home. I told myself, Mum, I'm going to give you what you never had in your life and you will get what you deserve. I felt that I was going to shift her life to another level and I saw she would be happy, in my imagination. Whether it was going to be true or not, I didn't not dare questioning, I decided to move on.

The following few nights, I didn't sleep at all; I was swung between joy and uncertainty, situations that my mother might encounter and vivid imagination about my long dreamt home that comes true, my dreams about the continent of darkness comes true. As a ship caught in a cyclone in the middle of the ocean, I was beaten left and right by my emotions. I realised that how the negative pole of human mind can coil around the positive pole, it was like an anaconda which coils around its prey. Every single thought pushed or pulled me into or out of fear, anguish, uncertainty, loss, or vanity. After fighting with overwhelming emotions and endless thinking, I get up like a buffalo that survived from a battle with lions. I felt quite depressed and started going back and forth in evaluating the decision that I took. And each time I see my mother trying to hide her sad face by an imposed smile which is not hers, it urges me to stay home.

Since everything is arranged and I had given a word, I stuck with my decision communicated to UNDP country office. The big day came over, my luggage were ready, my backpack was carefully packed with all necessary things, and my travel- and job-related documents are in order and the taxi confirmed the airport drop. I went to have my last bath for a few months in my favourite bathroom. I love bubble baths, staying in slightly hot waters, with bubbles reflecting over various things. I stayed around forty-five minutes, relaxing whenever I take a bath. The time I am passing in the tub is a treasure and a meditation. I started thinking all of a sudden that I might miss this time. Life is about to change, life will change, it is a chosen change that I have to face. I left the bathroom and put on my clothes to go.

When I came out of my room, my mum was at the door, waiting for me, as if she cuddles a little child, she stroked my face and head with unexplainable tenderness which seemingly contained a hundred thousand unsaid words, and told only 'God bless'. I hugged her and said, 'I will come in April for new year.' My mum followed me to the taxi, stroked my head again, and said 'God bless'. She is a Christian, though she didn't practice regularly, lived in her belief, and at the same time, respected other religions, too. She gave birth to two Buddhist children and fostered them properly in Buddhist discipline while practicing her own religion. As anyone else who lived through similar situations would feel the magnitude of what she said. She gave me blessings from the utmost profoundest place in her spirit and heart. With the fading view of my mum in the background of my house which was partially built, the taxi started to move. I heard the sounds of pieces of sand being grounded by the wheels of the taxi as it moves on.

My flight was scheduled at 20.35 on 15 February 2011; I was supposed to go to Monrovia via Dubai, Nairobi, and there was a stopover in Accra. When I reached the entrances of 'Bandaranayke International Airport', the main international airport in Sri Lanka, my mind was still left with home, and nothing about my destination was clear besides what is in the itinerary. I knew I was going to Africa leaving my home, and only 'free-time stories' were being visualised about where I will be. 'A bunch of black-skinned, curly haired people with painted faces, with bloody mouths, with javelins and bows in hand started dancing around a fire, where something is being roasted. I saw myself, standing in the middle of the jungle, lost and frightened, hiding behind a big baobab tree.' A slight sweat started appearing all over my body and I heard the announcement, 'EK653 to Dubai is boarding now.' The announcement pulled my hesitating feet towards the boarding gates. The last chance of turning back has passed.

The flight attendant woke me up for the landing in Dubai and I was deep asleep due to the emotional and physical draining during the preparation for the mission. When I reached Dubai by 2.30 a.m., I felt rested and refreshed. For the first time, my mind seemed to accept that I had left the country. As my next flight to Nairobi was in eight hours' time, I started roaming around the airport Duty Free shops to search whether there would be something interesting to buy. I always try to remain mindful and organised in every little thing I do. In addition, as a habit, I used to read a lot of literature about anything I'm going to do, prior to starting it. While I was wandering among the bookshelves in the shops, *Lonely Planet West Africa* caught my curious eyes that I grabbed one without a second thought as if I have already decided to travel in whole region. I located the next boarding gate, sat on an empty bench and started reading the book just like a student who was going to sit for an exam. When I heard a voice, 'Excuse me, Sir,' I just looked up. A man who is significantly tall, dark, and with Negro features, wearing a weird dress like a Russian Orthodox priest, in multicolours instead of black, was standing right in front of me. 'Is this the gate for Emirates flight to Nairobi?' I nodded my head. Am I already in Africa? When boarding time approached, I felt as if I was isolated in a totally different world and felt that it can be the bitter reality that I might face in my destination. People wearing various frock-like bright-colour attires of different shapes with weird decorations started to throng to the boarding gate like vultures around a carcass, with stuff full of cardboard boxes, plastic bags, chewing Biltong, talking in loud voices. The whole place became a common market in a couple of minutes. Before getting on board, I called my mum and sister to confirm that I was safe.

'Please take care, God bless you.' My mother's words pierced deep in to my soul but I did not have much time to think of them; a ground attendant called my name, 'Rupasinghe Arachchi Pramudith.' 'Sir, your hand luggage have to be sent as a checked-in luggage as there is not enough space in the flight cabin.'

I was startled and told them, 'All my original certificates and important documents are there, so I cannot leave it with you as a checked in luggage.'

'Sir, we do not have space, you decide!' The cold nature of the ground attendant created another uncertain situation. I opened my hand luggage, pulled out my file with certificates, and I gave him my luggage with a sharp constant eye contact. He hesitated to talk. 'This is how the clients of Emirates are going to Nairobi' I told with a bit high tone and a sarcastic smile.

I was unable to walk for a few metres; someone called me again: 'Sir!' I turned back. A lady, apparently a senior ground handler, called me.

'How can I help you, Sir?' My level of tolerance had already exceeded with what I encountered, and I didn't have any space for being more polite, I gave her my file of certificates, 'This is what happened to me.' She felt that I was not in a position to talk and called the guy who asked me to check the hand luggage in. After few minutes, she came back to me, with my file. 'Sir, can you please wait until other passengers get on board?' I panicked. 'Why?' I asked. I imagined the worse scenario which is simply impossible. I expected to hear, 'Sir, you will not fly today, no space in the flight.' Instead the lady explained, 'Sir, after everyone is on board, I will allow you to take the hand luggage in with your file. Please wait.' I felt that the constant level of cortisone and adrenaline in my blood, maintained during the time I left home, went down. I took a deep breath and sat on a waiting chair next to the ground assistant. Now for sure I'm going to go to Africa as I dreamt and planned, without having a clue of what will come next.

'Sir!' I looked. 'Here is your luggage, please proceed to boarding.' I rushed to the flight. '44J'. I showed my boarding pass to the cabin crew member at the entrance. 'Straight, Sir!' Following instructions, I started moving along the passage between the seats, all the black heads started turning towards me in a rhythmic way as I pass by, maybe wondering how I was able to take my hand luggage into the cabin. I stopped at seat number 44J, looked around seeking a cabin to put my luggage in; still everyone was looking at me. I opened the overhead locker of 44J. It was full of plastic bags and cardboard boxes; all the other overhead lockers were also stuffed with various things, like plastic bags, cardboard boxes, old clothing, and luminous and laser-colour hand luggage of all fake Haute-couture brands. I found a small space in another overhead cabin where my hand luggage can barely fit and I was trying to push my luggage through the gap between two large plastic bags. 'Hey, man! Do not spoil my food!' A scream broke out from the far end of the flight. I didn't have time to realise whether it's for me or not. 'You! be careful, my things are there,' he added, stood up, and started coming towards me.

'Your bag is too big, you can't push it here, find somewhere else!' A bold guy in a strange red and black costume like a magician said, supporting his continent man. 'Yes, thank you! Indians are spoiling our things, find somewhere else!' The guy who was the owner of the bag raised his voice and told victoriously feeling supported by his co-African, adding some gestures that brought my memory to *Planet of the Apes*, which crossed my limit of tolerance and respect to diversity. I always try my best put behind ethnocentricity, trying to understand the issues from the other person's perspective according to his or her sociocultural dimensions.

'Hey, do you think that I travel for free?' I started after a long silence. 'Your seat is somewhere miles away, you put your stuff here usurping someone else's space, how dare you tell me to not to put my stuff here?' I didn't let the man to talk, and continued. 'I paid the same amount like you, maybe more, and it is my nearest overhead which is 44f and as one of your brothers, who is like you has taken my space over seat 44j, I use the space left here. If you do not want me to push your bag aside, take your stuff out and go to your place! Do you understand what I say?' As I raised my voice coming very close to the face of the man, he backed off. I kept on looking at his face for few seconds and heard a voice of a flight-attendant running towards me. 'How can I help you, Sir?'

'Please can you find a safe place for my hand luggage?' I asked her politely. 'Sure Sir.' She took my hand luggage and went towards the area reserved for the staff. I felt relieved after a hectic start and returned to my seat and fixed my earplugs tight so that I will no longer be disturbed. Even before thirty minutes after the take off, the first sign that my flight will be a nightmare appeared. My neighbour starts sneezing all over the place as if he is telling me that 'you are in my continent and you have to bear any nonsense of me'. I pulled my eye mask out and put on my nose, as I did not have a mask to protect myself. I expected something every single second and was constantly monitoring the flight status in my personal monitor waiting anxiously until the journey comes to an end.

Time to destination 4h 23min
Distance 2,580 miles

I felt that the flight was not moving though it was mentioned in the screen 'ground speed is 734 kilometres per hour'. I was feeling very tired and fell asleep till I was awakened by a flight attendant in preparation of landing in Nairobi, Kenya. In Kenya, there was a transit of five hours in Jomo Kenyatta International Airport. My mind started wandering among my father's free-time stories about the wild life in Kenya. Giraffes, lions, wildebeests, zebras, hippos, rhinos, and giant Nile crocodiles in a live game in endless savannas and Masai people in their reddish costumes jumping high as if they are going to touch the sky became vivid in my eyes as if I was watching a film. Every single thing my father mentioned about Kenya appeared before me with full of life and colours, heightening my desire to see The Great Masai Mara. I did not have entry visa for Kenya to let me go out but I do not remember that I was unhappy of that but rather I was happy to set my feet in Africa for the first time in my life and to feel that my dream had almost come true. 'Thaththe! (*Singhalese word for father*) I am finally in Africa!' I told aloud. As a dark cloud laden with waters to fall down covered the shining Sun, my happiness ended up in a street of warm tears that invaded my eyes. He is not with me to see that his dear son has followed the whereabouts he related in his stories. Again, though it was not for the first time, I realised that life is too short for all of our dreams to come true and to share the joy with everyone in our lives. By the time some of your dreams come true, those who have shown us the pathways towards those dreams might already have had left this world. I felt that an achievement never gives you complete happiness as there is always a sad end in every smile.

Outside of the glass curtains, the weather beaten endless grass land and a few aircrafts were there. Despite a few craft shops and Duty-Free electronic shops loaded with Chinese gadgets, nothing much was found inside the airport. I approached one craft shop and started looking for something that I could buy as a souvenir. Among hundreds of extremely expensive crafts, after a careful observation for almost one full hour, I chose two oil paintings of iconic Masai people, just for US$3 each, which later on I framed and hung in my home in Sri Lanka as my first souvenir from the dream continent. Time seems not running as much as I wanted; I decided to have a coffee in an in-house cafeteria. As a result of my extensive reading about Africa, I knew a few words from key dominant languages in the continent, one among them was Swahili. My special interest on the Eastern Part of D R Congo was the reason behind my little knowledge in Swahili. I walked into the cafeteria and found a single-chaired, tall bar stool, which was comparatively higher than usual ones as if it was especially designed for Masai people. I tried to climb the chair, attracting the attention of not only the bar boy but also the clients. The bar boy came running to me. 'How can I help you, Sir?' It sounded to me as if he is asking whether he would help me to sit on the chair rather than asking me what I want to drink. 'One Kahaba, please' I told him in an ordering tone as if I were defending myself from the shame of not being able to sit on the chair at ones, though my reaction was not intentional. 'Sir, no no no, we do not have them here, go out in the town, you will find them enough in the street.' The boy said at one breath looking at me astonished, making me more confused and irritated.

'You do not have coffee?' I asked looking at the cashier who was just observing what was happening with me. 'Yes, Sir, we do have.'

'Please one strong black coffee medium size,' I told him.

'Sir we have one standard size.'

'It's okay' I made my reply short and clear to avoid further confusions. Looking at the passing passengers near the cafeteria, I sipped my coffee, enjoying my first moment of tranquillity after so many unexpected situations. I forgot the confusion that happened in the cafe after a while and, almost one year later, learnt about the reason behind the reaction of the bar boy. The Swahili word for coffee is *Kahawa* whereas *Kahaba* stands for Prostitute, but it was too late to know the right word.

After a long flight which is pretty much the same in terms of packed overhead cabins, yet interestingly significant differences I started to notice, of people in comparison with the flight I took from Dubai to Nairobi. Instead of tall Masai-like bodies, stout shorter ones were to be seen. Long angular faces were not the majority this time; their faces were round and with heavier and smaller eyes. It was like the unseen and unheard side of my dream continent being unfolded every single hour. I looked at them carefully, listened to them attentively with immense curiosity of knowing something more about these people about whom I had heard through the anecdotes of my father. My neighbouring seat was occupied by an African lady who I guessed was middle aged. I saw she was desperately trying to operate the personal screen, and I offered help. 'Madam, may I help you?' I asked politely.

'This does not work,' told she in a tone more of a complaint rather than in direct acceptance of help. I switched the screen on for her and opened the menu for her to select whatever she is interested in. As a fish taken from water, struggling to breathe, my tongue was anxious to start a conversation with her to know more about the place, where she is going, what does it look like, what is her language, how they live, and many more things. I was thirsty of first-hand information of Africa, just like a cattle running after a mirage, and trying to talk to every single person whom I was able to reach. 'Are you from Kenya?' I hesitantly asked, knowing that her facial features were a bit different from most of the people whom I met in Nairobi.

'I'm a Ghanaian,' she replied with a welcoming smile. As the rain falls to a desert, her words gave me a quenching sensation that I was waiting to feel since I was a small child. 'Ghana, Nkuruma's country,' words jump out of the tip of my tongue faster than a thought. After a brief in-flight conversation, my curiosities stretched to their maximum width and length and could not resist the feeling of visiting Ghana one day soon. 'Ghanaians are different, there are lot of tribes.' For me, all Africans used to be the same, now I discover the great differences in diverse dimensions that were not even noticed as nuances having being outside the continent. The word *tribe* in my understanding is a group of savages who do not wear cloths, who eat roasted or raw meat, perhaps human flesh, who just roam in thick jungles. Stories of Pigmies became alive in my head, dancing around a burning hunt, nude and uncivilised in our perception. Fufu, Kenke, and Bankun with palm soup entered into my subconsciousness as if they are alien food that I cannot imagine how do they taste or look like. The initial perception of the tribes in Africa, learnt through the free-time stories, started conflicting with what I hear throughout the journey and some evidences that I have encountered. But again, I had seen and have had an orientation about modern Africa through the media and as a result of my extensive reading about the continent. However, it is difficult to eliminate certain stereotypes and misconceptions that I conceived in childhood, hearing about something for the first time, remained profoundly routed during decades within oneself. Despite there is always a close relationship as well as a contradiction between the reality and the stereotypes.

'We have lot of things to see in Ghana,' she added. 'In Accra, there are a couple of things, Kumasi, we still do have famous Ashanti kingdom and in cape coast, there are live evidences of slave industry. It is our pathetic history she ended.

'Please fasten your seat belts and remain seated, we are flying over a turbulent area.' The personal screen shows that we are flying just over Democratic Republic of Congo, one of the countries I heard most often about during my childhood. Being a teacher in political science, my father had a vast knowledge in political history as well as keen interest in cold war and post cold war issues. In addition, he was an enthusiast of communism rather than a follower or a so-called comrade who believed that communism was the best theory of good governance. Many times, he talked about 'Patrice-Lumumba, the first Prime Minister of Zaire, and his remarkable leadership and bravery and immense sacrifices during the process of Liberation and post independent sociopolitical role. Whenever father told the stories about Zaire, he repeated one of the famous statements made by Dr Patrice Lumumba: 'We are no longer your monkeys' to the king Leopold II of Belgium. The tragic assassination of Patrice-Lumumba by his successor rebel leader Joseph Mobutu, in South East of Zaire, today called Lubumbashi, was always a part of his repetitions.

The strange carnivorous trees, venomous ants that attack in masses which can even kill a bull, mysterious tribes living in thick tropical forests, Pigmies whom he always talked about with smile and interest, should be within the infinite greenness in which there are blue in land and ocean-like lakes and rivers. A thought of repentance invaded my mind, all of a sudden. 'I missed my chance to experience this enormous land rich in nature.' If I had been lucky enough to get the first offer of UN, by this time I would have been in Goma, the regional capital of the Eastern Province of the Democratic Republic of Congo. Even though I was not lucky enough to get there, I had heard and read a lot about the country much more than any other African State. Modern warlords of the Democratic Republic of Congo; Laurent Nkunda, CNDP leader, and the stories of unbelievable inhumane atrocities committed by those recognised and unrecognised militia groups that shatter the life in the Eastern provinces; the child soldiers and abductions of children; and victims of sexual violence who are revictimised over and over again; Joseph Kabila, successor of his father Laurent-Deisrére-Kabila, who is the youngest president who ruled a country of total impunity were some of the issues I was familiar with despite nature's beauty and the immense natural resources that belong to this large country in the middle of the continent. My wandering in the free-time stories was interrupted. 'What would you like to drink, Sir?'. A flight attendant was serving drinks. I usually do not enjoy alcohol though I'm a social drinker. Whenever I fly, I drink only water and take light food. 'Water' I replied. While sipping my glass of water, I was looking at the route of the flight—DRC, Chad, Nigeria, Togo, Benin, Ghana, and Liberia. Civil war in Chad, Voodoo civilization and black magic from Benin and Togo, I had read about them during my childhood. 'Muru, I'm from Nigeria' was the first African child whom I saw in a photo in my English textbook when I was in grade 3 in school. Today, I fly over the places that I had read about and dreamt about, and tomorrow, I might be on the ground.

'We will be soon in Accra.' This time, it was not the usual announcement from the captain, but from Mrs Aggyman, my neighbour in the flight. Dry earth yet considerably green, gravel roads between the buildings spread unevenly like in a play kit of a child, and some paved roads started appearing clearly in the skyline with relatively high buildings that looked like some offices or else apartments. The heavy traffic circulation gave an impression that there are either lot more vehicles in the city exceeding the road capacity or there is no proper traffic control measure; the cars, buses, and trucks all were in the same road lined still. 'Cabin crew, get ready for landing.' In a few minutes' time, we reached Kotoka International Airport in Accra. Two more hours left to my destination; the flight will retain one full hour in Accra to board the passengers to Abidjan, capital of Ivory Coast. Mrs Aggyman wished me safety for the rest of journey and left the flight. The airport premises looked like a soccer ground in a village, with irregularly grown grasses and lack of maintenance although most of the key airliners were to be seen. British Airways, Lufthansa, Air-France, Delta Airlines, Ethiopian, Emirates, Turkish Air, Air Namibia, and South African were on the ground, making Kotoka International Airport look like the emerging air hub for West Africa. One by one passengers started coming in, and instead of English, French started being heard everywhere, each colonial power has left their dispositions deep into these cultures, including language and dress code. Till Ghana, most of the people were well dressed like most of the Africans do when they go out, and those who come in look more 'Chic' than well-dressed with apparently fake designer wear and perfumes that are strong enough to immobilise a person. Is this a voluntarily acquired trait from French, adapted to the socioeconomic conditions of Africa? Or else is it a typical Ivorian attitude to life? Every leg of the flight left me with something to reflect on and to discover. My longest flight comes to an end in two hours and then I will walk in the soils of Africa, I said to myself when I heard the captain announcing the take off. The sky was gray and gloomy, visibility was very low. 'Allo, pouquoi, le ciel est sombre?' I asked the guy who was sitting on the next seat. 'ç'est Hamathan' he said with 'un air normal'. That was the first time I heard 'Harmattan'. Later, I discovered that it was a climatic condition induced by the dust clouds formed upon the Sahara and moving towards the South as a shield of dust clouds against the sunlight, sometimes making air traffic impossible.

New continent, new ecological and climatic conditions, new race of human beings, and a lot of new aspects of life to explore and comprehend, seem exciting and yet challenging. Malaria, typhoid, rabies, Lassa fever, and yellow fever are very common in the zone; I was advised during the predeployment briefing, and now a light vigilance comes out, suppressing my bravery of coming here. Many times I had read that most of the expatriates get malaria in West Africa, and sometimes it leads to death. The closer I reached Liberia, the more that mixed feelings started dominating in lieu of the extreme enthusiasm and the urge to be in Africa. It was like a new phase of my journey. I was already missing my home, mum, and sister. Being the eldest and the only male child of the family, my responsibilities and obligations to my family, especially to my widowed mother who is aging, had already been translated to overwhelming emotions that brought a stream of tears along my cheeks, all of a sudden. The last moment, just before my departure, my mother's attempts of hiding her sadness and fears and the way she hugged me I started feeling as if I was at home. I heard the last few words my mother uttered to me, 'God bless you, my son,' over and over again, echoing inside my ears. If something bad happened to her I would not forgive myself for taking the decision which is solely for pursuing my childhood dreams. Though it was my father who was filled with this irresistible passion to discover the dark continent, he has already left us, leaving a more important responsibility to me to take care of my family, rather than pursuing the dreams of my childhood that stood apparently impossible together. I was lost in my thoughts which ran up and down in two poles about my choice but I cannot return for some time, at least I will have to work one month to earn to buy a ticket back home, therefore worrying is not going to change anything for sometime although it is not possible to not to worry about loved ones. First time ever in my life, I'm filled with inexplicable feelings of anxiety and fear and uncertainty of what would be in store in the future for me. It might be the first missioner's syndrome or else that of a first missioner from South Asia, or does everyone else feels the same? Maybe the whole humanitarian world might have gone through or be going through the same situation, or else it's simply human nature. I did not have much energy left for finding answers for the questions popping in my mind as bubbles in a boiling hot water pot.

'Ladies and gentlemen,' it was the captain. 'We will be landing shortly in Robert's International Airport in Monrovia, Liberia.' Most ugly things look beautiful at distance. My perception of Liberia was basically shaped on what I heard and saw in different media, but from a few thousand feet above, this tortured land by thirteen years of civil conflicts stands proudly and happily with infinite greenness and a cobweb-like interconnected network of water bodies. When someone comes over Sudan, Chad, Nigeria, and Niger, this green piece of land looks like a heaven full of life that is nourished by its widespread water sources and beautified by a strip of brown beaches where the Atlantic embraces the former paper coast, and that gives an impression to anyone: what else is needed for a life here? The scene took my breath away for a moment. Such an amazing country gifted by Mother Nature has turned to be a paradise poisoned.

Robert's International Airport is located in an apparently isolated area, obviously poorly maintained, and only our flight was there as a commercial air line, though there were several white colour MI24 fighter gunships with a large UN logo, and few other passenger flights of the United Nations. Only two staircases linked to canters were parked recklessly in a corner which stood as an evident of limited air movements in the airport. Signs of disconnectedness and isolation from the rest of the world ruled the horizon. After the flight came to a complete stop, everyone started rushing towards the exit, which reminded me of 'travelling in a minibus in Sri Lanka in the 1980s' where people push one another as if it's an emergency. With a pushing line of passengers, I finally came to the exit of the flight. It was sunny, hot, and filled with heavy air full of humidity, kind of a typical tropical environment; this is going to be my duty station at least for six months and I did not know how it would be and what will be in store in the future for me here. Finally, my feet touches the soil of Africa, I'm in Africa, in the continent of darkness, the Africa my father talked about, Africa that I dreamt to see, dream to explore, dreamt to experience, but it had taken almost three decades for my dreams to come true. I dreamt like a crazy little boy, I looked at Africa and Africans through my father's free-time stories when I was small, then I read various literature about this continent, I watched a lot of documentaries, and finally I'm here in reality, in Africa, with my long-lasted dream come true with an uncertain feeling of what will happen tomorrow. Once, my father told me, Africans do not worry about tomorrow. I proceeded to my immigration.

Chapter 04

MALAGUETTA—THE PAPER COAST

11 February 2011
'Malaguetta, The Paper Coast'

Malaguetta, you remained a virgin grace to Atlantic tides,
Nourished and protected the lives and woods untouched,
Bassa, Kru, Kpelle, and Krio beat the same beat and rhymed,
Malaguetta, I call you from the barren land of death.

Mark of emptiness with traces of fruitfulness days ago,
Shattered with gunpowder hundred thousands of dreams,
Born human living 'animalised' handicapped and deformed,
What cursed the fragility of your heart and tender hands?

Hope sailed across pacific and kissed you in Atlantic,
Journey for equality and respect, granted by Monroe,
Cracked earth, fallen heavens bargained life, death won,
Beloved land of Liberty, you are violated before puberty.

WHILE REFLECTING ON PROS and cons of my potential deployment to Liberia, many things invaded my mind and I just put them into verses and as a result this poem was composed. 'Malaguetta' was the name given by the Portuguese traders and explorers to the area which was unbelievably defended by rough Atlantic tides and fence like rock reefs, almost unreachable by the sailing ships, centuries ago. Grace to which Malaguetta was able to remain virgin, noncolonised, being one among the only two territories in Africa that was not colonised by any of the colonialists. But ironically, as a result of reintegration efforts of the African slaves in America during the time of President Games Monroe, Malaguetta's virgin coast was penetrated by some American ships that carried the Afro-Americans who expressed their willingness to come back to their place of origin, 'Africa', though no one among them had any clue of where in Africa their first seeds were as they were the products of 'Human Husbandries' of colonial masters and some of them partially carried the traits of colonial masters which is said that 'some of them can be slightly white or fairer as their parents served very closely for their masters', and which was seen as 'mulatto' from the African eye, which was derived from the French word *Mulatre*, hybrid of donkey and horse, which cannot contribute for an offspring. With the arrival of the Afro-Americans, the name Liberia came into being, naming it as the Land of Liberty for the Afro-Americans who were said to be freed as per the doctrine of Monroe, yet spreading seeds for the world's most inhumane civil wars, due to the fact that America, who dumped some of its black population in this 'newfound land', completely ignored the indigenous population that was 95 per cent and centralized power on 5 per cent of the newly freed ethnicity of Americo-Liberians, in a newly created 'American type of Republic of Liberia'. They named the capital as Monrovia in honour of Games Monroe, who freed them, and following that, roads, the flag, and even the model of governance, civil service, were named and created as per American model which created an impossible and superficial America in a poor, straying nation, on the banks of the Atlantic, in an extremely poor part of the continent of Africa. Instead of the dream of Liberty coming true, the friction between the empty superiority of Americo-Liberians, who used to be slaves once upon a time, and ever free indigenous population who lived in this piece of land for thousands of years, start growing with time and ended up with thirteen years of dark and bloody era of mass destruction and social deterioration, which finally created endless dependency in Liberian society and horror and atrocities instead of the freedom dreamt by the freed slaves.

Robert's International Airport looked like a rural post office in Sri Lanka; there were two counters painted in brown, one was empty, and there was one immigration officer waiting in the other, with his rubber stamp and mobile phone which was quite a third generation, with music on, and he was moving his head according to the music which was playing. 'Good, evening!' I said with a little high intonation, just to get his attention. 'Hm-passport and ticket please!' His tone was still sleepy and inattentive. I just gave him all my travelling documents along with the letter from the United Nations Mission in Liberia, requesting the immigration to exempt me from requirement of obtaining a visa for entry to Liberia. 'You are good to go,' he said and returned my passport. There was a stamp :VIP: One hurdle is passed without any problem and I proceeded to claim my baggage. I was advised and warned by the field mission as well as by the headquarters to have a few spare sets of cloths as there are often cases of missed luggage. But I was lucky as my luggage were just waiting for me at the entry of the baggage claiming area which was like a cell of a political prisoner. Finally, I came out of the airport expecting my colleague who waited for me, holding a board with my name as in usual cases. All of a sudden, a bunch of teenage-looking guys who are apparently selling mobile SIM cards and reloading cards gathered around me, and I didn't see anyone with my name and started wondering what to do as I did not even have a local phone to call any of the numbers given by the field office. All of a sudden, one guy reached me, 'Are you Pramudi?' I'm not used to partial pronunciation of my name, and it took some time for me to respond. 'Yeah, I am Pramudith. It should be Michael, I guessed ' 'I'm, Michael' he responded. He took my luggage and led me to the minibus with a big logo of UN in black colour. 'Michael, is it possible for me to buy a local SIM card for my mobile here? I asked. 'Yeah, $5 only.' I gave him US$10 and got my first Liberian telephone connection on the way to my temporary lodging in Monrovia, which is not yet seen. I felt kind of reassured and happy that I have at least the facility to communicate with the external world and gave my first call to Mum and reassured her that I'm safe in Liberia and call her the next day once I get to office. Michael started the engine of the minibus and started driving out from the airport. I felt curious and impatient to see the country as he drives by.

Before we reached the final exit gates of the airport, little boys and girls holding big baskets of pineapples, bananas, and mangos on the head started blocking us, asking us to buy some of them. As we slowed down, a couple of handicapped guys had already reached us in the speed of arrows. I could not believe my eyes, how come can these people run so fast with the aid of clutches. Signs of war and its remains are still around, after nine years. The first sign of child abuse and exploitation and live evidences of mutilation of human during the war, I witnessed even before five minutes of arrival.

Even though life seems reined by the rules of misery, nature stood intact amidst all disturbances as a huge Baobab standing with its victorious and prestigious personality, in the middle of a semi-desert. Immediately after we passed the gates of the airport, the horizon was opened to greenish land full of trees where there were few houses spread unevenly like a small herd of sheep spread in a feeding ground. There were people walking randomly on the road, ladies with firewood or clothes on their head, children with peanut, bananas, or fish in hand waiting till a vehicle stops to buy them. Here and there on the road, pieces of bushes were kept in the middle of the road which are followed by the overloaded old American trucks broken down along the way. It took some time for me to realise that those pieces of bushes are signs of danger ahead. After thirty minutes of constant drive along merely an isolated way towards the capital Monrovia, we reached more populated areas where there were little shops and more houses. People were out in the compounds, busy with talking to each other in groups and first time I heard loud music here and there, but almost a similar kind of beat as if someone is pounding wheat in a traditional motor. And here and there some girls were moving their pumpkins like butts up and down in rather a more sexually aggressive manner than rhythmically. And men were dancing behind dancing girls, to maximum proximity as if they were having sex in partial doggy style. But when it is seen with the weird expressions and the movements of their hands as they dance, it was seen more or less like two baboons were in action. Though I was curious to know what really is happening, I didn't want to disturb the driver who drives almost overspeed ignoring the alarm of the car-log system.

I had seen the taxies in the United States; here it's pretty much of a copy of everything in the US. Yellow colour taxies carrying more than ten passengers inside, packed like chicken, going on the road with full of authority in total impunity. They stop wherever they have someone to grab or to push out without any signal and most of the yellow taxies didn't have functioning break lights. You can always expect that a door opens suddenly on roadside and someone jumps right in the middle of road from any of the yellow taxies that stops abruptly irrespective of road signs or circumstances. 'Michael,' I interrupted my driver who seems bit angry because of a few taxies that blocked him going fast as he wanted. 'What are these taxies? those are government owned or run by private companies?' I just wanted to know. 'Those are yellow machines; if you have a car you can run a yellow machine, I have two of them, some boys run them and bring me money in the evening.' Some taxies were loaded with so many goods on the top, apart from the human weigh inside, making them look like carrying a mountain. And most of the taxies seem very old or either heavily damaged due to lack of maintenance. I posed my next question to Michael. 'Here, there are no buses or trains?' His reply sounded bit reluctant. 'We used to have, but now we have yellow machines and motos.' I received his massage well, when public property and systems destroyed during the conflicts, it's not easy to re-establish them unless the present governance have a strong will along with public support. So naturally, abrupt and irregular systems come in to being that exploits public and creating diverse side effects on society and economy.

We reached to a junction where the driver stopped nearby a little shop to buy something. 'Total' my eyes caught something that I had seen many times in France. I knew that Liberia was not an oil-producing country, but somehow, even this war-torn little country sandwiched between three war-affected countries, was unable to escape from the French oil giant 'Total'. Though they are relatively smaller, there was even a 'Bonjour' pick-and-pay shoplet in the 'Total' gas station. If it was a francophone country, I would not wonder how, but Liberia being extremely pro-American and anglophone territory, I started wondering how the French managed to take over the oil market in Liberia to this extent. However, someone provides to their standards and to their price, and the consumer has no choice and is forced to buy at the imposed rates and these people are not in a position to demand. I told to myself, 'Here, we will be in Monrovia in two minutes.' Michael started the engine and started moving, turning the vehicle to his right side. Within few minutes, some buildings started appearing along the road which was congested with all kinds of vehicles including motorcycles, trucks, cars, jeeps, and small vans. And on some of the motorcycles, there were five people seated and passing with high speed, through the small gaps left between other vehicles. 'Michael, why are there too many people on the bike?' I was wondering who are those people on the bikes. 'Those are motos, they take as much people as they can.' No one had headgears, and same as in the yellow machines, none of the lights were functional. Instead of the yellow machines in urban setup, motos were taking the lead in public transport. It did not take much time for me to realise that people drive here without any proper orientation and training, as the rest of the vehicles on the road do not differ much compared to the taxies and motos. And it happened many times that pedestrians cross the road like chickens without watching the road. While I was lost among my thoughts, Michael had already come to the transit house for United Nations Staff who come to Liberia. 'Here is the transit house, your temporary accommodation' He said with a relaxed feeling of having ended the stressful trip, and he blew the horn a few times, in front of the light-blue high gate that completely blocked the site of what is inside the fence. Slowly the gate opened; we entered to the compound which was fully fenced with high walls and on top were barbed wires. The house was kind of a poorly constructed cement house with thick window grilles with full of corrosion. Yet some efforts had been taken to renovate it by repainting and fixing some air-conditioners. One lady, middle aged, round faced, a bit fat, came running towards us and took the luggage and smiled at me with a gesture of welcome moving her head down. 'Welcome to Liberia,' she said with a very respectful intonation while taking me to the room where I was supposed to stay for next couple of days till I find my own accommodation. 'Here is your room, and you can choose any of those beds' said she, showing little beds that reminded me of military hostels in Sri Lanka. She handed over the key to me, and told 'when you go out, you need to give me the key.' Sounded like an order but I just nodded my head and closed my door behind me.

The room was dark and smelled foul because of fungus on the walls due to high humidity and lack of sunlight inside. The white wall was full of patches as moisture had retained in the walls for a long time, in some areas the wall filler has come out leaving brownish areas on the wall, matching with the old partially destroyed painting of an African woman carrying a baby on her back, hanging on the wall. Two metal beds that barely stood with heavily corroded legs on cracked terra-cotta floor, like a river caught to a drought, were placed near the windows that were covered with very bright-coloured curtains looking more like dusters that had not been washed for a few months. The air was smelling and not enough inside the room, and light was not enough even to read a book. I felt like being imprisoned and locked up in a country where I knew no one. I took my phone and rang my mother in order to change my thoughts. After an exchange of a few words, I felt sleepy and almost forgot that the bed was not stable.

When I woke up hearing the symphonies of birds, it was almost seven in the morning. It was totally disoriented by the natural alarm that I got used to in Sri Lanka. I didn't use an alarm clock to get up in the morning and used to wake up hearing the birds singing near my bedroom balcony. As I had to report to the United Nations Mission Headquarters by nine, I just ran to the bathroom, which was shared by all the tenants in the transit house. First time ever in my life, I was to sit on a commode without a seat and where there is no flushing system that functions. And the old terra-cotta floor was cracked like a sky full of lightning and has created small water paddles and streams full of green moss just like a Google hybrid satellite map of an evergreen forest in Latin America. The remains of what those who had come before had done were still there, making me feel like I had been sent to hell. I tried my best to resist the nauseous feeling and finally I had to listen to what my body wanted. I came out like an old Greek coming out of a vomitorium and crept into my room to get ready to go to office. I decided that I will find an accommodation with acceptable conditions, or else I will leave the job and return to Sri Lanka.

First time in my life I found myself standing at the roadside waiting to be picked. I was informed that I will be picked up by 09.00 a.m. by the office team. Having a habit of being on time, I left the compound ten minutes earlier to wait for the car and was watching what is happening on the roadside. The transit house was located in the 12th street, Sinkor, Monrovia, almost in a dead end of the street, yet a busy marketplace where almost everything on earth was sold. Women with baskets on the head were walking up and down in the busy market, calling for the clients with their loud and cemented voice. Local bread which reminds me of Fanthi bread (*a soft white wheat bread unique to the tribe called Fanthi*) in Ghana, served with home-packed mayonnaise bulb made out of polythene bags which is sold mostly among everyone who works in the market. The bread-selling woman is followed by an Atae (*kind of herbal tea usually sold by the Fula tribe across West Africa*) seller who looks like a Muslim with his long white dress, beret on the head, and unique beard left curled just under the chin. Bread with a bulb of mayonnaise and a plastic bag full of Atae is the common breakfast of every one in the market, and it was not rare that schoolchildren also stop and grab their breakfast though most of them go for the doughnut or cornbread sellers standing by the junction. I considered that my parents controlled me too much not allowing me to buy food from the school canteen but they made sure that their child is given hygienic and nutritious homemade food before he leaves home along with a carefully packed lunch box as well. During our childhood, it was rare for a child goes to the school canteen. Almost everyone is given homemade food, although we desired to go and taste canteen food that we thought a luxury. Looking at these children, who are dressed with dirty and untidy dresses, buying street food sold at dusty roadsides in dirty baskets, I realized how blessed our childhood was, with caring parents who looked into every single need of us, even neglecting their own needs. The uniformity and the signs of being cared for are not at all found among the students, and first time in my life did I notice a mother carrying her children along the roadside whereas they should go in the safe side. Seeing all these, the famous poem 'London' of William Blake came to my mind, 'Harlot's curse on newborn's cry.' Do children become consequences of the pleasure of parents? Witnessing some realities of some parts of the world can be traumatic and heartbreaking for those who are not from those cultures and places. Here, a growing life is a burden and let out neglected, whereas in my place, it's a treasure and protected by everyone around.

A woman carrying a basin full of different stuff stopped by me. Smiling at me, opening her mouth as wide as possible, showing her pearl-white teeth, she asked me if I needed peanuts. In her basin, there were little plastic packets of peanuts, mayonnaise bulbs, and some candies, placed like little hills erupted in a valley. I said no as I was advised not to try street food. Among the continuous roar of motors, loud voice of the sellers, and the constant blowing of sirens of vehicles, I heard someone calling me from a distance. Rather than a calling, it was more like shouting out. My driver, Michael, had come to pick me up and got stuck on halfway of the road as there is a truck broken down in the middle of the road to the market, no other vehicle except motors can pass. 'How is Liberia for you?' Michael asked with a smile. I was without words for a while and told 'It's okay', though it was not what I was exactly feeling. 'This is UNMIL HQ, and I will take you to check in and check out of the office where you have to check in.' He took me to an office of human resources for me to check in to the mission and the very first day of the work in Africa is to begin with United Nations' mission in Liberia. A dream has come to its realisation and so many other dreams are trying to pop up just like the air bubbles of fish breathing in muddy water in a tiny little paddle left in a stream hit by a drought. Human dreams always are not crystal clear but they do exist within and pop up over and over again, and never end, and each dream is connected to thousands of other dreams. One dream comes true making grounds for thousands of other dreams to pop up like mushrooms in the jungle, some of them might be picked and many of them will disappear unnoticed.

Chapter 05

BLEEDING STONES

WHEN OUR HIRED YELLOW machine reached Bo-Waterside border post, it was almost seven in the morning, hundreds of people were waiting to cross the border with swelled plastic bags and so many stuff ranging from kitchen utensils to livestock. The Bureau of Immigration Liberia—Mano River Union turned to be a busy place with friendly chats, voices of donut and cornbread sellers, women bargaining for a cheap moto or taxi, usual daily quarrels, and bleating of goats who wait to cross the border for the Eid. I took my passport to the chief of immigration, to his little suffocating chamber where hundreds of people try to get through the little door, not even sufficient for two persons to pass. 'Yes Sir, where are you coming from?' His voice was too serious compared to his tiny body and childish face. I felt that he wanted to show that I was the most important person among the crowd. 'I live here in Liberia,' I replied to him shortly. 'Where is your residence license?' I heard someone among the thick human shield at the door told, 'Let the man go.' 'I work with the United Nations.' He seems satisfied with my reply and took his seal 'Seen at the Departure and VIP'.

I came out and hurried towards the other section of the Mano River Union—Border Post where a clean green and white flag was waving prestigiously with the cool waves of breeze coming across the Mano river.

'How are you Sir?

How can I help you?

Have you got visa for Sierra Leone?

How long you are planning to stay in Sierra Leone?'

The immigration officer was kind of more controlled and polite and he manifested a client-oriented behaviour that made me feel relieved. 'I'm good, heading to free town via Kenema and Bo,' and I added, 'Two weeks.'

It was impressive the way Sierra Leone welcomed me with a warmer attitude that manifested through soft and pleasant voices and manners. After the formalities of immigration, my next task was to find a taxi to Kenama, my first destination, which is the most proximate township of South West of Sierra Leon, where the rebels of the Revolutionary United Front (RUF) reigned a couple of years ago, marking one of the most inhumane civil conflicts in the world. I was able to walk less than ten metres from the Bureau of Immigration/Border Services, and a bond of guys surrounded me and kept asking where I need to go. I looked at the crowd and called one of them, selected randomly, and talked to him, keeping a very confident and unbroken eye contact to make him feel that I'm not nervous being in a new place which is almost 'in the middle of nowhere'. I obviously didn't want him to know that it was my first time in Sierra Leone. 'I live in Kenema, work in Liberia,' I started by giving him a hint that I was not a first timer. 'I need a taxi to Kenema, nonshared,' I added. While I was talking to the taxi driver, again a bunch of boys had surrounded me as what ants do when they found a big piece of food. 'Money change, money change.' I didn't want to show that I had some good amount of dollars in hand as I was in a country where there are a lot of ex-combatants left with arms, there is a history of looting and robbing expatriates, and on the top of all, I was going to go on following a route which is almost isolated in the dense West-African rainforests where anything can happen at any time. Usually, I hide most of my bank notes in a belt bag so no one could guess and keep one or two hundred dollars in my wallet with some invalid shopping cards. 'What is your rate?' I asked from one young guy, while the taxi driver was trying to tell me his rates for the car. As exchange for US$200, I got a plastic bag full of Leones' local currency, making me feel like there is another Zimbabwe in Africa. I was amazed to see the level of inflation remaining in the country even after half a decade after the civil conflict. 'Sir, $170,' the taxi driver's awaited voice woke me up, making me quite surprised.

'No way! Last time I paid only $100, it was two months ago' I raised my voice. 'No vex Sir, 150,' he came down, as I was told that the road-trip to Kenema is almost around seven hours and a difficult terrain. Also, the month of August is the peak of West African pouring rains that make the gravel roads almost impassable. Only Peugeot 4×4 wagons are used as taxies in the route and each taxi is loaded with at least ten passengers and all sort of stuff including chickens and goats considered as luggage are loaded on the top and wherever there is space. When a taxi is about to leave, it looks more like a camouflaged battle tank. 'I can pay you only $120,' I said firmly. Allowing his unhappiness over my bargain, he said, 'Okay, no problem, but it's no profit.' I did not try to convince him in further as I knew he would not be paid the same for the whole journey, even though he has to take ten plus passengers along with things for a truck of one cube. I will go alone with only one luggage which is even less than ten kilos. The car was an old Peugeot 305 station wagon, equipped with three additional wheels in the back, two gallons of fuel, many tools including showers, a huge anchor rope, and a few woodblocks. All these equipment gave me enough clues to prepare psychologically for the trip. I got in and sat in the back seat in the second row and threw my bag to the last seat. 'Why do we not start still?' I asked the driver as it was getting late. 'I am waiting for my supporter.' Even before he finishes his reply, one young boy came with two cans of water and got it to the front passenger seat.

'He is my helper, we have to push the car in many places,' the driver added.

I felt like I was on the verge of a new adventure in an unknown zone, a warm current was slightly passing through my hair, I felt. After a few tries of igniting the engine, we finally started to move, along the same path where 'Blood Diamonds' were smuggled to Belgium from Sierra Leone; the sensations mixed with excitement, uncertainty, and a little bit of fear start pinching my nerve ends. After five minutes of driving along the paved road, we entered a gravel road apparently turned into a muddy lake due to the pouring rains in August. Despite a few Palawa huts of villagers, not much human presence were to be noticed along the way and the vegetation was getting thicker the further we move towards Kenema, I remembered a scene from the film *Blood Diamonds*, Leonardo Di Caprio goes into the south-western forests of Sierra Leone which is literally 'in the middle of nowhere', where exactly I'm heading. Kenema, the heart of *Blood Diamonds*, then I will proceed to Bo, another township soaked with blood in shadows of diamonds. The station wagon moves vigorously, falling brutally in the mud puddles shaking everyone inside. It is just the beginning but my back started aching and started feeling a bit of nausea. After a few more kilometres, the thick rain forest owned both sides of the road and the sky was barely visible through the green canopy of trees. 'Gauda national park' a board by the side of road at least gave me a trace of a human intervention in this wilderness.

All of a sudden, the scene in front of us was shocking to me, though it looked like kind of a part of life for my driver and his helper. Two big trucks loaded a few more metres beyond the top end of the trailer were completely stuck in creamy mud like two greedy flies stuck on an icing-topped cake. One of the trucks had already leaned on a tree partially fallen in such a way that it was going to be there forever. The driver of the other is trying all his expertise to take the truck out of mud but every attempt makes the wheels go deeper and deeper in mud, making the road almost impassable for the other small vehicles waiting to pass in a long queue. Everyone got out, so did I, in order to get some fresh air and stretch myself a bit, and then took advantage of the waiting time to address a call of nature, in the African way in the middle of the bush. It was around 11.00 a.m., but the sun is proofed by the trees that reach as high as twenty-five to thirty metres or more than that. Some trees stand straight, prestigiously, like giants who are protectors of the forest with their body circumference which is more or less bigger than a traditional lighthouse and the height can also be the same. It started drizzling though we did not see any sign of being able to pass through the mess created by the trucks. After a constant struggle for more than an hour, we were able to release our stress with a sigh of hope. The truck started moving up and slowly got out of mud. Just like how scared birds sing when the sun peeps after an eclipse, everyone started engines with hope of passing the incoming hurdle. It was obvious that it would not be that easy for us to cross, too. Our helper opened the back of the car and took a few of those logs and two long pieces of flat wood sheets and started walking ahead. Now I understand why the driver needed to wait till helper arrives and how important role of the helper is. He laid two pieces of flat wood on the muddy road, aligning them exactly to the wheel width making sure that the wheels are not sinking in mud. We were fortunate to move almost till the end of the muddy area and all of a sudden the rear wheels slipped out of the wooden support. 'Can you please get down for a minute, Sir?' My driver 'Mohomad' seems bit frustrated and bit angry. I opened the door and was amazed by the level of red mud gathered around the car. There was no way to avoid stepping on mud, and the first step of mine ended up making my foot penetrate almost one foot in the mud layer, and the second followed. My shoes stuck in the mud, leaving me with my socks pasted with a thick mud layer. I pulled my shoes out of mud and tried to walk out like a rabbit stuck in a snare. This is going to be a constant part of my journey till Kenema, a bitter reality of travelling by road in rural West Africa during rainy season.

The car was surrounded by more than fifteen teenagers and some adults within a few seconds as if they were hyenas rushing to a carcass, wrestling with one another to push the car. It has almost become a livelihood for some villagers: they come and wait near the muddy areas of the road where the vehicles get stuck, probably they make the place impassable by digging to make sure that they would be able to catch their prey easily, and once a vehicle gets stuck, they voluntarily come and push. As the final stage of the invasion of helpers, they ask something from you, it could be something equivalent to US$5 in Leone. They are very well equipped with logs, ropes, shovels, and hoes and manage to get their little something from each and every vehicle that passes through their hurdle point, and at the end of the day, they should be happy with what is left in their hands. The car was brutally pushed by the crowd, reminding me a tribal war. Everyone, including me, has a thick mud layer up to knee level; as if nothing happened, the driver got into car with his legs full of mud, and then the helper followed by me. We had made just about forty-five minutes out of full journey, many more hours to move and we were wet and full of mud like mine workers. Expecting the worse, I made myself ready psychologically for any adventure on the road, and as predicted, every thirty minutes, we experienced the same, like the cycle of life that never ends. Once the car almost slipped out of the road turning two times anticlockwise and stopped, stuck in a bush by the side of the road, heightening the adrenaline flow to my bloodstream. In case something happens, there will not be a single person to attend to the casualties till the next vehicle comes.

And it is more than certain the boys who are waiting on the road with shovels and hoes would rather loot causalities than try to help them. When there are less opportunities and resources, opportunism becomes the main means of survival.

After struggling immensely with the muddy road in the middle of the dark and thick tropical forests, we started moving on a relatively rocky gravel road passing across the villages. For the first time, we were stopped at a road block made with a rope attached to a red piece of cloth. The driver stopped the engine, pulled out some Leones, and ran out into the small hut. In less than two minutes, the driver came out and got into the car, saying something in Krio to the helper. I did not understand a thing but I rightly guessed the situation. It was a police checkpoint where everyone has to pay a little something which is called 'small-small' in Liberia, but I do not know what Sierra-Leonese call the small bribes that are imposed by their police officers and border control officers. It seems that it is an obligation to pay a couple of thousand Leones before you come to the final destination. After a couple of checkpoints, we reached a border inspection bureau at the midpoint of our journey where I had to pull out all my documents to prove that I'm travelling merely as a tourist.

'How long you are going to stay in Sierra Leone?' The officer in uniform asked me with a gentle smile.

'Just two weeks', I replied.

'What is your occupation?' while going through my bundle of passports annexed to each other, he asked me with a sign of curiosity.

'I'm a psychologist, working for the United Nations.'

He looked convinced by my reply and had a quick look at my documents.

'You are going to treat my mother-in-law,' he added with a laughter. 'She is a difficult woman, vexing too much.'

I politely thanked the officer and left for the car as I didn't what to waste a minute of the trip as we never knew what was there waiting for us on the way.

The herds of goats led by little boys, women fetching water near roadside pumps, and men talking in Palawa shelters set in front of their little huts became a common sight since we started travelling through the villages. The car stopped at a few more local police checkpoints to 'give something'. The driver probably knew each and every officer who was deployed and no one questioned me where I was heading, or else they did not bother to ask as they got their little 'something'.

'Sir, I will stop for a while over there,' the driver pointed at some little huts near the road. As we approached there, I realised that those were local restaurants and shops where you may buy anything you need such as groceries, gasoline, cloths, medicine, and food. A couple of taxies had come to the line of shops where they had a snack or a full meal with soup and rice before they reach the destination. Everyone who goes from Kenema to Liberian border or else the other way around meet here and update each other with every single thing that happened on the way. And once drivers leave the shops, they are well informed by their colleagues and they can prepare for the rest of the journey. After around thirty minutes, we started again for the final stage of our journey; although there were no muddy traps like before, I was extremely exhausted due to the hardship of the journey. I wanted to have a shower and lie down a bit but I knew we have to make at least one more hour to reach the hotel I booked in Kenema. It was almost 4.30 p.m. but darker than what my wristwatch says. The sky was laden with gray clouds and about to burst out with a pouring rain like a curtain of water. The next thirty minutes, we started entering to the township where a lot of motorbikes haunted just like in Liberia, but they were with headgears in Sierra Leone, a sign of a bit more safety consciousness. Most among these boys who run the bikes should have been a part of west-side boys who terrified the nation years ago. As a result of disarmament programs carried out nationwide by United Nations Mission in Sierra Leone, they have gone for the next easiest legal livelihood which is 'running a Moto' and in any chance they tend to get involve in robberies as if they cannot get rid of the traits of their past life as child combatants. As we drove along a very busy market road, it took some time for us to pass the centre of the town to reach the hotel. Finally, around five thirty in the evening, under drizzling rain, I got out of the taxi, ending my first and unforgettable road trip in West Africa. 'Thanks guys, have a good evening,' I said to my driver and helper. I could not wait to check in to my room and rest till the next adventure in the land of blood diamonds unfolds.

The hotel was small but quite clean and organised; it was more like a lodge than a hotel but it was like a heaven full of divine luxuries to me. I felt asleep immediately after I got to bed, and it was probably the longest sleep in my life so far. I got up by eleven thirty in the morning. But still I had pains in my back and neck as if I have been beaten while asleep. As per my schedule, I was supposed to leave by ten for visiting diamond mines and it was already late and I wondered whether the driver had already left. I made a quick call to the reception and got to know if he was still waiting for me. Over the phone, I ordered full English breakfast for him and a simple fruit breakfast for me in order to compensate his time I wasted. After a quick breakfast, we left to diamond mines. On the way, we had to pass the town of Kenema. 'Diamonds', 'Good diamonds', ' Diamond centre', 'Diamond cutting', 'Kamokai Diamond cutters'. I was surprised to see the name boards of the shops. Most of the shops look like very basic and for an outsider who does not know anything about the diamond trade here in Kenema, these can be like old retail shops in Old Delhi or in Karachi, but what they sell here is one of the world's most expensive commodities that has already shown the whole world its killing power, leading to two bloody civil wars in West Africa. I asked the driver to park by the side of the road and decided to walk into a few shops, pretending I'm going to buy diamonds. Being a Sri Lankan, everyone perceives me as an Indian; no one in this part of world has ever guessed my nationality correctly. 'Hi, good afternoon!' I said to the security at the door with a smile. Even without a word, he opened the door and let me in. The few showcases are with different small boxes where the fortunes from the earth are kept. One guy, apparently a Muslim with his identical beard and costume with beret, asked me, 'Want to buy a stone?' I had only US$2,000 which is for my stay in Sierra Leone and I did not plan to buy diamonds not because I did not like but because I didn't want to fall in a situation where I end up paying bribes lot more than the true value of the diamond or else my name appears in a Liberian or Sierra Leonian newspaper with a partially or totally manipulated news, along with my country's name and the name of United Nations in case I refuse to give bribes. But I was not able to resist the desire to touch a diamond. 'Can I see some good stones?' I asked. These are the stones that have claimed thousands of lives, caused hundred thousands of rapes, mutilations, and looting. Hundred thousands of innocent people lost their shelter, livelihood, and livestock simply becoming either refugees or internally replaced populations for which a stylish NGO abbreviation is often heard as IDPs. On top of everything, around quarter a million of children lost their right to education and to have a healthy childhood. Thousands of children were abducted and given Kalashnikovs instead of books, and they were trained to kill, rape, and loot instead of providing them with formal education. The tiny little shinny stone that is on my palm has left a nonerasable patch of blood in human history, yet it is extremely attractive and unique. One part of myself tried to push me to buy one of them despite all the evil that these stones have cause and potential difficulties I might face while taking a diamond back. But I resisted my urge, for the moment and thanked the gentleman in the shop and stepped out to the car. 'Let's go to mines,' I told my driver.

After another break-bone trip inside the district of Kenema which was again in the middle of nowhere, we reached to a point where we were not able to go by a vehicle. 'Sir, we have to take all valuables with us as we will be going four more kilometres in the bush.' It was Sassy, my driver. I pulled my backpack which was the only treasure where all my travel documents were. There is already a little pathway which is an indication of human movement. The sun has come to the peak of the sky and, hitting us through the canopy of trees, was still hot and humid. 'It will rain in the afternoon,' Sassy told while removing a piece of branch fallen, blocking the path. 'We have hippos here.' I felt a cold current all over my body. Hippos can be extremely aggressive towards the strangers. Though they look like very passive, heavy, and lazy, these monsters run faster than they look and their teeth can cause mortal damages. As I had never seen a hippo in reality except on TV or other media, it was quite a curious feeling to expect in its natural habitat though an intense fear has already conquered every cell of my body. Beside the little pathway we follow, mangroves stand like life savers of those who walk alone, separating the swamps, which open to the river that flows through the forest a few hundred metres away from us, an ideal transit paradise for crocodiles and hippos where they find anything and everything for their survival. But as we move further, the river comes closer and the defence wall of mangroves thins to an extent that we walk along the banks of the raged Moa river flows roaring with such an aggression, swollen high almost up to the bank, due to seasonal rains in August. One simple mistake can take you on a journey of no return while walking on the bank which is narrower than two feet. 'Wait.' It was Sassy who muttered. 'Look up there!' he said showing me a piece of rock that had popped up in the river. Taking advantage of the island formed by the rock which is still exposed in the swollen river, a huge crocodile is sunbathing with his enormous jaws wide open. 'By this time hippos should be in water,' Sassy added. Usually, hippos come out early in the morning before the day becomes hot and sunny they get back to waters. But it is not difficult to notice the presence of a hippo in waters due to their unique nozzles, eyes, and ears that are always kept upon the level of the water. With a constant thrill, we reached an open area which is full of mountains of gravel and gray colour soil, which is on the verge of the river. A part of the riverbed is dug with excavators, and the water is diverted into the area with care, and a couple of men wash the gravel in a round basin-like filter with a metal net at the bottom to filter the water from the gravel. Starting from the men who shovel the gravel, those who bring the gravel to the washing point, and those who filter, the chain of work which is absolutely manual despite the excavator that is used to dig the riverbed is a vivid example of absolute exploitation of labour. The owner of the mine is watching with his greedy eyes, fixed to the filters, just like a fox waiting to grab the neck of a chicken while the men who filter stay almost half a day in muddy water up to thigh level, washing the gravel for the little sum of Leone that they collect at the end of each day.

'How long have you been working in the mines?' I asked one of the men who was relatively older among the other workers.

'Twenty-seven years,' he said with a humble smile. Wasting their whole life in mines, socked themselves in muddy water, working hard the whole day like slaves and their lives end in empty air in the name of legally exported or illegally trafficked diamonds, that become nonidentical in luxurious five-star jewellery shops in Antwerp, at the end either hung in the neck of a mistress or a wife of a millionaire, or in a ring worn on the finger of a lady whose hands have never touched a kitchen utensil, in the name of prestige rather than true love.

'How often are diamonds found here?' I asked the owner of the site.

'It depends but this one is a new site and we found a good stone two days ago. If you are lucky, we might find one today, too,' he said with indifferent gestures which seemed to me that what he pays for the employers is not much significant compared to what he gets out of stones that he finds on and off. I could be wrong, but my instinct interpreted his indifference as his attitude of negligence to his employees.

I met 'Kamokai' in the mine, who was a mine worker, a middle-aged man with a limping leg and a short stout body, who has been working with Mr Mohomad, the owner of the mine, since 1995. Kamokai was supposed to go to Kenema to bring some stuff for Mr Mohomad, and as we have a car, Mohomad asked whether we could give him a lift. I was more than happy as it would open the door for me to know more about the industry in a mine worker's perspective. 'Kamokai, How are you?' I asked him before he got into the car, in order to make an acquaintance with him and to invite him to sit with me in the back seat so that I would be able to talk to him. He smiled and looked at Sassy as if he seeks his assistance. 'He doesn't speak English,' Sassy said, while translating what I said in Krio.

After witnessing the hazardous conditions of work in the mines, I could not wait to talk to Kamokai, though there was no direct way of talking due to the language barrier, at least through the driver, despite the fact that he would filter a lot of things as he knew the mine owner well, or on the other hand, Kamokai, knowing that Sassy is a friend of his boss, he would hesitate to speak his heart.

'How many times, you have found diamonds and what happens when you find one?' I asked Sassy to translate for us.

'I have found so many stone in my mining life, I cannot even count as I always did washing,' Kamokai said with pride.

'Our boss is always with us while we wash. We find a stone, we give to him,' he added as if he is not a part of the moment of happiness of his boss when a stone is found.

Does he give you at least a treat when you find him a stone?' I asked him directly. He smiled, looking at me when Sassy translated my question to him. It was a smile of sadness, smile of helplessness, and a smile of a victim who has accepted being exploited as destiny and no-right for rights.

'How many children you have, Kamokai?' I broke his prolonged pensiveness after previous question.

'He says now five children and one wife,' Sassy mentioned. 'Now five children means?' I was completely lost hearing that. 'His wife is pregnant and expecting one, two of his children has died and his first wife, too.' I was shocked to see Sassy's indifference to what he says rather than to Kamokai's life story.

'What happened to them?' I asked Sassy.

'Woman was killed by Rebels, they raped her in his presence, took her to the bush and never returned, Elder boy went in river and found four days later, eaten by monitors and fish.' I didn't have the courage to ask what happened to the next but Sassy went ahead. 'Little girl died few weeks after dog died; they must have had the same sickness,' he added. It did not take much time for me to realise that the little girl must have died with rabies as thousands of rabies cases are found in Sub-Saharan Africa each year. Sierra Leone, being a country where the access to health is very limited and health infrastructure, expertise, and facilities are poor, especially in the remote areas along with its high prevalence of highly contagious tropical Homeric fevers such as Lassa fever which is endemic to Kenema and Bo plus common killers in Sub-Saharan Africa such as rabies, malaria, and typhoid, life is very much fragile and death is more untimely than timely. I just wanted to divert my conversation to another sphere as hearing his story, which can be a common story for many of the miners or in larger picture many of poor Leonons, is traumatising.

'How much you are paid a month?' I asked Kamokai.

'Whenever he goes to work he is paid, not for the month,' Sassy said. 'How much per day?' Before I finish asking the question, Sassy replied '1,000 Leone'. One dollar is equivalent to 4,320 Leone and these mine workers get less than one fourth of a dollar per day, for the immense physical work they do under a great risk and at the end of the time they will find themselves left alone in a deteriorating little mud hut, which is not bigger than a goat cage, stuff with various useless old stuff accumulated for decades like the pains of their bodies popping up with old age that was accumulated over years of work, laying on the mesh made out of rough wood, looking at the stars through the holes of Palawa roof, flashbacking how their children died, how hard they worked, how many times they fell sick, and waiting for their time to come to embrace the eternal peace in paradise that was preached about by the priests and amans who grabbed their last penny left, in the name of all mighty lord.

As we reached Kenema township, Kamokai got down from the car, thanking us. I thanked him silently for being a live proof of a heartbreaking reality behind those symbolic stones for marital bound which bonds two hearts. I kept looking at how his weak legs struggle to carry his wrecked boney body hidden under the old, torn clothes full of mud and sweat. This piece of fossilised carbon that shines like a piece of glass, pure and transparent, starts its long journey in the middle of nowhere, creating various issues on its way, such as labour exploitation, rapes, massacres and looting and trafficked through the illegal channels, before they shine on an appealing female body dancing with a full-suited man in a ballroom in a luxurious five star hotel, or walking hand to hand with her wealthy husband unto a limousine.

One end of the world earns millions in exchange for this bloody and sweaty piece of carbon while hundred thousands of lives are suffering and dying for the same piece of carbon at the other endo fo the world. Do all luxuries of heaven belong to hell? Does heaven owe immensely to hell? If this is the governing factor of the universe, heaven have to pay it back one day sooner or later.

I gave up my desire to have a diamond from Africa, though I remember one day my father told me most of the best diamonds are from Africa.

The next scheduled destination was Bo, the next township on the way to Free-Town from Kenema, which is also a mining area, and an endemic area for Lassa fever outbreaks that occur often; it is almost the mid-point one the road trip which is a three-hour drive. But I decided not to stop in Bo as I would witness nothing but the sad side of miners' lives, hence we headed to Free-Town, which is the capital of the Republic of Sierra Leone, once upon time a paradise for newly freed slaves who worked in British ships and in recent past another West African capital with soil soaked with blood and air full of echoing wails of victims of another ruthless civil conflict but still hold some prestigious icons of its history intact.

The road from Kenema to Bo is an old but paved road, and the rest of the road till Free-Town was a new road; therefore, we drove fast as we didn't have any other agenda. After almost two and a half hours of drive, traffic started to get dense and little buildings started appearing instead of the isolation where we drove through, and I learnt that we have already reached the suburbs of the city even before the 'Welcome to Free-Town' signboard that stood by the road appears. It was almost noon and there were a lot of movements in the suburbs, and I asked Sassy, 'How long would it take for us to go to Congo Cross?'—the place where our hotel was, which is not far from city centre. He was silent for a while and said, 'At least two hours because of traffic.' I had heard about terrible traffic in Free-Town but two hours to go less than four kilometres is unbelievable; it's a distance usually one can run or walk in less than thirty minutes. We just entered to a street which is almost invaded by little temporary shops infested with Chinese gadgets, Atae bars, used cloth sellers, bread sellers, and women and boys who were selling peanuts, cakes, kebab, and various stuff, walking paving their way in human river flows along the road. Legally established shops which are in the buildings in both sides of the road are not visible at all despite their signboards hanging or painted on the top. The line of red break lights of vehicles, from container carriers, to the little cars, runs to the infinity along the straight road that is a bit hilly, just like a hazard reflector of a highway. Only motorcycles just like the same motos in Liberia, but with more life conscious or lawful riders who wear headgears, that on the other hand, perhaps, they are not left in total impunity like in Liberia, move like arrows, blowing their siren constantly, though the little spaces between vehicles stuck in the traffic. Pedestrians stream through the vehicles almost parked unable to move, as if the traffic is never going to be clear. Under the hot sun, breathing polluted air, constantly disturbed by the loud west African music, screams of sellers and on top of everything, frustration and stress caused by the feeling of being stuck for hours, I felt drained and wanted to get to the hotel pretty soon.

'Après la pluis, le beau temps.' This French proverb has supported me psychologically in many life situations that swung between hope and despair. As it is said, after more than ninety minutes, we were able to get out from the congested area, I left like a prisoner who was just released, I took a deep breath, looked around, and filled with life when I saw a strip of beautiful beach running parallel to the road we drove. Lumley beach, here is civilisation, and life, I told to myself while winding down the shutters to breathe some fresh air. After passing though the marine drive for a few minutes, we reached Congo-cross area where I had booked a hotel. And Sassy's duty was called over once I was dropped in the reception of the little hotel in Congo Cross, where I could see the port of Free Town, from the lobby. At least after a few days of hazardous, tiresome, and frustrating trip overwhelmed with feelings of uncertainty towards human suffering, of anger, and fear to some extent, I really wanted a day or two off just to sit, eat some healthy food, relax looking at the Atlantic from my balcony, and write while preparing to next adventure scheduled in two days' time in one of the roadside ghettos in Free-Town.

By six thirty in the morning, I found myself sitting in the balcony facing the port of Free-Town across the Congo Cross, the hilly town infested with little metal-roofed houses built with cement blocks, without the plaster, which are almost attached to each other, bordering to the sea reminded me Port au Prince in Haiti. I enjoyed the loneliness and silence in the hotel and the scene of endless waters in the ocean while having my specially ordered tropical fruit breakfast that I was craving for since the day of departure. I just finished my breakfast, was sipping my second coffee, when I received a call from the reception. 'Your driver has come to pick you, Sir.' I realised that my rest has come to an end till the evening. I pulled my backpack, took a bottle of water and descended the stairs to discover another sphere of diamond battle, not with miners, but with a victim of cocaine, Kalashnikov, mutilation and an lifelong trauma, who was a hero when the decision between life and death was at the tip of the trigger of a Kalashnikov or the length of your limbs will be determined by a machete held in a hand of a drugged teenager.

I went to an expatriate hangout called Montana Cafe in Lumley beach area not to be noticed by anyone that I was going to interview one of the ex-child solders. I did not want to create even a single milligram of suspicion in anybody's mind though there had been lot of documentaries and articles done interviewing the ex-child combatants in Sierra Leone, by different media, and by freelancers. Nonetheless, there is always a possibility that someone could take the advantage of the situation to grab something from you. T.I.A. This is Africa, I still remember my Ghanaian friend told me when a Moto-rider tried to grab my wallet when I was paying a banana seller at roadside in Monrovia.

My coffee was already cold, still I'm waiting for my guest, it's been almost thirty minutes. All of a sudden I received a call. 'Sir I'm Kamara, I'm near cafe, where are you?' A long awaited meeting is about to be a reality, I was so excited and stepped out. The scene melt my heart at once; I had never met Kamara before, I got his contact through a psychiatrist who worked in Free-Town a few years ago. A slim, still young man, on his wheel chair, unable to come in to the cafe as there were a wooden stairs, waiting for me outside. As I got close to him I noticed, his both legs were off just below knee level. Went to the reception and asked where the it was possible to arrange a table for two people in the beach near the cafe. As they agreed, We started our conversation, with first cups of Italian coffee, and as we went on talking the number of cups of coffee consumed kept on been added.

'I'm the only male child among seven children for my father, my father was killed during the war. They cut his head and put on a stick in the intersection. He was a village chief. We had a big cattle, goats, and chicken, they looted everything and abducted me, I was only 12 years.'

Kamara looked at me as if he wanted a reassurance. I told him that can talk freely anything and everything, can take your own time and I will be listening with without judging.

'That was the last day I saw my family.' I allowed his silence.

'They took me to the bush, where they had a training camp, there were some other boys too, the youngest was 11 years old. We were locked up in a small old house that looked like an old farm house, full of dust and old cloths of men and women, which hints that there had been people locked up here before. Everyone was crying, frightened, and lost. I do not remember whether I thought of what happened to my parents and sisters; that night, I witnessed my father was chopped into pieces, my mother was raped at gun point, but the terror of abduction hindered my grief and I was completely possessed by an intense fear. The whole night, I was not sleeping. I cried calling my mum to keep me warm and safe, forgetting that she might have quitted this earth already. Every footstep I heard during the night gave me palpitations. Times of silence at night were times of uncertainty for me; I didn't know what comes after silence. For us, mice are just a part of life; in West African villages, mice dominate over our lives, they are in every corner of house, but they were able to hold my breath every time they run across the place where I was lying down. One time I heard someone was talking closer to the window of the building. There was only one window which was nailed so that it cannot be opened. It was breakable even with a good kick but I always heard that there was someone near the window, which prevented me from trying to break it. I peeped through a small gap between the piece of wood nailed to the window frame, whenever the sound comes, the last time I peeped through, it was daytime, should be morning and there was a boy with a radio and a gun. He was smoking like a chimney while muttering some pieces of songs, moving his hands and head like a hip-hop singer. I kept on looking at him for a while; this boy who was slightly older than me, seems happy and powerful with his gun in hand.

The creaky noise of the door repositioned me among the boys even without my knowledge, almost after thirty-six hours, a light came to the room but along with armed rebels, then I realised we were not a few, there were around fifty children, some were beaten to bleed and had scars everywhere: those should be the ones who had resisted. "Come out all, hurry up!" one rebel screamed and started beating us with bamboo sticks. We were blindfolded and pushed in to back of a cab. I felt a kick on my butts when I was trying to get into the cab; I was almost thrown inside; a piece of meat thrown to the cage of a tiger. I was starving and still under shock. After around twenty minutes' drive, along a very difficult road, that almost shook us as if we are in a boat caught by a cyclone, the cab stopped abruptly. "Hm get down all!" It was another order. We were pushed brutally down from the cab. There was a minute of silence, and we heard the cab started and drove away. Still the pieces of clothes tied around head covering the eyes were intact.

"I'm Lt Bangura, commanding officer of this area." He kept on revealing his full warlord autobiography before us in a very boasting yet a serious tone. I did not know whether we were attracted to his long speech, full of elements of hatred, impulse, aggression, bravery, and determinedness. I would rather be scared about the next moment and surrendered unconsciously to his speech out of fear and terror, so do the other boys, I assume. "Your parents are weak, they are farmers, carpenters, but you are soldiers, you are strong, you are respected, you have power, you have a gun, the best gun on the earth AK 47, gun of liberation, gun of killers, gun of common people, the gun that brought common man to power." His voice came nearer and gripped my arm. I left like a rabbit in the coil of a hungry python. "You, you are a strong boy, you are going to be a man now, a man! A man! Powerful man! Like none other!" I was terrified and numb as he was talking to my ear. "Take this and pull their trigger!" he yelled like a devil, placing a gun on my hand, and putting my right index finger on the trigger of the gun. I was numb and I did not move. "I told you! Pull the trigger! or I will pull my trigger!" He yelled touching my head with a cold piece of metal. I knew it was a gun and I had no other way. *Tik tik tik tik*, the gun started firing as I pulled the trigger, I almost fell down because of the backfire. The gun is silent, and hot. I'm frozen and lost. The rebels started cheering while one among them was untying the knot of the black piece of cloth covering my eyes.

A man is lying in a lake of red blood, still bleeding, and the wall near him is sprayed with blood, like in a horror film. Still they were cheering me with their AKs up in the air, dancing in hip-hop artists. Other children are still blindfolded and see nothing. I could not believe my eyes, I felt as if my feet went under the earth, I felt like I was about to faint. "You are a man now," Lt Bangura, whose face I can see now, reminded me 2pc, told me with a rueful laughter. I looked at the gun, my shaking hands, and again at the body lying in hot blood, my heart started pounding as if it was going to come out, while my eyes were dry though I wanted to cry.

I do not remember whether anyone among us did the same but I slightly remember I was given an injection and everything else went blurry. The next day, I woke up in the same room where we were locked up the day before, with the same group of boys. Few weeks, we were given intensive yet very informal physical training which made us like dead bodies at the end of training session. In addition, a simple mistake, or else in case you are overwhelmed with the exercises and get tired, you will be beaten till you restart. Every day I had new bruises and wounds somewhere, especially on my back and legs. One day I was beaten by one of the rebels who trained us, till I bleed out of my nose and I thought I would run away that night but it was impossible as we were guarded every single minute by boys with AKs and one attempt will make them pull the trigger without asking a single word. As one of the boys tried to run away one week after the abduction, he was shot on his legs and brought to us as if they wanted to show us the destiny if you try to escape. They beat him brutally and mutilated him to death.'

For last two days in Freetown, it was very common to see people without hands and legs, which confirms to me what I had heard, read, and seen about mutilations during the war. Apparently more than 100,000 individuals, both male and female, children and adults, across the country have become victims of these inhumane atrocities in Sierra Leone itself, and many more in Liberia, too, as the civil wars in Sierra Leon and Liberia have very close relationship, which led the former president of Liberia, Charles Taylor, convicted for fifty years in prison by the special court for Sierra Leon in 2012. When the conviction was pronounced, I was in Liberia and the UN mission in Liberia broadcasted a security adversary restricting the movements of UN staff on that day, expecting demonstration or any sort of acts of violence from the local population as there was a belief that a lot of Liberians still support and consider Charles Taylor a true leader of people whereas there was not even a single demonstration or any violence despite that the local newspapers had published diverse articles for and against the conviction.

'After few weeks I was given an AK and sent me to another section, where I met Lt Nero, whose real name was unknown, who was my commanding officer.

One night, Nero came with one man, by ten in the evening. Hurrying, he told me, "You are going to fight the war." He took out a injection-syringe and injected me with something that I had already been injected at the end of every long training day, which made me feel nothing but unreal and flying like a kite. "You will be bulletproof, a real warrior, an iron soul of RUF and you will no longer feel the pain!" His words were echoing in my head, repetitively, over and over again. And I was already feeling lost and confused, after the day I shot the man down, the scene comes to my mind, live and vivid every night, I hear the rounds of gun, his scream, and I wake up in horror, sweating, and it takes a few minutes for me to realise it's a flashback. Afterwards, I could not sleep for hours. Whenever I hear gunshots, I start palpitating and sweating. Now I'm with a gun and ordered to go and fight the war, or else I will be shot from behind.'

The stages of Kamara's life are just like that of the life of a herd of lions in an African savannah. Whenever the male lion of the herd is unable to protect himself against the invading males, the whole offspring of defeated lions will be massacred by the invaders and helpless lionesses witness the playful cubs of their own blood and flesh, being fed with milk from their heavy breast laden with love for the little ones. And next moment, the grieving lionesses find themselves making love to the assassins of their kids, hosting the descendants of assassins in their wombs, and ultimately, after couple of months, new cubs, the offspring of killers, become the new beloved cubs of the lionesses till the next victorious invaders cross the grassland from the other side of the savannah. Kamara was abducted by the same RUF who killed his father, raped his mother and their herds and house, probably his sisters may have become victims of rape or forced prostitution or either killed or mutilated, and now the abducted child of twelve years has been transformed to a powerful man by the glorious AK47, by the assassins of his family, perpetrator of rape and loots, and he is about to fight for them, probably would die for them as if the destiny of a victim is constant victimisation no matter whose hands he or she is in.

'Under the influence of Brambram, which is mixture of gunpowder and cocaine, you cannot feel the risk you are under; you behave brave and inhuman as your judgement is almost totally impaired. I remember I was shooting in the frontline, as they always sent us, little children in the frontline, always under influence. We used to shoot at anything that we meet along our way. We didn't talk but with guns, which cannot determine who is fighting the war and who is not, who is the foe and who is not. Hypnotised with Brambram and empowered with AK, storms into the villages like Lake flies in Malawi, destroying almost everything on our way, for us a man is an enemy and woman is a prey irrespective of their ages, creed, and religion; those who resist us were treated either with AK or machete.'

It was unbelievable to hear what Kamara describes as it's all about how a gun and drugs have transformed a victim to an obedient servant of his own enemy, and repeating what he went through as a victim, victimising innocent villagers, looting them, chopping their hands and legs, raping women in the same way his mother and probably his sisters were raped. Every single thing that came out of Kamara's mouth at this stage reflected on cycle of victimisation, revictimisation, and transformation of a victim to perpetrator as a result of unconscious revictimisation. While this cyclic process occurs within the individual, thousands victimised perpetrators like Kamara add into the growing pyramid of antisocial criminals in the conflict-torn society and in the nation in a large picture which is apparent to the external world.

'Have you chopped hands or legs?' I asked.

'Few times whenever we found enemies,' he said. 'In case if they find us, they chop us with machetes.'

'Who are your enemies?' I asked out of curiosity.

'Oh, all except those who fight for us, especially those who wanted to go and vote.' His reply is simple as such, and it looked like rest of the country except the Revolutionary United Front and their allies are enemies. This vague explanation is quite enough to comprehend the complex nature of the civil conflicts of this part of the world. Forcefully recruited child soldiers know nothing but torture and kill anything that moves and the high command just use them for their survival. The value of the life of a child soldier is less than that of a chicken in the village.

'You cut hands and legs of villagers?' Kamara took some time, and his face started changing. His heavy lips started tremors by themselves as if they want to disclose something that his heart had kept locked for years. And his eyelids were not strong enough to resist the warm flood of tears that erupted like a damn-break, and ran all over in his cheeks.

'Sir,' he looked at me.

'I had to use the machete many times; we cannot disobey the orders.'

'What were the orders?' I asked.

'We were ordered to prevent people to go for voting,' he said calmly.

'We were ordered to cut the hands of those who were going to vote, so that they won't be able to vote,' he added. His voice started wobbling and he turned his head away.

Tears running along his cheek and his trembling hands were evidence of unsaid pain caged in an ex-child solider, a double victim of African civil conflicts, another bleeding soul because of someone else's greed for power, and finally, a sacrifice for a diamond which is worn by someone who is totally unknown to him.

'I did not feel any human feelings but the feeling of superiority, powerfulness, super-man-hood, and revenge, that have been pumped deep into my mind by our commanders, to my body by Brambram, and kept on chopping and killing villagers, like an armed mob rather than combatants, as other child soldiers did. But when we fight with government soldiers, where there were also an unofficial wing of forcefully recruited children which is the most virulent part of the army, we were driven by the fear factor, we fought mostly under influence, without knowing where we were heading, how to protect oneself while fighting as we were not properly trained, often we were sleepy and experienced blurred vision due to drug and when we're sober we were terrified and afraid. In such situations, I wanted to go and hide under the bed of our little hut in the native village which is now just a memory of my family members, who were lost, killed, and raped. I forget that our little hut, made by my father and uncles, no longer exists and the village is just abundant and haunted by armed men who are transformed into devils with Brambram and AKs. Sometimes I cry the whole night while in the ambush, though I was told that soldiers never cry.'

As I had been hearing stories of a few other ex-child-soldiers in Liberia as well as in Sierra Leone, I was able to understand and visualise the chronology of events in Kamara's life as a 'freedom fighter' in the eyes of the chief commander of the Revolutionary United Front, Foday Saybana Sankoh, as well as the next door rebel leader, ex-president of Liberia, Charles Taylor, leader of National Patriotic Front of Liberia, who was responsible and convicted for outbreak of fighting in Sierra Leone. The words of glory, patriotism, revenge, power, manhood, and god along with hypnotic extracts of poppies in conflict beaten Afghan valleys, and with the universal symbol of terrorism (AK)*Kalashnikov*has usurped not only his past but also his present and his future. The same machete he used to cut hands and legs of innocent villagers, cut his one leg and one hand off, which reminded me of the cycle of karma taught in Buddhism lessons in school twenty years ago when I was not interested in learning, but today I witness the live evidences of those teaching.

Today, Kamara is living in Freetown, as a especially abled single young man, selling used clothes as his livelihood. He had learnt that his mother is no more, and one sister is living in Freetown with her son who is born as a result of being raped by rebels. She works at a supermarket, after returning from Guinea where all of them escaped during the war. Others did not return and completely disconnected from Kamara and her sister. With dreams shattered by the conflict, his brighter future that his parents dreamt of is already almost darkened forever by a bright piece of fossilised carbon. Kamara is just one of them, one among thousands of ex-child soldiers who are lost in the society of Sierra Leone and there are victims of these victims who represent a significant proportion of society, are living with lifelong trauma as live evidences of cruelties committed by their own brothers.

It was almost 18.45, the sun was dying, sinking in the infinite Atlantic, as if the evening sky reddish like a bloody cloth does not want to give light to this part of world anymore. I left Montana Cafe, thanking Kamara for unfolding his story before me. Though there were obscure ends, he gave me an insight of the life of a child soldier in Sierra Leone and he reminded me that nothing is perfect and nothing is hundred percent sure like the cups of Italian coffee left on our table, with dark deposits of coffee in the bottom covered by white ceramic layer

The next morning after my usual early morning breakfast, I decided to walk in the city, covering some of the attractions that I highlighted in my *Lonely-Planet West Africa*, to see what really the commoner's life in the city looks like. Walking along the streets, referring to my map, took more public attention than I thought of; however, after moving through the crowded, dusty, and dirty roads, I was able to locate the famous 'Big Market' of Freetown, a place that every tourist who come to Sierra Leone does not miss, where, most of the Sierra-Leonian handicrafts are sold for touristic prices, that can be even ten times higher than the local price.

The old building with two stories is full of different small stalls full of wooden crafts, African Batik cloths, ready-made traditional attire, cane work, paintings, apparently old coins and masks sold as antiques but in most cases they are kept buried for some times for making them look like antiques, small ornaments made out of wood and plastic, and most iconic and famous 'Country Clothes,' very heavy and abruptly woven thick cotton cloths painted using natural colouring of extracts of trees, where the sellers are bit aggressive in their manner of trying to impose what they sell on whoever comes in. Also, the competition between the sellers is very tight and everyone wants you to buy something. While roaming inside the market, avoiding the annoying sellers, I was looking for buying something as a souvenir of my visit to Sierra Leone.

'This is genuine Hippo teeth,' a seller came to me with some white-colour carvings and jewels. Small statues, pendants, and rings made out of Hippo teeth are unique to this place. Though the carvings are not sharp and refined as professionally done, they were acceptable but unless you know how to identify a genuine hippo teeth, it's is not advisable to buy as there is less accountability and genuineness in such markets where there is lot of foreign buyers who come just for one visit. However, the amount of items made of hippo teeth silently reveals another story untold to the external world. Poaching of elephants and rhinos are widely discussed but I had never heard about the hippo poaching, but in reality, including the smaller species of hippos called pigmy hippos endemic to West Africa, all the hippos are more or less vulnerable to extinction and some of them have already become extinct. Having an approximate population of 3,000 pigmy hippos left, Sierra Leone has the highest density in the world, but despite what statistics say, the pigmy hippos in Sierra Leone have been already classified as endangered by IUCN. Looking at the carvings and jewels made out of hippo teeth, a similar feeling that I had in the diamond shop came to my mind. Almost everything that looks precious from Africa are products of exploitation, blood, pain, deprivation, and injustice and most of us from other parts of world are not aware of the bitterness that remain latent in those precious things that we long to own as symbols of luxury and prestige. It looks like the colonisation has its virtual or distant form through which not only those who scrambled for Africa, hundreds years ago, but also the entire rest of world has colonised Africa in a passive yet in a lasting form that sucks all the resources from the continent, not only creating intercontinental conflicts and environmental issues but also making the whole world's human and animal population and ecosystem endangered.

A tourist who came to Freetown will never miss the famous 'Cotton Tree' icon of Freetown, which stands like a giant who is a guardian of the country's history since 1792 when the Nova Scotians, the Afro-slaves of British America, landed in St George Bay, the point where the settlers' history in Sierra Leone began. Near the national museum of Freetown, right in the middle of a meeting point of three roads, a gigantic tree under which the first Baptist service in African continent took place on 11 March 1792, by reverend David George, silently shading the surrounding from hot tropical sun and the wind that comes across the Atlantic embraces the leaves, gently generating a soft melodious sound as if the first song of liberated Afro-Americans still echo within the tree.

Awake and sing of Moses and the Lamb,
Wake! Every heart and every tongue,
To praise the saviour's name,
The day of jubilee is come,
Return ye ransomed sinners home.

I'm still able to recall that my father used to tell me about the 'Cotton Tree' of Freetown while he was telling stories about the slave trade in West Africa and he showed me an old photo of the cotton tree we're standing near; there is no much difference between the photo of the tree he showed me fifteen years ago and now, and he is no longer on this earth but the memories would not fade till you embrace them and they determine the moments of smiles and tears.

Generally, the historic places except 'Cotton Tree' are not given much importance and are not very well maintained. 'Wharf Steps and the Guard House' the colonial constructions, stone steps, and commissariat building, built in 1818 by government of Wharf, which was often referred to as Portuguese steps although there was no relation between the Portuguese and these constructions as they had already left Africa in 1800s, today they are left in ruins and abundantly covered with garbage. There is no more cascade running along the steps as it used to be, originally

'King's gate or gateway to the king's yard,' which was the hospital and asylum for the rescued slaves by British valour and philanthropy, which is at the other end of the road where the 'Whaf Steps and Big Market' are, was my next destination. An arclike structure next to the General Hospital of Freetown still remains graceful as the hospital is operational and maintained. Despite some ruins of forts and some remaining city boundary canons, nothing much of the manmade landmarks of history is retained at present in Freetown. In addition, the national museum of Freetown owns more or less traditional heritages and a significant amount of evidence of colonial history, as Freetown remained the capital of British West Africa because of the strategic importance of its geographical location and position of the biggest natural harbour in the continent, even though the Leonians were very resistant to colonial rule.

Contrary to the manmade tourist attractions in Sierra Leone, the country is gifted with breathtaking natural attractions such as River Number 2 beach, Lumley beach, Sierra Leone river, and many national parks. As one of the wettest countries in the world, the seasonal monsoons affect the accessibility of tourists to those sites. Lumley beach and river number 02 are both exotic tropical beaches of the Atlantic ocean, with shallow waters and golden sands, along which are a couple of cafes and restaurants that serve good local and international food, but it's not advisable to go alone as there are cases of arm-robbing the foreigners especially late in the evening. As arms of the civil conflict roam free in the hands of the unemployed youth, even after the disarmament programs implemented all throughout the country, the probability of a weapon being used for looting for survival is significantly high in this zone.

After all of my walking up and down in the city, I just came to my favourite place where I interviewed Kamara two days ago. I sat at a table very near to the beach, at the wooden balcony of Montana Palace, by six in the evening. The chants of Hausa Mosque is slightly heard, blending with the sea waves, and the sinking sun at the horizon altogether gave a sense of relaxation after a hectic week and a kind of a pause to the panorama of terrific incidents and stories being visualised in my mind.

I enjoyed the sight of the breaking of milky waves in the blue ocean as if it has built resiliency to remain happy and joyful irrespective of the misery of the land it embraces full-heartedly. This Atlantic should have witnessed the atrocities committed on this land, during the devastating civil conflict, but remained calm and insensitive as the world on the other side of this immense blue waters. I ordered my usual cappuccino, undid the first two buttons of my shirt, and opened a book that I had bought a few years ago, which describes the indigenous beliefs, customs, and rituals existing in Sub-Saharan Africa, known as Juju, Marabou, or witchcraft among local populations. Witchcraft is affiliated with everyone's life here in Africa, Sometimes it can be the only explanation given, accepted, or understood by the local population for a sudden untimely death, sickness, loss of something, harmony of a relationship, marriage, miscarriage, or any unexpected event in human life. And in African context, some people are witches and they are evil and demonic. In western and central parts of Africa, witchcraft determines many things in daily life than in any other part of Africa, although in general, whole Africa believes in the existence of witchcraft and their power and these indigenous beliefs and practices are known in different names in different parts of the continent. I kept on reading while I was sipping my coffee, and it seems to me that another horizon opens to be discovered in the same zone where I am.

Instead of taking the same road through Kenema and Bo, I decided to go by air to Monrovia, the capital of Liberia, and I headed to Lungi International Airport of Freetown which is situated in an island separated from the city. By three thirty in the afternoon, I was in the ferry looking at the city moving away from me, and on the other side, I noticed that the Arik-Air flight to Monrovia has safely landed to the one and only runway of Lungi International Airport, meaning that I'm leaving Freetown, finally Sierra Leone, with stories of diamonds and child-soldiers roaring within me.

Chapter 06

NOT EVERY ONE ASHANTI

Kodjo Opoku, an akan, before he became a Ghanaian, was my best friend in Liberia, with whom I shared my house for around three good years. He was a principled and overtly religious person who believed in depth that the prime purpose of life is to serve God. The endless arguments broke out between me and Kodjo whenever he tried to impose his Christian vision to life. I, a realistic individual, rather than being influenced by any religion, including Buddhism, which is my religion by birth, deny the existence of God, whereas every single story started and ended with God with Kodjo, despite that we used to have productive times, often discussing subject matters in international development, sociopolitical and environmental issues as development workers. As most of the people talked about, he fell into the stereotypical category of an extremely God-fearing, disciplined, educated, and reasonable individual, which Ghanaians are seen by the rest of the world. We used to have our after-work conversations in the balcony of our apartment, while sipping tea, looking at Liberian kids playing football in a barren land near a swamp bordering to River Doe. And one day I happened to disclose my motivation to come to Africa and intention to write about my first-hand experiences in the continent. 'Why don't you come to Ghana, I will take you around.' His words were genuine as always and the following weekend, I packed my bags for the next destination in the same western part of Africa but with an expectation of seeing a difference.

Kwame Nkuruma was known to me since the time I was even unable to understand what a politician is, but I had seen his photos in paper cut-outs and in some old magazines and I can slightly recall that my father was repeating this name during his regular political science tuition classes for students who are preparing for university entrance exams. That was the only name familiar to me from Ghana, 'Gold Coast' in colonial time till I came to Africa. However, after being based in West Africa, I was able to explore detailed information and knowledge about Ghana as there were a lot of Ghanaians in Liberia in all layers of society, starting from fishermen to senior-level professionals in corporate and nonprofit entities with whom I used to interact in a daily basis at work as well as in social settings. In addition, there was a Ghanaian restaurant in downtown of Monrovia, where most of the Ghanaians used to go to eat their Bankun, Kenke, or Fufu, with goat soup, fried fish, pepper, or peanut soup that they were missing in Lebanese or local restaurants in Liberia and finally end up emptying few Guinness Dark, a British brand of stout bitter beer which is very famous in Ghana, and plunge themselves in never-ending conversations about anything comes into their heads and very seldom the conversations turn into hot arguments. Being a part of such companies, accompanying my friend, I became familiar with many aspects of Ghanaians and Ghana. The tribal and linguistic diversity of the country, gastronomy, as well as politico-economical aspects had become a part of everyday discussions in my life, in addition to my reading on history and environment as predeparture preparation to Ghana. Basic conversations in Twi Akan language, which is mainly spoken in Kumasi, and Ghan which most of the people in Accra speak, and some Fanthi words, along with almost total familiarisation of food have been acquired, grace to prolonged interaction with Ghanaians.

The designated destination for R&R, rest and recuperation for the staff of United Nations Mission in Liberia, was Accra, the capital of Ghana where a free UN flight flew twice a week, every Friday and Sunday, enabled some of us to go to Accra for weekends for free of charge. Most of the time, those who were based in Liberia had to transit via Accra as there was a wider choice of airlines to fly to any selected destination. Hence, most of the time, I used to transit via Accra for the last six months, which provided me with some opportunities to build contacts as well as to experience Accra from time to time.

On Sunday, 8 January 2012 at 11.28, UN151, United Nations Shuttle Flight, Boeing 737, safely landed at Kotoka International Airport. I was planning to stay one week in Ghana to explore the country that bear the remains of a dark history of slavery and where some the Afro-Americans come to see the traces of their ancestry and where their forefathers left their native continent through the gate of no return.

Stories of slavery used to be a very exciting part of my free-time stories as a little child. I used to have hundreds of questions to which my father was unable to convince me with his answers. Having never had his feet on this continent, merely basing on what he had learnt through extensive reading, that could be someone else's indirect experience or else quoted from somewhere else, he had accumulated an adequate level of general knowledge about Africa, which provided me light to find my pathways in the continent of darkness. After completion of the immigration formalities at the airport, which took some time as the number of immigration officers and their level of efficiency are insufficient when a couple of flights landed at the same time.

'What you brought for me?' one immigration officer asked.

'I brought a valid passport and a valid visa on it,' I replied, knowing what he meant. It looks like they are used to Indians and Chinese businessmen who are residing in Ghana, from whom they can easily grab some dollar notes while stamping their passport. For sure, I look like an Indian, being a South Asian, but my passport says precisely where I'm from. He stamped the passport even without looking at me. When I came out of the airport, it was around 12.45, the sun was shining at its fullest and I felt as if I was in an oven, the air was heavy with humidity. At a far corner in the exit gate I saw my friend Kodjo waving at me. My quest in the Gold Coast had just begun.

To an outsider who does not have a clue about the difference of the various nations in West Africa, all of these people would look alike despite their slight differences in height, colour, and of course the languages and gastronomy that one cannot see from a distance even though there is a great diversity that exists between the nations and tribes within each nation. The moment I reached Ghana, I noticed the differences of colour in the general population, a bit darker than that of Liberia, which is an immediately noticeable nuance, but the underlying differences are greater, which are revealed slowly when you interact. Kodjo and I first went to a roadside restaurant near the airport where some Ghanaian delicacies are served. The first time ever in my life I had a roasted guinea fowl in my plate, a conserved animal in Sri Lanka, and some villagers raise them at home as a guinea fowl usually is concerned about intruders and call with their loud, high-shrieking various identical voices for different threats. A bit of a dry and chicken-like roasted bird that I would never eat in my homeland is in my plate, and some slices of tomatoes, French fries, and shito (*shito is the Ghanaian version of chilli paste which is oilier than the Chinese chilli paste*), which is pretty similar to Chinese paper paste but more oily and with more dried fish inside, are on the table for lunch. The order of my friend came to the table in a large clay bowl, a fufu, placed almost sunk in hot goat soup like testicles of a goat in a bowl served with red curry. TIA, common abbreviation for 'This is Africa', I told Kodjo. He laughed as he knew already the story about the guinea fowl back at home. 'Bonne appetite!' We had to rush as we were supposed to cover some of the attractions in Accra that afternoon.

As I was advised that money exchange is more profitable in private places in the city than in the airport, we drove to a shop, a black money market kind of a place, to get some dollars converted into Ghanaian Cedis. 'Thank you, Sir! Here is $2,000 in Cedis,' the good-mannered gentleman at the cashier gave me 4,300 Cedis, which made me feel completely deceived and pissed.

'How comes you give me 4,300 Cedis, for $2,000 whereas the exchange rate is 1$ = 9,100 Cedis?'

That was the information I had heard and read of. The cashier looked shocked and kind a totally confused. 'Sir, you are mistaken,' he told while trying to be calmer than he is.

'What is your exchange rate?' I asked with a tone of suspicion.

Replied the cashier, '$1 = 4.3 Sir, which is much more than what you get from the bank' and he showed me the computer screen with the latest exchange rates via an online converter which is reasonable enough as a proof. But I, too, had my reasons to know what happened, and I kept on questioning why the rates I was informed and present rates are different. There was a moment of silence between us and all of a sudden he put his hands on his forehead in gesture of surprise. 'Sir, you talk about the old Cedis that are out of use since 2007 and the new Cedi is equivalent to 10,000 old Cedis,' he told with a smile and showed me a piece of paper related to the currency exchange rates that changed in 2007. Finally I was convinced, thanks to the cashier for his patience and professionalism that he manifested and I left the shop with 4,300 Cedis for my expenses in Ghana.

Prior to the visit, I had booked a hotel in Accra, which cost me around $170 per night, quite expensive considering the quality, but as Accra is the most expensive city in West Africa, nothing cheaper could be expected, but I strategically avoided paying for my full stay to shift to another place in case I find a better one for a cheaper price. After checking in, we left for driving around in the city.

It was already 15.00 h, still hot like a frying pan, we just drove through the streets of the city where the vehicles moved slower than the pedestrians, and I was able to imagine how this circulation would get worse after office hours when everyone comes out to the road to rush back to home. Simply, the number of vehicles on the roads is not bearable for the infrastructure though the roads are quite good and wide with functioning automated signals, compared to poor road infrastructure in most of the other West African countries. On top of the heat and terrible traffic, air and noise pollution are overflowing in Accra. At the very moment I entered the city, I felt like burning and on the very first day in the city I started sneezing as if I was under a poisonous gas attack. There were some true and visible efforts to make the city as green as possible which took my mind back to my time in Colombo, capital of Sri Lanka. Despite some beggars who are waiting near signal lights, the city looks normal and calm, but lively as any other African city where all types of people are found on the same surface at the same time, just like pepper soup in which you will find vegetables, spices, all sort of meat, and fish altogether which are separately prepared and served in the other end of world. Again TIA, this is Africa, and this is the African way and this is their life which is good enough in their eyes, I thought. The buildings, roads, vehicles, and people you see in the city says that there is a big difference in terms of development and attitudes of people in Liberia and Sierra Leone, people are competitive in progression, although there is apparently lack of planning and organised nature.

The Mausoleum of late Kwame Nkrumah, ex-president of the Republic of Ghana, who was a pioneer in gaining independence for the Gold Coast, and then pumped blood and flesh into the Republic of Ghana, is brought and erected in Accra, though it was originally in Kumasi, heart of Ashanti kingdom today. A very seldom case that a Ghanaian raise his voice against the days of Nkrumah, instead most of them highlight those days as golden days of the nation, which gives an outsider a strong message. In addition, Nkrumah is considered as the father of the nation, not only because he was the forefront leader in the independence of Gold Coast, prime minister in Gold Coast, and the first president of democratic and sovereign republic of Ghana, but probably because he was a Nzema, an ethnicity related to the larger group of Akan with royal blood. He is one of the leaders who advocated for Pan-Africanism, along with Jules Nyerere, in Tanzania, Patrice Lumumba, in Zaire. The names to which my ears are very used to since my little age. Dr Nkrumah brought Kente, the traditional attire of Akans, to the international level, as a symbol of Ghanaian nationalism, yet there were a lot of other ethnic groups in Ghana that I discover today. The colourful and heavy-looking dress, pretty similar to the dress of monks in shape that Nkuruma wore among international community, was an eye-catcher to anyone who sees it first and would come to a quick judgement about the Ghanaian national dress, whereas it's not holistically representing the nation, especially those who feed the nation.

There is no way that a foreigner comes to Accra for leisure misses the shopping mall of Accra, a medium-sized shopping centre where one would rather do window shopping than buying anything. The prices are high up in the skies and look like they are meant for extravagant tourists or high-class locals but not for the commoners of a country where the average gross domestic product per person is less than $3,000 a year.

At the other end of the city is Makola marketplace where most of the common people as well as the tourists go to get something for a reasonable price through your ability of bargaining while trying to safeguard yourself from pick-pocketing as well as the stream of people running in the market like flood. In case you do not know how to tackle the sellers, you would end up paying a very high price, higher than what you pay at expensive malls, for something which is not even at a desired quality, but if you are used to crowded African common markets or else accompanied by a local, you would find best buys.

The first African national dress that I had seen on photos is Kente, and now that I'm in Ghana, I wanted to buy one for me as a souvenir of Ghana, that again comes back to the idea of seeing Ghana entirely, nearly through symbols and heritages of Akans. I was taken to a place where they manufactured Kente cloths in the suburbs of Accra where I was able to see how these multicoloured handmade clothes come to life using manual weaving techniques with the help of basic wooden weaving machines. This piece of cloth, the symbol of royalty, put on by Akans in Ghana, Togo, and Ivory Coast, today is everyone's dress irrespective of your clan, caste, ancestry, nationality, or class but still remains a symbol of Ashanthis and a heritage of Ghana. Every little piece of cloth had different colours and designs, and as per Ghanaians, the Kente in Togo and Ivory Coast are different from the ones in Ghana, in terms of design and colour, which made me more curious to add one more destination to my itinerary in Ghana to discover Kente more in depth. I ticked Kente village in Ashanti Region.

In the evening, I sat down with my friend as I started drafting the itinerary of my visit to Kumasi and Cape Coast. Kumasi is the heart of Akans, the capital, or else pretty simply, the last piece of protected territory of Ashanti empire at present, which had been expanded from north till Ivory Coast at one point of history and the capital of Ashanti since its formation during the time of King Osei-Tutu I. On the other hand, Cape Coast is made of the crystallised tears of the ones in history who wept because of the slavery of Ghana under British colonial rule. These two places are the most visited areas of the tourists coming to Ghana, but in Accra and the suburbs, there are a few other attractions that lie in silence, unnoticed. As I was already tired of road trips in West Africa, after the disastrous, break-born trip to Kenema, I decided to take a domestic flight to Kumasi, which is more time effective and comfortable than taking nonshared taxi that costs almost the same. As it was Harmattan season, the dust clouds from Sahara come and cover the whole sky, making it sometimes impossible for air transportation. In January, it's the peak of Harmattan. Therefore, I had a second thought about my first option, but as my friend says, this is Africa, nothing much we can do, pray to God and will see tomorrow.

'Thank God!' I heard from the other end of the receiver when I informed Kodjo about my safe arrival in Kumasi, though for me, it was the technical suitability and ability of pilot, favourable weather, and nothing superstitious or spiritual. I had been referred to one of the relatives of Kodjo, so that I will be guided during my time in Kumasi. 'My name is Kofi, pleasure having you here, welcome!' He received me at Kumasi Airport 'KMS', which is known as the second busiest airport in Ghana.

I had learnt that Kumasi is one of largest metropoles in Ghana, so I expected a city like Accra, with slight differences in size, but the nature full of the flora and fauna, which was extremely exotic and breathtaking, took my breath away for a moment. It was still a city of real African model, a marketplace which is literally impassable, like any other common market of the country, taxies speeding up with constant sirens like devils who possessed the roads, there were garbage and dirt all over the place, and it what as hot as Accra, but there was something that the trees and flowers have brought to the city and it makes a visitor forget about the disturbances and the heat that conquers you from head to toe as you stand outside. Kofi took me to a local restaurant as it was almost lunch time. 'Ethisein?' His first word took me to the time I was participating in gatherings of Ghanaians. Everyone talks in Twi where I was trying to catch some words, some obviously I had caught were most of the basic greetings which are sufficient enough for understanding the menu and for simple use in a restaurant. The lady, the waitress, replied, 'Boko,' which means 'cool' and took our order. I ordered boiled yams and spinach stew which was quite familiar to me back in Liberia. Kofi went for his favourite Kenke, which is like a ball of flour wrapped with banana leaves. Kenke is another heavy Ghanaian dish made out of fermented corn flour and often served with various local soups and fried fish or meat. I did not dare to taste Kenke as if you are not used to such fermented meals the smell itself can make you nauseous. The culture of food, especially soups prepared with meat, smoked fish, and vegetables, all together with minimum use of spices, makes it smell fishy and bloody, which is an aroma that provokes the appetite in West African context whereas in South Asia, a lot of different spices are used to hide the smell of fish and meat and make it aromatic with diverse essences of spices. In West Africa, I learnt that those two food cultures can never cohabit.

Ashanti kingdom is the pride of Ghana, only the presently existing kingdom in West Africa, though the king does not have dictatorial and autocratic full executive powers like the King Swati in Swaziland or countrywide position of nominal monarchy given by the constitution of Lesotho for King Leste III; King Ashanti, Ose-Tutu, is given informal authority, high recognition, respect, and loyalty not only by his own Akans but also by most of the Ghanaians.

Manhiya Palace, the official residence of the king of Ahanthi Kingdom, presently King Osei Tutu II, which is built by the British in 1925 as a present, may be in replacement of the former palace Asanthehene that they destroyed and burnt to earth during second Anglo-Ashanti war, an immense building of a variety of oblong courts and regular squares entablatures exuberantly adorned with bold fan and trellis work of Egyptian character. They have a suit of rooms over them, with small windows of wooden lattice, of intricate but regular carved work, and some have frames cased with thin gold. The squares have a large apartment on each side, open in front, with two supporting pillars, which break the view and give it all the appearance of the proscenium or front of the stage of the older Italian theatres. A drop-curtain of curiously plaited cane is suspended in front, and in each we observed chairs and stools embossed with gold, and beds of silk, with scattered regalia, which stand today prestigiously showing the glory of kingship and say much more about the wealth enjoyed by the royal family rather than the wealth of the kingdom.

'Have you ever felt that the Kingship have to be abolished?' I asked Kofi.

'Hmm, I do not think so, as he is a part of our traditions, and every single social activity is linked tight with the royal family.'

He added, 'Royal family is the main pillar of our society, we as Akans.'

What Kofi says is what the majority would say but I felt there should be a growing minority which is significant who have some other opinions like anywhere else in the world, when the democracy creeps into social systems where the eyes of public are blindfolded with strong traditions, their minds are fenced with iron walls of absolutism, and their reason for obedience is fear for life and marginalisation.

In Sri Lanka, there was a tradition that the true owner for the kingship should own the 'Sacred tooth relic' of Load Buddha, which protects the nation and the kingdom. A similar association is revealed with regard to the 'Golden Stool' of Ashanti royalty, which is believed to be conjured by fetish priest Okomfo Anyke from the sky, and landed on the lap of the King Osei Tutu I, who was the founder of Ashanti kingdom and Akanthis are made to believe that the nation resides in the 'Golden Stool' so people must protect and respect it. As a result, they strongly believe that Ashanti people would disappear from history if ever the Golden Stool were taken away from them. Covered with pure gold, the Golden Stool is never allowed to touch the ground. When a new Ashanti King is installed, he is merely lowered and passed over the stool three times without touching it. Whenever the Golden Stool is taken out on special occasions, the Asantehene follow it. Behind the superstition, the strategic approach in social control within the territory of the kingdom is the rationale behind the stories about the Golden Stool.

Although I was not fortunate enough to meet His Excellency King Osei Tutu II (Omanhene), my path crossed with that of one of the most important women in the kingdom, the mother of the king, 'Her Excellency The Queen Mother (Obahenma)'. Although Ghana, in a large picture, with Akans as a unit, had a patriarchal social system where the father is the centre of the family, also, polygamy used to be a common practice of the ancient Gold Coast and it still exists in some distant villages; however, the position that the Queen Mother has been placed to by the Ashanti society is pretty contradictory to the common reality. She is the nucleus of the kingdom, the one who plays the parental role for the King. Her symbol is the egg out of which all other chiefs came. She is the King's (Omanhene) counsellor. When Omanhene's stool is vacant, Obahenma names the next candidates for the position of Omanhene. She is expected to consider all factors such as the character of the available candidates, their royalhood, and their contribution to the royal family. Mostly, the lineage and order of birth are given a paramount consideration in the selection process. Although found in other traditions, the position of Obaatan does not fit into the Akan Chieftaincy structure. The one who suggests and nominates Omanhene is the Obahemma (the Queen Mother) in the Akan tradition. I heard from Kofi that the rights and privileges of the Ashanti Royal Family are constitutionalised in Ghana not only because of their symbolic value but also because Akans have developed their own hierarchy of governance alongside of the democratic system in the government which is a pretty exemplary governing strategy for other countries in the region where there are conflicts between the democratically elected governors and the traditional chiefs. However, Ashanthis in the larger group of Akans are not the only ethnicity in Ghana; no place in Ghana is ethnically homogenous.

In the 1060s, approximately 100 linguistic and cultural groups were recorded in Ghana. Although later censuses placed less emphasis on the ethnic and cultural composition of the population, differences of course existed and had not disappeared by the mid-1990s. The major ethnic groups in Ghana include the Akan, Ewe, Mole-Dagbane, Guan, and Ga-Adangbe. The subdivisions of each group share a common cultural heritage, history, language, and origin. These shared attributes were among the variables that contributed to state formation in the precolonial period. Competition to acquire land for cultivation, to control trade routes, or to form alliances for protection also promoted group solidarity and state formation. The creation of the union that became the Asante confederacy in the late seventeenth century is a good example of such processes at work in Ghana's past. Even at present, the diversity that exist in Ghana, ethnically and linguistically, has not been melted away, even though Ghana is always seen through the symbolic letters of Twe, the language of Akans; Kente cloth, the traditional attire of Ashanthis; and the Ashanti royalty. Everyone is not an Akan; there are many others in the composition of this West African Nation. By the time I asked her permission to leave the palace, Obahenma had overwhelmed me with various information about the Kingdom of Ashanti. In her brownish Kente cloth, a simple woman with her curved, high forehead, a mark of wisdom, she is in sooth a bank of knowledge, courageous, and a determined female leader who is completely dedicated for her clan and kingdom. She is humbly proud of her Akans, their history, present, and hopeful about the future, which might be the reason why Akans are seen as the essence of Ghana, a heritage, and the lens through which the whole nation is looked at.

Kofi had a plan for me, which I did not know, but I wanted to visit Kente Village. 'We will try some yams with stew first, then let's go to Kente Village' Kofi told. 'You might be able to get a good Kente,' he added with a bit of humour. But I really wanted to buy one, as when I was a child, I used to make associations with African Dresses with Nkuruma's attire which is a Kente, I assumed that everyone in Africa wears such things, or else pieces of branches to cover their male or female parts. The very moment I saw a Kente cloth in Kotoka International Airport, my mind went back to the free-time stories about Nkuruma, and a few days after my first sight, I'm now in the very place where those royal cloths are being weaved and coloured and where they come out as a refined royal attire, which represent a unique and iconic dress of a nation in West Africa.

'Kente cloth' is a royal and sacred cloth worn only in times of extreme importance. Kente was the cloth of kings. Over time, the use of Kente became more widespread; however, its importance has remained and it is held in high esteem in the Akan family and the entire country of Ghana. In Ghana, Kente is made by the Akan people (including the Asante, Fante, and Nzema). Kente is also produced by Akan groups in Cote d'Ivoire, like the Baoule and Anyin, who trace their ancestry back to Ghana before the rise of the Ashanti Empire. Kente comes from the word *kenten*, which means 'basket'. The Ashantis refer to kente as *Nwentoma* or 'woven cloth'. Truly, when the unisex attires are concerned, not only is Kente the most popular in Ghana, but Kente is also the best known of all African textiles.

Kumasi is the centre of the nation, roof of culture and a place of heritage, most precisely, the jewel of Ghana. Even though I was not able to stay for a long time for experiencing the profound and special aspects of their rich culture, I was completely positively impressed by what I experienced for three days. Though it was quite expensive, I bought my first, lifelong memory from Ghana: a royal attire, a Kente. Kofi put it on my shoulders even though I didn't know whether I was offending anyone or disrespecting the Ashanthis. I looked like an African version of a Buddhist monk.

The following day, I returned to Accra to take a taxi to Cape Coast. After an impressive story of a proud history and its remaining heritages, I was to excavate the ruins of a partially buried painful story of the old Gold Coast. History is a wheel of defeats and victories along the time of struggle for survival; the fittest always wins, adding another stone of time over the dead and the blood of the defeated as the wheel moves forward. As a result, hundred thousands of Ghanaians were taken thousands of miles away from their native lands, to the Caribbean, as slaves, and some of them ended up in the sugar cane farms and some of them in human husbandries. I had heard so many stories of Africa and slavery, some of them beyond my imagination as a child; twenty-five years ago, I was looking at my father's face, surprised as if I was watching a thriller film, unable to connect the imaginary pictures popping up abruptly in my mind: curly-haired black people, naked with no pubic hair, chained like dogs and being fed like cattle in a farm are being taken away by force in ships to an unknown island where there are cages where they are kept. But I can recall that I was questioning about why they were chained, and why they do not wear cloths, and so on, to which my father replied simply that they were forcefully taken away against their will. His explanation made my visualisation more weird about the slavery in Africa and judgmental about the western world, in sooth white people in general as I didn't have much detailed and profound knowledge about the slave trade despite tiny parts that I picked from the free-time stories. I thought all whites are cruel blood shedders who torture the blacks and treat them as animals. When there is no detailed information, it's natural that anyone would pick a generic picture of something based on a short little part of a long story and mistakenly misinterpret and see the world through that misconception, especially when you encounter such incidents when you were at developmental age. My father had a very open attitude to all races, nations, creeds, ethnicities, and religions; married to a native Christian lady from a strict Christian family, he never had even a single issue related to my mother's faith. Instead, he used to walk in to church with her while sticking in to the principles of his own faith. And I cannot remember that he ever uttered anything against the Tamils but of course against LTTE insurgents. He treated the east and the west in the same spoon and he never had double standards. But as a child, the partial information I picked up created a prejudice which eventually disappeared during my adolescence grace to in-depth reading and exposure to international community. I'm standing in front of this majestic castle painted in pure white, standing solid and peaceful just like a sacred religious building as if the huge heavy walls want to keep the dark history suppressed and buried under them. Like South Asian politicians who live a 100 per cent religious life after their tenure in Parliament during which they commit all dirty deals existing on this holy earth.

Dating back to 1650s, first built by the Swedish West India Company and being captured by the Dutch, then the British, and almost destroyed by the French naval attacks in 1757, yet again restored by the British in 1920s, Cape Coast Castle is a mirror of colonial history of Ghana. Today, except for the traces of British, the existence of other colonisers has been vanished under the sands of time. On the staircase, paved with stones, guarded with a carefully and evenly made railing, which adds a royal look to the castle, it is claimed, you will enter the main hall and then to separate dungeons where the slaves were kept. Before entering to the cells where the slaves were concentrated till they are sent to the selling points in the Americas including Caribbean, anyone who comes in after 2009 would notice a signboard left in memory of the visit of the president of the United States, Barak Obama. There are two separate concentration dungeons, one for male slaves and other for the females, each cell can accommodate about 200 slaves, and there are five of them in each dungeon, which all together, the castle can trade 1,000 male and 1,000 female slaves at a time. When you look at the cells, the space is barely sufficient for 200, and there is a canal in the cell itself for urine and faeces to flow into the Atlantic Ocean, but it is imaginable how these human beings, looked at that time like animals, were kept in extremely unhygienic conditions, walking and sleeping on each other's faeces and urine. When in times of transmittable diseases like cholera or typhoid outbreaks within the slave population concentrated in the dungeons, almost everyone is affected due to the poor hygienic conditions within the cells. It is beyond one's imagination that female slaves' stay in cells with blood and mucosa when they are having periods, besides faeces and urine, making it like butchery. Poor ventilation, lack of light, had made the conditions worse for them as there are small openings like rat holes through which a bit of light and ventilation creeps. And the openings where the guards were watching the slaves, whether they try any attempt of escaping, or else fighting with each other, are believed to be used by the soldiers to spot whom they want in female dungeons and take them for quenching their sexual desires. There used to be pregnant slaves whose children were sent to the care centre in the castle who never knew who their parents were and where they were, so did their mothers. An opening from the castle to the coast of the Atlantic Ocean, not high enough to walk straight, is called 'Gate of No Return,' which is the last point where those slaves kept in the dungeons were packed into slave ships, under very similar or worse conditions of life than what they were living in the dungeons, and sailed to the Caribbean and the Americas. Once a slave crosses the 'Gate of No Return', he or she will never return to Gold Coast. That is the end point of one chapter of a life of a slave where many more chapters are to be written accordingly about what is in store on the journey to the final destination and so on. But mostly and certainly, the worse was waiting for them at each stage and some of them were not able to make it to the final destination. No one among those who were behind the 'Gate of No Return' knew about the destiny or whereabouts of their loved ones; it was an eternal separation from all senses of place, culture, family, ecosystem, and sometimes from life, and they never returned.

I do still remember the guy, probably a teenager, school dropout, who came to me to guide me, in reality to make his living of the day by telling me some stories about the castle to any tourist who comes here, repeated what Obama had told standing near the gate of no return. 'We toured Cape Coast Castle, a place for centuries where men, women, and children of this nation and surrounding areas were sold into slavery. I'll never forget the image of my two young daughters, the descendants of Africans and African Americans, walking through those doors of no return, but then walking back those doors of return. It was a remarkable reminder that, while the future is unknowable, the winds always blow in the direction of human progress.' It seems to me that he had studied the quote by heart and repeated it with a heartfelt pride. As Obama felt, there is a strong emotional association of this castle with the Afro-Americans who come not only to Ghana but also to Gambia, Senegal, and other places in Africa, where there were slave trading points, seeking the traces of their ancestry. It can be an obsession rather than an emotional need to find out the true traces of ancestry, for a West Indian or Afro-American who doesn't know who is his forefathers and where they came from. Mostly, they do not get the accurate answer for their burning need as most of those ports were slave trade centres for neighbouring countries, too, hence finding out the origin is literary impossible but having seen the traces of where their ancestors were probably sent and where they were kept may fuel their wrath towards the white world rather than helping them to build a kind of an association or a liaison with their assumed past.

Today the strip of beach near the 'Gate of No Return' is infested with Fantis, a tribe, part of a larger Akan groups who are mostly living in coastal areas, fishing as their livelihood, and their canoes. Instead of the lamenting female slaves, resisting male slaves and slave traders with their whip, there are fishermen and women who sell their harvest right at the beach for retail and whole buyers.

The castle is built very solid and equipped with draining systems, backup water system, offices, and with accommodations for those rankers who worked. And the constant threat from the other colonial powers to this castle built in one of the most strategic points can be seen by the number of cannons fixed along the defending wall of the castle along the beach even though French naval attacks were able to demolish the castle almost fully. Today as a museum of bleeding history, next to a crowded fish market, overlooking the immense Atlantic, the castle of Cape Coast remains silent and white as if it is still indifferent of the suffering of those who were forced through the 'Gate of No Return'.

After every slave story I heard when I was a kid ended up with a perceptual set of whites catch the blacks in the bush and carry them forcefully into the unknown islands. The reality is that more local leaders are involved while the colonial powers penetrate into communities and take villagers as slaves. Each head of chiefdom was paid a price for every single slave sold to the foreign traders. And it was the local leaders who caught people and sold them as if they sell other commodities such as gold, spices, or any other thing that the foreign traders used to buy. But the local potion of involvement which is the primary part of the slave trade is always forgotten or rather ignored by most of those who talk hysterically about racism and slavery. As everywhere else, media, though intentional or unintentional, by ignorance or knowingly, changes the worldview. Sometimes, the sympathy of the audience is for the perpetrator who is highlighted as a victim, when the major and most important parts of the story are omitted on someone's interest or ignorance. While dismantling my Nikon DSLR set, sitting near a canon bravely facing the infinite waters of the Atlantic across which the whites took blacks as slaves, where as the other side which is behind me that I do not see, covered by the castle that is visible to everyone, there stand the immense land, which expands to the whole continent of Africa approximately, where blacks ruthlessly sold their own people for a penny to whites who came in.

Irrespective of what will happen in the future, today Ghana is one among the most stable countries in the region when socio-economical and political aspects are concerned. In addition, Ghana has a diaspora that brings a lot of remittance to the country and with its significantly developed human capital that attracts foreign investors into the country. Yet, poverty, health, and infrastructure remain as a main challenge as most of the countries encounter in this region. However, the peaceful environment and Ghanaian hospitality and strategic geographical position in air traffic where Accra is considered as a hub for air traffic in West Africa, a handful of tourists come in and Cape Cost and Kumasi are ticked as high priorities in their tour but Ghana has much more to show to the world in terms of culture, wildlife, nature, and history.

Though I am from a tropical country rich in wildlife, my desire to experience the West African wildlife had not been quenched so far. Ghana has a very rich and diverse wildlife with insects, mammals, birds, reptiles, and marine animals, but unfortunately, there is no one place where a tourist can experience all at the same time and most of the places are far away from Accra and requires a long drive, in some cases two days or more. 'Mole National Park', which is the largest wildlife refuge, situated in the north-western part of the country, was my next and final destination. I had booked a room in Mole Motel, which costs a fortune considering the conditions, around 250 Cedis a night, and the safari package separately and left Accra to Mole which is around 735 kilometres, a distance that takes almost ten hours along a road which is in good condition, as the airfare for Thamale which is the nearest domestic airport for Mole is quite unreasonably expensive, around $400. When I reached the accommodation, Mole Motel, it was almost 18.00 h, and darkness had already started swallowing the whole world. I was extremely exhausted with the long trip, sitting immobile on the vehicle, wanted to have a tea and sleep, as the next day early morning, the safari would team would pick me from the hotel, after a very early morning breakfast. A safari guide met me at the reception, while I was checking in and briefed me the agenda of following morning. I nodded as if I understood everything as I needed to go to my room and chill 'ASAP'. I ordered my tea and went to the room. The alarm rang like an alien invasion, which startled me during the most relaxing part of sleep, and then I realised I had completely been disconnected from this world for the last nine hours or more, which my body and mind were craving for.

After a quick breakfast, we got in to a semi-open safari 4×4 and left to Mole National Park; the sun was still lazy to light up the jungle, though there were no completely nontransparent canopies like in the forests in Sierra Leon. Mole is on grassland savannah and riparian ecosystems at an elevation of 150 metres from the sea level; therefore, the green canopy is not much dense and in most of the areas, despite huge wild syringa trees which stand alone or in families, in the grassland, there is no canopy at all, resembling to a typical savannah in the eastern or southern parts of Africa that I had seen on television. Shortly after we entered the national park, I was fortunate enough to come across the first African elephant of my life. Not only between humans, but also between the species of animals, there is a significant difference, from continent to continent. Huge ears and round head with tougher skin instead the fatty skin, small ears and head with easily noticeable division on the top Asian elephant looks like a younger brother to this huge beast in Africa. I remember the programs on Discovery Channel about elephants in Africa and while watching them I was dreaming to see one of them in their natural habitats one day, but it remained merely a dream for more than two decades, popping out from time to time when triggered by pictures and articles in magazines and newspapers, programs on television, or else during casual discussions with friends, but most of time remaining like fire under the ashes, silent and hidden. But they never disappear from me. Today, the little boy who dreamt to see a real African Tusker is a 30-year-old man, when the dream comes to a reality, which made me realise that dreams cannot sometimes be time bounded, but they should not be given up, which is a hard exercise of extreme patience. As long as you have a dream, it will lead you to where you dream of, but initiatives taken towards it by oneself is paramount to seeing the final result. Today, after twenty years, after two decades of dreaming, swinging between hope and desperation, looking at an African Tusker, the largest animal on earth, that is calmly enjoying a mouthful of acacia, while my eyes are zooming in and out impatiently with happiness flooding in like an urban flash flood, uncontrollable, spontaneous, and real, another dream comes true. The driver started moving the jeep slowly, and the beast disappeared into the bush, leaving its immense image live in my mind.

Mole National Park is rich, with lot of fauna and flora as well, and Mole River that flows across the national park makes its ecosystem very rich and abundant in resources. Antelopes, monkeys, grass-cutters, and porcupines, which took me back to my trip to Kumasi, as it's the symbol of the Ashanti and Kumasi region, were a few among the wildlife I witnessed in Mole.

Under the burning sun in Accra, where money turn in to vapour in less than a second, I started my quest in the old Gold Coast, then along the royal pathways, in Kumasi, I came to know an extremely rich culture that this silent nation has inherited. Looking through the gates of no return, at the endless dump ocean that expands to infinity, I felt the tormenting experiences laden in the history of these people, and I vented every single heavy feeling conceived in Cape Cost, into the receiving freshness of Mole. Ghana is a wonderful country, a nation that has not forgotten their history yet learnt how to lead the future through the lessons learnt in the past. Ghanaians are warm, calm, and vibrant characters who are famous for their hospitality. When I saw the big billboard 'Akwaaba' with a 'Kente' background, while I was entering the terminal for international departures in Kotoka International Airport, I felt the warmth and genuineness of this word—it was not like an American 'Hi'.

Chapter 07

FETISHIANS

'VOODOOS, THEY WERE MAGICIANS, witches, as well as healers. An empty bottle of shampoo triggered the conversation. 'Voodoo', for us, to a Sri Lankan commoner who has no exposure to Africa, is just a brand name of cosmetics. Simply, the first thing that hits one's mind in my society is just an olive green-coloured plastic bottle of perfumed powder or a piece of soap wrapped with an olive-green paper. That was the first stimulation of looking behind reasons of every name. He explained that every name has a meaning, which is consciously or unconsciously given, and there should be a reason for every name, which could be unknown to the others except for the one who gave it. I was not too little to comprehend the profound philosophy in it. I guess he found me confused and took me to his lap and said, 'When you were born, I was happy, I was happy to an extent I completely forgot to ask whether the child was a boy or a girl.' He laughed, shamefully, which made me laugh, too.

'I just went to Mum's house and informed everyone the child was born.' I was looking at his mouth, without knowing what would be next. Something exciting should come out now, I thought.

'When they asked me whether the child was a son or a daughter, I did not really know,' he laughed again. I was unable to translate his feelings behind his behaviours at that very moment when his first child was born, the very moment he became a father for the first time in his life, and the very moment he and his beloved wife became my father and mother; however, I found the story amusing and funny when I was listening to him and today I can feel how he had felt that time.

'I was happy and I wanted to name you Pramudith, which means happiness.'

That was the day I learnt the meaning of my name. And I was still having the shampoo bottle in my hand.

'A magical beauty, or miraculous beauty product, or some sort of a magical touch, the company might have wanted to give to this product,' he told to my uncle, his first younger brother who was immediately after him. I, being a child of six years, was more interested in the magicians and witches of Voodoo that he mentioned than boarding business topics. I remember, the word *Voodoo* became a hum between my lips. I was singing 'Voodoo' when I was alone as if it was the chorus of a famous song.

'Voodoo, do do,
do do voodoo.'

When I was playing cricket with my classmates during the physical education period, I used to sing, and one of my friends, without knowing what was that strange yet kind of a melodious song, was probably thinking that it was a part of a Hindi song and started to follow me. We sang 'Voodoo, do, do do'. The following week, we had a few more followers, and it invaded not only the time of cricket but also whenever there was no teacher in the classroom, we sang. Later, the singing was accompanied by clapping and dancing. Everyone unconsciously had acquired a set of words muttered with a melody that even the one who sings did not know, and finally ending up naming one of my best friends 'Voodoo' as he was caught by the teacher singing 'Voodoo do do do' during English period. The teacher asked him to come in front and sing to everyone. Since that day, everyone called him 'Voodoo', 'Voodoo', which no one exactly knew what it really was aside from being a bottle of cosmetics.

One stormy evening in April, the thunders started cracking down the sky with pouring waters of rain. Even though it was late afternoon, the gray sky had already covered the whole area with its mystic blanket of darkness so that the sorcerers and witches started boiling their poisonous potions looking at the whole universe through their magical mirrors, closely watching which one of their enemies were around to poison in the silence of darkness and in the roar of rain of curse. A ball of thunder tripped the breaker of the road and electricity went off. We wanted an thriller to make the moment complete, which my grandmother stated, and my father who joined later to our story diverted it from its ultrasuperstition and added some believable substances, coming back to the story of 'Voodoo'.

'All these are just human thoughts induced by irrational but deeply rooted beliefs that people are holding on to for generations.' An expression of disagreement was marked across my grandmother's pale face. But she did not try to argue with my father.

'If you believe in witches, you will at least see them in dreams, even though they do not exist in reality,' he added. Another thunder strike, like an aerial attack right on our head, and raindrops started falling like stones on the roof. And Grandma was stuck between my sister who reclaims her to continue the story and my father who was trying to negate the superstition of the story, and I was waiting to hear more about 'Voodoo'. Stuck in the triangle of three different interests, opinions, and needs, that chance I had to talk more about 'Voodoo' with my father entered to history as an attempt, and we did not talk about them again. My 'Voodoo do do do' song was never sung by me again as per my recollection and my friends were fragmented into different classes in the next academic year and we rarely met and it was never the same. I made new friends in my new class so did they, and everyone forgot 'Voodoo do do do'.

However, it was my father's indirect influence that I grew up in an environment where there was not space for superstition, though in Sri Lanka, superstition and supernatural elements had a lot to do with folk lifestyle. The unseen gods, devils, spells, and the evil spirits controlled a greater part of the life of Sri Lankan villagers even though the practice of rituals has significantly been given up; the beliefs do exist in the core of village life. Some of aspects had been integrated into the modern beliefs and religions and giving them an extended existence in modern world. For example, worshiping the God of wrath, Kaliamma, or Shiva, to destroy one's enemies is widely practiced by the Buddhists as well as some Christians in Sri Lanka whereas both of those religions have nothing to do with keeping grudges, cursing, or wrath. Yet again, it was common to see some devil dances and rituals including sacrifices of some animals, for curing some diseases especially in the southern lowlands of Sri Lanka where witchcraft is well renounced. Sending spells is another famous activity done by those traditional healers who call themselves 'Kattadiya', the individual who is gifted with skills to handle the devil and evil spirits. The 'Kattadiya' usually are engaged in a wide range of witchcraft and healing activities ranging from sending a spell against an individual, family, or a group of people; cutting a spell sent by someone; healing the individuals possessed by evil spirits; free the house and villages from the haunting evil spirits; and guard or break ancient treasures protected by a sacrificed soul. All these activities demand a series of rituals that deal with sacrifices, body parts, poison, different animals, and many more things merely based on mythical believes but for those who believe in them, they really do work which is the psychological impact of witchcraft.

I had heard stories about the Kattadiya, traditional healers taking out dead bodies of people to extract some organs for spells, and in some cases, a figure similar to the target person is cut out of flesh of the dead body and the 'mantras' are chanted over seven nights to make sure that the spell-doll comes to life and become active against the target, then whatever one does with the spell-doll will be felt by the target person. For example, if the spell dummy is stabbed, the target person will feel the pain of real stabbing. Cutting a spell, which is negating the power of a spell, requires similar procedures and the one who did the spell will have visible consequences in a frame of time given by the traditional healer. All these weird things I had been hearing from different sources especially when the friends of my grandma come home, such stories were often heard. But my father's constant denial of those beliefs and the truth that the others talked about them had shaped my attitude to them. I took them as things without essence and no one ever could make me believe either in witchcraft of devils or gods. And I was born in a time when our society had already rejected what did not have scientific proof, rational, and pragmatism.

'It is witchcraft my man, no Ebola in Liberia.' A Liberian, well educated in the United States, told me. I'm not able to recall how many others told similar things during the early stage of Ebola outbreak. A lot of health professionals from different parts of the world had to sacrifice their lives just because of mythical beliefs that exist in the continent. Ebola and witchcraft are a subject that the whole world is aware of today because of the unprecedented humanitarian crisis that erupted in West Africa which still has not come to its end. But the deeply hooked believes that they have more profound and long-lasting impact to their daily lives, lifestyle, and the future of the continent.

'My friend who is a priest heals the HIV patients.' It was one of the trainees who worked under me, addressing an international audience. I felt as if I was nude in front of all of those people. A trained peer-supporter who had already undergone training on HIV/AIDS related issues and emotional first aid, talking nonsense to educated health professionals. I called him personally during the lunch break and I did not have enough patience left; I called him an idiot who tries to show the empty skull to the whole world.

'I swear he did it, the man does not have HIV now.' He started defending his statement which obviously pissed me off. It was a situation where the type of statement one makes would have a severe impact on the organisation as well as on a specific unit where we worked. This was just a randomly noticed incident due to the fact that he opened his mouth at the wrong time in the wrong place whereas there are more than hundreds of thousands of people who seriously believe in miracles of indigenous witchcraft-related healing. Instead of taking antiretroviral treatment, mostly known as ARV, which is freely available in many of the Sub-Saharan countries, accessible to every layer of the society, most of the people in use fetish medicine made of grounded organs and bones of animals, sometimes humans, mixed with herbs and other substances that the traditional healers use to treat a viral infection that weakens the human immune system with no understanding about the behaviour of the micro-organism that causes the illness. I met one Congolese from Goma who was asked to have sex with an elderly woman so that his viral load will be absorbed by the older person, while taking the fetish medication given by him. However, he was lucky enough to be diagnosed and referred to an allopathic doctor known to him and fortunately he was able to undergo proper treatment for coinfections and been given ARV for sustaining his life and to fight against the illness. Beyond everything, he was prevented from being victimised by another person in a ritual of remedy for his infection. But it is not a lie that thousands of people have been victimised unknowingly or forcefully by those who follow the instructions of those fetish traditional healers. In some contexts, instead of the elderly, the infected person had been instructed to have sex with underage virgins, which has also significantly contributed for increased rate of rape and HIV in the younger population in some areas, especially in Congo and some other countries in the Sub-Saharan African region. It has been for decades that the fetish, magical, bush, or witchcraft healers could not treat and heal a single HIV-infected person, instead aggravating the condition and, in many cases, promoting the spread of the virus. But in most of the rural parts of Sub-Saharan Africa, people have more faith in witchcraft and traditional healers than in proper medication, which is one of the major challenges in combating HIV/AIDS in Africa.

My interviewee, 'Kamara', ex-child soldier, mentioned once that he had been washed by a traditional witchcraft man to make him and the other recruits 'bulletproof'. I gave a dumb ear to him at that time as I had not heard much of it and again it sounded complete nonsense. 'Andrew', a Liberian ex-army soldier who fought for Charles Taylor, ex-president of Liberia who has been convicted by the International Criminal Court on charges of the civil conflict in Sierra Leone, told me that he remained bulletproof since the time he entered the secret society and started his rituals which he did not want to disclose. I found him rather ignorant than merely a boaster and asked him, 'In case if you were hit by an RPG?'

Rocket-propelled grenade is usually used for attacking armoured vehicles, which can penetrate the armoured plates and cause the second deadly blast inside the vehicle.

'My man, black magic? Believe me! We do anything, what is an RPG for black magic.'

'We survive even artillery in Africa with black magic,' he added, making me laugh to death. I never expected a mid-level professional to be superstitious to such an extent. If he was not trying to fool me through his pseudo-heroic stories of not being hit by enemy bullets during the war, he should be either absolutely unexposed to science or he is out of reality. I was not ready to generalise the fact that in most of the civil conflicts, Voodoo, witchcraft, or black magic has been widely used to brainwash and mislead the uneducated, underage, and helpless youth and children to fight with the fear factor and send them to the frontline. A member of Mai Mai militia in Congo told me another version of witchcraft to be able to stay untouched by the enemy.

'The priest gave me three medicine balls which are made during his dialogue with the witches and it contains 'Kindoki' the power.'

He kept on explaining the process.

'On the third day before rise of the sun, he asked me to have sex with a child,' he said.

My question broke the fence of teeth like a raged elephant breaking a defence wall in old warfare. 'So you raped a girl?'

It was too quick and charged with my impulses hearing the worst thing that happened in the region which had already become a humanitarian crisis in the eastern provinces of DRC, especially in North and South Kiev. Today there are more than 100,000 victims of sexual violence are in both provinces; among those, a significant amount had been encouraged by 'Voodoo' beliefs and advices given by the traditional healers.

Till the point where it did not reach my personal and official territory, I considered 'Voodoo' as something that I had nothing to do with. Back at home, traditional spellbinding-related stories I treated with indifference and never believed. It was an end of performance cycle of the year; I had just sent the PDP of my subordinates with my comments, highlighting the areas of development and with some additional points which were however perceived otherwise by one of the staff members, unlike the others who took them constructively.

'You know, wicked people do not leave Africa alive.'

'Black magic is powerful for true, you know that?'

He came to my office and told me as if I was the one who was targeted by his comment. I obviously had to ask what his problem was even though I knew that it was normal to have disagreements over the reviews of a supervisor on one's professional development plan which should be raised, discussed, and agreed upon during the discussion of the plan between the supervisor and the subordinate. But seeing 'black magic' invading my office and trying to influence official decisions was something beyond the feeling of anger or irritation. It was almost a shock for me to hear a professional threatening another in an international working environment using 'black magic' as a weapon, which is first not a rational and pragmatic approach to solve issues. Second, it was a threatening and abusive behaviour which is not encouraged in any workplace, and it is something that does not make sense to a stranger who does not believe in what they do.

That was one of the few moments in my professional life when I completely went blank with anger. I was like a volcano that was about to erupt, with anger bubbling like hot magma about to erupt in the form of words with no refinement, but the so-called professionalism guarded my immediate reaction like a piece of rock on top of the volcano formed out of fossilised lava as a result of an eruption long ago. My experiences in spells of anger in the past had already given me the stamina to prevail in similar situations indifferently and I asked him in a very calm tone without showing my anger that was trying to push my tongue out of my mouth and eyes out of my eye sockets.

'What you mean, Mr Koli?' I asked.

He was expecting a word of surrender out of fear of black magic and of course a favourable review of performance appraisal.

'Lot of people who came here died because of witchcraft,' his words picked the same ascending intonation as it was a few minutes ago. Then he paused, looked at me as if to check whether I was tamed or afraid.

'When they became rude to the locals, it happens.' His chin was just about to hit my forehead.

'You do whatever you want, but I have not done anything which is against you,' I felt my voice was rising without my knowledge.

'I have graded you better than your actual level of performance and remember that the areas you have to develop, you need to do. It is vital and imperative,' I added with a look of confidence and authority. It was an unpleasant situation that I never expected, I never thought 'Voodoo' had unlocked the doors of office spaces in Africa and come in to the professional development systems and official discussions.

My interests in finding more about witchcraft known as 'Voodoo', 'Muthi', or 'Juju' or in many other names across Africa were given wings by the encounter with my colleague at the office and a funeral of a colleague of mine whose cause of death was told as witchcraft by his relatives.

'He was a strong man, just died like this,' a relative of the dead said with a gesture of surprise.

I was listening without making any comment but I was watching him. He looked around restlessly and fearfully as if he was trying to steal something and he broke the silence.

'It is nothing but witchcraft, man had no sickness,' he whispered into my ears while watching the surroundings.

I nodded in accord because I did not want to have a prolonged discussion with a villager who believes nothing but superstition while most of the people around us were grieving on their loved one who had passed away. For them, the cause was not important but he had left them, no longer among the living. I moved to their side of the tent erected for the visitors where there was a group of people talking causally. I sat near them just to avoid the man who was talking about witchcraft. I pretended checking my phone and was killing the time as it was not polite to leave a funeral all of a sudden.

'It happened quick quick,' One among the crowd said. Some West African dialects of English always sound a bit limited and significantly lack proper grammar and demand a lot of attention for one to catch a word.

'He was possessed,' another added.

The third person confirmed: 'The woman is from Sierra Leone, they are good in witchcraft.' It seemed that they had a clue about a suspect.

'Woman is a witch,' the next one added her part to the story which is being concocted. It looked like the whole community had concluded that the cause of death is simply witchcraft. I was amazed by the depth that the roots of witchcraft had gone into African society. When the postmortem examination had already proven that it was cardiac arrest, no one was ready to admit the forensic laboratory result, and the witches seemed to have taken over the roles of scientists and investigators, and rumours about the death fly faster than the news about the true cause and in no time the whole neighbourhood and then the village had come to believe that it was witchcraft that had ended the life of the man. That was the day I came to realise that the truth is not which is true; in some societies, it is often what most of the people believe.

My first deliberate attempt in discovering what really was behind the witchcraft known in different names in Africa was my visit to Maryland in Liberia. Maryland remained as an independent state for some time, sandwiched between Liberia and Ivory Coast before it was absorbed by the republic of Liberia. It is very well known that killing for taking human organs for witchcraft occurs more in this southern tip of Liberia than any other area in the country. Also, among the expatriate community in Liberia, there was a rumour on the cause of death of an international staff who worked for a nongovernmental organisation who was mysteriously found dead in a closed area on the beach in Harper.

'It was not by drowning, some parts were missing.' It was a part of a discussion between two expatriates who were having a so-called social drink just beside me in a famous beachside pub in Monrovia.

'His penis was missing,' the guy in flip-flops and dirty jumper said with an inappropriate laughter provoked by excessive intake of alcohol.

His companion, a fat, short guy who looked Russian more in his style of drinking than in his outlook said, 'They grind penis to make some indigenous medication and spells.' He inclined too much toward his glass as if he was going to fall on it.

'Hey, come and join us,' I thought it was for someone else, even though I wanted to hear the story in detail, as I had heard a different version of it at the office in the morning of the same day.

'Hey my brother, you!' The guy in the jumper sounded clear and more sober than the other. Even before I went there, he poured one glassful of scotch, even without asking whether I would take drinks or not. I was anyway not surprised by his behaviour as Friday night in Monrovia is the time of discharge of all negative energies accumulated in expatriate minds and bodies. Any wild thing can occur after the hot sun sank in the deep Atlantic when suppressed desires and unmet fantasies are trying to conquer the darkness with the power of alcohol that dilutes the shames and consciousness.

'By the way, I'm Oleg,' he confirmed my guess of him being from a country of ex-Soviet confederation.

'You know a friend of ours was killed by witches,' he told, taking his own time between each word of the sentence. I nodded, took the swap poured by the guy in jumper, turned the bottom of the glass up into my mouth, and said enough before he pours the second swap.

'They grind the bones on a piece of stone and add different stuff and make a small medicinal ball that has a lot of powers.'

Oleg continued, barely keeping his head straight, which was already heavy for his neck, which reminded me of a dead chicken.

'My friend, believe me, they swallow that medicine ball and fly like birds.'

I resisted my laughter with a lot of effort. It was unbelievable how even the expatriates had come to believe black magic, sometimes it was to an extent which is not really convincing but people just believe. A man flying after drinking a ball made out of grounded human bones which is composed mostly of calcium cannot be believed today. And even a school child could give a scientific explanation on the nonexistence of any chemical trait in human bones that enable another person to levitate like the witches in old mystic tales. However, these two drunken aid workers sitting near me were not the only ones who were taken by the tornado of witchcraft. There were a couple of expatriates whom I met who had come to believe in the mirage of witchcraft after coming to Africa. Among those, one American lady working in Harper, at her sixties, was complaining about her housemaid for making her sick with an infection and chronic bronchitis using witchcraft.

A week after I met the drunken men, I was on the way to Harper, Maryland, by a United Nations regular helicopter, but unfortunately, due to a technical failure, we had to stop in Greenville, the midpoint between Monrovia and Harper, which is almost a few brick buildings and a couple of mud and Palawa huts left completely isolated in a thick jungle. I had a wait desperately till a replacement comes from Monrovia for three hours, but thanks to the Chinese-formed police unit of the United Nations Mission based in Greenville, I was able to fight my hunger with delicious Chinese food till the journey resumes. Finally, another MI-8 was sent to Greenville to take the passengers stuck in Greenville, and we reached Harper four hours later than expected.

Bordering to the blue Atlantic Ocean and away from the dusty and noisy Monrovia, Harper is full in its untouched beauty. Once I entered to the town, I saw the ruins of old mansions and administrative buildings by the side of deteriorated paved roads which still treasure their once prestigious past as an attractive seaside elite residential area where, to the naked eye of an ordinary person, one would not notice any clue of the existence of mysterious activities such as witchcraft, but the beauty of the ocean and the immense destruction caused by the war to a town that once shined at the coast attracting all elites of Liberian society, as a lighthouse to the sailing ships in the Atlantic.

I was provided accommodation in a prefabricated container in the compound of the formed police unit from India, which was on a hilly area just on the verge of the sea. The monotonous sound of the wind and the waves that break was swallowing all the other noises, like how the small fish goes into the mouth of a whale, and made me sleep like a child after a frustrating and tiresome journey, but as usual, my body clock made my eyes open by five in the morning without any alarm. I made my instant coffee that I carry everywhere when I'm in the field and came out to breathe fresh air by the sea which is a few dozen of metres downhill but still clearly visible. With a chilling sensation of the cold breeze, which is not often gifted in Liberia, seeing the rising sun with a hot cup of coffee by the sea side was a rare luxury for a peacekeeper. A few lights, apparently the flames of gas lamps, were moving in thinning darkness, that I was unable to recognise as returning fishermen from the sea, even-though I'm from an island. Later on, the canoes that were clearly noticed in clusters returning from the sea made a panoramic and vivid image of a naval battalion rushing to the enemy targets in the coast, which gave me a flashback of colonial time, the way the Portuguese, Dutch, English, and French might have come into the continent. Over the hill, an island surrounded by anchored canoes in turquoise waters is seen from the veranda of an old high-roofed church which was abandoned since the time of war. The blackish walls and broken windows with colourful glasses remaining as an evidence that it was a church, even though abandoned. This is one of the key places where the residents believe that 'secret societies' meet and craft their spells and do other rituals known as witchcraft. My colleague who invited me to Harper briefed me about this place even before I decided to come. It had a faded prestigious look that belonged to the past and the present has added nothing but a haunted and mysterious outlook.

'We can take you inside the church first and have a look at what is there,' Satheesh, my colleague who invited me to Harper, said. He knew my intention but it was apparent that he did not want to go inside with me even though he wanted to help me in my interests. He showed me the door of the church and said with a hesitant voice, 'I will stay here, you can see inside.'

I felt the latent content of his words. I smiled and walked towards the old door, passing the giant concrete pillars in the front veranda area, getting closer to the entrance, which is barely covered with the old door with old carvings, barely attached to its broken frame; hearing a human voice, I was startled.

'Where are you going?'

A man with beard and dreadlocks who was in rugged clothes rather screamed than asked me where I was going, even though it was clear I was heading towards the entrance of the building.

'This is for society,' he started walking towards me.

'I can go in anyway, right?' I asked with a bit of an authoritative voice. I just wanted to intimidate the person as he looked like an informal caretaker of the building. He came closer to me and looked at me as if I was an intruder.

'Sir, it is for society people. Others do not go,' he said.

'Others are not allowed to go?' I did not allow my voice to soften.

'No, you can go, but it is a society place.' I did not respond to what he was repeating and tried to open to door which was almost hanging on the old frame. It was just like a snare; it fell on me along with the frame. I nearly got my head injured.

'What the fuck is this?'

'How those society people open this trap?' I was vocal again and the man with the beard and dreadlocks had disappeared. Probably he knew that I was not going to stop and will end up having the heavy door and its frame on my head. Or maybe I might not be the first one who tried to go in and he might have escaped from a potential risk of being a witness of a death caused by a doorway tragedy which would not be easily defended as a cause.

The fallen door had been the curtain between two different worlds. Skeletons of different animals, candles, boxes of matches, pieces of stones, parts of trees, firewood, a few kitchen utensils and some pieces of cloth were fragmented carelessly on the floor. The air was stiff with some foul smell which I could not recognise—it was probably a decomposing piece of flesh of an animal or a human organ, I assumed. Or else it could be a rat that had died due to a natural cause, but seeing all these strange signs and elements spread on the floor, it is natural that the worst and most horrifying distortions would come to one's mind. I felt my bravery was being swallowed by a feeling of fear while the determination which took me this far had already faced a reversed effect; I did not have the courage to move forward. I felt a sense of danger and turned back. Satheesh, my friend who was hesitating to come in, was at the door, looking shocked and immobile as if he was frozen at the doorstep. He was trying to tell me something but I heard nothing. It could either be my shaken mind that impaired my hearing or he might have been frightened to such an extent that his voice would not come out.

'Something is wrong somewhere.' It was him; finally, after few seconds, he raised his voice. His reaction pumped blood into my heart.

'They had been doing rituals with all these strange things,' I added upon what he said. He walked in and joined me. We walked a bit inside again, even though we had fears as it was the first time in our lives that we encountered something this. It was rather dangerous than thrilling as if the members of the society had already known about us, maybe through the man with dreadlocks, they would have done anything to prevent the news leaking out. Such things had happened in many places, not only in wild Africa but also in other places on earth. Therefore, we decided to head back as we found nothing else.

Even after I returned to my accommodation, things I saw in the old church building were full of my mind. What might they have done inside using those stuff. All the weird stories I had heard about witchcraft, which I discarded with no regard, saying it to be unreal and nonexistent, seemed existing and happening in reality. Harper gave me another path to follow in the continent of darkness, a dark story, probably might not be darker than most of the realities I had witnessed in Africa such as stories of child soldiers, victims of rape, and victims of torture, but I knew for sure this would be another journey through darkness, with no clarity as many things I had seen here within the frontiers of Africa, maybe just another obstacle for the process of development of the continent such as the extreme belief in the concept of 'God'. I booked my tickets to Togo, via Accra, to adventure the world's largest fetish market which is in Lome, capital of Togo, seeking answers for all of my boiling questions which were about to be gazed and explode within me.

In West Africa, having been colonised majorly by the French and British, even though there are two long retained Portuguese colonies (Cape-Verde and Guinea Bissau), there exist two significant linguistic blocks: French-speaking West Africa, where most of the countries of the region belong and where there is a common regional currency, CFA—Central African Franc; and the English-speaking block which is more fragmented geographically and less integrated than the French speaking countries, even though a few strong economies of the region, such as Ghana and Nigeria, are within them. It is vital that anyone who travels and especially those who plan to stay a long time in West Africa should know at least the basics of both languages. Switching my English mode off since the time I boarded in a jetliner of Asky Airlines, a regional airline from Monrovia, to Lome, I changed to French mode, which would make my life easier in Togo. When the flight landed in Tokoin International Airport, known as Gnassingbé Eyadéma International Airport, my anxiousness to see this well-known but hidden part of African life, known in many different names and interpretations, some of them gris, Voodoo, witchcraft, black magic, Loodoo, charm, spell, mojo, etc, was provoked by the fact that I was safely landed in the final destination in my attempts in discovering the magical lights of the dark continent which are lights of darkness to the scientific progress of the continent, especially in rural Africa.

'Akudessewa' is well known among the Voodoo practitioners in the region. Lome being the heart of witchcraft known as 'black magic' to the non-Afro world, Mojo among Afro-Americans, Loodoo or Voodoo, charms of spell, especially in Asia, Akudessewa fetish market is considered as not only just a market where the Voodoo practitioners come to buy the necessary things for their rituals but also a centre where the rituals and consultancies of experts take place. In other words, Akudessewa is the heart of the Voodoo world, a university in the discipline of witchcraft, a hospital for physical ailments as well as psychological issues, and spiritual healing is complementary. I had heard about Akudessewa from many people who visited Lome as tourists but not from any Togolese as I was not able to make any contact with a Togolese for last three years that I stayed in Africa. As a result, based on what I had heard and read, I had a perceptual set and an imaginary picture of fetish market but being a visual person I craved for seeing it to reconfirm what I had heard and read and to understand what really all these weird practices were and to discover whether there is any truth behind those that science cannot explain within its limits. I walked down to the lobby with my backpack on my shoulders and requested the lady at the reception to book a taxi for me in the next fifteen minutes to go to Akudessewa fetish market.

'Are you coming back, Sir?' The lady threw a strange look at me as if I was a thief and asked. I guessed my backpack was the reason why she thought so. Probably she might have thought that I was trying to leave the hotel after having a nap. Such a thought was ridiculous but such things can happen in Africa, I thought. Sometimes, one might find the behaviour of another either strange or offensive but we usually jump into judgements without having a clue of what those people have gone through or what or who made them acquire such behaviours.

'Non madam, je vais renter, mais je prends mon sac à dos avec moi' I replied politely reassuring her that I would come back but I take my backpack with me. She smiled and called the taxi. In next twenty to thirty minutes' time, I would add another once-in-a-lifetime experience to my life and would be able to see with my very eyes, hear by my own ears, and touch by my own hands what remained like a poison tree in biblical literature. Instead of the fears and hesitation that I experienced in Harper, in the old church, I felt that I had come to the end of one leg of my journey in Africa, which still remains a mystery to the rest of world.

'Sir, Moussa is your driver, he is here,' the lady at the reception told me. I thanked her and followed the driver to the car. I requested Moussa to wait until I come back when we reached Akudessewa as I did not have an idea how long I could or would stay.

From a distance the place looked like just a dusty deserted lot lined with wooden tables. As I entered, I saw the piles of heads, tails, skins, and limbs of various animals, and I realised that I was in the right place, 'Akudessewa Fetish Market', the world's largest fetish market. Amid the dust and noise of people, I crept inside the market which took me to an ultrafuturistic scenario of forensic investigation of a mass grave of all sort of animals. The smell of dried body parts of every single living thing on earth was combined into one Akudessewa version of odour, which reminded me of a remote atoll of the archipelago of Maldives where the dried fish industry is everyone's business. Odour, noise, heat, and dust all together do not allow any stranger to stay long in the market. I wrapped my scarf around my face, just like an ISIS, to minimise the odour of the dead animals that was making me nauseous, and stopped by a shop which was full of heads of buffalos and some stuff that looked like dried skins. Immediately, a weird-looking fairly old man in a traditional Togolese attire which is more like Ghanaian handwoven tops but with dead colour instead of bright ones that one would find in Ghana, approached me, noticing I was a foreigner. He greeted in French, 'Bonjour,' and asked, 'On dit quoi?' which is typical to the West African region, which means, 'How are you?' even though it has nothing to do with formal French greetings which are either 'Comment allez vous, comment va tu?' or 'ça va?'

I replied, 'Dieu Merci,' in the same dialect of French, which literary means 'Thank God' and contextually 'Je vais bien or ça va bien' translated as 'I'm fine' in English.

He is the Voodoo chief of the place and he offered me a tour of the whole market. I felt that he expected something at the end of the tour even though he did not mention it. I had made my mind to pull out some small CFSs and place them in his palm after we finish the tour.

He observed me carefully while walking, from head to toe, with a look of a jackal that anyone would encounter with the Gypsies who come from house to house as fortune tellers in Sri Lanka. I felt as if I was with a Gypsy fortune teller.

'Ta femme?' He asked me 'your wife' in an interrogatory intonation which was like a try to find a clue to start with.

'Non, tout le monde va super bien, je suis tourist et vais rien acheter.'

I made him clear that everyone in my family is okay and I'm not going to buy anything but visiting as a tourist. But he did not give up and started showing me different animal parts and strange talismans, as per him, that could bring me fortune, drive away the evil spirits at home, and solve all existing and potential problems of one's life.

'Cela vous portera le bonheure' which means that will bring you goodness. He repeated every time he showed me some skull of an animal. Another man who was around his late fifties or early sixties arrived to the store. By their gestures, I concluded that they should have been friends; he took some rope-like stuff out of his bag and each of them started examining them carefully. I was like a little kid at a toyshop, curious and reluctant to leave the place, watching at the deal that those two men were trying to make, and my curious eyes noticed that those ropes are with heads and for sure those were snakes. Dried snakes, just like ropes, are left on the dusty wooden table. I was wondering what on earth is wrong with these people to choose to deal with these creepy stuff.

'Monsieur,' the man who brought the new supplies interrupted my thoughts and introduced himself as a Voodoo priest who was practising a few stoles down the row. He said he can cure any human illness within his treatments of seventy-two hours. I had been hearing such things from different people in different areas in West Africa and did not believe much as I did not see any rational or scientific truth behind what they told. He asked me to follow him to his store. It was just like an outdoor pharmacy where various animal parts, bone statues, and herbs take the place of conventional medicine.

The chief of the place left me for a while with the Voodoo priest whom I was following and went to attend to group of tourists looking like French. He might have thought of monetary benefits of handling a larger group. The Voodoo priest called me into his store which was relatively a bigger one, and there were animal parts that no one on the beach except those weird Voodoo practitioners would ever be able to describe. He showed me a pot partially filled with some black powder, and told me that this is a universal medicine for not only treating any ailment but also used for overcoming any barrier or difficulty in life. After I had heard about the universal medicines in Hindu mythical stories referring to the ultimate power of God, I heard about the existence of a universal medication in

Akudessewa. I was rather sounding sarcastic even though I did not want to offend the priest, and asked him, 'Comment tu peux traiter toutes les choses avec un seul medicament?' 'How do you treat everything with one single medication?'

He used the most powerful word that they use for anything that cannot be otherwise explained: 'magic'. It was magic; that was his explanation. Once it is magic, you should not question it. That was the rule. I knew that it was the only defence that he had and to prevent me asking more questions.

'Black powder' is made from ground up animal parts and herbs that have to be rubbed into the flesh of the 'patient'. Sure the person has to be cut on the chest or back three times before they apply the magic powder, but outsiders were not allowed to know much further about that. It was beyond imagination that a lot of people still do go to those fetish priests/ healers even though they have the access to allopathic medication in many hospitals for free. Looking at the herbal substances and the parts of the animals and how they were being kept, instead healing one's illness, one would acquire many more infections and allergies due to the level of contamination and accumulation of poisonous substances in these traditional medication which are processed with 0 per cent accountability. But it looked like that deep-rooted traditions remain as a tooth of a snake stuck in someone's feet.

I was taken to many other shops where the same stuff were sold and we stopped at a place where there were different scary-looking statues of humans, gods, or devils that I was unable to demarcate properly. The shopkeeper, who was also a Voodoo practitioner, rushed towards the man who took me there, greeted him, and turned towards me as if he found a treasure. And within a few minutes, a few others gathered around me like a group of ants around a piece of sugar. Everyone wanted to sell me something, anything from a paw of an ape, gazelle head, snake, or at least a souvenir. I did not ask for anything but everyone started asking me my price for different smelly dried pieces of animals and old dusty wooden statues. It is truly a crazy place where everyone tries their best to get under your skin and make you buy at least something even though they have nothing to do with your life. Voodoo merchants have products collected from every single place of West Africa, and no matter what your problem is, they're bound to have something for you. They claim they can help everybody in the world, and whenever someone has a problem and runs out of options, they come to Akodessewa to look for ultimate solutions.

To be successful in competitive exams, to win the elections, to win football matches, to be successful in business, to win the heart of the girl or the boy whom someone loves, or else to untie the marriage or send the mother-in-law or father-in-law to rest in eternal peace and for many more social issues are brought to the attention of the Voodoo priests, and they assure that the burdens will end if the client follows what they exactly advise even though, in most of the cases, it's a long-lasting process that sucks almost every single piece of wealth from the clients, adding many more problems for Voodoo priests to address.

All sort of illnesses which can only be managed even by modern medicine are believed to be cured by Voodoo healers. Diverse herbs, some of them highly toxic blends with animal parts, are given to the patients. They are not supposed to know what they are taking, that is an imperative. Irrespective of level of education at the school and how much money one has, Voodoo has apparently conquered every single corner of Africa, appearing in different names, for example, Muti in the southern part of the continent. But its origin is believed to be in the western part of the continent, where today's Togo and Benin are, which are known for Voodoo since centuries.

However, even if I was not intending to get any Voodoo treatment or craft, it did not let me go for a while as it had its own culture, a leftover of an old tradition still not being consumed my modernity. And, still the people believe in it to its very profounder. Voodoo is like a linnet to the leaf called West African life. It is obviously disgusting to see the smelling animal heads staring at you piled on dusty desks and snakes dried like ropes and kept in boxes but it was not only an outdoor indigenous pharmacy but also a university that offers theoretical and practical education on West African conventional medicine which has an integrated treatment approach that treats the physiological ailments while simultaneously healing the psychological aspects, but unfortunately, the methods and products have not been advanced since many centuries and instead in a vigorous process of being buried under the sandstorm of modern science that invades the continent across the Sahara.

Chapter 08

BUSH FEVER

I'M FROM A TROPICAL country where there used to be malaria, especially in the dry zone of Sri Lanka, but there is nomore malaria in Sri Lanka since 2012 grace to the strict and very efficient anti-malaria campaign launched by the ministry of health in Sri Lanka. Probably, my country could be the only country that has beaten the cause of the highest number of deaths in tropical zones all over the world. Nonetheless, my parents' generation had dispositions of traumatic memories of terrible symptoms which they call 'break-bone', of the fever known as 'bush fever' among the rural farmers in the North, North Central, South East, and East provinces of Sri Lanka which is Vivax malaria, the most common plasmodium species in Sri Lanka. Malaria caused by *Plasmodium falciparum*, which can escalate to severe cerebral malaria, used to be known as 'Brain fever' among the commoners. As a result of sensitisation campaigns and community mobilisation along with clinical interventions and public health measures taken by the government in collaboration with communities, as a nation, we beat the malaria threat in Sri Lanka. But unless a miracle happens and this little island which is not more than 65,000 squared kilometres would be thrown in the sky and fall in somewhere out of tropics, all the hazards favourable for malaria, especially Anopheles mosquito, which is the carrier, would be in the island. However, Malaria is a fear inducer in my society in all layers, irrespective of the low death rate that existed even during the time when there was a significant prevalence of Malaria, though it was endemic to some provinces and easily managed even at very rural health facilities in the country. Always a hair-erecting reaction can be expected from whoever hears that you are going to go to Africa. 'There is malaria' will be the very first thing you would hear. And their Halloween-like facial expressions make you really scared as if you are going to be left to die in a mud hut, in a bush in an unknown continent full of savages. Every time she cried, wept, and remained pensive in deadly silence, my mother may have thought of 'bush fever', too, but I barely remember whether she warned me about it. It could be because of her own experience with malaria, when she had been deployed as a fresher, just after her diploma, in an extremely hardship duty station in the North Central province where by that time, in the Seventies, there was a high prevalence of malaria in Sri Lanka. She had found an accommodation in a house of a wealthy farmer in the village, whose whole family was involved in farming, often were victims of malaria. 'They used to go to farm in the morning and in the evening they become totally bedridden, weak, and shivering the whole night as if they were going to pass soon. And the following morning, they turn to be normal and go back to the farm,' she added, 'I used to sleep in the same house for three years and never got malaria. It was her first-hand experience with 'bush fever' in Sri Lanka. That was the only time I heard about malaria till I read the predeployment documents I received from the United Nations.

A skinny man, under drips, lying on a bed with rugged bedding, his eyes are almost about to jump out from his eye sockets, his veins are like a brail map, embossed on his bony hands and legs, limbs are just bones covered with wrinkled skin like the spare parts of an old bicycle covered with a wet cloth, he barely speaks or not at all, barely noticeable up-down movements of his skeleton-like rib-box is the only evidence of his being still alive and his face is just like a skull covered by an oil paper. The media had made us think that Africans die like that. It's always

HIV AIDS, and then you will see the famous picture of a vulture waiting for the child to die taken by Kevin Carter in Sudan, and some similar photos taken by different journalists about famines in various places in the Horn of Africa. But to my part of world, nothing else was familiar. Not even a single free-time story of my father had a single word about malaria. To me, twenty years ago, Africans die only in famine, AIDS, and conflicts and hemorrhagic fevers like Ebola, Marburg, rift-valley-fever, or Crimean-Congo hemorrhagic fever. Malaria was out of the horizon of my imagination.

It was a sunny Saturday morning, fresh and energetic after a six-month long depressive rainy season in West Africa. I felt like a Norwegian who saw the sun after the long dark winter. I had just completed nine months in Africa and one of my friends just arrived in Liberia from Uganda, and we planned a beach side 'Brai' to welcome him. I just had my morning coffee, by six thirty, in my balcony, looking at the Doe River that silently flows across the green marshy lands in Monrovia, took my Nikon DSLR, monopod, foldable camping chair, few cans of Heineken, and a book to read if time permits me and rushed to the car to get to Marshall's beach which was around forty kilometres from where I stay. Marshall area itself is a lagoon opening to the Atlantic Ocean, of brackish waters, where most of the expatriates go to have a safe swim, as in the Atlantic the currents are deadly and the fresh waters of West Africa are also dangerous as carriers of schistosomiasis or in common terms 'snail fever' pathogen are common. Hence, Marshall's lagoon area has become a safe haven for those who want to have a BBQ, drink, and a swim on a weekend or on a holiday away from dusty and smokey Monrovia with generators running twenty-four-seven as there is no central electricity in the city. It was an ideal escape covered by bushy forests from one side and open to ocean from the other side though infested with plastic bottles, disposable cups, plates, condoms, and underwear that the locals who come to the lagoon left behind with live evidence of their shared attitude and behaviour. And every beach and dark corner in Monrovia becomes Sexoriums in the dusk, where the bodies are sold for less than US$1 or for something ranging from a can of coke, corn bread, donut, or a full dinner, and only the traces of activities are left behind in the morning which retain for months and months, probably years, as there is no regular cleaning or not at all as if the garbage is born out of gold, they are kept at roadsides forever.

After a short swim and staying on the beach for a while, I returned home in the evening, by 18.00, bit lifeless than just tired. It made me seek the comfort of my sofa bed; just after a brief wash, I went to bed. All of a sudden, I woke up in the middle of the night, completely disoriented, shivering as if I was in a freezer. I switched off the air-conditioner, hating that it was probably the cause, but in a few minutes I realised it was not the cause. I was having spells of chills and trembling like an old Ford 3000 tractor engine encountering a blockage in diesel filter. I looked at the clock hanging on the wall. It marked 2.45, early morning, almost six hours to go to see a doctor in the UN clinic. My instincts told that this has something to do with mosquitos.

By this time, I had visited many people in the mission who has fallen critically sick with malaria and witnessed some unfortunate untimely deaths of some of my colleagues caused by Malaria. Once Philippine solider who completed his official tenure of twelve months in the UN mission in Liberia was happy to get his extension for another six months, but unfortunately, he died of cerebral malaria, just one month before his extended time, and was sent back in a metal casket with his all dreams packed inside, leaving only grievances with loved ones back at home. On another day, my colleague from Nigeria was hospitalised because of malaria and ended up talking to his dead grandmother as if she is near his bed. In addition, as a clinician, I had met several clients in the workstation who manifest strong constant somatisation, as if they have malaria every other day. Witnessing all these horrible physiological and psychological drama that this little parasite called Plasmodium can cause, I felt as if I was not going to return home on my favourite seat on EK788, seat number 50B or 50F the last aisle seats near the toilet and the kitchen where I can access easily the basic necessities without waking anyone up, while flying a nine-hour long flight across Africa, instead in the checked-in luggage cabin in an aluminium box as a fallen peacekeeper, not because of a rebel attack but because of a useless mosquito bite.

After 2.45 a.m. I was unable to fall as sleep, instead I wrapped myself with two blankets and tried to wait till morning, wondering among weird thoughts about death and afterlife. For the first time in my life I felt that

I had done enough good to be reborn as a human but not sure whether it would be sufficient to not to come back to Africa in my next existence. First time, after I arrived to Africa, where I dreamt to come for almost two decades, I wanted to go back home. A feeling of repentance crept into me like a Cobra creeps into a termite mound, deeper in the dark underground where it hibernates for a long time after a good full meal. By eight, I drove to the clinic directly, met a doctor, and explained my symptoms. By that time, chills were no longer there; instead, I was feeling hot, sweaty, and weak with a strong headache including the neck area. I felt as if an iron shaft is being screwed through my neck up to the brains.

'We have to do the test for malaria.'

The doctor's words confirmed that I was in the club, but it was just a clinical diagnosis and the lab test will confirm what he assumed. After one hour, I was called back to the clinic. I saw the doctor writing the prescription, even without looking at me. He looked at me as if I was a victim of an antipersonnel bomb who was going to lose a leg for the rest of his life.

'You have malaria.'

I smiled at him, I remember. But I didn't know whether it was for what. If I saw my smile, how I smiled, I could have told what was in it. It was my first reaction to the bad news. Reconfirmation of bad news. Either it was an effort of acceptance, or denial.

'Here, I have prescribed you lumapharine; it is a very strong medicine. You have to eat well and take more fluids.'

He added in a tone of a warning, 'You have falciparum malaria; be careful, take medicine on time.'

I did not say anything and thanked him and left the clinic with the card of medicine given at the pharmacy attached to the clinic, along with my sick leave form.

Instead of fear or weakness, all of a sudden, unknown heroic feelings started oozing in to me, slowly. May be it was a deliberate effort to overcome the extreme fear which was latent and unconscious. I bought two big packets of Mars and Milky-way chocolates, yogurt, mineral water, and some other stuff enough for at least five days as if I was going to have a week full of sweets and high-calorie supplements. After a heavy meal, even though it is common among malaria sufferers to have a very low appetite, I was lucky to have my appetite intact and took my first dose of medication with a hope of diminution of all the pains that come out from the core of the body and spread all over as if I was possessed by an evil spirit like in Greek mythical stories. As a result of regular intake of paracetamol, the feeling of feverishness had already disappeared, instead the weakness and dizziness together had brought a miserable feeling that sometimes you feel like wanting to give up life. I remembered TIA of Eric, this is Africa, I told to myself while preparing my corn-flour-based thick soup, just before the next dose of medication.

The first twenty-four hours passed and I had chills in the night again and night sweats; it was like a super fast journey between Nordic zone to Sub-Saharan Africa or the Middle East. It was time for another paracetamol. It was almost impossible to sleep with the severe neck pain and joint pains, along with sudden spells of chills and sweating. I remember the Singhalese folkloric reference to Malaria symptoms 'Break-bone feelings'. Whenever I woke up with chills or sweating, I ate something and drank a glass of warm water, following what the doctor said. But it was not easy to be hopeful when you experience a constant stage of pain all over the body; it's easier to give up than fight with it. Every moment is either a moment of flight or fight. Most of the time, I stayed awake at night sometimes falling asleep for few minutes and wake up with a horrible dream of death, completely disoriented and frightened.

By the third-day morning, I had developed severe weakness, though feverish feelings, night chills, or sweating had disappeared gradually and instead my appetite had been severely affected by gastritis induced by lumapharine, which is a very strong medication. A disgusting feeling retained in the mouth with a nauseous feeling whenever I saw seafood, and the tummy was full and hard like a rock as if it's full of something that cannot be digested for the next few days, probably a week before I end my first encounter with the number one killer in Africa, which, first time in my life, after coming to Africa, was able to create a psychological scar with constant thoughts of leaving the continent, which gradually diluted with time.

Unconsciously, I had confronted fears about malaria after my recovery from the first encounter, and with time, I had developed a psychological resiliency to malaria and accepted it as a treatable parasitic infection rather than an instant death brought by the tip of a mosquito beak, which obviously helped me to cope with the next couple of times that malaria took me into its lap. I was given different medication as per the availability in the country as it always happens like that in Liberia. There is no constant flow of commodities coming into the country, including food, medicine, clothes, and so on, if you get one medicine today, tomorrow you will get another variety which is an alternative. Life in West Africa kept me reminding constantly that I was far away not only from the luxuries but also from basic needs. However, I did not experience the same weird feelings which made me feel very prox-imate to death.

Today, while writing this chapter, I'm under medication, artesunate and falcidar, with malaria for the fifth time in my life. Nonetheless, I have come to a realisation that malaria is a part of life in this part of world and everyone who lives here has to deal with it, as my local colleagues who simply say that they have malaria, whenever they are found sleeping while at work or like watchers in my apartment mourn the whole night shivering with chills, almost every two weeks' time. Most often, when the seasons break, either from rainy season to dry or the other way around, many locals become almost like at the end of the world. When you ask 'how are you?' they will reply 'trying small small', meaning that they are not good, most probably the cause is malaria.

By the way, life goes on, irrespective of 'bush fever' which visits almost everyone every year, couple of times. Most of them win the struggle against the tiny little microparasite that comes with the song of the death from the mosquito, and some go with it, adding up to the annual number of deaths each year; this tiny little parasite eradicates around 400,000 lives out of the total population of Africa every year, which is 54 per cent of total deaths caused by Malaria globally, and 3,000 among them are children who are the future of the continent.

Chapter 09

OVER THE SAND DUNE

AUGUST IS THE LONGEST school vacation in most of the years as there is an advanced-level examination, a university entrance competitive examination, that takes place in many senior schools and which is followed by paper marking in a few selected schools that takes around two more weeks. Most often, my father used to go for paper marking which happened often in Colombo, the commercial capital of Sri Lanka, and unlike other vacations, we would have a chance to enjoy something rare every evening when he returns from home. He never forgot to bring either an apple, mandarin, pears, or panibundi (a traditional sweet usually sold at roadside small shops) every evening. When *tuk tuk tuk* sounds at the door between five thirty and six in the evening, it was no one else. We knew he is not empty handed. It was a honeymoon time for us, little children who did not understand much of the horrifying reality that our little island was going through. For my mum, in the morning, when he leaves home to catch the train, I hear she was telling 'God Bless you,' which I do not hear her often say. She is a Christian, practising in her heart, not in public; she is also more Buddhist than any of us whose birth certificates were endorsed as Buddhists. However, her religion, which she inherited or was imposed by her parents, has conquered more space in her that she might feel an extra weight in herself than anything else, which is reasonable and believable. Until late adolescence, I did not really understand what she expected by her saying 'God bless' every morning when my father was going to Colombo.

Since a minority among Tamils who formed an armed front called LTTE started its atrocities specially in the North and East provinces, in which they were demanding for a sovereign 'Tamil Elaam' state that Tamil diaspora and some extremists among south Indian were dreaming about, even though the majority of Tamils in Sri Lanka lived in harmony with Sinhalese and Muslim ethnicities with no difference since the time of history known to us, the security of the country became more and more fragile. By late 1980, LTTE had been already transformed to a well-organised terrorist army from the stage of being a rebel group and spread its operations beyond just attacking an isolated and under-resourced police stations or a military camps as reported Northern or Eastern provinces or killing innocent civilians in border villages, cutting them into pieces while they were sleeping. They had made a radical shift in their attacks by launching suicide bombing in key areas of country, especially targeting civilians and major buildings that are critical for financial, administrative, and political functions of the country. The public places and public transport became no longer safe for travelling, but as the majority of Sri Lankans had no other alternative but to take the public transport which is being vigorously and constantly attacked by LTTE, as an alternative, most of the couples who were parents chose to travel separately at different times to avoid their children to become orphans. And once one goes to work, till he or she returns alive, the family members used to 'boil eggs in their stomachs'. My mother was one of them whenever my father goes to Colombo for paper marking. We, being children, did not understand what was going on in the country; despite some traumatising photos of victims of roadside bombs or attacks in a train or else sounds of explosions that we heard on and off, we did not feel the gravity of what the population was going through.

When we grew up, the fear which is constant when someone lives in prolonged vulnerability, invaded our adolescent lives imposing a lot of limits that our age did not really deserve. Unlike other conflict-ridden countries, except the children in LTTE-controlled areas, we were not deprived from education, access to health, food, or from any other basic necessities of life. On and off, the children in border villages, villages that were situated in areas under so-called LTTE control, were deprived the right to education as a result of sudden unexpected attacks of LTTE on civilians. But most of the time, our schools were operational. Workplaces were functional, shops and markets were open, and life rolled on as usual but with an intense fear that controlled every single activity of everyone under the superficial life that one would notice as 'normal'. We as Sri Lankans, not as Tamils, Muslims, or Singhalese, had adapted a new lifestyle in the course of the first fifteen years of the ethnic conflict of Sri Lanka which one would see continuing until 2009 when the military phrase of ethnic tension was officially over with the victory of government forces of the Socialist Democratic Republic of Sri Lanka.

The schools were daily guarded by the parents who were rostered by the school administration. At least once a month, every parent had to take a day off from work and come to serve as a guard at the school gates under the hot sun burning and dehydrating them the whole day. Guarding schools became a new part of parental responsibilities besides the newly adapted standards of travelling, mother and father do not travel together, which can also be considered as responsible behaviour. Upon the shoulders of the teachers, the responsibility of checking the bags of each and every student fell, as there were suspicions and there are also possibilities that they might use children as suicide bombers. Usually, in many of our schools, there were more than 2,000 students, and instead of opening the bag of each and everyone, schools imposed another regulation, asking everyone to use transparent bags so that any suspicious object can be easily noticed. However, there were no cases reported that LTTE had used children to bomb schools; instead, they tried a couple of times with suicide bombers who came as caretakers, housemaids, or parents to accompany children. However, the new regulation of transparent bags created a new market which was retained till the end of the war in 2009.

At least every other month, there were suicide attacks in the capital, Colombo, despite the ongoing battles in the North and East provinces between government forces and the LTTE. Except the children who lived in border villages, the rest of us were not much familiar with the reality in the North and East, despite the news published in papers, telecasted and broadcasted in TV and radio channels. But most of those news were closely filtered and some were manipulated. We often heard about the victories of government forces and less about the aggressive advances of LTTE against the military of Sri Lanka, but the attacks on the civilians were highlighted after. But, as if the LTTE was warning rest of population about their existence, they constantly targeted the civilian population in different places in the country, especially in Colombo, and other towns with historic, commercial, and political importance. Besides all that, the pistol team and suicide teams of LTTE were fragmented everywhere in the country in pursuit of VIPs such as political leaders and leadership of government forces, who launched planned suicide attacks when the right time comes for their long awaited hunt. Photos of human remains in pieces, burnt and blasted human flesh on roads, monks cut into pieces like pigs and cows in butcheries, and heads of attackers on rooftops or treetops were not rare in public media that everyone was exposed every single day, day and night, irrespective of age, gender, or other dimensions of human sensitivity to traumatic graphic illustrations which obviously have traumatising impact on everyone in the nation irrespective of the ethnicity. And we had learnt to hate each other over time. The media had done a lot in creating gaps and raising detestation between ethnicities in Sri Lanka, besides the opportunistic politicians who used the ethnic conflict widely and deeply in their favour. For us kids, it was the Tamils who killed the Sinhalese, and for the Tamils, it was the Sinhalese who killed them—our heads were filled with nothing logical except what we heard and we were told.

It was one of the days in 1994 when my mother was on a class in Colombo and the LTTE attacked the crude oil refineries in a nearby location in Colombo district, Dematagoda. A series of explosions, one after the other, started shaking the whole place, and we learnt that the trains had been halted at a nearby area to prevent being attacked. That was the first day I felt that I was going to lose someone in the family, and when my mom returned late that day the feeling that embraced my heart was inexplicable. That was the day I felt the weight and the sense of my mother's 'God bless' whenever my father goes to Colombo.

'It's hot like Sahara,' he stepped in showing his white cotton shirt with round collar, soaked with sweat, and even before he changed his shirt, he kept his leather bag on the stool, opened it, and pulled out a paper bag, which had clear evidence of what was inside. There should be fried jumbo peanuts or Panibundi inside the oily paper bag. Till he comes back from bath, which usually takes some time as we had a traditional water well which is annexed to the house just like a bathroom but one has to pull water from a bucket, we started munching our share of fried jumbo peanuts.

'What a great feeling,' he comes back after the bath with a towel on his back. His next ritual is his tea, which is usually sweeter and stronger than what we usually drink. He wants his tea to be made with at least three to four teaspoons of sugar and well brewed with Ceylon black tea. When his tea is ready, he is ready to talk, share his day, talk about anything we are interested in. When he was coming in, he was talking 'Sahara,' it was my little sister who picked up the word and started repeating 'Sahara, Sahara, Sahara'.

'Chooti, you know what it is?' he asked my little sister.

'No, no, no, sahara sahara sahara,' she kept on saying it like a song.

'I know it is a desert,' I replied.

My mother had an extraordinary knowledge in geography, and she had told me about different places on earth which I was also quite interested in. Therefore, considering my chronological age, my knowledge in geography was quite higher, grace to my mother.

'Yes' my mother who was sitting next to us told in recognition of my reply.

'That is the largest desert on earth and it's still expanding,' she added making all three of us her audience.

'How come?' I asked with surprise.

By early Nineties, 'Climate change and adaptation' had not even appeared at the horizon, but her reply was simple enough for me to understand that it was because of heat. She said, 'It's because of series of droughts that the area experiences since a few decades.' Droughts of course I had seen on television, in Hambanthota, southern Sri Lanka, Somalia, and Ethiopia, which was adequate for me to understand what an 'expansion of a desert' looks like.

'Chad Lake, which is in the Saharan region, is shrinking gradually.' When my mother mentioned that, I could not help my urge to run to the old bookshelf of my father and bring an Atlas. I really wanted to locate these 'shrinking' and 'expanding' elements of nature. But unlike modern time, there was no Google Maps or any other Internet-based facilities to search for geographical locations. An atlas is the only material which we had to depend on when it comes to maps. I remember, I located Africa by its shape as my mum always used to say that it was a like a sugar-apple. It was not difficult to locate Sahara, which was indicated in 'yellow', and then finally the small blue spot which was lake 'Chad'. I was rather proud than happy having been able to locate it. Then I heard my father was breaking the silence.

'You know the name "Chad" in local language is "a large reserve of water". This used to be enormous, much bigger than Caspian Sea in Russia. This is the biggest water source for a population around 65 million who live in this Saharan zone. And the occupation of these precious resources at the very edge of Sahara desert was vital for everyone in the region. That's why the history had stories of hundreds of fights over "Chad Lake".'

He took the atlas and showed me the 'yellow' zone.

'This is the division of the continent.' He showed me the 'green' part, which was right under the 'yellow' zone. I was always a curious child and wanted to know more even if I was not able to understand certain things.

'Why it is divided?'

'Is it by the desert?'

I kept on asking my endless questions out of curiosity.

'On one hand, the desert was a barrier to cross for many people who wanted to penetrate into the green area, which is known as Sub-Saharan Africa. On the other hand, it was a natural border between two demographic groups in the continent.'

It was not a right explanation to quench my infinite thirst of information. I was barely 8 years old when I spent the whole evening looking at the different maps of Africa in the atlas. And I found out that there were other 'yellow' areas in the southern side of the continent. It was the point of time when my inquisitiveness on what my father said about the difference between the 'yellow' and the 'green' parts started growing.

A couple of years after the very first discussion about Sahara and the differences between 'yellow' and 'green' zones, I came into contact with new names, such as Sahel Region and Sub-Saharan Africa, during a geography lesson in school.

'What are the differences between the Sahel Region and Sub-Saharan Africa?'

It was my voice, which is rare to hear in the classroom. I used to be a quiet student as I was more of a visual learner and I used to reflect and try to understand by going through additional literature, whenever I have access, about subject matters which I was interested in. I rarely asked questions in the classroom or gave my opinion on something. I would rather observe the others and try to find the answer to my questions by further reading. From the teachers' viewpoint, in a country where educational psychology or developmental psychology had not come to the forefront of the stage called 'teaching' in the Nineties, I was looked as a child who was not studious. There were two major labels in schools at that time, mostly labelled by the teachers themselves—'studious children' and 'those who were not'. And the teachers were not equipped with skills to adapt their teaching methods to be sensitive to the diverse styles of learning of children and tried their conventional colonial type of teaching with the power of the cane stick or terrifying children with screaming. In case the children do not respond to their methods, the child will be classified as 'those who are not studious' and will be a trash for the rest of his school life. Sometimes, teachers used to mock at children or bully them. But there were teachers who were made to be teachers even though they were a few. I was one of the 'those who are not' studious.

When I talked, it was a wonder for the class, especially for the teacher and the students whose confidence had been uplifted beyond what they were, being classified as 'studious'. The geography teacher, Mr Haturusinghe, was a person full of ego, and bit of inferiority also made him act superior in front of the students, sometimes before his colleagues.

'Rupasinghe, what do you mean? What differences do you refer to?'

His voice was quite suppressing, as if I asked a irrelevent question which was not supposed to be asked or else I was not supposed to ask questions as I was already classified under the 'those who are not studious' category.

'Can you please tell, what are the differences between Sahel Region and Sub-Saharan Africa?'

I was inquisitive as a student, but probably because of his own perceptual set which he had based in his own prejudices and stereotypes, he might have perceived my question as a question formulated to test him. That was what his gestures and response signalled to me. He threw a threatening look at me and said, 'Do not hurry, you will learn in the next lessons!'

He immediately turned towards the blackboard and started writing some questions down for homework for the weekend. And we did not talk about Africa again in the class.

Sitting in a traditional family hotel in a crowded medina in Marrakesh, while sipping a cup of traditional Moroccan mint tea, talking to the owner, quite an old gentleman who lived all his life in Marrakesh, looking at the busy and vibrant medina, I was completely disconnected from the thought that I was in Africa. By that time, I had already visited dozens of countries in the Sub-Saharan region, and I had witnessed cultural, demographic, gastronomic, linguistic, and historical diversity as well as connectedness among Sub-Saharan African nations. It was always a gradual transition of cultural features when you travel East to West and North to South in the Sub-Saharan zone, which allows the traveller to speculate and anticipate what he or she would come across when he or she makes the next 500 miles, and this prevents him or her from being surprised with cultural shock or a feeling of lost in an alien world. As most of the Africans in neighbouring countries would day, ' We are the same people,' which is true in the Sub-Saharan region when it comes to subregions even though extreme differences are found at the end of each pole of the continent, but those would become noticeable along the line. And when it comes to demographic diversity, there are significant differences, but still, the key elements of Negroid nature are well preserved in every tribe and ethnicity in Sub-Saharan Africa. But beyond the hot sand barrier of the Sahara, life is different: the people, cultures, and life itself. Even though some traits in the countries like Mali, Sudan, Niger, and Chad that possess the progressive transitional traits when one travels from south to east of those four countries, still there is a difference that cannot be suddenly digested by the tourists if they were not familiar with the historical background of Sahel region.

Amazigh, a slender yet energetic person irrespective of his age, which is very well shown on his extremely wrinkled face and gray hair on head and wide gray eyebrows with long hair like antennas, is a pleasant supportive person, yet he has his first Arabic trait, 'a good businessman' who counts every single cent that he earns; he started in his own Moroccan Arabic when he saw me first. I gently said in French that I do not understand a thing in Arabic along with a 'fomule de politesse'. His roadside small lodge and tea shop full of traditional and colorful moroccan decors offered a real ground-level experience of medina life to a visitor. Under the arch of Bougainville creepers with full of violet flowers, just like a gate to a royal park, we entered to the internal little garden surrounded by a wall painted in dark orange, which reminded me of some traits of colour combinations of old buildings in Senegal. The place was old and full of authentic architecture, carvings, tiles, paintings, and crafts which obviously reminded me the old French magazines, especially *Geo*, with their articles about Arabic arts with graphical illustration similar to what I see in reality now.

'I have five rooms all the same except their proximity to the road and view from the window,' he told while walking in a small marbled passage opening to another small open area. He opened one room, just at the corner, probably the smallest hotel room I had ever seen in my life, with a single bed, with clean beddings, a small table, wall-robe, and bathroom with a separate shower area with walls and floor with brightly coloured and decorated tiles, despite the small window which was just like a fanlight of a toilet, and did not allow me to change my mind to go for a luxury boutique hotel in the other side, calm side of the city as I had already felt the level of security and the comfort was acceptable in the downtown, medina, from where I would smell, taste, and feel the real Moroccan life of the people on the ground, who live on hot sands in the Sahel region which was told, heard, and seen differently from the 'green zone' of my father and 'Sub-Saharan Region' of my geography teacher.

The first day, as I arrived in the early afternoon, I was invited by Amazigh to have tea with him. When I was crossing the Bougainville arch, I was marvelled by what was on the round metal table with fancy rod iron legs that looked like it dated back to the Roman era, a table cloth which was full of handmade decors with golden threads, on which the tea set that is a heritage to this colourful culture is placed prestigiously, adding some kind of a royal ambiance. The teapot, which is shiny metal and rich in unique decors, carefully placed right in the centre of a metal tray which looks the same in terms of craftsmanship which has royalty in it, and two tiny glasses just like Russian vodka swabs but quite more colourful than them were waiting empty till I arrive at the table, and Amazigh, with his smile that extends to his ears, aligning all his wrinkles evenly distributed all over his face making his smile more genuine and face more expressive.

'Good afternoon, I hope you like my little place,' he told me when I was reaching the table.

'Of cause, I find it homely and warm.' It was my honest reply.

'Thank you,' he said with a humble gesture.

'Shay bi Naana, this is our traditional tea.' He poured tea into one glass while talking to me, then to the next. I was almost lost in the hospitality, ambiance, vibrations, and colours of the living little city I happened to come to. I was still wondering where I was, and whether I was still in Africa or not. Waking me up from my thoughts that never had a rest since the moment I landed in Morocco, Amazigh started.

'This is your first time in Morocco?'

'Yes, and first day,' I said. 'But may not be the last time,' I added as the first impression had already made me want to come back for a longer vacation, one day.

Amazigh was a man who talked with control, politeness, respect, and sage and he always left room for me to talk once he finished, which stood as a wall between my usual experience in Africa with what I was experiencing with him. In Ghana, Nigeria, and Kenya, many people easily get into one's skin by breaking one's talk even in a friendly discussion, but every single world I had with Amazigh reminded me of what my father used to say: 'yellow part' is different from 'green part.'

'Allah Hu Akbar' blend with the air in the reddish skies, reminding me of my time in Indonesia where the morning prayers of the mosque were my alarm of the morning and the prayer at sunset was the warning for stopping the work and return home. I usually do not like noises and detested when there were events in my neighbourhood in which loudspeakers were used. But, I do not know why, but for some reason, I had become very used to the prayers of the mosque, which I never considered as a disturbing sound, instead a pleasant calling Amazigh knows that his time for sacred prayers had come and looked at me with his humble smile as if he was begging me pardon to leave the table, which I felt before he verbalised it.

'Yes, Sir, please go for prayers, I will wait for you here.'

'Are you Muslim?' He asked me with a bit fearful and reluctant intonation.

'No, but I have lived in and visited Muslim areas,' I said, acknowledging my sensitivity.

'I will leave the menu here. You can order anything from it, then we will join you for dinner.' He left.

I was listening to evening prayers, looking at the road which is still full of life, and at a corner in a roadside spice shop, an old man was praying, his head that goes up and down caught my attention to the shop. I was just having a look at the colourful small mountains of spices which reminded me of a Hindu town in India during the Holi festival. Marrakesh is a city of contrast, colours, patterns, and life—a place which does not come to immediate imagination about Africa to an outsider who had not been to the continent.

'Monsieur, vous avez déjà commencé votre dinner?'

I knew that voice already. It was Amazigh returning after his prayers and he was checking on my order whereas I did not order anything as there was enough food for my eyes and for my mind at the roadside. I was enjoying the site through the arch-type windows in the tea shop and completely forgot about my dinner.

'This is a place of wonders, I was spellbound by the place and forgot to order the dinner,' I said with a kind of sense of humour.

'I can see,' he responded while taking the menu.

'By the way, what do you want? You need my help to choose?' he added.

Being in France and Africa, I was not very much distant from North African and Middle Eastern food. In many African countries, it is very common to find Lebanese restaurants where most of the North African

135

delicacies are served. On top of it, in France, finding a Moroccan restaurant was not difficult. Beyond everything, I, being a person who lived alone in Africa for almost half a decade, have tried to cook many African delicacies, among which couscous was my favourite.

'I will go for couscous,' I said spontaneously even without looking at the menu.

'Are you sure?'

'You are ordering what you know, right?' He was right. I wanted to start with what I know rather than going for a completely new kind of food on the very first day. That was my principle during all of my trips in Africa, which spontaneously popped out here as my subconscious knew that I was in Africa even though I was marvelled by the wonders of Morocco.

'If you give me the privilege to select for me today, probably I might be able to offer you a delicious dish.'

Amazigh finally convinced me.

'Okay, go ahead.' I said with a gentle smile.

That was the first time I had such an amicable conversation with a hotel owner in Africa who is from Africa, even though I had met many hotel and shop owners with the right and helpful attitude in Africa who were not Africans, including the owner of Semonkong Lodge in Lesotho who was from France. Amazigh is exceptional in terms of his public relations and client orientation and he was adding wonders to what I was experiencing in his motherland which is just on burning sands of Sahara, blessed with the cooling winds across the Mediterranean and guarded by the High Atlas.

'Here it is, have a look.' He broke my pensiveness again. It was him who was serving, instead of the waitress.

When he placed the plates saying, 'Boneless sirloin, breast of chicken, kofta and assorted vegetables resting on saffron rice,' I felt that the presentation of food had kind of an enhancing effect on the surrounding which already have an 'out of Africa' feeling.

'Am I somewhere in the Mediterranean?' I was giving him a compliment.

'It's is over there if you want to go,' he added with a humble gesture along with his usual smile.

After a delicious dinner with an amicable conversation, I left Amazigh almost forty-five minutes before midnight. And he mentioned he might not see me again till I leave as he will be leaving to Casablanca for two weeks to see his family. And I was supposed to visit the attractions in Marrakesh and around for a few days and leave to Fes, Casablanca, and then to Tunis in Tunisia. It was late night, I was thinking of the unbelievable change that I have been witnessing since the moment I crossed the sand dune that my father told about the 'yellow' part of the continent. I was in a state of mind that I was unable to realise that I was in Africa in reality. I did not sleep at all. A hot floor of positive energy was running in my veins. A feeling that I had not often experienced in the Sub-Saharan region of Africa, even when I was in national parks in South Africa which I loved more than any other experience in the continent. I was even thinking that my unforgettable experience of wildlife in Africa was kind of fading before the colours of contrast of Morocco, in tongue-binding tastes of Moroccan cuisine, lively culture that is warm like a fur blanket for chilling nights in Sahara, and soothing music that cools down the burning soul by the ruthless sun laughing over the desert. When my alarm started ringing, I realised that it was morning and I had not slept a single minute since the time I came to bed.

Before leaving Marrakesh, Amazigh had already arranged my transportation for Fes as well as made available one vehicle, on standby, in case I needed to go somewhere beyond the limits of the city where I cannot walk. Such a welcoming hospitality I did not see in Africa, probably because the level of hospitality which is world renowned in Asia especially in Sri Lanka, where I have come from had influenced my baseline in comparison. Predeparture prejudices which are created by various information on the Internet and other literature were nearly proven to be not true, even though I had not completed one third of my journey. Being an Arab country and being in Africa, there were a lot of biased news articles and old horror stories of kidnappings, swindling, disease, and generalised ill-will. Probably, it would be too early to conclude what I felt instantly and I did not encounter anything to question my perceptual set induced by the very first impression. I felt free to enjoy my vacation and worried less by the sense of travellers' vigilance.

In Marrakech, I spent several nights awed by the acrobats and storytellers of the Jemaa el Fna, determined to see each performance through to its bitter end. Snake charmers and monkey dancers who are usually gypsies are often found in my part of world, South Asia, especially in Sri Lanka and India. The sight of a snake charmer or the music of melon-horn of a gypsy would rather make us avoid than see them. No one back home dare to touch or get close to those snakes which are furiously rushing out of the round cane bag and run all over the place, sometimes into the crowd who are watching. The sight of a snake charmer in Marrakech instantly bridged my mind with Sri Lanka, a back-at-home feeling without the usual reserved feelings to the charmer, unlike to the gypsies back home. I touched the fanged cobra belonging to a snake charmer, for the first time in my life in Marrakech and for the first time ever in my life I gave money to a snake charmer, I gave him a few dirhams, which I usually do not do to a gypsy back home or somewhere in Sub-Saharan Africa. And I did another 'don't' back in the 'green' part of Africa. I sampled various Moroccan foods from the evening vendors. Trying street food in most of the parts of the Sub-Saharan Africa ends up with travellers' diarrhoea or typhoid. The presentation of the medical section in the induction briefing of the United Nations Mission in Liberia kept on echoing within my ears every time I see roadside grilled meat, corn, or any other food in many countries I visited in the continent, but not in Morocco.

Throughout my three-week journey from the imperial cities of Fes and Marrakech to the dunes of the Sahara, I was treated like a desert prince by everyone I met. Not only did I visit fabulous Casbahs and wander fragrant Palmeraies, but I also learned history from the Roman ruins of Volubilis, perfected the fine art of haggling in the souks, developed a real taste for Moroccan gastronomy, and took to saying 'Shukran' instead of 'thanks'. Morocco, by its outlook, and its profounder had an invisible power of taking the tourists into its hands of charm, just like the dancing snakes following the melodies of the charmer.

In Fes, while navigating the old medina, I enjoyed getting lost. It was just like solving a complex puzzle to find the way back through small but extremely crowded pathways through little shops. I marvelled at every shop which had something unique that reflects on the colourful culture of Morocco. In small huts found in corners of the medina, craftsmen paint wooden furniture and do carvings, adding life to the market-place. Despite the sellers who do not want to let anyone out without buying a little thing, my whole experience of medina was an exciting adventure which was beyond my imaginary Africa.

Each morning, I empty several glasses of Shay bi Naana, looking at the street which is awakened by the birds. After long walks in crowded medinas and dusty streets in town, under the burning sun, upon the Sahara, several cups of Shay bi Naana reenergise me. Every lovely evening, with reddish skies upon the colourful world full of life, I empty several tiny glass cups of Shay bi Naana, plunged in reflection of the wonders around me, deeper than what one's thoughts can reach, and at the end of the journey, I had probably emptied several dozens of pots of Shay bi Naana, having discovered another culture centred around a pot of tea but which is not just about tea but more about how it is served, the amazing craftsmanship that reflects the hypersensitive artistic skills filtered through the culture which is a blend of Arab, African, and Mediterranean features, the quality time spent around the teapot and the long conversations that follow every sip of tea, that never ends just like cycle of life.

I had already three tickets in my hand, one for Tunis and extended to Cairo and the third one for Accra, Ghana via Addis Ababa. It was crystal clear for me where I was heading to from a culture of a multitude of colours, true human warmth, with the smell of human civilisation, healing melodies, and the first bit of thought that Africa is not the same Africa I lived in for almost half a decade of my life. My father's reference of 'yellow' and 'green' parts came to my mind over and over again when I was in the train to Casablanca and these three tickets would either affirm or disapprove his allusion. But I had already experienced a difference that I could not deny existing, a true difference which is multidimensional.

I stopped at Paul's in Mohammed V International Airport, Casablanca; before proceeding to the gate, I pulled out my phone and rang Amazigh. I just wanted to thank him for his outstanding hospitality and the human kindness he expressed to me.

'Monsieur Amazigh, Je suis déjà à l'aéroport pour partir à Tunis, Merci beacoup pour votre gentilesse et pour tout ce que vous m'avez fait. Merci encore! Je vais quitter le Maroc physiquement mais je quitte jamais psychologiquement ce magnifique pays,' I told him my honest feelings. I might have been probably overwhelmed by emotions but I told him what I felt in its own form without changes. I heard the slight sound he makes when he smiles followed by a 'Merci'.

'Vous êtes toujours bien-venu chez moi,' he added in his polite voice which one may easily misunderstand as 'submissive'.

Amazigh would remain in my memory with a positive note not only as an individual but also with the name of his country. One of the most wonderful trips I have ever made—a destination of diversity and contrast that I did not find anywhere else in the continent of Africa.

It was early in the morning when I reached Tunis–Carthage International Airport, from Casablanca, which was, according to the popular news and tourist information, moving from secured area towards volatile Arab lands where violent protests, roadside car bombing, shooting in public areas can occur at anytime. That reminded me of the three decades of ethnic conflict in Sri Lanka. I, being a Sri Lankan, who lived in my country during the terrifying peak of the conflict, have not only first-hand experience of how it affected us, but also how foreign media tried to 'fish in muddy waters', exaggerating the situation and misinterpreting the whole situation, making it best sold in the world market. The popular diction such as barbaric, terrorists, killers, extremists, violence had already been repeated over and over again in liaise with news in Tunisia since 2011 protests and regime change. Another Arab territory, which is potentially volatile, is being born through CNN and BBC terminology, and it's neighbouring countries Algeria and Libya are already being labelled as volatile, unsecured, or countries of dictatorships which the Western world cannot admit that the people are living happily in the kind of administration or rule that they have just due to the simple fact that they do not fall into Western democratic governing framework which leads to market liberalisation, ensuring the access of resources within the territory to the external world. I visualised Tunisia behind CNN and BBC's lens, a country with a great history, culture, and a vast geographic diversity, simply a paradise that is at the northern tip of Africa, over the sand dune of Sahara, just like the bottle-neck to Europe and Middle east—a blend of many cultures of dominant empires that existed in world history.

Tunisia used to be the heart of the Carthaginian Empire which was founded by Phoenician settlers from Tyre and Sidon which is today Lebanon. The power of the Carthaginian Empire was a major challenge for the Romans during the antiquity, even though Romans were able to conquer Carthage in 116 BC after a series of tough battles that were never easy for Romans, known as Punic Wars. As a result of being a part of the Roman Empire, doors of new civilisation were opened for Carthage till the next occupant, the 'Vandals', came in and then followed the Byzantine Empire, Arabs, and finally the Ottoman Empire till Tunisia fell under the sway of European imperialism as a French protectorate along with Algeria. After the independence from France in 1956, Habib Bourguiba ruled Tunisia for thirty-one consecutive years, leaving zero space for the rise of Islam extremism within the territory of his country while ensuring equal rights to both men and women like in no other country in the Arab world. But today, unfortunately, young Sahara is burning with the flames that came across immense Arabian desert and seeds of extremism and violence have penetrated into the frontiers once heavily guarded by Carthaginians which even Romans could not enter easily. The Jasmine Revolution, in 2011, was the first event in the so-called Arab Spring, which ended up overthrowing the existing rule and electing a new government yet leaving ongoing protests all over the country. On the top of it, Western media fills the gas into the balloon of extremism, making it bigger and flying higher so that the whole world can see it.

Pushing myself out of the gates of the airport, I searched for my driver from the boutique hotel where I was supposed to stay in Tunis, who was supposed to keep the placard with my name on it, among those hundreds of people who were holding placards of different names. First I carefully looked at the names on the placards from the beginning to end, but I did not find my name. Then I looked for names that could sound like mine as I usually find my name misspelled in many occasions. 'Pomdir' instead 'Pramudith' was on one placard held by a quite lean young guy. I approached him and asked whether he was from the hotel I made the reservation.

'Yes Sir,' He instantly responded. I was sure that I would reach the hotel I booked, which is the first part of a successful trip in an unknown destination. When I saw the small board lying on the dashboard of the van with the name of my hotel, I was convinced that I would not be kidnapped or taken hostage by an unknown group who would later claim themselves as Islam militants by releasing a video on YouTube of executing me with a razor blade while the 'Holy Koran' is being read rhythmically in the background. Passing the city, we headed to north of Tunis, avoiding the main resorts as I was quite tired of areas crowded by tourists, which I found as a common negative element in Moroccan cities. But compared to Marrakesh, Fes, Rabat, or Casablanca, Tunis remains neglected and underrated. The media campaign on Islam extremism and the series of violent protests have significantly contributed for that. But my first impression while riding the taxi was that there was less hassle than in Moroccan touristic cities probably because of phobic picture which is given to the external world.

An old merchant house converted into a hotel, which are called boutique hotels, white walls with blue wooden doors and windows that suggest some Greek heritage than Arabic architecture, blending with typical north African and Arabic marble work with its breathtaking view of the Mediterranean sea from the courtyard did not allow me to think twice about what I paid for the hotel. Just a few dozens of metres away, the beach that stretches to infinity unfolds before my very eyes, taking me on an imaginary journey back to the sandy beaches of Sri Lanka, which made me feel like at home. In the mean time, 'feeling like home' triggered the fear induced by potential terrorist attacks. Since the beginning of my journey in Tunisia, I was like on a roller coaster, swinging between two poles: fear and Joy. I tried my best to overcome the fear that is underlying whenever I come across something which reminds me of the Halloween tonality and cold-blooded expressions of CNN and BBC news presentations. Yet again, whenever I look around, I see the life and serenity condensed in Tunis that sits on the bay overlooking Mediterranean, picturesque and tranquilising, just like a heavenly medicine for body and mind.

Roaming around the main street, through the crafts shops, I did not hesitate to grab some street food and sate my hunger even though it was not the right place to buy crafts which are unreasonably overpriced. The main street 'Rue DJamaa Ezzituna' leads to 'DJamaa Ezzituna', the great mosque of olive tree itself, which is a symbolic masterpiece of architecture of the harmonious cohabitation of Turkish and Arabic cultures. As the city gets crowded with the day trippers from cruise ships, and the sun rises overhead, the tranquillity of city centre started to be interrupted. I took a yellow taxi which reminded me Liberia and told the driver to take me to Carthage, which was the only city which was able to challenge the Romans.

'Ne me joudgez pas si vous m'aimez autant. . .' the song of Swat and Atlas, Franco Algerian musical group, was one of my favourites when I was in school. I did not know how many times I had been listening to that song. I loved Maghreb French music, which is a melodious combination of Arabic and French, probably the only way the French and Arabic worlds can be in the same rhythm. Swat and Atlas, Bruel and Faudel were my favourite Maghreb musicians. When I was in my early twenties, I was tightly bounded by the exotic charm of Northern African countries which have not the same exoticness that one would experience in South Asia. Probably, it was just the difference which attracted me, but I loved to visualise the Maghreb along with the songs, just like an imaginary journey across Morocco, Algeria, and Tunisia. It was a dream that never came to the surface of myself as a strong urge and I never thought that I would be able to trample the sands of Magreb. Today in my early thirties, after a decade, I'm in a taxi, in Tunis, travelling to the ancient power bank of ancient Tunisia, Carthage, listening to one of my favourite songs from the region.

To my surprise, even after almost two thousand years, the ruins in Carthage seem standing straight against the fast-changing modern world as if to show the robustness of the Carthaginian Empire which was the only empire that was a challenge to the Romans, which reminded me of the ancient cities of Sri Lanka, such as Anuradhapura and Polonnaruwa, which date back to 2,500 years ago. But Roman influence was vivid in Carthage as it was rebuilt by Romans after demolishing it during the invasion. And later on, it became one of the wealthiest cities in the Roman Empire.

A feeling like I was in the heart of the Roman Empire while entering to a museum in the northern tip of Africa which was known as a part of Arab world was hard to believe. But the museum in the heart of the city is live evidence that the Romans had left behind, a surviving collection of ancient mosaics in Tunis.

Just before my departure, after four days in Tunis, which was another 'lost in wonders' kind of an experience over the sand dune of the Sahara, I felt an irresistible urge to go back to the main street and buy some colourful hand-painted plates for my wife. She loves blue colour, which was not hard to find in craft shops. I walked along 'Rue DJamaa Ezzituna', navigating through the craft shops crowded by tourists searching for a shop, which I noticed when I was there for the first time. At last, after an exhausting exercise of bargaining skills, which is always needed in this part of world, in which I am not good at, I was able to buy six hand-painted plates, which are my only physical memory of Tunis against thousands of pleasant, colourful, melodious memories of this relatively unnoticed yet magnificent city which is in my opinion more homelier and exotic than many of the better-known Moroccan destinations. The heart of the city, old medina, which is the old city, a mirror of Arabian and Turkish rule and 'Nouvelle Ville' which is just outside, built by the French in early nineteenth century, has given birth to a paradise on a gulf where several civilisations have put their colours, patterns, and skills together to create a human-made heaven at the northern tip of Africa, where cold moist breeze blows across the Mediterranean, cooling down the heat of burning sands in the Sahara. I had the feeling of wanting more which was suppressed by the lack of time that ended up with sadness when I checked in at Tunis–Carthage International Airport for Cairo, Egypt, in quest of a civilisation that is a subject of tense arguments between 'yellow' and 'green' parts of Africa, claiming its ownership which remains controversial.

It was like not long time ago, even-though it was more than two and half decades, my father taught me about four great ancient civilisations on earth. He talked about India—Indo-basin civilisation; China—Ho-wan-ho basin civilisation; Iran—Euphrates and Tigris basin civilisation; and Egypt—Nile basin civilization. I still remember he added that Nile is the longest river on earth but I was unable to visualise how long it was, especially to think that a river would cross borders of several countries as it was not a Sri Lankan experience as we are islanders and as a child of eight I had not been exposed to the world to think beyond the context of my country. The he talked about the most hair-raising and fearful yet interesting part of the whole history lesson.

'Pharaohs, the nobles, and the dynasty of Nile basin civilisation are mummified and resting in peace in colossal rock tombs called pyramids.' He explained showing a picture of a copper-coloured statue with a strange head like a hood of a snake.

'This is a mummy,' he said.

'The ancient Egyptians used different traditional techniques to preserved dead bodies for thousands of years.'

I did not speak a word, yet I was excited and kept on looking at his mouth with my mouth open with surprise.

'It is believed that they rolled big cubes of heavy rocks to carry them to build these amazing masterpieces of ancient architecture.' He showed me a picture of a pyramid, which made me absolutely lost in the mist of history.

'Is it like Anuradhapura?' I asked him with a curious tone. Anuradhapura is first kingdom in Sri Lanka, in which a lot of smooth rock work had amazed the world. When my father mentioned about rock work, the only thing that came to my mind was Anuradhapura, which was familiar to me. I was unable to imagine something beyond that. Unfortunately, we did not have access to educational television channels in Sri Lanka by that time and we did not have a television at home as my parents did not want us to sit in front of the television every evening. Their total focus was to see my sister and myself studying better than others to maintain their names as well as to secure our future. Every parent in Sri Lanka wants their children to excel in education, pushing themselves up in competitive examination processes that start as early as when the child is just 9 years old, which deprives the freedom of the child to grow as a child. A lot of play time, leisure time, and interaction of the child with nature and society remain significantly limited during the twelve years of school life. The time a child would learn from the environment and society does not exist for us in Sri Lanka during our childhood, and we were completely inclined to the books and exams. As a result of the system and parental attitude towards intensive education as the only way for a prosperous future, I had to forget about further quest on the pyramids as my junior scholarship examination was approaching. Everyone was pushing me to study hard for a better score and to be selected by a more recognised school in the capital. I guess I did not give any importance to the scholarship exam and I was unable to meet the high expectations that my parents had but I succeeded in the exam that allowed me to be selected to the school where my mother worked which was in the same township where we lived. The school was not a new place for me as I used to go there with my mum and most of the staff knew me already which gave me kind of a comfortable feeling of being in a familiar place and at the same time I felt a bit restricted as I knew whatever I do would be informed to my mum right away. I was not known as a studious child but I had my favourite subjects in which I was more knowledgeable than the 'studious' group even though I often remained silent in the classroom. Being a visual learner, I hated lecture-type sessions; I could not concentrate on long stories that teachers often related to students, but I loved library period that gave me an enabling environment where I could read and learn. I used to go to a corner in the library, so that I will not be interrupted, and read, most often the librarian would come, tap my back, and say, 'Period is over.' One day, I was searching for a book to read during library period and found a think book called *A Civilization at the Heart of Sahara*. First time ever in my life, I trafficked a book from my school library, not with the idea of stealing it but with the intention of reading it till its end. I went to one of the abandoned three-storey buildings in the school premises of which entry was prohibited as it was under threat of collapsing due to very poor construction. I found myself tranquil and peaceful and started to go through all the colourful pictures with descriptions and read the narratives as if it was a book for my end-of year's examination. That day, I did not hear any of the bells in the school except the last one which was louder and longer than the usual bell that signals break of periods. I decided not to go to this classroom to get my school bag and get caught for not being in class; instead I took the book home.

My father always had a soft end for us, whereas my mother was often seen as a police officer spying on what the children do and questioning, followed by relevant punishments in case found guilty. When I was crossing the stick of wood which is across the entry to the compound, she had already noticed that I did not have my school bag with me.

'What happened to your bag?' Her authoritative voice was loud and clear up to the entry of the compound. I anticipated her reaction and I had already formulated an answer when I decided not to go back to the classroom to get my bag.

'I was in the library and the monitor had lost the key so we could not enter. They were trying to find it but I came as I did not want to miss the school van.'

I knew that was enough for the next eighteen hours, till next morning. When my mother goes to work the following morning, she will get a detailed report of my absence in class since library period. I did not worry about it much as I had a proof to show that I took a book to read and I read it within the premises of the school. I knew that my parents would not speculate that I would go outside the school for anything. However, in case I mentioned about the library, my act of trafficking the book which is classified as 'not for lending' or 'reference' will be caught but I thought that I would be able to handle that situation better and easier as a child of a staff member.

There was a test cricket tournament between the Sri Lankan national team and West Indies being broadcasted that I had been listening to since its beginning. And the final day of the final and decisive test match which would determine the destiny of both teams was being broadcasted that evening when I came home. Instead of going to the living room with my usual cup of milk tea that my mother prepares for me and listen to the live broadcast, sitting on one of the two wooden veranda chairs that my mother had brought on my grade five scholarship exam, I went to my room with my milk tea and the book that I got from the school library. I remember that was the first book and probably the last book I read overnight during my school time; I read till I heard the alarm on the next morning. I could not believe my eyes that it was the following morning and I had to go back to school which I did not want to do as I had not finished the book yet but my school bag was left in the classroom, so I had to go. It was always a thrill to go back to class after violating regulations in the school and the teachers are following up closely with 'those who are not studious' whom I was classified as. For my luck, first period was physical training and everyone had already gone to the playground when I reached the class. My bag was still under the desk. I pulled it out, put my book inside, and headed to a Wetakeiya bush near the playground from where I could see the classroom as well as the children playing in the ground so that I will be able to read the rest of the book at least for another forty-five minutes. I ignored the sun that I always hated; it was a sunny morning and rays were hitting me right on the face. I kept on reading till the end-of-period bell rang. After I came back to the classroom, I realised that I had burns on my face and it felt as if I was caught in a fire and I later developed a bit of temperature, which I turned into my favour. I went to my mother's class in the interval time and told her that I had developed a slight fever and I wanted to go home. My mother touched my forehead and said 'I will send you home.'

When I heard that, I felt like I was in seventh heaven. It was what I was longing to hear. 'Yes' I would have a whole afternoon followed by the weekend for me to finish the book. Instead of doing my usual school work, I spent my whole weekend completely plunged into the book and by Sunday afternoon, I had already completed the book. That was the longest constant reading I had ever done so far, and at the end of four days, I was equipped with some knowledge which was sufficient to surprise my social study teacher by defending myself or even challenge him with my spontaneous and elaborate responses to his attacking questions thrown to the 'not studious' group of children. On top of everything, that was the moment my dream to visit Egypt germinated within me. Yet it was another dream that I did not know how to reach and by that time I also came upon my miscellaneous African dreams, and they already piled, one upon the other. That day, I realised that dreams without means are like helium balloons, just flying in the air with no goal, no direction, just straying in empty space. I felt vain and useless. I had a few pen-friends from Western Europe who were in the same age as me and had visited few countries in Africa. A current of sadness and helplessness ran through me for some time for being born in a poor country where there were limited opportunities for growth and where there are not much choices of a path for the future. I went through, over and over again, every single page where photos of mummies, paintings, and pyramids were, and without my knowledge, a deep sigh released my hopelessness to the empty air as if there will be a day that would take me to where my dreams live. 'A sun would rise with the rays with hopes and as it set a moon full of accomplishment and achievement would melt the darkness of the sky—pyramids,' I wrote in my notebook and eventually forgot about the book and many facts I read, but not the dream.

Ninth of July 2011. My Sudanese colleague, who was a Harvard-educated lawyer, met me in the cafeteria of my office for the usual morning conversation during breakfast time.

'Today we are independent,' he told me with his usual pleasant smile, which was always special as his pearl-white teeth surrounded by an ebony black wall of lips are fully shown whenever he smiles, which made his smile more than an official and diplomatic smile of a colleague. I congratulated him for the newest state in the world, 'South Sudan,' but I raised my concerns whether separation from the Arab part of Sudan and being an independent state would address the underlying issues that were the root causes of decades of prolonged series of dynamic conflicts in the territory.

'They claimed our ancient civilisation as theirs. We are Nubians and our territory had extended till the southern tip of Tanzania and Northern tip of Egypt; now they say that it is their civilisation.

He was referring to Nile basin civilisation which is a subject of endless contradicting information about who were the real owners of the ancient Nile basin civilisation. Egyptians with Arab origin claim that it is theirs, while Negroid along the Nile basin, especially from Sudan, and some parts of Tanzania and Kenya, claim that the pyramids belong to a black civilisation. I remember one of the Afro-American academics had made a detailed documentary on civilisations of Africa including the kingdom of Nubians. When I was watching his documentary, for some reason which was unknown to me, it gave me a real feeling. One scene in the documentary was unforgettable; that one young black man with completely dominant and pure Negro features from Zanzibar says that he was not an African but a Nubian who is an Arab. He was adding more obscurity into a truth that had already been buried in the darkness of the history of sands in Sahara which had already created a friction between 'green' and 'yellow' parts of the continent. My conversation on the freedom day of South Sudan, rejuvenated my old dream to visit those amazing wonders standing in burning sands, against the running time and I already had passed the difficult passage of life in which the means for pursuing my dream was the obstacle. I had earned sufficiently for my dream voyages. After a few weeks of our conversation, I was on board MS844 of EgyptAir which landed in Cairo International Airport when 1845h was indicated in my wrist watch. I had five days ahead of me to discover in reality what I first heard when I was a kid, then read in a book when I was an adolescent. I had never experienced anxiousness and restlessness when I just reached a destination before. I was just like a football coach who was watching a round of penalty shots in a match where his team had equalised the score of the opposing team. I was going to see the most ancient civilisation so far on earth that my father and mother taught me when I was a kid. Time had passed by in such a pace that I had already lost the narrator of my first Egyptian story and I have already a man of 32 years and still his dream of childhood was alive and young.

The most precious thing about having worked for the United Nations at international capacity, especially in peace keeping operations with larger missions, is that one would make contact with people from almost every country of the world. I did have a couple of friends from Egypt. An ex-police officer who served as a police advisor in Liberia had organised my itinerary from airport pick-up to drop-back to the airport a couple of weeks before I had arrived. Grace to his super-organised nature, I was able to have a detailed yet very budget type of tour among the lost world where millions of wonders had been left for modern archaeologists and the which scientists debate on. And on top of it, instead staying in a hotel, I stayed in his home and he emphasised as his first condition that I should not deny I was able to make my stay a typical ground-level experience than a touristic one. And Ahmad became my chauffeur guide since the time I arrived and till the moment I left this country and his protective and caring hospitality took all my paranoia and fears created by the media away.

'Okay, this is the plan' when we sat for breakfast. The following morning, he pulled out a small piece of paper which was quite crushed one with some irregular and faded scrubbing with a blue pen. The paper reminded me an old piece of map of ancient Arabic sailors. He unfolded it carefully till it expanded into two A4 sheets.

'First we will go to Giza, where you can see the pyramids and then we will see other things in and around Cairo,' Ahmad had indicated the attractions in and around Cairo while explaining the itinerary. After his detailed briefing which made me feel that I was about to take another humanitarian assignment, I felt as if I was undergoing a predeployment briefing.

Just after breakfast, we headed to Giza which was around ten miles but heavy traffic in the city pushed our scheduled time thirty minutes back about which Ahmad was not happy even though I was quite realistic and flexible enough to take it as a normal situation. Almost after an hour from our departure, a silhouette of an extraordinarily shaped giant pyramid started appearing at the dusty horizon just like a giant warrior appearing through the flames. A moment of dreams that came true was triumphing within me silently, while my memories of the book I trafficked from the library started to be refreshed. The world of mere dreams and the world of reality was bridged again, that I was unable to think of a possibility, years ago. It was a wonder that the wonders of time brought me to the wonders of the world.

The moment I walked near the Great Pyramid of Giza, widely known as Pyramid of Khufu or the Pyramid of Cheops, the colossal structure standing firm and prestigious for more than 4,000 years, almost intact, reminded me of an association with ancient cities that dated back to 3,000 years, in Sri Lanka. More than being surprised by seeing a pyramid in reality, I was rather trying to recollect the pieces of my old readings. I stood just in front of the entrance and just closed my eyes. I wished to see the great pyramids that I used to see when I closed my eyes. For some reason, I did not see any of those, probably because I was on the ground of reality descending down from the skies of dreams. I guess I was there a couple of minutes with my eyes closed till my old dreams appeared within my eyes before I entered the world of reality, and heard Ahmad calling me.

'Let's go in.'

We entered through the new entrance to the structure which is called 'Robert's tunnel'. A mild coldness of fearful feeling of entering to a world of mystery was trying to coil around my mind as I was entering. It is a tomb but it did not give the same sensation when I was crossing the huge arch entrance in Taj Mahal in Agra, India, which is also a tomb.

'It is believed that this was built as the tomb for Pharaoh Khufu,' Ahmad told when we were walking along the passage in the grand gallery which says more than what the world can believe about the artistic skills of ancient Egyptians that defies one of the theories of construction of pyramids which is that the slave labour was used for construction of the pyramids.

'Khufu's vizier, Hemon, or Hemiunu, is believed by some to be the architect of the Great Pyramids' Ahmad added just like a professional guide which amazed me.

Actually there are different theories about the construction of the pyramids but still not one is certain how these massive structures have been built on the sands to remain not only across the generations but also millennia, resisting and surviving the extreme heat, rains, earthquakes, invasions, and many other miscellaneous destructive forces, standing superior to modern construction methodologies.

I had learnt in the book I read at the school that they were massive tombs constructed on the orders of the pharaohs by teams of workers tens-of-thousands strong. This is supported by the discovery of a pyramid builders' settlement, complete with areas for large-scale food production and medical facilities. The belief that the slaves were used as labour for heavy work is most dominant among the commoners despite that a lot of excavations on the Giza Plateau have provided solid evidence that the slaves were not used, as highlighted in many Hollywood films, but an organised and trained workforce of Egyptian farmers. During the flood season, when the Nile covered their fields, the same farmers could have been redeployed by the highly structured bureaucracy to work on the pharaoh's tomb. In this way, the pyramids can almost be seen as an ancient job-creation scheme adapting to the seasonal calendar ensuring constant livelihood opportunities for citizens. And the flood waters made it easier to transport building stone to the site. But despite the evidence, many still won't accept that the ancient Egyptians were capable of such achievements. So-called pyramidologists point to the carving and placement of the stones, precise to the millimetre, and argue the numerological significance of the structures' dimensions as evidence that the pyramids were constructed by angels or aliens. The moment I started to see the evidences of genius craftsmanship demonstrated by the builders of the great pyramid of Giza, Anuradhapura, Polonnaruwa, and Segiriya era of Sri Lankan history where the enormous stone statues, palaces, temples, and many other crafts amazed the modern world, hit my mind. Coming from a country with an ancient civilisation where there were a lot of similar evidences of smooth and sharp engineering of old time, absorbing that these are made by skilled human hands guided by sharp minds.

After the great pyramid of Giza, I had the chance to witness a most seen icon of ancient Egypt via media. The great Sphinx of Giza is the first image that would come to one's mind when thinking about Egypt. During my school age, the image of Pharaoh is merely Sphinx and whenever I thought of a pyramid, Sphinx appeared as an annex. At the moment I saw immense limestone statue which is believed to represent the face of Pharaoh Khafra but with a body of a lion in reclining position, again my thoughts were immediately connected to the stone statues dating back to thousands of years in Sri Lanka.

'We call it Abū al-Haul which means father of dread or fearful one,' Ahmad said showing almost an intact face of the Sphinx, which might have fought its long surviving battle with changing weather and human intervention. The cracks and visible damages of Sphinx tell us its struggle of survival through millennia.

'This is the largest monolith stature and the oldest monumental sculpture on earth, believed to have been built by ancient Egyptians during the time of Pharaoh Khafra,' I said to Ahmad, quoting one of the unforgettable passages from the book I read about Egypt during my school time. I looked at the still yet determined face of the Sphinx that seems looking ahead in time with anticipation of something that we had not yet thought of. Over the years, several authors have commented on what they perceive as 'Negroid' characteristics in the face of the Sphinx. This issue has become part of the Ancient Egyptian race controversy, with respect to the ancient population as a whole. The face of the Sphinx has been damaged over the millennia. From history, what we the present generation know about the Sphinx might not be the truth and the future would have its own plan which is not anticipated by present generations. My thoughtfulness took me to my mental archives of the documentary made by an Afro-American academic who tried to bring forward the argument of Egypt as a black civilisation, which makes the audience think about erasing the truth after invasions which presently happen with Islamic State Groups, known as ISIS, in many countries in the Arabic world. The documentary stimulates the audience to reflect on something similar to ISIS activities. Instead, demolishing or changing certain elements to change the identity of the originals might have been happened, which was quite a common strategy followed by the invaders irrespective of geographical zones or demographical differences.

Even though I wanted to stay more in Giza, the time to return had already been reached as we did not want to get stuck in traffic again. On top of everything, my mind was tired as instead of clearing my doubts and knowing unknowns, I found myself in a complex puzzle of different views, opinions, hypotheses, and assumptions about ancient Egypt. Ahmad told me there was heavy traffic on the way back but I did not even notice what was on the road and how long we took to get back home. My mind was completely engaged with a never-ending cycle of thoughts about pyramids and pharaohs.

'It was like trying to make a time machine to go back in time,' I told to Ahmed when we were having tea with his family in the evening.

'Did you navigate through time?' He immediately used his sense of humour which is always spontaneous from his end even when he was working with me.

'No, I could not make the machine,' I said with a laughter, followed by his laughter.

'I realised that even if I made the machine, it would not go all the way along the line of history, so I gave it up,' I added.

The next few days, I was with his family on navigating Cairo, visiting a couple of my old friends who worked with me, visiting some attractions such as the Egyptian museum in downtown Cairo, the Islamic Art Museum, shopping at busy markets places like Khan-Al-Kalili, and a cruise in the Nile to see the attractions along the back of the river, on the day before I left Cairo to Addis Ababa for a short stay till my next flight back to Accra, Ghana. Ahmad always tried his best to make my stay a balanced one; at the latter part of my journey, when we had time, he talked about the progressive rising of Islamic extremism on their soil, which I had been hearing and seeing in media over and over again.

'We used to live peacefully with everyone for centuries,' he expressed his sincere views with a bit of frustration.

'Today, we fear that these armed groups would create turmoil in our country as they did in Libya and Syria,' added Ahmad. I really did not have anything to say, but I felt the heat of the sand expanding all over the dune, across the width and along the length from Western Sahara through Tunisia, Algeria, Libya, Egypt, Sudan till the Horn of Africa where Somalia stands at its peak with Al-Shabab. Unlike during the ancient time, where the sands of Sahara was a hurdle for invasions, today, across the 'yellow' zone, the 'green' zone had been penetrated by the unprecedented heat wave of terrorism of Islamic extremism in Africa making Mali, once a peaceful country with its rich and colourful culture which stood as high as Mosques in Timbuktu, one of the largest battlefields of extremists movements such as Tuareg and ISIS, Niger; a dessert soaked with blood, Nigeria; a hunting ground of Boku-Haram, Central Africa; a guerrilla war of Anti-Makala, Sudan, still unstable even after its legitimate division and establishment of new state 'South Sudan' and Mauritania a silent husbandry for extremists by transforming the Sub-Saharan and Sahel Region the battlefield of the modern war of Constantinople between Colonial God and the God of Islam fundamentalists devouring millions of innocent lives, displacing millions, and destroying and demolishing properties.

Ahmed's words of concerns reminded me of the time before 2009 in Sri Lanka, a state of incertitude where no-one knows when death waves hit you and how. Maybe a sudden crossfire in a shopping mall or a busy bazaar, a suicide bomb at roadside or an intended attack in anywhere can take your life. The ammunitions or explosives are not sensitized to faith, creed, colour, age, gender, or the kind of language one speaks and do not care how many innocent woman become widows and helpless, how many children become orphans, how many people become disable and traumatized for life but they just explode leaving nothing but a massive human and property destruction which I could see clearly as I had gone through the same in my own country. Any moment a bomb could blast anywhere, changing lives of thousands of people in less than one second. Today, hundred thousands of mothers in many of those countries would feel the same feelings that my mother had felt when my father went for paper marking during the time of terror in Sri Lanka, in which, we as little children did not feel it at that time but when we grew up we realised that what our parents had gone through more than a period of three decades. When you go out of home, you would not know whether you would return or not, whether you would be able to see the little waiting eyes of your children and hug them with warmth. Probably, you might return home in a casket along with body parts of many other unknown people and still the children do not know why their mother is crying holding a closed casket, and they play with their toys on the soft woollen carpet on which the strange box has been placed. The day they realise that 'Papa had gone', it's too late; they had already lived several years without paternal love and protection. Life is not the same as it used to be.

An Africa which is geographically one single continent but demographically and politically two continents, that might be what my father was trying to tell to his 11-year-old boy. The 'yellow zone' is different from the 'green zone'. But today, the 'yellow zone' has already become 'orange' with flames of extremism, and expanding to the 'green zone' across Sahara, burning down the life of lives remained protected from the sand dune for Millenia.

Chapter 10

WAIL OF EAGLE-OWL

 TODAY, AS A RESULT of significant advancements in humanitarian response in many dimensions and spheres, the victims of natural and manmade disasters are not seen as victims but rather dignified human beings with equal rights, just like others. But two decades ago, sympathy-driven stand-alone assistance and aid were given by diverse actors based on various biases such as individual preferences, political affiliations, ethnicity, race, religion, and so on, duplicating the aid or interventions while the most vulnerable and severly affected population is not reached. Parallel to the ad-hoc aid and assistance, the media used to be involved in selling human suffering for the rest of the world, publishing traumatising illustrations and video clips along with manipulated, and always exaggerated news heading which are always all the time were bias. As a result, the crisis in ex-Yugoslavia and Rwanda genocide and famines in the Horn of Africa were shown to other parts of the world as if the end of the world was in the following hour. As a result of cyclically telecasted videos about Rwandan genocide and the literature published in many French news channels and papers, my humanitarian imparatives were triggered and showed me Africa which is 'in-need' when I was a teenager but I did not expect that those atrocities telecasted on television would penetrate the frontiers of Rwanda and expanded to the whole region as an unprecedented regional conflict that highlighted the fatal consequences of imposed borders of colonial powers that split the tribes and ethnicities and locked them divided into new states called postcolonial national states. They drew lines across the natural distribution of the tribes, dividing into subgroups, separating their relatives brutally, broke down the chiefdoms and kingdoms, deprived their right to live with their indigenous governing system, and finally pushed the newly formed national states into a never-ending series of conflicts which usurped the opportunity to development. Making Africa look like the battlefield of children where all old AKs and RPG from all around the world finally reach as their finally destination to blow out houses of innocent villagers, kill millions of civilians, and to pump strength and confident for rebels as well as trained government forces to rape women and loot property of innocent people.

It was couple of years before the Rwandan genocide that my father was talking about the dynamics of power struggle in postcolonial Congo. He used to repeat some parts of the famous independence speech of Patrice Lumumba delivered at Palais de la Nation in Leopold-Ville, today Kinshasa, on 30 June 1960. Lumumba was one of his favourite personalities in African politics, not because he was one of the icons of the rise of communism in Africa but because of his immense audience and directness in his words and action unlike many other political leaders in the content of Africa. Though I do not remember all, most of the stories of my father about Africa was about Congo, which was Zaire, Congo Leopold-Ville those days and DRC today. Probably, he did not know about the existence of the Republic of Congo, known as Congo Brazzaville as his world was always associated with the old literature that he had read when he was young and the world had already moved a long distance since that time when he was narrating those stories to me. In reality, the flow of knowledge was slower than today just like any other aspect of life of those days compared to the modern days. However, as time started running faster than the old time, with invasion of information technology into the human life in form of modern technology which turned to be a basic necessity in our lives, I was able to fill the gaps in his old time stories, catching up the changes that time had already done to the places and people who were in his stories. But my dreams of seeing the heart of the dark continent, that stretches across three time lines from East to West, was kind of blurred like in many other dreams I had that needed financial support and I did not want to ask for support and determined to work on applying for employment opportunities in Africa with different organisations as an entry-point to the continent which worked after decades.

The day found myself in North-Kivu and Democratic Republic of Congo, at the peak of the conflict in Eastern provinces DRC, M23, had already taken Goma under their total control, I found myself in the middle of dozens of militia groups and it was not the Zaire that I had heard about from free-time stories.

It was not a surprise for me to see armed men and children in every single place I visited as I had heard about the constant arm struggles that are common in the zone but instead of the resourcefulness and the proud Congolese people, I witnessed a life which was torn into pieces and covered with misery and disparity. Literary the resources that are sufficient to make the immense territory a pure heaven have turned it to a hell on earth making it a paradise for several killer rebel groups who kill innocent civilians, rape women and sometimes men, loot almost everything of poor populations who are forced to choose fleeing or death, and recruit children into their forces. The armed men and children seemed still at the stage of rejoicing their victory over 'FAC' Force Armée de Congo and roaming in old double cabs as if they were the rulers of the universe, intoxicated with victory, paralysing the life of everyone for another time. It was common to see abandoned mud houses with broken doors and windows, abandoned village farms, and immense refugee and IDP camps in many places with new and old tents with highly visible emblems of different nongovernmental organizations and UN agencies. Roads were busy with old wrecked double cabs and jeeps of Force Armée du Congo, armed patrol vehicles of United Nations peace keepers, and the white jeeps equipped with long antennas of radio sets and with flags with emblems to prevent being attacked, and the people who carry their last left belonging moving from their villages to the IDP camps which were already overpopulated has not been properly set as the dynamics of the battle pushes the people further away from the places where they are currently. Most of these IDPs have been moving for days from the rebel hit areas with diverse difficulties, baring various losses including the lives of loved ones, and being traumatised over and over again not only in the way to IDP camps, but also from time to time, constantly for the last fifteen years.

I was received by one of my friends who worked with an aid agency operating in Goma and he accommodated me in his place in his official residence in Goma which was a most compliance accommodation as per the security standards of the organisation, he worked for. Just like in Liberia, Sierra-Leone, and Ivory Coast where conflicts had significantly changed the public life, the accommodation looks like a prison to me. With high walls with barbered metal wires on the top, high iron gates with no grills, windows with metal bars, flashlights that are used all throughout the night enhance the visibility during night, metal doors that were exactly like the ones of a prison, and a generator that keeps beating the ears all night, the house made me feel like I was in a military camp in the front line. By eight in the evening I realised that it was not just the hypervigilance of the organisation that imposed such strict and rigid security in the accommodation when I started hearing exchange of fire very close to the accommodation. We were in the front line in reality which was not just a bad dream and my first night after a long travel remained a sleepless one, listening to the gunshots, trying to identify from where they came from, whether they were moving in or moving out. It was a night full of distortions and fearful thoughts. I had only three things that I did not want to give away, my had drive where I had copy of my book which I was writing my passport where I had a lot of valid visas and my life. I had my laptop, camera, and around $7,000 in cash for my stay in DRC and expenses for next destinations which I could easily give up.

When we met for breakfast by seven in the morning, my friend smiled at me in a quite ambiguous way and asked me, 'Hope you slept sound?'

I knew very well how he put the words together which always sound ironic.

'Are you kidding me? Do you think gunshots are like classical music?'
He laughed loud at me.

'I was the same when I first came here,' he told with a kind of seriousness.

'But now I know that is the reality of the place and the situation we live in. I gradually learnt to live with this,' he added.

'You mean you disregard the sound of shooting and sleep sound?' I asked with amazement.

'I do' I could not but laugh

'You have become that much indifferent to all these?'

He finished the cup of tea in few gulps and said, 'This is normal to this area, everyone sleeps well till they come and knock on your door one day.'

He had been working in Goma for over eleven years, and according to his role in the organisation, he had to cover most of the villages under the control of different militia groups; therefore, he had already developed some good relations with the rebel leaders of all sorts and he was one of the few among foreigners who could meet those so-called warlords at any time with a short notice. My next adventure was about to begin in the middle of nowhere in the eastern part of DRC, interviewing a so-called warlord but before that there were preconditions imposed by my friend as it was his connections which will be used to give me an opportunity. But this time, unlike any other times, he wanted to see my questions and type of information I needed from them. My intention was to extract the maximum whatever possible about anything of their lives, mission including few direct questions about rebels being accused for raping the civilians including children and men, and recruitment of children as rebels.

'Well. . .' my friend paused.

'You can ask those but what you would disclose about your identity?' He was concerned.

'I would tell them that I'm a freelance writer and would like to write about the rebel life in eastern DRC. Hope they will be satisfied with it,' I really did not have a well-structured answers for the probable questions that they might ask. It was my friend who had been interacting with rebels for last eleven years who gave me some practical hints about what to say and what not to say in such a way that not even a one milligram of a suspicion arises.

Next day early morning, once the curfew was over, we packed some food and water in a field type land-cruiser and started the journey along the gravel road passing abundant villages that had become unlivable due to constant fighting. My friend informed me that it would take at least two hours to go to the unspecified location where the meeting was scheduled. This is a very volatile region where anything can happen to anyone at any moment. This time, I was going to push myself in to a live conflict area where a proud soldier who will have to wait five more years to get his first pubic hair could determine whether I would return alive or dead. An unintended mortar can fall on us or else an intended RPG can burn us till the bones. Also, we could be targeted by any one of the fighting parties as a mistake and no one would bother to take responsibility or else as dead we would be held responsible as we were the ones who decided to cross the last UN checkpoint and proceed into the rebel-controlled area taking a risk. As a person who had travelled enough in Africa, from North to South and East to West, I had not let my fears to override my confidence except a few times but this trip had some unexplainable thrilling sensation mixed with an intense fear not because they carry guns and they were rebels, but merely because they were children whose judgement is impaired by the pride of having an semi-automatic assault rifle in their hands which were still growing. The roads, as many parts of eastern, western, and central part of Africa, was gravel and full of holes and only a 4×4 could pass many of the areas as a result of Mobutu's strategy of maintaining the road network weak and hard to pass and to keep main townships disconnected from each other to prevent probable uprisings against his rule. Mostly, domestic jets are used to travel from one place to another which is a significant risk at this time in DRC as at anytime flights can be shot down by any of the rebel groups or by the Force Armée Congolaise. It is usual to see chicken on the road wherever human habitat exists in this part of Africa, but they were gone long time ago, just partially broken mud houses and broken fences hold witness of human existence few months ago. And the children holding the rebel icon 'AK 47s were here and there in so-called rebel checkpoints that block the gravel road with a log, where bribes are taken from every vehicle that passes through, became more common than chicken on the road.

'These ones do not understand our language; they use weapons to talk. Just small children who do not think and intoxicated with the power of gun can do anything to anyone. Let's follow what they ask us to do. It's their guns which speak, not them.' It was the Congolese driver who was telling. However as we had informed the leadership of rebels about our arrival, they had already informed every single check point of them about our trip in to their area which was visible from the first checkpoint where we entered their territory. When we reached the entry checkpoint to M23 controlled area, one rebel got into our jeep who was designated to guide us to the place where I was supposed to meet, General Sultani-Makénga, who is the military chief of M23, that allowed us to pass even without asking where and for what we were going inside the rebel-controlled areas. That is, the rebel law in eastern DRC everyone finds their survival grace to an old AK or a Light Machine Gun with a belt of ammunitions. After one and half hours driving along the gravel road infested with armed rebels which were off limits for UN staff who were working in DRC, even-though many NGOs working inside, we turned to a partway where we had to drive with extra care as it was known as a very sensitive area of militia groups as their leaders reside. We were stopped at a check point again, this time It was not just children, there were some matured men carrying AKs were there. One armed man showed us an area to park the jeep. The rebel who was with us said that we had arrived to the venue where we would meet the so-called General. They checked the jeep carefully, and then we were checked in person and then were allowed to proceed.

'No mobiles?' One man in uniform kept on telling a list of prohibited items beyond the check point. We had a radio in the Jeep and old mobile phones which we left in the car and there was only one ball-point pen and a note book in my possession despite my cloths. I heard they were talking on the radio getting permission to let us in even-though we had already informed the chief on our visit.

'We do not have any above' my friend told the man.

Then one boy checked whether we have anything hidden and then allowed us to go in with two other rebels who walked into the compound of partially broken brick house. Three armed men carrying AKs came out, checked us again without exchanged of a single word, and escorted us to the commander. He was a slender, relatively young guy, lying in tranquillity in his portable recliner chair while his camouflage barrette was resting tight on his head and the jacket is left open. He reminded me of a kind of a young boy who was completely lost whose purpose of life, a kind of a character living in a fantasy far away from the real world. However, he was very pleased to receive us and show his boys that we were also under his rule even for a moment which reminded me one of my colleagues told one day 'Africans love power'. I did not really look at them with a perceptual set which is biased but sometimes it was proven that my friend was right to some extent even though everyone has more or less the hunger for power in manifest layer or latent layer of the character.

Two men behind us and two men behind the commander, holding AKs guarding him.

'This gentleman I had not seen before here.'

His words proved that my friend was not a new person here, and he might have brought a few other people to meet the commander.

'This is my first time here' I smiled gently and replied.

Clearing his throat, the commander got up and sat at the large single recliner next to me, rocked it a few times, and looked at me again. All these behaviours are roles that many people play when they feel empty inside, just to show others that they have control and power over others.

'You are a journalist?'

He asked me with a voice in disguise.

'No no he is a freelance writer,' My friend replied as if to take the commander to the proper channel.

'I was giving interviews for Journalists and they ask the same thing over and over again'

He added.

'You are going to write about me?'

His intonation started ascending and his expressions became serious.

I pulled out few chapters I had written about Africa, and gave him.

'You can read this if you want, I had not written anything beyond what I have heard from people and mentioned nothing beyond what they expressed consent to.'

He went through the papers as if an old gambler going through a notice in a betting centre, nodding his head as if he understands every single detail of what I had written on it.

'Well,' he said which I perceived as a go-head signal.

I was more than happy that I was given a chance to ask some questions at least irrespective of what I would get as responses. I intentionally avoided asking certain questions that were extremely sensitive in terms of the situations and position where they were and in the meantime I tried my best not to pose any question that would create any suspicion or provocation as he was feeling at the top of the world because of the victory over the other militias and being able to take control over Goma in total and being able to succeed over the existed leadership of M23. Lost in the glory of the victory and power he enjoyed, his impulse, if triggered by any slight mistake, could have taken our lives in the middle of nowhere, unknown to the rest of the world. As I was given a very short time which shattered my high ambitions I had before I met him, I decided to ask only most important questions and get the detailed answers from him.

'What are the key demands of you that was not met or addressed for you to take this vigorous military action that brought you so far till conquest of provincial capital of North East province, North-Kivu, Goma?'

General Sultani-Makénga reminded me some traits of Laurent Nkunda, former warlord in North Kivu, ex-leader of CNDP, ex-general of Armée Congolaise. Unlike Nkunda who had at least some acceptable level of education, diplomacy and ability to make a point to push across systematically, Sultani was in a constant struggle to make him look like a matured orator, an intellectual, and at the same time, a visionary rebellion leader.

'As per the last peace accord in 2009, we were integrated to the Armed Forces of the Democratic Republic of Congo, but we do have a lot of grievances.'

His attempts of formulating a rich response in diplomatically and politically correct diction were very well manifested in each and every attempt of answering.

'We are deprived from promotions and we have not been given promised increments, and the level corruption of Kabila's government is very high, we are a rich nation but most of people are poor.'

He was making a point, in truth, since the liberation in 60s, despite short period of Lumumba, every single name that follows in the line of rulers from Mobutu till Laurent Desire Kabila came to power with the power of bullet, not the ballet. They saw themselves as emperors and gods and craved for being in power for eternity, building palace-like mansions not only for them but also for their family members, creating a massive gap between the ordinary and governing class in terms of wealth. When the governing class reach the zenith, the majority of Congolese were pushed below the line of poverty, transforming Congolese society from the first potential state of development in Sub-Saharan Africa into one of the poorest nations on earth where tension, frustration, distrust, injustice, and helplessness raised as key ingredients, while with secondary and peripheral parties who had interests in enormous deposits of natural resources easily pulled the country into a never-ending conflict in which dynamics were completely unpredictable and incomprehensible. For nearly a decade, since 1994, when Great Lakes region became fragile in terms of security and safety, after the genocide of Rwanda, diverse militia supported by neighbouring countries, specially Rwanda and Uganda, even though the leaders of respective countries always deny their hands behind it, have been engaging in a continuous war in taking control over the resources in the eastern provinces of Congo. Some would say that they were fighting to protect the Tutsi population in DRC and others believe that their presence is to protect the Hutus when those who are lead by Babma in the northern part of Congo where he has the complete control says his fight is for a better tomorrow for DRC. And Ernest Wamba Dia Wamba who is the leader of RDC and later RDC-Kisangani, based in Bunia, says that his struggle is for good governance and a transparent democracy in Congo whereby the country would reach its optimum development. And every-single rebel leader that emerged in Congo strongly share the notion that Kabila government is corrupt and they can ensure a better Congo for Congolese. And their bloodshed is for a better future for Congo which I heard many times via media interviews with the rebel leaders starting from Laurent Nkunda, Ernest Wamba dia Wamba and today while interviewing so-called warlord of M23 Sultani Makenga.

'I saw a lot of children with guns in your forces, would you think that is right?' I directly sautéed to my first preplanned question.

'Yes, all of our members are volunteers; we do not force them to come in. You know, people in Congo are fed up with the Kabila government.

They want a better life. From the child to old man, they are ready to fight for it.'

His justification, even though he thought right, did not convince me at all. Each rebel group in DRC, with no exception to M23, just like all rebel groups in many parts of Africa, use children as their main front-line force. Children, being easier to mobilise, especially when they are in extremely helpless situations, are often used in rebel movements as child soldiers. During the civil conflict in Liberia, the ex-president of Liberia, famous West African warlord who is convicted for war crimes in Sierra Leone, used a slogan, 'You kill my mama, you kill my papa, I vote for you.' The children, once child soldiers, were singing loud on the roads, as an electoral slogan which sounded not real but was real. In most cases, in DRC, children who were abducted will never see their parents, or volunteers who join the forces as their last sanctuary of survival. These children probably would not see their loved ones and never go back to school. Also, a significant number of them sacrifice their lives in the battlefield as a result of going to the front line without proper skills required for survival in a warfront, as mere basic knowledge in manning a very fundamental assault rifle does not make a child a solider but a victim of war. As per Sultani Makenga, children fighting for him were volunteers, but for me, they were children whose ability to take a right decision in complex situations especially when they are at vulnerable end of the story, completely impaired. And sometimes, inspiration for volunteering is based on a false assurance or else just the sight of other children who are often seen as powerful when looking at them from a position where helplessness reins each and every corner of their lives. Sometimes the type of volunteerism that Sultani Makenga was referring to is granted out of fear of death, at gun point, otherwise there is no way that a human being would volunteer for fighting with someone who killed his parents, raped his sisters, and tortured the devil out of him.

'Do you think that they are capable soldiers who can defend your territory against a systematically trained armed force?'

I did not refer to the Force Armée Du Congo, in which the integrity is a major concern as there is a lot of ex-rebels from different groups integrated without being properly intervened before integration. On top of that, the soldiers are not properly trained, not paid enough or not paid at all, most of them do not even have proper uniforms or basic necessities such as boots, head gears, and so on, and enough food in most of the cases. Yet again, though the authorities deny screaming at the top of their voice, the fact that children are fighting for FAC, Force Armée Du Congo, there is a lot of children that I had witnessed fighting for Force Armée Du Congo in two forms, first as recruits at the war front, mostly by force and children who are rebels for the allies of Force Armée Du Congo. Hence as an armed force, Force Armée Du Congo, in local terms force de Kabila, engage in almost all the activities that rebels are engaged in, killing civilians, raping, looting, and using children in the warfront, that no one expects from a national army of a country. When competence is nonexisting, discipline is not at the desired standard and integrity of an army is endangered, it is obvious that they always end up at the losing end of a war which is also one of the main factors behind this never-ending series of wars in DR Congo. My question was specifically focused on the level of confidence and alacrity of Sultani as the head of military wing of M23 to face the intervention brigade to eastern DR Congo which is composed of mostly South African and Tanzanian forces with a stronger mandate to confront armed groups.

'We are here for last few months, and this is our land and we know the terrain, Kabila's forces cannot defeat us, not even UN, in case they attack us we will retreat.'

He was overconfident, which manifested his immaturity as he sounded overwhelmed with unreal emotions evoked just because of the victory of overtaking Goma, even though not completely. And even though the peace talks were still on going in Kampala, between Kabila and political leadership of M23 Jean-Marie Runiga, Sultani Makenga is not only determined to go to Kinshasa but also his words sounded like a plan. But for a rebel group to reach Kinshasa to far west from the other end of an immense country like DRC, where there is a lot of geographical and demographical challenges, would not be easy.

'We will move to Kinshasa next.'

He was kind of hypothetical and completelyblind with the occupation of Goma.

'A lot of people are forced to flee, in many cases they are displaced from the places where they had been already living as internally displaced

populations, would you think that people of Congo want this anymore?'
I asked to see whether he would be grounded.

'They want a better Congo. This is a war, displacement is a normal thing.'

The life in Great Lakes area has been shaped by the constant conflicts for over fifteen years. Displacements from the places where one had been already resettled after a displacement had become cyclic in North and South Kivu but all that has been caused by the conflicts which are caused by the armed groups whose interests are not centred in the population of the host country or host region and their leadership sounded contradictory to how they operate. It was not only Sultani but also other famous rebel leaders in the region such as Laurent Nkunda, Ernest Wamba Dia Wamba, most of the 'Mai Mai' militia groups in the region did and do the same. Those so-called war lords manifest zero sensitivity to the population in the region and rather trying to tighten the grip on resources and the power.

When someone is intoxicated with the glory of a victory, the words slip though the gates of lips without being filtered through the rationalism. I thought that it was the ideal time for my ultimate question comprising all what I was dreaming to ask from a leader among any one of the rebel groups operating in eastern Democratic Republic of Congo.

'Hundred thousands of women have been victims of sexual violence in these areas since last one and half decades, are you aware that your soldiers are also following the path of other rebel groups who were here before?'

I threw my verbal bomb at him. He seemed survived from the surface but his denial of such cases reported hinted that he was hit inside but in reality he does not care as long as his boys can defend the captured territory.

'I'm not informed about such cases,' he replied with a voice apparently sounding like a fat lie as since the day M23 started their offensive in 2012, there had been a number of rape cases reported to aid centres in Goma. There is no doubt that Makenga is aware of what his boys are doing out in the villages.

'There are other armed people in this area,' he added, probably as a predefence.

'They support you? right?' I wanted to make a point that the allies are also under his command.

'Yes they do, that's why they are here' Sultani Makenga, as a rebel militia leader had succeeded to some extent but his tactlessness in discussion highlighted his immaturity as a potential ruler.

As many other rebel leaders and some politicians in the Africa who have come to power as a result of military coups or conflicts, Makenga also had selected his rank by himself. He was a colonel in Force Armée Du Congo, after being reintegrated in to national army, but now, commanding M23, he had chosen to be a general by himself. Those stars and rank, just like what Idi-Amin did, calling himself as a full general, are not acquired as a result either of skills, special services or experience as it happens in a systematic military environment. As a result they behave like ruthless killing machines, not only harming the individuals, families and communities, but also so many generations to come.

As Makenga had to leave, leaving some of my questions left within me, I was lead by the same guy who brought me into his place, to the jeep where my friend and driver were waiting for me. I was feeling contented as I was able to ask some among the long awaited questions that I was longing to ask either from Laurent Nkunda, Ernest Wamba Dia Wamba, or else anyone who was a rebel leader in Eastern DRC but time and the circumstance allowed me to meet Makenga, as other were not accessible and some of them were arrested before 2013.

'You looked drained,' my friend told with an ironic tone, seeing me coming to the jeep like a zombie. I did not want to respond and instead I smiled as I knew well he was aware of how I was feeling as he had been working with different rebel groups that emerged here in Kivu like mushrooms popping up in bushy mountains in early summer. Talking to a person who demonstrates at least a minimum understanding towards what you say or ask does not suck your energy in vain but those who strictly believe that they are right even when their consciousness is full of fears and uncertainties create impenetrable defence wall in any discussion, even prior to you ask something, which obviously drains energy. When leaders do not listen to the public and make attempts to understand their grievances before they are translated into actions of violence, conflicts are inevitable. As a result, just like a cycle that never ends, suffering remains within the radius of the common population and never penetrates the ruling class, irrespective of their form, military or democratically elected. At the end of the day, innocent population sacrifice their whole life on behalf of someone's political or economic motives, but their strategies for reaching their goals have transformed society in the eastern provinces of Congo into a completely disconnected and dependent displaced society from a self-sufficient economy based on farming while social fabrics have been torn apart and shattered into pieces whereby the values and norms existed had vamoosed into empty air in sighs of IDPs, leaving only a self-centred survivors attitude. However, being impartial and neutral, listening to the stories of the affected IDPs who were still afraid to open their mouth, and warlords who talk pompously, behind the triggers of AKs of child soldiers and under old and torn blankets of IDP's who are limited to a few square meters of shelter survive in chilling nights in Goma, millions of issues remain unheard, unmet, and suppressed that should not only be attained by the local authorities, but also by regional, zonal, and international actors who are involved in political humanitarianism. Rather than remain stuck in the conventional thinking box, in which exploitation of resources, involvement of Rwanda, Uganda, in the conflict, and victims of sexual violence as a weapon of war, where every advocacy group and the humanitarian actor is stuck in, no one seems interested in plunging deep into the root cause of the conflict and come up with questions such as 'why' to explore deep into the conflict and discover the interest, demographical traits, geographical features involved and come up with a sustaining solution for this series of conflicts that had literally transformed a heaven with resources into a hell of never-ending suffering. It is apparent that the modern world still believes that the frontiers imposed by them during the time of scramble to Africa should remain the same irrespective of extreme suffering of Africans who are forced to live in territories given by their masters. While the so-called frontiers marked by colonial masters remain as borders of national states in Africa, Africans blame the white world for supporting the conflicting parties and destabilising Africa. However, as national states, the public in respective states have the ultimate solution for making a change in their territory, including re-marking the territories, instead of putting the blame to each other, allowing millions of human lives to succumb, hundreds of thousands of women and children to be raped and mutilated, and millions of people to be displaced over and over again, paving the path to diverse militia to gain power in different areas of one country, threatening its sovereignty.

When the dynamics of the conflicts of eastern Democratic Republic of Congo are considered, it is vivid that the formation of new groups out of old groups, coalitions of different rebel groups for specific target, or on short-term, being integrated into national forces or separation from national forces, or else fight one's own little war for a little piece of resourceful land as a Mai Mai group that operates at its utter independence. However, the impact of constant fights have escalated into a humanitarian crisis where a solution is not visible at the horizon but there are always possibilities of breaking out of fights, creating new trends in the region.

Since the beginning of the conflicts of Kivu, many militia used to target innocent civilians as a strategy of forcing them to flee from the areas occupied by the rebel groups. The Democratic Forces for the Liberation of Rwanda, one of the most powerful rebel groups operating in eastern Congo, is believed to be supported by Rwanda and the west, formed by the perpetrators of the 1994 Rwandan genocide. While the original soldiers were Rwandan exiles, most of the current FDLR soldiers have been recruited from refugee camps in eastern Congo. The National Congress for the Defense of the People was born as a resistance of constant threat from Hutu-led FDLR. Founded in December 2006 by Laurent Nkunda, the CNDP reportedly sought to protect the Tutsi minority in eastern Congo against discrimination and maltreatment, particularly at the hands of the FDLR. Prior to the founding of CNDP, Laurent Nkunda was a major of another rebel group, the Rally for Congolese Democracy, or RCD, which was a major player in the Second Congo War from 1998 to 2003. Until it became a political party in March 2009 and was renamed the ex-CNDP, the CNDP was one of the most destructive groups in eastern Congo, committing heinous human rights violations. In 2008, the CNDP participated in a full-scale war against the Congolese national army and international peacekeepers. An unbelievable feature in Kivu conflict is the Mai Mai groups, which are a loosely grouped collection of Congolese militia operating in eastern Congo. There are at present six main groups operating in the Kivus: the Mai-Mai-Yakutumba, Raia-Mutombogi,

Mai-Mai-Nyakiliba, Mai-Mai-Fujo, Mai-Mai Kirikicho, and Resistance Nationale Congolaise. Mai Mai groups are often formed by combatants who refuse to participate in Force Armée Du Democratic République du Congo reintegration processes and ascribe to autochthonous beliefs, meaning they believe the land should belong to its original inhabitants. Mai Mai groups feel threatened by Rwandophone communities Hutu and Tutsi which they see as foreigners trying to take over their land and power. They are not unified under any political or racial affiliation, but they target anything that crosses their way irrespective of colour, creed, religion, or any other affiliation. Sometimes Mai Mai militia groups make coalitions with main rebel groups or with Force Armée De République Democratic Du Congo depending on the circumstance. Amidst of such a complex and loose system, there are many other groups of rebels that emerged from time to time, such as the emergence of several armed groups in Ituri conflict between Hema and Lendu. And finally, M23, as a result of inability of Kabila's government to uphold its side of the 2009 peace agreement dated March 23, 2009, the date of the peace treaty that integrated the National Congress for the Defense of the People, or CNDP, into the national army, which started terrifying the population in Goma, making history repeat over and over again. And tomorrow, probably another team will appear from the dense forests behind the mountain that shadow Lake Kivu. However, as a result, the innocent population will suffer irrespective of their ethnicity or language.

We returned to the accommodation after the interview with Sultani Makenga and I was happy to be alive. Even though there was a strong belief that they would not harm me as I was accompanied by my friend who was very close to every single fighting thing in the zone as a humanitarian, but looking at the type of things that they were doing in the villages, it was hard to believe that they respect any living thing on earth, not even themselves. The evening turned to be different that the previous one; heavy artillery had already joined the gunshots I used to hear for last two days. It was a sign that something was about to change, was changing, or had already changed. After a tiresome trip and staying constantly in a stage of uncertainty during the interview, I did not expect a sleepless night with full of adrenaline in my bloodstream.

Next day, early morning, there was a new sun over the mountains, and instead of little children who were carrying guns at temporary checkpoints, the members of Force Armée De République Democratique du Congo were rejoicing at the victory of pushing M23 from their initial positions in Goma, but still all the strategic areas in Goma were under the control of M23. When the things started changing, with the support of the intervention force of the UN, I got in to another land cruiser heading to Bukavu, regional capital of South Kivu, where the CNDP shattered the life of habitants into nano-pieces in such a way that their lives would never be the same again.

The Democratic Republic of the Congo, and the east of the country in particular, has been described as the 'Rape Capital of the World,' and the prevalence and intensity of all forms of sexual violence have been described as the worst in the world, especially by militia. Rape in the Democratic Republic of Congo has frequently been described as a 'weapon of war', and the United Nations officially declared rape a weapon of war in 2008. War rape makes a particularly effective weapon because it destroys not only its physical victims but entire communities as well. War, violence, and instability have ravaged the DRC for decades, and this has led to a culture of violence in war and civilian life that often takes its form in a sexual nature.

Eleven years after the Democratic Republic of the Congo gained independence in 1960, President Mobutu renamed the country Zaire in 1971 and ruled the nation under an autocratic and corrupt regime. Under Mobutu's regime, sexual abuse was used as a method of torture. Mobutu ruled until 1995, when after the 1994 Rwandan Genocide, many active participants of the genocide fled across Rwanda's western border into the DRC in hopes of escaping censure. Hutu extremist militias were reformed across the border, particularly in Kivu, the DRC's easternmost region, bringing crime and violence to the DRC. This influx of militants and fighting in Burundi catalysed the First Congo War and the end of Mobutu's regime. Spurred by the violence, the Alliance of Democratic Forces for the Liberation of Congo, AFDL, led by Laurent Kabila, launched a rebellion against Mobutu regime in 1995 in the eastern part of the country.

The epidemic of rape seems to have started in the mid-1990s. That coincides with the waves of Hutu militiamen who escaped into Congo's forests after exterminating 800,000 Tutsis and moderate Hutus during Rwanda's genocide thirteen years ago and developed in an unprecedented form spreading it into other communities. And today, hundreds of thousands of victims of sexual violence are in DRC, especially in the eastern provinces of the country, making DRC the most dangerous place on earth to be born to as a woman. Rape, as related to the conflicts, is the most prevalent form of sexual violence in the country. However, civilians are also the perpetrators of rape. Hence, in resumption, DRC is a country where rape had been used in many forms during different stages of its history, but today, more than 200,000 women live in silence as victims of sexual violence which ranges from rape caused by individuals, gang rapes, destroying or damaging genitals or other body parts after the rape, and suffering from various secondary consequences of rape, such as severe infections, fistulas, HIV, and other STIs.

When I reached Bukavu, it was almost 3.00 p.m., and Josephine, a pseudonym used for maintaining confidentiality, was waiting for us in the community centre where psychosocial support is provided for the victims of sexual violence in many villages of the eastern provinces of the Democratic Republic of Congo. She had two kids: one is born to a Tutsi father who was unknown by name but was well known by the act that he committed to her, and the elder one who was from her husband who was brutally killed by the armed men of CNDP years ago. That was all that I was informed about beforehand by the peer-supporter, Matilde, who was working at the community centre, providing emotional support and practical assistance for those who had been victims of sexual violence. For the first time in my life, I was about to work through an interpreter as I did not have a clue of local languages. And it was a strange feeling when your questions are interpreted through someone else and the answers you get too are coming back to you through the same channel. It was a feeling of mild suspicion mixed with having second thoughts about being confident on someone else's interpretation when you seek direct and detailed answers for complex and sensitive issues which are not often talked about.

However, the little French she knew helped both of us to build a passage of confidence through the buffer zone of language orientation which at least helped me to build a healthy rapport to continue with her story, even though she was aware of what I was going to ask. However, as she was still undergoing therapy, I had already agreed to conduct my interview in a supportive manner, giving her enough time and flexibility, even allowing her to refuse from being interviewed in case she feels uncomfortable or anxious. After a brief discussion between us, she mentioned that she did not want her to disclose her real name, but she was okay to describe every single event, inhumanity, torture she went through, as they believed that it was her moral obligation to disclose those to the rest of world that she believed was indifferent and passive to what was happening in her part of the world. She said that she wanted to make her story heard and see that her daughter who was still not born would not be a victim of torture and aggression. Even before she started her story, tears started coming out of her big, glass-ball-like eyes and ran down along her cheeks from both sides of her wide, flat nose centred in her small face which clearly showed her origin among the conflicting tribes, which is also the most proximate cause of her having her story as a victim of sexual violence which is about to unfold in front of me.

'I was at home with my child and husband, when rebels started attacking the villages. I was breastfeeding my child in the evening around 6.30 p.m. when six armed men broke into our little mud hut. My husband was down with malaria and he was lying down near me. They just appeared from nowhere, usually they come from the bush, as our house was bordering to bush and kind of isolated from the rest of the houses as we had a small area of land where we had cultivated crops which separated us from other houses from a considerable distance. That evening, as my husband was sick, his food was left in the pot which was on the clay oven, still hot. Two of them first appeared and then one took the pot out and they ate it. I was trembling with fear as I knew that they would not stop there. They had attacked our village many times, and most of the time, we hide in the bush to be protected. I did not even have time to react, I was frozen. I did not have voice to talk or to scream. Sudden presence of armed men made my child cry. She was my first child, born to my husband. One man among them came and grabbed the child and dashed her on the mud floor. She became silent, like a little mouse and before I got up one of them jumped over me and grabbed me like a mongoose that pounces on a snake. He did not give me a chance; I tried to resist, biting the hands of the man who grabbed me. Then another joined him. He kicked my head a few times and stepped on my right hand. While I was struggling, I heard my husband was screaming and trying to struggle with others. They were beating him brutally with the guns. They tore my cloths and raped me over and over again. Over and over again in front of my husband. Every time he tried to move or scream, they beat him with gun, on the head, on the back, and they kicked his male organ.'

She seemed not really chronological in telling her story and she was repeating 'They raped me over and over again' a few times, which is an evidence of the psychological impact of the event. I did not want to interrupt the flow of the story as what is said so far have told many things which were the key elements of the story as many of the stories I had heard from the victims of sexual violence in the eastern provinces of the Democratic Republic of Congo. After a while, she was trying to recall where she stopped, and then with the support of my interpreter, Josephine started her story from where she stopped.

'Last time I remember my husband was beaten on the head and he was bleeding and fell down just like a tree pulled down by a storm. When the last one got up, I tried to push myself towards my husband who was lying down. I did not know he had already gone. One man covered my mouth again and held my head between his knees so that I could not move while the other one tried to come to me again. One among them again raped me. I was feeling numb and unreal. They did not let me scream, even though I wanted so much. They always held my head just like stuck in snare. Later they tied my hands and mouth and took me to the bush, into their camp, where I was kept for two months.'

She fell in a deep silence. I noticed that the interpreter was not prepared for a situation of emotional fluctuations. I gave my bottle of water to Josephine. She looked drained and anxious. After a pensiveness of a couple of minutes, she turned her head towards us and started talking again.

'I later realised that there was a commander of a unit which was based in a camp deep in the bush. He was the first one who raped me first and he had wanted to take me to the camp with him. That was the reason why I was taken to the camp many miles deep in the forest. Then I was given food and I was with Gahiji, the one who raped me first, and he was using me for sex every single day even without considering my physical conditions. He forced me to have sex with him every single time when he returned from somewhere. However, I was given enough food as he had ordered his boys to treat me so. After some time, two other very young girls were taken into the camp and I was not treated the same by Gahiji. One night, he called his boys and threw me at them. They grabbed me just like a band of wild dogs and tore my cloths into pieces in seconds. I saw while being forced down on the ground, Gahiji was laughing loud while watching how his boys were raping me. They did it over and over again. Over and over again.'

She said 'over and over again' and broke into tears.

'You know, I was bearing all of those thinking my daughter was still alive somewhere, I thought that my neighbours might have found her and she might have been with them. Otherwise, I would not choose to bear such pains over and over again, I would have chosen to die, trying to run away. One time, I thought of grabbing a gun from one of those small boys who were guarding us and kill myself. But I believed that my daughter should have been living somewhere, most probably with the neighbours.'

My interpreter, having heard the story before, as she was proving her emotional support several times in the past while she was hospitalised, sat closer to Josephine and held her hand.

'One night, I heard gunshots very close to the camp, and everyone in the camp was kind of confused and they were anticipating something on which they were focusing on fully. And it was a full moon evening and I felt not that afraid of walking into the jungle. I was determined to find my path back home. I was waiting the whole night patiently. The men in the camp were not focusing on us anymore. They seemed having more serious issues than guarding us. It was just after the first bird started singing in early morning. I noticed two other girls were sleeping and no one was around me aside from two men who had already walked far towards where the gunshots we heard, but there was a visible distance from where they could reach me in no time or shoot me instantly.'

She plunged into a deep silence again. I offered her water, she did not refuse. While taking a gulp, she said with an awakened voice, 'I felt that was the only chance left in my hand, last chance to be rescued, last chance to escape from hell.'

'What you did? You ran?' I asked with surprise as being caught trying to escape from such savage rebels can result in death or further torture.

'I slowly walked into the bush.' She looked at me.

'Then?' My curiosity was not actually about how she escaped but about what happened next as she was not the only one who tried to escape from sex slavery, of different armed groups in eastern DRC. And most of those who tried to escape had encountered extremely inhumane treatments.

'I walked into the bush and could not remember where I was taken from. Therefore, I chose to walk against the direction where I heard the gunshots to prevent being caught back by the same group or another group. I was aware of how they would treat me if they found me escaping. I walked for hours, without water, nothing to eat. It was not because I could not find sources of water or else anything edible in the bush, but I was horrified by the feeling of being caught while escaping. After several hours, I was able to feel a little relaxed and found a small stream of water where I drank enough for the next few hours. I was feeling weak and hungry even though I was no longer thirsty. But still I was not in a mind to search for something to eat. I was wishing to see a village before the nightfall, which sooner became just an illusion. I had been going to the bushes and used to walk for long time, even with a lot of firewood on my head. But this time, I was feeling very weak and dizzy. I wanted to vomit a few times but just some boil and saliva came out. I did not have anything else to throw out. I did not know what really happened to me, I felt that I could not move anymore. Night had already fallen in the dense forest before the sky. I sat near a tree and I did not know what happened after that till I woke up hearing sounds breaking of branches and voices of men. It was already morning, and I pushed myself into the bush near the tree. I saw a few of them walking against the way I was going. Had they been in search of me all night? Or else they were returning after looting villagers? The gave me a direction, which confirmed that the direction I chose was not wrong. But my fear was that there would be many others who would be returning from where the others came from. I chose to hide in the bush for a while as I anticipated that there would be more of them coming from the same direction. After several hours of hiding, I started walking. With every single step, I felt my legs were becoming heavier and I was becoming weaker, I was unable to complete my journey. I had fainted and fallen down. After almost a day, some women who came to the bush from the neighbouring village had found me. Later on, people in the village had taken me to the village, dressed me with clothes, and referred me to the counselling centre of the village, that's where I met your interpreter. She was my first counsellor.'

Matilde looked at her with a partial smile, yet honest and empathetic. 'She was just like a skeleton when I first saw her. She was traumatised. She did not have tears to cry and she did not know she was pregnant, pregnant with a child from a Tutsi father, Gahiji, who was the commander of the camp,' Matilde said.

'Then we referred her to hospital for medical attention; she had multiple mild infections but her overall physical health improved faster than anticipated so that she was able to become a mother in the following months, but we had to refer her for a professional mental health practitioner for doing interventions for the impact of trauma she had gone though. She was searching for her daughter who she believed was alive, but was dead on the very first day she was raped. Her husband and their daughter were brutally killed before she was taken to the camp. When she got to know about the deaths, even though she had accepted the death of husband, she did not accept the death of the child. She was in constant denial about the fact that the child had already passed, killed by the rebels. Her condition in terms of mental health started deteriorating during the last few months of her pregnancy and she was treated in-house in the hospital. I still remember the day this adorable child was born.'

Matilde gently pulled the little boy who is around six years towards her. It looked like that she was not a stranger to him.

'Josephine did not want to look at him for some time, she refused to feed her the first day, she was asking for her daughter constantly. After a lot of effort, she started accepting the child. For the first year, Josephine was with my sister who lived in Bukavu and then moved to Goma where she lived before she came here. She was referred to a counselling centre there and we sometimes followed up on her whenever we went there. When I saw her in Goma before she was referred here again, she was in her farm, working hard with her little son who had grown almost two years. Then we were disconnected as war breakout in Goma again. I did not hear from Josephine till I saw her in Panzi hospital in 2010. I identified her at first sight even though her face was fully covered with cotton bandages and the little son was with her who ran to me when he saw me. Today, Josephine is not the same person whom I met in Goma. Her life has drastically changed, with new challenges over the old ones, piling up one upon another as many of the victims of sexual violence in this part of world.' Matilde paused with a long sigh.

Josephine was listening to what Matilde was telling me in French, but she did not understand in depth. However, we briefed her about what we discussed as we did not have anything to hide from her, and of course I did not want to drain her psychic energy asking her a lot of question on ultrasensitive ones as Matilde already knew her history. By the end of our discussion, Josephine was showing interest in telling the rest of her story, and I rather encouraged her than discourage her attempt.

'I went to Goma, my village was not existent when I went there. I learnt that the village was attacked by the rebels many times and people were forced to flee or die. Many women were raped and men were killed. They had been looted to nothing. My little daughter had been buried in the village with her father and some other villagers who had been killed that day. I went here and there and finally went to my sister whose husband was brutally killed by rebels a couple of years ago. But she did not want to take my boy into her house. She said he would be a curse to her house, who will bring nothing but bad. I broke into tears. I knew that no one in a Hutu village wanted a Hutu woman that comes with a child born to a Tutsi rebel who is roaming in the villages killing Hutus, raping women, and looting properties. My sister said that she could do only one help, to give some money and food, and after that, she asked me to leave the house in the darkness not to be noticed by anyone in the village. She said no one in the village wanted to see a Hutu woman with a child born to a Tutsi. She pleaded me not to come back as that would endanger her life. I left her house with tears. I looked at my little boy who was growing like a little plant. We left the village in the night and walked as much as we could, along the roads without any direction. That night I felt like killing my child and killing myself. We reached Goma again and then I found myself in an IDP camp with my child. I was given a little shelter where I used to do everything. Cooking, sleeping, praying, etc, etc. When it rained, whole area got flooded and this boy fell sick many times there. But at least we received some dry food rations. Therefore, I decided to stay there as I did not have anywhere else to go. One day, I thought of my aunt who lived in a small village towards north of Goma. She had a good house, her husband was dead a long ago, and she did not have anyone like children. On top of everything, she was the only one who used to help me when I was young. I thought to go to her, leaving the camp. I had a little hope that she was alive and she would accept me and my boy.'

'You left the camp and went to your aunt?'

'Yes,' she replied

'I went to her, she was rather surprised than happy to see me after a long time. I explained her every single thing that happened to me, except about the father of the boy. She knew I was married and I was pregnant. I pretended that the boy was the child of me and my late husband. However, I managed to work with her in her little garden where we had cultivated crops with some other ladies in the village. However, aunt was happy that someone was there with her. She loved my little boy and I was satisfied that he at least got a grandmother who was telling him stories and keeping him happy. Every day I used to go to the bush to collect firewood with a couple of other ladies and we used to work in the garden on crops for the rest of the day. Life just begun to be routine and normal, I had only hope which was flourishing, it was this little boy who was growing with his smile wide till his ears. It was a usual morning; we left for collecting firewood as usual. I did not know that something bad was in store the following few hours.'

As I did not understand Swahili, I was observing the facial expressions of Josephine and gestures and movements of Matilde whenever there was a moment of silence, or kind of a hurdle for Josephine to move on with the story. She was silent and her head was in her hands, and suddenly she started sobbing. I was anticipating another dark corner of her life story, things that I never wanted to hear or see human beings go through in their lives but which remain as utter realities on the same earth where we live.

'We had already finished collecting firewood and were returning from the bush. I had a very heavy load of firewood so did the rest of us. We were almost a half away back in the bush when four of them appeared before us. When I saw them my legs became suddenly paralysed. I started feeling all what I had gone through since the time they appeared in our hut and till the day I fled from them. They grabbed one young girl who was with us and pulled her cloths and tore them into pieces and I tried to scream pleading them not to harm the girl. Then they turned towards me and beat me on the face and pushed me on the ground. They raped me over and over again. And one of them pushed a piece of wood into myself and another peed on me. I knew only that. Then I found myself in the village. Someone had put some medicine on my wounds, I did not know who, but it was very painful. After a few days, severe pain started and I started smelling foul. My belly became big and shiny. One day, I felt terribly bad and puss started coming out of me. I was shivering with fever; chills were so strong that I thought it was the end of my life. That evening, one white jeep came and they took me to Bukavu to Panzi hospital where I was treated. If they did not appear on request of my aunt, I would have been dead by now. This kid would have been dead or an orphan by now. Thank God, I'm back to life now even though I do not have strength to work as usual and I'm constantly under medication that makes me dizzy and lifeless. My only worry is the little child who is also sick, but my boy is big now, he will be able to take care of the little one till he survives. I pray every day and night for the future of my boys but one of them will not stay long, I know. It was the life forced on me and them, we did not choose to be like this.'

When Matilde stroke the head of the younger child, Josephine was looking at her with a sympathetic look. Is this the common phenomenon of almost 20 to 25 per cent of victims of sexual violence in the Democratic Republic of Congo? Matilde told me later on that she was infected with HIV as a result of the second assault. And she had become pregnant with second child after the second assault and the second child whom she referred always as the little one was also living with HIV. Even though the fistula and the secondary infections that she was suffering from were successfully treated, she has now a lifelong illness to manage. She and the little one are under ARV that would at least facilitate them to live a little longer than what their cruel destiny imposed on them. Josephine was just a randomly selected individual among hundreds of women and children who are being treated in Panzi hospital in Bukavu, and there are thousands of Josephines who had already passed away from this world among the bushes, some of them are afraid to come out because of stigma, fear, and myths; some are still waiting outside to be hospitalised as the facilities on the ground are not sufficient at all to meet the demand. Not every victim comes to the aid centres; the women who do are the ones who know that help is available, and who are strong enough to walk there sometimes on a journey of several days. Because rape is usually accompanied by a systematic pillage of their homes, these women sometimes have to borrow clothing from a neighbour. What's more, before they set out, they have to scrape up enough money to bribe the soldiers at each roadblock, and for the medical care they think they're going to have to pay for. Few of them know that the aid centres charge practically nothing, an exception in a country where the public health system is supposed to pay for itself. First and foremost, the victims who do seek help are those who have dared break the taboo, the stigma that attaches to any woman who's been raped.

Around 20 to 25 per cent of the female victims test positive for HIV/AIDS. Almost 50 per cent of the victims are syphilitic, a condition that greatly increases future risks of HIV infection. It is estimated that two thirds of the fighters, regulars and irregulars, have HIV/AIDS. To a populace ripped apart by a long, cruel war, feeling abandoned by the national capital, Kinshasa, and the world, these statistics on HIV/AIDS are so horrifying that leading public figures in Kivu have denounced what they see as a Machiavellian extermination plot, if not attempted genocide. Another argument is raised: The wave of rapes is said to have begun with the regular Rwandan army, early in 2000, around the time when Kigali decided to use eastern Congo as a buffer, having abandoned as impractical idea of turning the entire country into a Rwandan satellite. Presently, it is crystal clear to everyone that all the armed groups, without exception, commit rape en masse, with the worst offenders probably the armed Hutus. It all began in 1994. Rwanda's Patriotic Front, dominated by ethnic Tutsis, seized power in that country and halted the genocidal attacks against the Tutsi community planned and perpetrated by the Hutus, in which an estimated 800,000 people died. Perpetrators of the genocide escaped to neighbouring Congo, herding along with them 1.5 million Hutu refugees whom they then forcibly enrolled in a struggle against the new Rwandan regime and later claimed to protect Hutus in Congo. To stamp out the insurgency, the Kigali regime launched its first invasion within Congo's borders in 1996, during which 200,000 of these refugees—men, women, the elderly, and children—were slaughtered as 'genocide criminals' because they fled the advance of the Rwandan army. With the collapse of Congo's economy and the disappearance of any semblance of law and order, violence in eastern Congo became commonplace. It's a culture characterised by acute spasms of violence, fuelled by ethnic hatred that is fed in turn by confrontations between radicals from both of the Rwandan sides, all of which spilled over into Congo. This violence includes rape, carried out intentionally as a genocidal act as the woman is the nucleus of the family and the pillar of society, so destroying women is the worse ever damage that once could commit against a society. They often torture women and rape them in front of their husbands for humiliating them for not being able to protect their women against the perpetrators.

Since the beginning of 2002, the sexual assaults have followed patterns so common that they are becoming commonplace. Several men gang-rape a woman repeatedly. The husband is tied up in the hut, often after being heavily beaten, and in the worse case being cut and brutally killed; the children are brought in; the whole family is obliged to witness the humiliation of the wife and mother. The victim passed out well before the men had finished with her. Increasingly, the assailants force fathers to commit incest with daughters, or brothers with sisters, which was a common feature in many civil conflicts in many parts of Africa such as Liberia, Sierra Leone, and the Central African Republic. They even sodomise men, an act that is unimaginable and extremely disgraceful in the African countryside, even as part of consensual sex. The victims can be anyone, boys to men, little girls to elderly women, ranging from 4 years to 80 years. While I was hearing many other stories of women and men of different age groups, I came to realise that every single word found in languages used by humans had come into being because of human acts; some of those words that we hesitate or are told bad or dirty are in our language because of the same reason above, even though civilised society condemns the words, but in the bush, such words like 'motherfuckers' do stand for a sense as they do exists.

While listening to an interview of Paul Kagame of Rwanda, I heard the same old story that many people say in Africa, that the Western powers are sourcing minerals and are buying them from traders who finance rebel and government troops. Minerals, such as cassiterite, gold, or coltan, which is used for electronic equipment and cell phones, are an important export for Congo, whereas a UN resolution states that anyone supporting illegal Congolese armed groups through illicit trade of natural resources should be subjected to sanctions including travel restrictions and an assets freeze, but so far, no one had been subjected to sanctions and the UN maintains its largest mission on earth in DRC. Blood curdling and unnerving cry of dozens of Josephines are emitted into humid air in thick rainforests and hit the green hills and sink deep into the deep still waters of kivu each night and day and remain unheard forever, just like most of their stories.

Chapter 11

VALLEY OF POLIGAMY

WHEN I FOLLOWED THE path of conflictology, psychology, and sustainable development in the humanitarian domain, my sister, the only sibling of mine, my father's petty-doll, whom he always used to call 'Chooty' which means 'the little one' and always right whatever she does, followed natural sciences with specialisation in virology, bacteriology, and started her career as a scientist and a researcher in the academic domain, affiliated to the University of Duke and University of Washington in USA and many other direct and indirect collaborative initiatives with various local and international universities. She used to be a critic of humanitarian organisations as a result of constant exposure to progovernment political discussions that always placed humanitarian agencies, including the UN, under suspicion of international conspiracies in overthrowing the left-wing government. That was a common illusion in most of the university staff in Sri Lanka, an acquired perceptual set from in-house politics that vamoose in the wind once one goes out of the system. We, Buddhists, believe that it is Karma that places you where you belong, whereas others believe that it is the Almighty God that makes abrupt shifts in one's life;

however, on December 2012, my sister got an offer from 'Medicines Sans Frontieres' for an epidemiologist/lab advisor position for HIV and TB programs in Swaziland; ironically, like an act of destiny, co-audience of free-time stories, she was also brought into Africa.

Simultaneously, the official visit of King Mswati III, the king of Swaziland, to Sri Lanka triggered my desire to go there once my sister is established. 'The king has so many wives, every year a new wife is taken to his palace,' I was listening to my father as he is relating a surreal story about another planet. When I saw his arrival in the news, I thought he is just a savage polygamist who just covers only his sensitive areas with his red piece of cloth barely hanging from one side of his shoulders which is bit like Masai traditional cloth in colour combination and the way it is put on. The next immediate thought that came to my mind was that this piece of cloth might make his conjugal life easy as it is just a matter of undoing only one knot whenever his libido is provoked by anyone among his pool of wives. Nonetheless, King Mswathi III's piece of cloth remained as a hot topic in Sri Lanka for a few weeks after his visit to Colombo, blending with different rumours, including that he had taken a wife from Sri Lanka, he was HIV positive, and so on. Knowledge of an ordinary Sri Lankan about Swaziland was limited to polygamy, HIV, AIDS, TB, and nude dance of ladies, which is an iconic festival called 'Reed Dance' when King Swati selects his wife of the year, each year. Beyond that, as an ordinary Sri Lankan, I knew nothing much about this wonderland where this semi-nude king landed from.

After five hours' direct flight from Accra to Johannesburg, another short flight of forty-five minutes in a small jet of South African Air-link, where there were only ten passengers, took us over the green valleys and mountains, which is obviously an amazingly beautiful landscape, and landed in the only international airport, Mastapa International Airport, of the wonderland of King Mswati III. For such a small nation, occupies a small piece of land, sandwiched between Mozambique and South Africa, it does not need an airport like a modern city. Small but clean and with extremely friendly staff, Mastapa International Airport gives sufficient good impression about the country irrespective of its being unorganised and its ineffectiveness that everyone encounters at the immigration and security counters. I did not have a visa but a special authorisation granted by the Ministry of Foreign Affairs of Swaziland, requesting the airport immigration to allow me into the territory. The immigration was not actually notified about the letter and they did not have a copy of the document sent by the central office; however, instead of making my life difficult because of the fault of their central office, they took my information and the information of my sister who is the sponsor for me during my time in Swaziland and let me in. Instead of what I had heard about the country and the impression given by the fancy dress of the King Mswati, Swaziland gave a homely warmth that I will never forget. Lively smiles, welcoming words, and warm gestures of the first few Swazis I met at the airport made me feel as if I was in wonderland.

My sister received me at the arrival gate. It was after her 29th birthday, the second birthday she had celebrated without my presence, and it was a fact that many more birthdays were to come for her to celebrate without me as we were in two separate places, although it was extremely painful and emotionally difficult to stay apart after we had grown up together for the last twenty-nine years. It was a moment of joy, reunion, and celebration, we held each other for an unknown time and then headed to the car that was waiting for us.

'This is Chikumboussa.'

It was my sister who introduced her driver, the biggest human being I had seen on earth, a giant like Incredible Hulk, probably much bigger than him, too. He was the first Zulu I met in my life.

'Nice meeting you,' he groaned, like a lion while mating, in his cemented deep voice that would scare the shit out of anyone if heard at night. It was more ghostly than human. Along with his size, he had everything to kill anyone with a cardiac arrest at first sight. As we drove through the clean and perfectly paved roads in Manzini with a higher speed that I had not experienced in this continent before, Chikumboussa and I exchanged a few words, which was sufficient for me to understand that he was much more fragile than what his appearance and voice suggest. But unless you speak to him for a while, what comes to the mind of anyone is an image of an underworld thug, or a evil spirit in Greek mythical stories, and any woman who comes across him may have stuck in her imagination a modern Shiva Linga, the holy penis of God Shiva in Hindu mythology.

'See you Sir! Enjoy Swaziland!' It was his last verbal exchange with me as we reached my sister's home. I did not see him again. The modern, really incredible Zulu hulk was forgotten in the next couple of days.

Manzini, the commercial capital of Swaziland, is a small but a full city where there are a lot of things to do compared to cities in West Africa, and quite modern with enormous influence of South Africa. In short, it is a vibrant place full of life. Modern supermarkets, shopping malls, classy restaurants, entertainment centres, vibrant night clubs though infested by prostitutes who can be considered mostly HIV positive with no doubt, and with many more, along with acceptable road network in the city, offer a tourist an exciting experience for a low budget. And as per what I heard, though it is in South Africa, bordering to KwaZulu-natal, the criminality of the city is very low, which allows tourists to have an authentic experience of the city and the country at large. And though it is a kingdom, which looks like an authoritarian reign to the outside world, everyone looks free just like in any democratic country, even though some people hold their own opinions which also are reasonable to some extent, such as that most of the Swazis do not have the right to an international passport, which technically means that they do not have the right to go out of country. But a lot of Swazis travel a lot, too.

'Swazi candles', the world might not know much about this, but those who come to Swaziland are truly passionate of the skills of Swazis in handmade candle making. From wildlife to fantasies of sky or ocean, everything existing in this universe is available in the form of Swazi candles. Candles, made out of usual paraffin, with extraordinary designs that one's eyes cannot believe, such designs as cheetah skin, giraffe skin which seem real, baobab trees, elephants, and giraffes embossed in the candles in such a way that the light highlights them when lighted are just miracles of the sophisticated aesthetic skills of this little nation stuck in the valley surrounded by mountains protected by killer thunder strikes and scary lightning like the heavens fall down burning. Sometimes, some cultures, ethnicities, or tribes in imperialistic terms, remain hidden to the rest of the world, protected by natural factors such as Mordor, inherit their long-dated skills unshared with the commercial part of the world, without being exploited by competitive commercial trends. Though expensive, I was unable to resist my boiling desire to buy a few Swazi candles with unique designs along with the mounts and stands made of ox horn, as a souvenir to take back home. Maybe my children or my nephews or nieces would have a chance to see the touchable traces of my parkour in Africa, even though I personally believe that the height of imagination and curiosity generated by nonvisual materials a child gets into contact with such as free-time stories can be hindered to some extent when a child see some visual materials. If I profoundly dig into my latent factors of motivation, the paramount is the height of imagination and lack of visual and tangible proofs of what I heard when I was a child. The curiosity and thirst for proofs brought me to Africa.

Mbabane is the administrative capital of Swaziland, situated approximately forty kilometres from Manzini and two cities are connected with a well-maintained highway, where my next destination is situated, where the curse of Swazi Valley is going to be witnessed. Manzini government hospital clinic, financially and technically supported by an international nongovernmental organisation, receives more than a hundred patients a day and more than 90 per cent of them are with secondary infections due to HIV/AIDS, and mostly tuberculosis, with its drug-resistant variant, MDR, or extremely drug-resistant TB. The number of patients, with different age categories including little children due to mother-to-child transmission, young men and women who could have a perfect life ahead, severely ill people who look like skeletons, are sitting on the benches, waiting for their turn.

'Hardest part is the adherence' a psychosocial counsellor in the clinic told me, showing a good-looking young girl who repeatedly comes to the clinic, after giving up her TB medication a few days after each time. Due to confidentiality reasons, the clinicians could not let me talk to the patients, but some of the stories that the staff mentioned give enough clues why Swaziland still is not ready for overcoming the major challenge for them, having the world's highest HIV prevalence, which is 38 per cent in its population under 35 and +50 per cent among the females over 35. As everywhere else in the world, the prevalence is higher among females than among males because of biological reasons, as they are the receiver during sexual intercourse, and Swazi lifestyle, especially the one of men, contributes to the bushfire-like spread within the society.

'Every married man in Swaziland has at least one girlfriend'

One of my Swazi friends once told me, with a tone that is wrapped with a kind of a pride that I perceived as utter foolishness. In a country where the HIV prevalence is 38 per cent in average, having multiple partners whose sexual history remain a mystery, practising unprotected sex is an act of suicide. When testosterone dominates over common sense, it is natural that the penis decides the length of one's life.

One time, a staff of the clinic who was a nurse working with HIV-infected patients, who witness the endless suffering of the people living with the virus and with coinfections, told that she was still negative and kept checking constantly as she did not know the whereabouts of her husband. She sounded triumphed after each time the rapid test kit does not show the two lines, but tomorrow, she might get it from her beloved husband who is a passionate love-maker for many other women in a piece of land where HIV is just a condition and polygamy, having multiple sexual partners, is a norm.

Amidst this social catastrophe, the head of state, King Mswati III, gets ready for his fifteenth Hymen-hunt, which is an extreme encouragement for the commoners who are merely guided by their level of testosterone. Umhlanga, 'Reed Dance', is an annual Swazi and Zulu cultural event, tens of thousands of unmarried and childless Swazi girls and women travel from the various chiefdoms to Ludzidzini, where the royal villages are to participate in the eight-day event, some of them with pride of being a virgin, others just being single, with the hope of being selected by the king as his wife of the year.

The ladies gather at the royal village 'Ludzidzini'. After arriving at the Queen Mother's royal residence, the women disperse the following night to surrounding areas and cut tall reeds. The following night, they bundle them together and bring them back to the Queen Mother to be used in repairing holes in the reed windscreen surrounding the royal village, as usually every traditional village and house in Swaziland is fenced out of reeds, a tall straight piece of wood.

After a day of rest and washing, the women prepare their traditional costumes consisting of a bead necklace, rattling anklets made of cocoons, a sash, and skirt. Many of them carry the bush knife, which resembles a machete used in West Africa, they used to cut the reeds as a symbol of their virginity.

Today's Reed Dance ceremony developed in the 1940s from the Umcwasho custom where young girls were placed in age regiments to ensure their virginity. Once they reached the age of marriage, they would perform labour for the Queen Mother, followed by dancing and a feast. The official purpose of the annual ceremony is to preserve the women's chastity, provide tribute labour for the Queen Mother, and produce solidarity among the women through working together.

The women sing and dance as they parade in front of the royal family as well as a crowd of spectators, tourists, and foreign dignitaries. After the parade, groups from select villages take to the centre of the field and put on a special performance for the crowd, and subsequently, the king selects a new wife, but in the present context in which the country is severely affected by HIV and in the modern world where polygamy is a taboo and violation of the rights of women, 'Reed Dance' looks like a tribal ritual that endangers the nation, plunging its population deep in the trap of HIV/AIDS. As many parts in Africa, Swaziland is another place where traditions have blinded the eyes of the nation, or else the traditions are used by the high powers to keep their pleasures legitimate while the whole nation walks unto the hands of death.

'Ncwala', the ceremony of the fresh fruit, is another event that the nation gathers to observe a series of traditional rituals chronologically set up for about one month's time. Although not a tourist event, visitors with an interest in Swaziland culture are always welcomed. Respect for total privacy is required on certain special days when the nation gathers for its own focus, without outside interference, especially the day the king of Swaziland is believed to be having sex with a black ox to make it sacred for the feast, which is a guarded highly from the outside world.

The festival takes place over three to four weeks; the first period commences at the new moon when the Bemanti or 'water party' journeys to the Indian Ocean in Mozambique to collect the foam of waves, which is believed to have healing powers. Upon their return to the king's palace, they hold a ceremony called 'Little Ncwala'. Wearing traditional outfits, they chant sacred songs. When the moon is full, 'Big Ncwala' commences with a mammoth journey by young men from all over the country, who gather branches from the 'Lusekwane' tree to construct a sacred enclosure in the royal kraal, the cattle enclosure. The following day, a sacred black bull with which the king had sex, is driven into the king's kraal, captured and slaughtered, ready for the next day's feast. The next day is known as the main Ncwala day. Warriors and guests assemble in the royal compound. The warriors are typically clothed in traditional dress of animal skins and cow tails that cover only their genitals. They dance in the sacred boma, singing slow ritual songs, until at last the king moves forward into his sacred enclosure. The fifth day is dedicated to rest and meditation, to be followed by a huge bonfire on the sixth day, when articles are burned to represent the beginning of a new year.

The ceremony itself takes place over more than a month with various important aspects occurring on a day-by-day basis, but most of the parts remain secret to the outside world.

Swazi traditions could be found a little bit weird and not civilised from the viewpoint of outsiders, yet for Swazis, those are vital parts for their culture, and the king is the jewel for their tiny kingdom. Maybe because of an isolated, totally landlocked country, bordering to rural parts of South Africa and Mozambique, Swazis were able to preserve their traditions with minimal external influence and interference. However, when closely observed, it seems that the culture has taken the upper hand over their health and against the globalisation of this little nation left in a beautiful valley.

Milwane and Hlane, though those Zulu names make your tongue twisted with hidden N, M, and TL, are two of the most famous wildlife refuges in Swaziland where there is a rich wildlife and sufficient logistical support for tourists to have a classy experience. I remember, my mother had bought me a toy zebra that I used to ride for some time, till it ended up losing its legs, then finally its neck, turning into firewood. It was in 1980s, a good three decades ago. That was my first zebra encounter, though it was not a real one, that was the time I got to know the existence of an animal like a horse with white and black lines on this earth. The first wild animal I met in Southern African bushes was a zebra, the one I knew from my childhood. I told my sister, I had a wooden one of them when I was small, and you were not born yet. When I saw the first live one of my childhood toy, almost 10,958 nights full of dreams had passed, and I travelled almost 6,555 kilometres away from home. It was in Milwane National Park. My sister and I had a free bush walk of almost nine hours, continuously, grace to a favourable climate. In Milwane, one will not encounter the big five—elephant, lion, buffalo, giraffe, and rhino—not even cheetah cats, therefore anyone can go on a bush walk without a flight-or-fight response despite some wildebeests that I had seen only on Discovery channel, in programs about animal migration from great Masai Mara to Serengeti and the other way around, which crossed my path in real time during my walk, which made my hair raise. One time I was trying to take a photo of a herd of spring hogs, using my DSLR in manual mode, sitting on the verge of a mountainous pathway in Milwane, ended up rolling down along the steep as a crazy warthog cub ran into me. Those little scary creatures are very well used to tourists who feed them and do not have a single milligram of fear to humans, as if they rule the sanctuary. It was my first time witnessing the strange wild-boar-like animal I had seen in the *Lion King* cartoon series when I was a kid. The dance of the animated warthog in *Lion King*, waving its head which is proportionally larger than the body, had not been erased from my mind since that time. I felt like a dream had passed through the time and come to reality. Every little thing I dreamt of is live in-front of my own eyes. In the savannah-like forest, I walked with an immense pleasure for almost around nine hours, till my legs refused to move, though it was not enough for my mind which was on a honeymoon of a dream come true.

My parents met in a very remote village called Mahavillachchiya, in North Central Sri Lanka, while both of them were on their first government assignment in 1972, though they were originally from the same township called Gampaha. After work, some days, my father used to accompany the hunters, as it was a new thing for him and might have been kind of a thrilling experience for a young man of 27 years. And he was a red meat lover too. When friends had a good hunt, he also got a share of it, often it had been a good fleshy piece of a wild boar which is pretty similar to a warthog but an extremely aggressive animal that often attacks anything that crosses its path. He used to talk about those rare delicacies that he tasted while being deployed in the wild part of the country and always used to connect with wildlife in Africa, and I do not have a clue whether we had a conversation about the preservation of wildlife, instead we talked about how people survived in the wild, which sounded more exciting and thrilling. Also, one can be persuaded to experience the wilderness that is seldom found, especially those of us who live in urban settings where our plates are tired of holding broiler chicken, Chinese pork, and domestic beef, and as human beings are open to experience, and find luxury in rare things. I guess that was the reason why I found myself in a forest, a restaurant with a plate full of wildebeest, Warthog, and Spring-hog meat or else an unconscious carnivorous desire remained in my latent subconscious and had come out after seeing all these lively and tempting wild animals. As we used to define the character and the likings of individuals based on their zodiac sign they are given at birth, taking diverse horoscopic factors such as proximity of the moon, time of the day, the Earth's position in the orbit, into consideration, unlike the Western pattern of assigning a zodiac sign, taking the period of the year the child is born, being a Leo, the typical behaviour of my zodiac sign might have come out once I was in the natural habitats of lions. I think I was not sensitive enough to recognise what meat was of which animal as all tasted like beef or lamb to me. However, when I watched the song 'Hakuna matata', I did not even think I would see that strange dancing thing, and eating its meat has not even reached my thoughts. Swazis, in general Southern Africans, are good in meat, it being a vital part of their meal. The portions that anyone else except them cannot finish, yet delicious and perfectly seasoned and well done, tempt anyone, even a long-practised vegetarian to untie the discipline. Starting from Milwane, each stop for meal in Swaziland, I did not forget to feed myself with the finest meat in the Southern Wilds, prepared for centuries and carefully preserved with Swazi and Zulu methods. Simply, I became a gourmet of Southern African non-veg gastronomy, giving a kick-restart to my meat-eating habit that I got rid of ten years ago.

Swaziland is demographically, culturally, and linguistically influenced by South Africa Zulu ethnic group though this tiny 100 per cent landlocked country had developed unique social norms and mores that have been added to typical Swazi lifestyle in a large picture, portraying a vivid image of a unique nation isolated in a valley in Southern Africa. Zulu lifestyle, gastronomy, traditional dress—specially the dresses worn by men during Ncwala and Umhlanga festivals—and the traditions linked with major life events such as birth, marriage, and death have almost been totally shared by Swazis as if the colonial borders had failed in their cruel attempts in separating people.

'I gave 100 cows to my father-in-law as "bride price",' a citizen of France who is married to a Swazi lady with a Zulu ancestry told me I had heard about the bride price in the eastern part of Africa, some parts of Kenya, where daughters still remain unmarried as there are no such rich men who can pay the price set for women by their greedy fathers, who think that a female child is a lottery whereas there are hundreds of thousands of South Asian women, especially in India, who are not in a position to pay the dowry, the wealth demanded by the groom's family, and grow old single. But, till I came to Swaziland, it being my first Southern African state to visit, the cow as a unit of measuring wealth or exchange had not come on to the scene in my horizons of knowledge.

'How did you find cows?'

I asked kind of an irrational question but with curiosity.

'I bought them prior to the marriage ceremony.'

The size of the herd of cows, in other words, the cattle, reflects your wealth in this part of earth. I did not ask him why he did not negotiate to give the amount of money equivalent to 100 cows and escape from the hassle of finding cows. The bottom line is, customs should remain as customs, and they remain as customs, that itself is a custom. Later on, he showed me his wedding photos. He was in a traditional Zulu warrior's costume, with a couple of others who were obviously Swazis, also in traditional attire, which reminded me of the famous Sinhalese proverb: 'Where the heart goes, you build your palace.' During the time of Dutch, British, and even Portuguese in the next-door Mozambique have mixed with the local community, resulting in the third race in the region, 'Mulatoo', 'Malatoo', or 'Coloured', whose one parent is black and other is white, and they are gifted with fairer skin relative to the indigenous, more Caucasian features, and with less curly and silkier hair than Negroid hair. 'Mulatto' is quite an offensive word, although most of the people are not aware of it, which is derived from the French word 'Mulatre', meaning 'mule', which is the result of crossing between a 'Horse' and a 'Donkey', considered as unable to have its own offspring. The Europeans are symbolised by 'Horses', whereas 'Donkeys' have been used in Africa since antiquity for transportation purposes, especially in the Southern

Highlands. The fires of hatred and disguise caused by Southern African racial tensions are still remaining under the foundations of modern highways connecting countries in the region, under the foundations of every building on their ground, every little drop of water that embraces dry earth, every single thought that comes to their mind, but remain silent, waiting till another time comes, to come out. Racism has its own dynamics; it is neither a white man's attitude nor black man's fate, it is a trait of the side where more power is accumulated in a given time period or an occasion and used as a multidimensional weapon to suppress the less powerful. Colour is not what makes a person inferior, but the attitude. A racist is a white one time and a black the other time. When races are diluted into subraces, mixed races, mulatoo, coloured, racism by itself will find its hideout in history books with no applicability to the present, though it would require ten thousand full-moon nights and social education.

During the time of thunderstorms, the Valley of Polygamy becomes nearly a cemetery, pleasure turns into fear, festivity is hidden behind the mountains that transforms to Star Wars. The lightning and heavy thunder send a few dozens of lives into the hands of eternal peace behind the rocky Drakensberg every year. Dry winter, mostly with no snow, makes anything dry like firewood, and when the summer sun comes in, the whole place becomes a hot plate, where one can make a good brai without a coal grille. Under all these extreme conditions, Swazi life remain vibrant, relaxed, easy-going, and after all happy in the Troy of His Excellency Mswati III, and they are asleep while the Trojan Horse of HIV and tuberculosis, a terrifying collated army, hunts down every single life within Maswathi's Troy.

Chapter 12

KINGDOM OF CLOUDS

EVERY SUNDAY EVENING AT nine thirty, everyone, except my mum who is always busy with household affairs, throng around the television like ants surrounding a melting piece of sugar on the cement floor. 'Salanhanstle', a kind of a travellers' documentary program, probably the first such televisions program in Sri Lanka, started with a documentary on Lesotho. That was the first time we heard about the existence of such a country on earth. My father was quite curious about every single information in the program and he went through his small pocket atlas and showed me the country, like a piece of chicken pie within South Africa. When the Lesotho chapter was over, I was left with a notebook full of notes on every tiny piece of information about Lesotho, but it was my limit by that time. We neither had access to the Internet nor published literature about Africa. 'Salanhanstle' remained in my mind, the notebook remained intact in my little library at home, time passed by, and I was hopeful not to have a chance to go there but to find more information to fill the gaps in the story about Lesotho in my mind and to find answers to my curious questions popping up constantly. In year 2000, I typed on the keypad of my first computer, a second-hand Pentium 3, connected to dial-up Internet connection, 'Lesotho, Kingdom of clouds'. The very first words I ever typed in the search box of MS Internet Explorer that expanded my experience about Lesotho into a virtual discovery from carelessly taken notes with information that do not connect with each other in a notebook. Dreams are like liquid lead, till you are unable to reach them, they remain intact; once you reach them, they split into hundreds of other dreams, which could be the reason why humans have advanced as their dreams never end. I wanted to see the kingdom of clouds with my own eyes, but I did not know how, with my salary of $35 as a teacher.

November 2013, almost fourteen years after 'Salanhanstle' was telecast, my sister and I—by that time my father had left this world— were on board to go to Maseru, the capital of Lesotho. Our plans were to go to Namibia, but due to the time-consuming visa process, we decided to go to Lesotho where Sri Lankan citizens do not need visa to enter. As a result of Namibian bureaucracy my dreams to be on the Roof of Africa is on its verge to become a reality.

Shining galvanised metal roofing sheets appeared in clusters under the clouds of the second existing kingdom in Southern African region gave an impression that I'm landing somewhere in West Africa where roofs are usually metal. Even before landing in Lesotho, it was clear to me with the aerial view that Lesotho is not the same as her sister kingdom of Swaziland. It seems that the people do not want to forget the old fashion of close communities. When the flight was landing, I felt as if I was an eagle dreaming to grab its pray while reaching the ground. I did not want to lose anything that I dream to discover in this little paradise lost and locked in South Africa.

I said to my sister, 'Salanhanstle', when the small jet of South African Air-link landed in Moshoehoe International Airport. Despite the very hot sun as it was summer, the weather was perfect for travelling. The typical Basotho welcoming and warm smiles and friendly reception were impressive at the immigration except for few taxi drivers who were waiting like vultures to grab the few passengers coming out of arrival gate. 'What country are you from?' The lady at the immigration was puzzled as if she has not heard of a country called Sri Lanka. 'I'm from old Ceylon and I do not need visa for entering the country,' I added to convey to them that I'm aware of the visa and immigration procedures as I had learnt a lesson from my visit to Sierra Leone while I was on my way back to Liberia. I was glad that my perceptual set about the Basothos didn't change, I was given access to the country for fourteen days.

'Enjoy your vacation in Lesotho, Sir,' the lady added with a warm smile.

I had made arrangements in advance to pick us from the airport, but unfortunately, as a consequence of miscommunication, the driver did not show up. Therefore, we had to pick a taxi randomly among a couple of taxi drivers fighting like vultures on a carcass of a deer, on a few passengers. We came across a female taxi driver whose rates looked reasonable, with two options as most of the places in Africa, shared or nonshared, for LSL200 (Lesotho Malothi, official currency of Lesotho which is equivalent to South African Rand); each person on shared basis we agreed upon. As the minivan taxi started leaving Moshoehoe International Airport, we started passing by empty landscapes which told us nonverbally that the city could be a little far from the airport. Approximately after thirty kilometres, the first impression of Basotho city life started to be revealed, while the assumption I made seeing the aerial view of Lesotho was becoming true. Compared to Mbabane or Manzini, Maseru was a smaller capital with a poorer outlook. The roads were busier, full of traffic, than the ones in Swaziland, though the roads are acceptably maintained, roadside little shops made out of galvanised sheets have added an air of slummy urban area, like an abandoned slum in Rio de Janeiro. Most of the people whom I noticed along the road, probably those who belong to the very poor social layer, gave me an impression that the number of HIV and TB patients is more in Lesotho than in Swaziland. As we drove into the heart of the city, hundreds of people who were returning from work had gathered in bus/taxi stops to catch a minibus which is exactly the size of a Marshrutka in Ukraine or Russia, to get back home and invade the road like a herd of sheep, whenever they see a minibus come. Once we drove out of the centre, another part of Basotho city life, which could have been the reason for the high density of population in the city, unfolds. Thousands of youngsters flood out to the roads from the industrial zones. A lot of South African–owned industries, especially textile factories, are in the suburbs of Maseru that attract the youth from rural Lesotho, creating a significant increase in the urban population of Lesotho and again fuelling the spread of HIV/AIDS and TB epidemic in the country. Cheap labour, illiterate rural population, and extreme poverty in remote Lesotho have turned the kingdom of clouds into a hunting ground for labour exploiters who steal the sweat and blood of innocent villagers in exchange of a few hundred rands a month in addition to the social and health issues that follow the early stages of industrialisation with minimum control from the host government.

When we reached 'City Lodger', the hotel I had booked for us, it was almost 19.00 hours and the sun was creeping down from the range of mountains in front of us. And the road near the hotel that heads to suburbs has formed a line of lights with its heavy traffic congestion, adding some unusual artificial allure to the sunset that could have been very natural and beautiful without it.

I had my precious memories still alive with me, my little notebook, in my hand luggage, beside all modern and hyper-informative tourist literature, such as *Lonely Planet* and *Discovery*. Though it was not a long tiring flight to Maseru, the trip from the airport to City Lodger was a bit energy-sucking, but some unexplainable feeling was trying to keep my nerves stimulated as if something exciting was going to happen. It was probably the motor restlessness evoked by the eustress caused by the sense of accomplishment. I went through the notebook, read every single note that I had written with my barely readable handwriting. Some of them were totally unclear because of the blurred letters caused by exposure to moisture in Liberia, but I felt the emotions laden in the pages. I started having flashbacks of every single dream conceived within myself while I was scribbling on these pages.

'If I won a lottery, I would be able to see Kome.' Written on 15 February 2000, this sentence, written with a blue pen, probably 0.7 ballpoint, remained intact in the last page. In Sri Lanka, government-sponsored lotteries are a source of illusions of hundreds of thousands of poor people. Every day, most of the people buy lotteries, spending ten to twenty Sri Lankan rupees, which is around $0.20, most probably those are the last few notes left in the wallet, expecting a better tomorrow. They do not think that if they save those small bank notes for decades, instead spending them on socially accepted gambling, they will be able to save more than the jackpot amount they dream to have. However, the social trends can be translated into individual habits, and likewise, individual habits can contribute in creating social trends. As a consequence of one among those, I developed a habit of buying lotteries whenever I go out of the town. The desperateness and nonaffluence might have been the reasons for me to choose such an unrealistic way to reach my dreams. But, by that time, I did not see any other option to keep my dreams alive.

The next morning, just after breakfast, we started our journey from Maseru to Semonkong, a small town in central Lesotho, about 120 kilometres from Maseru, which is approx. four hours of drive, where we planned to stay for four days to explore Basotho village life. Once we left the outskirts of Maseru, the road appeared to be a road to the skies, ascending continuously spirally around the mountains like an anaconda coiled around a pray. The more we drove, the higher we reached to an elevation, where the common nickname for Lesotho, 'Kingdom of Clouds', was proven to be true: clouds were floating below us like the melting ice floating on waters, picturesque like a painting, a masterpiece of nature. The next few dozens of miles transformed our trip into an adventure. The road was under construction, and the one line which was edging to the steep like holly hell was the only one allowed to be used. Not even the most experienced driver would dare to look down while driving and a slight mistake in judgement can determine life or death. Almost around a couple of hundred metres, a sharp precipice waits below you like a crocodile waiting for its prey, and when a vehicle comes up, the one who descends has to park at the edge of the steep and leave the space to the one who comes uphill. Every time our pickup cab stopped at the edge of the road, my chest was about to burst with palpitations; I did not know whether it was because of the low level of oxygen due to the altitude or panic attack provoked by fear. Besides what I was going through, I felt my sister was gripping my hand, over time we got closer to the edges, and her sweaty and icy-cold hands told about all that she was feeling. Such times, being a Buddhist, it was not easy to fight with the reality in front of my very eyes. I could not simply pray to the God whom I have never seen or met, but rather stick into the rational that prevention is the only way out and there is no space for anything else. But when everything is in the hands of another believer, whose religion I didn't have a clue of, besides telling the driver to be more careful and attentive, I prayed to his God who was unknown to me. By 16.30, we reached safely to Semonkong Lodge where we were supposed to stay for the next four days, a four-star adventure lodge situated right at the bank of Semonkong River, where a lot of South Africans come for the world famous abseiling in Maletsunyane falls, which is the highest single-drop waterfall in Southern Africa. I desperately wanted to have something to change my blood chemistry, to lower the adrenaline level in my serum induced by the road trip between life and death, I left my bags in the room and went to the pub.

Semonkong is all about Basotho folk life, peasants who were mostly herdsmen with the symbolic Basotho blanket on the shoulders travelling on pony back is more common than the people taking taxies in cities like Johannesburg or Manzini. They appear from the top hill like the horsemen in Medieval times and disappear into the valley. Some come alone, and some with their fellow-peasants followed by their sheep and donkeys. With the traditional blanket on shoulders, head covered either with a woollen winter hat or a scarf made with sheep wool, stick in the hand, they resemble to mystic figures, ancient magicians, or witches. The main source of travelling is surefooted Basotho ponies, offspring of European full-mount horses and South African donkeys, and for transportation of goods, donkeys are widely used as the terrain is almost impassable by any vehicle. Just after the breakfast, the next day morning, we left the hotel for our own experience with Basotho horse trekking in one of the highest peaks of Lesotho, Maletsunyane falls, the continent's tallest single waterfall and height abseiling experience, I told my sister that we would try our luck today.

First time ever in my life, I found myself on a saddle, holding the ropes, technically speaking, the steering of the horse, and my sister followed me on another pony still with the assistance of another well-trained Basotho boy on horseback. Galloping across the green valley, against the wind that blows strong enough to push us down from the saddle, my excitement of riding a horse did not remain more than few minutes. Wherever domestic cat goes, it always knows its way back home. Just like that the horses started going uphill, with such a confidence like no other knows the terrain better than them, gradually they made us understand why

Basotho life and horses or ponies are inseparable. The higher they moved, the surer they become in all their body language, and the fears of seeing the precipice that looks like the end of the world started to become a part of the journey though the horses did not even a single sign of fear, As we reached to a kind of a flat land on the top of a hill, my eyes encountered the first Basotho hut at a reasonable proximity, though I had seen many along the way to Semonkong from Maseru. Unlike the Swazi hut which is like a dome made out of Palawa with the little entrance and fenced with reeds, The Basotho hut is made with mostly flat yellow stones and stuck with mud in a round shape, roofed with strong grass that lasts twenty to thirty years, which keeps the inside cool during summer and traps heat during winter, without a drop of water seeping through, and there is a special feature which is unique to the Basotho hut, the short wall made of rocks and mud, either in front of the hut or beside it for keeping ponies, and herds of sheep. Most of the Basotho huts do have at least one plant of spiral aloe, the national flower of the country, which is endemic to Lesotho. The uniqueness of the hut, which is symbolic to this little landlocked kingdom that is above the clouds, makes it irresistible. I pulled my DSLR from the backpack while the horse is on hold and tried to take few shots from a short distance, then I noticed an old lady sitting on the rock with her walking stick in one hand, looking at what we were going to do, I got down and walked up to her. She was delighted by the presence of a smiling stranger and greeted me in Sesotho, 'Dumela' which means 'Hello' or 'Good day'. I greeted back with a little Sesotho that I came to know during my long journey to Semonkong from Maseru.

'Dumela, Mama.'

'O Kae?'

She was quite surprised to see an Indian-looking man, probably she might have concluded that I was an Indian as everyone else in this continent, speaking in Sesotho, and looked directly in my eyes and smiled again as if she wants to reaffirm her humble pride to see a stranger talking in her mother tongue. And she said with another humble smile, 'Ke teng, wena o kae?' ('I'm fine, how are you?').

While talking to her, I had a close look at the strange creation of Basotho-men, with its unique architectural features, though the light was not much inside, the temperature was very well controlled, and after all, it looked homelier than a hut, though in modern eye it is seen as a hut, it is a simple healthy home that is engineered to mitigate the impact of the seasonal changes of the year. And every space is fully functional and useable, every little corner has a specific use, though it is inside or outside of the house. No extra spaces are wasted or are not in use. This little Basotho hut, though the round houses are considered as unhealthy as per the modern science, gives a strong message about eco-friendly living style and proper use of resources without abusing them. At a distance of couple of metres to downhill, usually the Basotho huts are erected in hilly areas, there is a place fenced with rocks and mud for ponies, donkeys, and sheep, as every single male born in rural Lesotho grows up as a herd boy and then a herd man, finally. Donkeys, ponies, and sheep are an integral part of Basotho life. Livestock is the fuel for existence in these impassable mountainous terrains, located totally disconnected from the modern world. The essentials of our so-called modern world, such as Internet, social media, and modern gadgets do not interrupt the serenity of Basotho life, their day starts with bleating of sheep, neighing of ponies, braying of donkeys, without alarms, ends with the Sun set that brings the darkness to the hut, time for rest. They do not share anything virtually, via blue tooth or infrared, whatever they share is heartily, one to one. Life goes on a very natural interface, as it is meant to be, and I felt that a calmness that words could never describe wraps around me, away from the sinking competitiveness of modern world. I felt that the life in its real sense existing here. Simple rules of nature govern life, whether it is human or animal. The level of hopes do not rise to the level of ambitions, its frontiers are drawn by the pony's back. The sanity of being harmonious with nature is the backbone of Basotho life. Once the sun hides behind the mountain, everything except the nocturne birds keeps silence, till the Sun re-appears with a new day, the ponies neigh, sheep bleat, donkeys bray, and symphonies of birds announce a break of another day.

As time cannot be held, we had to get back to the ponies to head to Matsupalyane falls; in a few minutes, we reached the second layer of the mountain ring, a part of the Drakensberg mountain range, where the falls break. After few hundred metres of climbing horses started along a very narrow pathway, which is not more than three feet of width, bordering to a sharp steep, which makes anyone dizzy and lose equilibrium, where below the river flows like a raged snake chasing a prey. I had no other option than leaving my life on the instinct and four feet of a beast which was my God, defender at this very moment, no other superpower could decide whether I would return in one piece alive or in many pieces dead. But surprisingly, the ponies walked as if they go home, confidently, calmly, and safely, but I was frozen on the saddle, rigidly holding the ropes with no movements. The roaring noise of falling waters involuntarily turned my head towards the steep, at the other side of the bank, milky waters of Maletsunyane falling from almost 200 metres and kissing Maletsunyane river down in the precipice; simultaneously the ponies located themselves in a flat area in front of the falls. When fear dilutes with the bubbles of falling waters, I got down from the pony and lay down on the ground and took a couple of deep breaths in order to release fear-induced stiffness. Matsupalyane falls is an amazing piece of art of nature, though reaching there is a death trap, and it had taken few lives including a tourist. The rainfall from October to April makes this place smoky with drizzles broken out of falling waters, while the wail of falling waters turns to a vigorous roar, like a hungry lion. When winter creeps into the Southern Hemisphere in May, the river freezes with a dead silence, Maletsunyane hibernates in cold, while once green mountains turn white and Basotho people start their annual fight of survival covered with traditional Basotho blanket and a fireplace. Central heating is not in their vocabulary.

As we moved uphill, Matsupalyane stayed back and the wailing waters left only an echo inside my ears. Ponies moved along a pathway, probably carved by their own shoes, towards the other side of the mountain range, where there was a little village in the valley. The place was full of donkeys, ponies, and sheep in clusters. A boy or a man, with a blanket on his shoulder and a stick of wood on his hand, was waiting, either wandering or sitting near the herd and it was common to see a dog with the herdsman. Kids were playing while mothers were busy processing food. The existence of a life simpler than the word in its real sense was proven to be true at the altitude of 2,275 metres from the sea level in utter isolation, but in fullest freedom, protected by the law of nature. By late afternoon, we were more exhausted than the ponies and called it a day full of adventures and memories. The first pony ride ever in my life left me with something to reflect on, I loved the beast, its sensitivity, and wanted to try another ride the next day with a fully mounted horse. That was the beginning of my passion for riding horses, which continued since that day and I tried in every single continent I visited, except Australia. But so far, no other can be as sure-footed in mountains as Basotho ponies, the amazing breed exclusively born for mountains.

By six in the evening, we used to sit outside the Duck and Donkey Tavern, on a wooden donkey bench, facing the river, though I usually do not enjoy alcohol, I do not hesitate to sip anything which is a delicacy or unique to my destination. I ordered a cocktail with Amarula, a South African–made creamy alcoholic beverage, made out of Marula fruit which is endemic to the Southern African region, and sip it for hours while planning the next day with my sister. The women along with their kids walk down from the rocky hilltops, along the steep to fetch water before darkness appears behind the hills when life becomes immobile in obscurity. And over the bridge appear the returning herdsmen, on pony back, some with their herds of sheep, some with their donkeys with stuff that they bought from town, on the back. Sitting in tranquillity of sunset, every evening at Duck and Donkey Tavern, I used to watch the winding down of Basotho life for the day, once they cross the bridge, on pony back, everyone in the villages calls it a day. I used to wait a few minutes till my T-bone steak comes, along with traditional Basotho bread, which is just like Pita bread of Lebanese but thicker and fleshier like a pizza base. After dinner, we used to creep into the cabana and try desperately to light up the fireplace for at least ten minutes; often the firewood provided were wet. Once the fireplace is set up, the last challenge of the day is over, and the day ends.

Lesotho is very rich in water, as a mountainous country, many water sources of the area starts from Lesotho and drains down across the frontiers. Water has become one of the incomes for Lesotho, as it trades water across the frontiers. The water reservoirs with multiple dams such as Mohale and Keste bring a lot of remittance to Lesotho, although the South African companies that manage them have more control over the resources, still the revenue cushions up the economy of the country at an average of $50–60 million per year. Our next destination is Keste, where Africa's second largest concrete arc dam is built on Malibamat'so River, which is a part of the larger Lesotho highland water project which is meant to trade water to South Africa. With this huge dam, a reservoir can provide South Africa with hundreds of thousands of cubic metres of water annually. Despite the water value that adds into the economy, Mohale and Keste dams have become tourist attractions. Passing through the same disastrous and dreadful road to Maseru till Morija road junction, we had a time-consuming and tiring trip, and from Morija junction to Keste, the road was paved and well maintained despite the fact that any highway in Lesotho can be invaded by a herd of sheep headed by a herdsman and a pony at any time. And every five minutes, we came across a Basotho man either on a donkey or a pony on highways, as if they were licensed vehicles. 'As long as they serve the same purpose, they can use the highway,' Mpho, a Basotho man, told me when I was asking him why he was riding the pony in the highway. When a halfway is made from Morija road junction, while driving along the highway, a world of blue waters was way below the steep which were manmade reservoirs, the wealth of Lesotho. However, unlike mountainous regions where almost everyone is a herdsman, farmers are the majority in lowlands. As a result of water projects, thousands of farmers had lost their livelihood and migrated to the urban Maseru, making it one of the most densely populated cities in Africa. We reached Orion Katse lodge, an Orion Group, four star lodge with a wonderful view of the reservoir from the rooms and the location of the lodge was very near the Keste botanical garden where one could see the endemic flora and fauna of Lesotho.

Next day morning, just after breakfast, we walked to Katse botanical garden from where the reservoir appears like an ocean with sapphire-blue waters, and a few mountain tops that had popped up from the reservoir pretend to be islands of an immense ocean. And one of the workers of the garden told us that those little islands disappear when the rainy season comes. Spiral aloes were the most noticeable and known plant in the whole garden, and we didn't bother to find details, mostly written in Latin, about the other plants and instead enjoyed the fresh air and mild sun. However, the Katse botanical garden serves in the conservation and sustainable use of botanical resources in Lesotho and in education, to raise awareness and build the capacity of botanical resource users and visitors. The garden has been in existence for a mere thirteen years (1996–2010), and when we visited it, it was fully functional. It hosts a large plant propagation area and extensive pathways that conduct the visitor to pass by the displays of Sesotho traditional medicinal plants.

The garden has a unique collection representing the dry Senqu River vegetation, rare and endangered plant species. Other activities at the garden have resulted in the assembly of a large seed bank and scientific and horticultural collaboration with other regional and international botanic gardens. The implementation of outreach programs has proven to be partially successful as local communities are now visibly proud to be associated with the showcasing of their national flora. Some villagers are participating in plant propagation projects focused on commercially viable species, which bring revenue to areas of high unemployment. The tar road ends at the gate of the Katse botanical garden, a real gem in the crown of the Mountain Kingdom of Lesotho.

Approximately after two hours, the clouds started gathering over the waters, light green mountains turned to a mysterious gray colour when drizzling started and we did not expect the sky to crack into pieces. The rain was just a drizzle but thundering started terrifying us to death, lightning cracked the sky into small pieces, burned and earthed as if the burning pieces are falling in to the ocean. That very moment of short thunderstorm, which was around thirty minutes, was like a surrealist painting for me; I had never experienced a thunderstorm with such a magnitude. It was not second to the hellfire-like thunders that deprive the right to life of Swazis every year. Almost after half an hour, I lifted my eyes and saw my sister's pale face that had lot of untold words written on it; we rushed back to the lodge, running like spring hogs chased by cheetahs.

Through the long, full-glass windows of the restaurant, I was watching the falling rain on waiting waters and mingling with them while the gray sky is getting ready for another fire show as the storm resumed more vigorously. Once position determines how the things are seen, how one feels. Instead of feeling frightened by the thunder and lightning, I was looking at the aesthetic designs of the lights that they draw in the sky, just like a masterpiece of an artist. Unfortunately, I had to make a choice between our lives and the boat trip that we had planned in the reservoir in the evening and decided to stay in the lodge as we were supposed to go to Morija next morning.

On the way to Morija, we passed by the University of Lesotho, which was one of the oldest universities on the region, which used to be an educational institution common to Botswana, Swaziland, and Lesotho, that I had seen on a TV program in Sri Lanka. Though the university is very small compared to the places I had been before, it was quite well built, equipped and sufficient to the small population of the country. Unfortunately, a greater proportion of the students are HIV positive and infected with TB, that fate of the future of the country was on the hands of death, being third in the world with 25 per cent of HIV prevalence, only behind Botswana and Swaziland. After around three hours, we reached the place where I had booked for the next four days for the visit to Mohale, Morija National Museum, hike for watching the dinosaur footprints, and to discover another side of Basotho life. I booked 'Our Lady's Lodge' online via 'Trip Advisor online travel facilitation site' two months before my arrival to Lesotho. Based on the information, including photos and maps, besides a couple of e-mails exchanged between the management of the place and myself, I found 'My Lady's Lodge' kind of a typical village setting with cabanas like Basotho huts, traditional cuisine where nearby villagers are employed. The advertisement indeed was appealing for a tourist who wanted to have a real grass-roots Basotho experience, so I decided to book 'Our Lady's Lodge' for four days. As per the map, we reached to the location indicated in 'Trip Advisor' and found an old church instead of a lodge, and I rang the contact number which I contacted prior to the departure from Ghana two weeks ago. The same lady answered the phone and I asked her we were in the location indicated in the map and we were unable to locate the lodge. Travelling is always an adventure, sometimes exciting and sometimes frustrating. A sister appeared from the church with another lady who was skinny, like a skeleton, and stood in front of our taxi, smiling as if she is there to welcome us. She was still with her mobile on and I could hear her conversation with the other lady. I was completely confused with what I saw in front of my very eyes and did not know whether to smile back at her or scream at her. My instinct didn't allow me to send the taxi back. I asked the taxi driver to stay till I return. I asked the lady, 'Where are the cabanas?'. She smiled again and asked us to follow her. She was walking like the boss, with the lady who is apparently a very sick person who sould not be working, and we were following her. She lead us to the next old building in the complex, she showed us an old room where there were two single beds, one rickety chair, and a fan that was creaking. Neither the windows nor the doors had locks. No bathrooms attached but the cost was almost the same as a three-star room. I was more than shocked and cheated, cheated by a religious missionaries who had come to civilise Africans in the bush, cheated in front of the holy cross that millions of Africans are made to kneel down and pray every day, cheated at the house of God, and my directness invaded my tongue, loaded with a spell of anger provoked by being cheated by those who appear like 'holy', and asked her where we were supposed to urinate and defecate, instead of asking where is the bathroom. It was my consciousness that posed those words through as it was truly a 'dirty' and unreasonable' business. She walked like a duck across a pathway and showed me a toilet without a door and a shower which is completely open. Everyone has a threshold of tolerance. I tried to master my patience but wanted to tell how I feel. My anger was about to be translated into damn dirty filth before an insensitive and cunning human being who is holy superficially and dirty within oneself. 'Sister, you know what? Please do remove your fake profile from "Trip Advisor". We are not going to stay here and please do not lie to people anymore.' The whole vacation would have turned to a horror movie if we stayed in that holy hell. Maybe we were the first to come there or else we were just one among hundreds of others who faced the same reality once they reach here. The lady's duck walk turned to be a walk of an ostrich and ran to the church and came back with another sister. 'We cooked for you and you need to pay half of the price.' That was enough for me to pull the pin of the verbal grenade I was holding at the tip of my tongue. 'What do you say? Look at dirty place you showed us? This is completely different from what you have posted.' When encountering with the truth, some people's strength turns to be a weakness, that's where the guilt tries its last option of defending, transforming its outfit from wolf to sheep. Mop violence is a common phenomenon that lot of people worry about but 'Mop sympathy' becomes often the escape of the perpetrator. The lady started crying. I pulled 200 Malothis from my wallet and threw in the face of the so-called holy thing and got back to the taxi. 'We go back to Maseru and find a hotel,' I told the driver. They turned the religion to a business to such an extent it exceeded the limit of exploitation and abuse. If Jesus Christ was alive in this era where his teaching has been transformed into a path to hell, instead to paradise, he would either crucify himself or burn himself to death. With dominant negative thoughts and a frustrated mood, I was unable to realise that we had already reached Maseru; it was very late in the afternoon.

. 'Out the Roof of Africa', held in the Mountain Kingdom of Lesotho, is considered to be one of the absolute toughest off-road endurance events in the world, attracting the world's best extreme-endurance competitors to take on the challenge. In 2013, the event was scheduled during the last week of our stay; therefore, most of the hotels and guest houses became fully booked at least three months before the event. By that time, finding accommodation in Lesotho was nearly impossible. We went from one hotel to another, passing by more than twenty different places, but we were unable to find a single room in the whole city. I was already drained out from the encounter in Morija, at 'Our Lady's Lodge', I did not have a single drop of energy left, my only strength was my little sister who knew me from childhood. I left the rest in her hands. 'Do you have anyone known to you here?' As she had been in the region for more than two years, I asked her. 'Tracy's mother lives here, she is a Zimbabwean.' She rung her friend in Swaziland and things appeared to be hopeful. 'Drive back to Morija,' my sister told the driver. It was around seven in the evening and darkness was peeping behind the mountains while everything was about to shut down, we were on our way back to Morija with a piece of hope on someone's hand.

After another tiring two hours, we came back to Morija and, seeing the old lady, Patricia's mother, waiting for us near Morija National Museum, gave us consolation. We were happy to be accommodated in a comfortable and well-maintained house with a warm person as host who had a lot to talk about Zimbabwe which might be one of my next potential destinations. I remember one time my father told me that one can be desperate but not completely desperate because in this world still there are choices left for people to make. If someone says that there is no choice left, it is simply lack of willingness.

'After the obscurity, there should be a ray of light,' as it was proven to be true, we heard from the old lady that we were very near to almost all the attractions that we planned to see in Morija. Geography, wildlife, and history remained my leisure time readings since when I was a kid. My father had a small library at home, where there were books of different disciplines and a few books among them I used to read over and over again. The images are still vivid in my mind and the footnotes of each image I used to remember by heart, of the book about the dinosaurs. The little child of 7 did not have a clue of what was called a 'fossil', but the photos were exciting; the animals were like from another world. Once I asked my father whether there could be a possibility that they still live, at least a few of them, hidden in the Congo forest. He said they are declared as extinct. Then I watched *Jurassic Park* of Spielberg, then *Lost World*, though I was in my early adolescence, I invested a lot of my psychic energy in thinking of possibilities of what is considered prehistoric being merged into the modern time as a result of scientific misadventure. But my thoughts were never ever associated with either a dream or a probability of seeing a fossilised dinosaurs, though in many documentaries I watched I had seen scientists excavating fossils. After I saw the details about the fossils of the dinosaurs in Morija, the photos I had seen in the old books of my father's library, started to flash back like a panorama. 'I'm on the verge of seeing what the prehistoric beast had left of the modern age.' We first proceeded to the mountains to see the footprints of dinosaurs and planned to come to the National Museum of Morija where there were a lot of fossilised bones and many more details about the evidence on the existence of dinosaurs in the area which is called Lesotho today.

With a guide provided by the Morija Lodge, from where the hike is organised, we proceeded to the mountains on Basotho ponies once again. As per the guide, pony back is safer than going on foot. And I was looking at the peak of a rocky mountain that was almost touching the skies, where the guide told, 'Over there, the footprints are.' It was like another hair-raising adventure, I felt a moment that adrenaline and cortisol ruled my whole life. One time, the back legs of my pony slipped around one foot or probably bit more, and I just closed my eyes while gripping the saddle like a hydraulic wrench. A cluster of houses in a village was visible as a little mirror down in the valley, probably a few hundred metres below that no one would dare to look at twice. 'Here we have to get down from the ponies.' It was our guide. We left the ponies in a small flat terrain on the hill and walked to a rocky area. 'Here are the footprints.' He sounded like a teacher. I wondered how the hell had those beasts come to this point. As I'm neither a geologist not an archaeologist, I decided not to become conclusive at this point and to find out the most proximate and reasonable assumptions that the research scientists have made for all these puzzles that are created by this small print of a prehistoric beast. I was unable to believe my eyes that I was on a place, presently a piece of rock, once either a marshy land, just soil or burning lava, where a dinosaur had walked. The imagination of prehistoric time merging into present modernity just invaded my mind as if I was with all sorts of strange beasts, some were in the waters, as huge as rocks; some were flying; some carnivores chase vigorously after their prey; the lowland which was in front of my very eyes looked like a game park of the Palaeozoic era. I allowed my imagination to dominate over the reality till our guide interrupted me, suggesting to go back as the gray clouds started to conquer the whole sky. Soon, there will be *Star Wars* in the theatre of sky instead *Jurassic Park*. When we reached 'Morija Lodge', it was already drizzling, and the fire show was almost about to start. We called our first-ever dinosaur trail complete. We headed to Morija National Museum under a heavy shower that was just a drizzle few minutes ago.

Morija National Archives was not what I really speculated; instead of a government authority that controls it, a white guy from Netherlands was in the room of the manager. My curiosity of external interference controlling the national assets of Africa was stimulated in many occasions in Lesotho, especially when it comes to water. But in this case, it was all about the heritage of a country and its history, which is undoubtedly the pathway to the future of a nation, owned not only by a private and external entity but also by just a single individual. As per him, the archives are better maintained and protected under a private entity. It could be true as well according to the level of corruption that occurs in government entities in Africa in general, and I felt that Lesotho cannot be an exception. However, the archives had been very well protected and organised as per record management standards, besides that, the staff were very well oriented in client-centred service delivery and equipped with knowledge. And they had their publication on diverse themes of Lesotho which were in truth resourceful documents where a tourist can learn about the history and prehistory of the country.

The first site of a dinosaur bone, which was almost the size of my whole leg, made me nearly accept that they had been really huge beasts, unlike today's world. The concept of cars in the modern days compared to older makes came to my life. During the Palaeozoic Era, there might have been enough space for these immense beasts to move around; unlike today, there were no cities, no vehicles, and in the real sense of the word, the whole world used to be theirs. Huge beasts who once reigned the world and enjoyed full freedom without human interference today has become a subject of study, and their right to dignified life after death is usurped by humankind today. Lesothosausrus, the species of dinosaurs found in Lesotho, is very small relative to the huge beasts like the Tyrannosaurus Rex or any other big species and believed to be herbivorous, but there exist an ambiguity about its classification and origin as it was originally considered an ornithopod. However, more recent work by Paul Sereno, a scientist, has suggested that it may actually represent one of the most primitive of all known ornithischian dinosaurs. The taxonomic history of Lesothosaurus is complex and it has long been confused with Fabrosaurs, another small ornithischian from the same locality. And in Lesotho, not only in Morija, fossils of prehistoric animals had been found. There are many dinosaur footprint locations, with sites at Subeng Stream and Tsikoane close to Leribe, Moyeni, Matsieng, and Mohale's Hoek where there were some other species of dinosaurs were found such as Massospondylus and Heterodontosaurus. I spent one or two hours with the fossils and the dummies of the Jurassic beasts of Lesotho, which was simply unexpected yet it was a moment in an obscure and unclear history that might not be repeated. While pursuing the dreams in darkness, the probability of encountering unexpected opportunities is high. I felt a silent current of happiness taking over the moment I looked at those glass boxes where the fossils were kept safe. I was already one of the lucky chaps on this earth who witnessed at least the remains of a family member related to the beasts on the photos of the old book that I read when I was seven, and the beasts I saw in *Jurassic Park* and *Lost World*.

'The present Lesotho, then called Basutoland, emerged as a single polity under King Moshoeshoe I in 1822. Moshoeshoe, a son of Mokhachane, a minor chief of the Bakoteli lineage, formed his own clan and became a chief around 1804. Between 1821 and 1823, he and his followers settled at the Butha-Buthe Mountain, joining with former adversaries in resistance against the Lifaqane associated with the reign of Shaka Zulu, today a region in South Africa, from 1818 to 1820.

Subsequent evolution of the state hinged on conflicts between British and Dutch colonists leaving the Cape Colony following its seizure from the French-allied Dutch by the British in 1795, and subsequently associated with the Orange River Sovereignty and subsequent Orange Free State and today Free State in South Africa. Missionaries invited by Moshoeshoe I, Thomas Arbousset, Eugène Casalis, and Constant Gosselin from the Paris Evangelical Missionary Society, placed at Morija, developed orthography and printed works in the Sesotho language between 1837 and 1855. Casalis, acting as translator and providing advice on foreign affairs, helped to set up diplomatic channels and acquire guns for use against the encroaching Europeans and the Griqua people.' All these guns and other traditional weapons used during those defending efforts of Basutoland are carefully preserved in National Museum of Morija, and I kept on listening to the lady who was briefing me the history.

'Trekboers from the Cape Colony showed up on the western borders of Basutoland and claimed land rights, beginning with Jan de Winnaar, who settled in the Matlakeng area in May–June 1838. As more Boers were moving into the area they tried to colonize the land between the two rivers, even north of the Caledon, claiming that it had been abandoned by the Sotho people. Moshoeshoe subsequently signed a treaty with the British governor of the Cape Colony, Sir George Thomas Napier, that annexed the Orange River Sovereignty that many Boers had settled. These outraged Boers were suppressed in a brief skirmish in 1848. In 1851, a British force was defeated by the Basotho army at Kolonyama, touching off an embarrassing war for the British. After repulsing another British attack in 1852, Moshoeshoe sent an appeal to the British commander that settled the dispute diplomatically then defeated the Batlokoa in 1853.

In 1854, the British pulled out of the region, and in 1858, Moshoeshoe fought a series of wars with the Boers in the Free State–Basotho War, losing a great portion of the western lowlands. The last war in 1867 ended when Moshoeshoe appealed to Queen Victoria, who agreed to make

Basutoland a British protectorate in 1868. In 1869, the British signed a treaty at Aliwal North with the Boers that defined the boundaries of Basutoland, and later Lesotho, which by ceding the western territories effectively reduced Moshoeshoe's kingdom to half its previous size.

Following the session in 1869, the British initially transferred functions from Moshoeshoe's capital in Thaba Bosiu to a police camp on the northwest border, Maseru, until administration of Basutoland was transferred to the Cape Colony in 1871. Moshoeshoe died on 11 March 1870, marking the end of the traditional era and the beginning of the colonial era, and was buried at Thaba Bosiu. During their rule between 1871 and 1884, Basutoland was treated similarly to territories that had been forcefully annexed, much to the chagrin of the Basotho. This led to the Gun War in 1881.In 1884, Basutoland restored its status as a protectorate, with Maseru again its capital, but remained under direct rule by a governor, though effective internal power was wielded by traditional chiefs.' After a long story about the prestigious history of Lesotho, at the museum, by very competent local historians, we said bye bye to the museum and headed back.

The late afternoon we had some free time left after the visit to the museum. The mum of my sister's friend was quite a heavy woman but she was very active at her late sixties. She lived with her grandson who was schooling in Lesotho. 'Let's have a walk around the village,' she suggested. Crossing little gardens, farms, we arrived to an old church. 'Here we can go down and buy some groceries,' the old lady sounded like a professional guide. We went down to the shop and the presence of a Chinese girl in the middle of nowhere in a black village, not even a town, rather shocked than surprised me. Morija is not even a big town, and where we stayed was far interior, going to a Chinese shop where the shop manager does not even speak English properly is something beyond a common thing. I was wondering what really these Chinese sell to the villagers. To my amazement, I found one of my favourites in childhood that we used to taste during intervals in school: water ice packets. The first time ever in my life I bought a packet of water ice in Africa, the cleanliness of the environment in Morija along with my craving for water ice persuaded me to buy it even though I had not bought any food that had any possibility of contamination. We felt safe and relax. We sat on both sides of an archway a few metres away from the shop and enjoyed the conversation with the old lady while tasting the water ice, as we used to do in Sri Lanka with school friends while we were on the way back home from school. Habits never leave you even though you try to leave them. After a couple of hours on the archway in villagers style, we left for accommodation as we plan to pay a visit at the palace of King Letsie III, the king of present time in Lesotho. Letsie III (born David Mohato Bereng Seeiso, 17 July 1963) is the reigning king of Lesotho. The palace was pretty close to the place where we stayed, and the old lady who hosted us had some contacts in the royal palace. But unfortunately, we were unable to go in as we were already late when we reached there. From outside, unlike a royal palace, it looked like a house of a moderately rich man, despite the fancy fence with the national symbol of Lesotho 'Besutho Hat', which is unique to the country.

Unlike the monarchy in Swaziland, he is a constitutional monarch, most of King Letsie's duties as monarch of Lesotho are ceremonial. He succeeded his father, Moshoeshoe II, when the latter was forced into exile in 1990. His father was briefly restored in 1995 but soon died in a car crash in early 1996, and Letsie became king again. Hence, it is reasonable that there is not much absolutism and corruption centred in the traditional yet ceremonial head of state. After our visit to the Royal palace, we said bye bye to Morija as one of the most exciting journeys to see the live evidence of Lesotho's cannibal history was awaiting for us at Ha Kome.

Passing Teya-Teyaneng, another Basotho township, we turned into an interior road that looked quite abandoned to go to Ha Kome where there is a remarkable village where cave dwellings have been carved out under towering rocks. The families still living there today are descendants of the original people who 'built' the caves in the nineteenth century and the site is now a National Heritage Site. The people living there now still live much as their forefathers did almost two centuries ago and those who have occupied the caves over the years have left a rich cultural history. We first reached the Kome Visitors Information Centre, we were given a guided tour of the caves and I pulled out my DSLR as we went there on foot and took some shots, framing the same photos I had seen in the articles as well as in the television program back in Sri Lanka. It was a moment of accomplishment. A few cave houses are intact, grace to the preservation efforts for tourism purposes. The caves have been partitioned using clay and pieces of rocks, and plastered with clay mixed with ashes, the doorway looked unique to 'Come caves', as per the guide, the blood taken from ox is mixed with clay to paint the frames of the doorway. The orange colour of the doorway is composed of ox blood and clay.

Gruesomely, this area was once home to cannibals and past generations of Basotho fled to the caves to hide from them. And the guide added, 'When cannibals caught someone from the cave dwellers, they hang the clothes of those who had been caught to signal that they were in hands of cannibals and would never return. Some believe that the ancestors of the Kome dwellers, too, were cannibals at one point; however, the very first photo with the descendants of cannibals was taken by my sister, dated 17 November 2013. My father had never thought that his son would go to meet the cannibals in Africa. But time had already taken him to the history, just like the stories of cannibals in Ha Kome, he would not see my photo in Kome. History is full of memories, some are faded, some are fading, some will fade, and few of the wil be retained like the fossils in Morija, while the present is on its way to become history in the future, through the same process, and I questioned why people say "History repeats".'

As the last leg of the tour, after sixteen days, we returned to Maseru, just to spend some hours before the departure, in the modernity that Maseru could offer us, but I was sure that nothing serene like in the Basotho villages was waiting for us in one of the most dense cities in Africa. Restaurants like 'Ocean Basket', shopping centres like 'Pick and Pay', or any other South African entities that I had already experienced during the visit in Swaziland and South Africa were not in my list. My mind was searching for something, just like a Bluetooth device. There was a mental signal that something was lacking before I leave this country. The famous Basotho blanket and a Basotho hat were icons of this little nation, this little kingdom, the kingdom of clouds, without which I would not be ready to board on a flight to Johannesburg. Hearing my conversation with my sister about buying traditional Basotho handicrafts, my driver suggested to go to 'The Basotho Hat', a shop located in the commercial city centre, looks like a typical Basotho hat in design, where one would find almost every single fine handicraft made in Lesotho, ranging from

Batiks, Basotho hats, Basotho blankets, scarves made out of sheep fur, and many more. A skilled nation lives in isolation with its resources unknown to the external world, yet silently cater to the endless demands of water of neighbouring South Africa. I did my last buy with Malothis, a Basotho Hat and a Basotho blanket that will be presented to my mother upon my return to Sri Lanka.

Chapter 13

CHARM OF WILDERNESS

At 22.30H ON A hopeful Sunday evening, I was on board in a jet airliner of South African Airlines; my final destination according to the ticket was Johannesburg, where I had been several times in transit during my visit to Swaziland and Lesotho, but even I was not sure about my final destination this time except I had hotel bookings in Grand Kruger Lodge in Kruger National Park in South Africa, Zimbabwe, and in Masai Lodge in Kenya, visa for each country on my passport, eighteen days of approved leave from the office in addition to a boiling desire that had been cooling, boiling, cooling down, and reboiling over and over again like a teapot on a roadside teashop, to see the wildlife of Africa in renowned savannahs which I had been watching over and over again on Discovery and National Geographic channels. Swaziland had already quenched some of my irresistible desire of seeing a live zebra, which was, as an experience from my childhood, a wooden toy being seen alive after three decades, but the frontiers of dreams about the 'Wild Africa' were certainly beyond the horizons of what the 'Kingdom of Polygamy' could offer me.

From after almost six hours of constant yet smooth flight, I arrived to Johannesburg where as a UN staff, life can be easier with immigration officers who change like weather, and as predicted, I was able to transit to the domestic channel to take a flight to Nelsprit to get to Kruger where I planned to stay five days with my sister who was celebrating her birthday. She had already confirmed her arrival to lodge which gave me sort of a reassurance as she had decided to come by road, which was around a four-hour trip on Southern African highways where mortal accidents are common. By twelve in the afternoon, I was able to reach Marlot Park, a fenced wildlife sanctuary which is bordering to Kruger National Park. Then after going up and down in gravel road within the park, where there are more than a dozen of game lodges, my driver was able to locate 'Grand Kruger Lodge'. After a quick light lunch, we were provided with a 'game watching schedule' that included a bush walk, an eight-hour game drive, walk along the crocodile bridge, and a night game drive which was quite a loaded package for a vacation, but the thrilling experience anticipated overrode my second thoughts when I remembered the scenes from National Geographic and Discovery that I had watched with infinite enthusiasm, realising that such a charm exists in the African wild.

The long awaiting moment for decades arrived next day early morning. We left the lodge by five, in a Safari jeep, partially open, with thick blankets wrapped around us, yet the cold wind pierced through the blanket and hit the bones, and the fog was thick like a white cloth hung before us. Over the acacia trees, behind the thick fog, a silhouette which was familiar started to be caught by the strong halogen beams of the anti-fog lights, a giraffe, then the sound was followed by a third started appearing just a few yards from the jeep, a fantasy was coming true in front of my very eyes; it was a moment of something inexplicable beyond just joy.

I never had a desire to go to the zoo and see animals; when I was small, I felt sorry to see caged animals. Later on, as an adolescent, I reasoned why I hated it as keeping wild animals caged and kept for exhibition is depriving their freedom, lifestyle, health, and finally, their right to life. I had read the stories of orang-utans in Colombo zoo that died eating food with polythene packs thrown by a visitor. Today, as an adult, I without a doubt stand for animal rights and always preferred to observe wild animals in their natural habitats while their behaviour remains natural with minimal human interference. Most of the time, when I had time, especially during vacations, after August and December as April vacation in Sri Lanka keeps us busy with New Year's festival, I used to go to bushy areas near by the little town where we lived, with an old binocular of one of my friends. Hiding behind the trees, we used to observe the birds and little reptiles. Later on, collecting pocket money given my father, not more than seven cents US$ a day, over a time of a few months I was able to buy my own binocular that got lost in school after three years; that day I felt as if I got blind and put a temporary stop to my bush walks and probably lost enthusiasm in it after the experience of loss. In 2005, when I was transiting in Dubai International Air-hub, I noticed a Nikon binocular that did not allow me to pass without buying it. 'It's got your name on it,' the Filipino who was the shop assistant told me, probably having seen the way I was admiring it while it was in the showcase. I pulled my credit card and walked to the counter. I felt like a gulp of cold water went through my thoughts after a long walk in the desert, though one side of mine was repetitively in denial of what I did. 'It was too expensive, you could have done many more things for $900,' I heard from my other side. And later on, I developed a passion for wildlife photography and went for a Nikon DSLR camera and a set of different lenses including telescopic, wide range, and fish eye. The day I bought my camera, a thought came to my mind: what if I do an exhibition of African wildlife. Later on, the little thought grew up into a dream. I took my first shot of a giraffe, a silhouette of its long neck and head over the top of shades of trees, in the background of the sky that was slightly lighted by early morning sunrays.

As we were crossing the bridge of Crocodile River, my eyes caught the second member of the African big five, a wild buffalo, with its curved horns and the upper head covered with the base of the horn like a shield that protects its head, which is a completely different feature compared with the Asian water buffalo that I had been seeing throughout of my life in Sri Lanka. I wanted to get a close shot even though the Cape buffalo is well known for its aggression towards any living thing that it encounters, especially towards humans. The guide did not show any positivity to my request: 'It is at your own risk but please do not go very close, it can charge at any moment,' he advised me. I was able to take just a one shot and the beast, hearing the clicking sound of the camera, raised its head abruptly and started to dig the ground furiously, coiling his tail like a whip, and I moved back soon to the vehicle as I did not want the wild beast make its next move. Just at entry point, I already felt the dreadfulness of a ferocious Cape buffalo that the Dutch and British took glory and pride in hunting down. My old notebook had accompanied me in an outer pocket of my backpack, all the way to Kruger, as it did in every single mile I made in quest of the footsteps of free-time stories, which remained hidden for decades under the dust of time and locked in the cell of nonaffluence. There was a piece of a magazine, just a piece of small paper carelessly torn out and fixed with natural glue that most of us use in Sri Lanka, gum of cashew tree, which remained attached to the book for more than eighteen years, 'African Big Five', a prestigious Cape buffalo with its crown-like horns was just under the heading. I showed the beast to my sister and said, 'Three more left.'

I was at a honeymoon stage of an illusion induced by sites of two out of the big five in less than ten minutes after we entered the game park, but as we moved on, I came to realise that seeing everyone in the big five family in one day is seldom. We moved up and down the roads inside the park for more than four hours, but we were unable to see a single lion, rhino, or an elephant, despite the kudus, impalas, wildebeests, waterbucks, klipspringers, and warthogs, which are very common in the south-western part of the savannah that spreads to the horizon. The sound of an areca nut cutter dragged my attention from a family of warthogs massacring the grassland in their funny feeding position that reminded me a group of people worshiping a Buddhist monk. I noticed a bird that I assumed to be a turkey, but in an instant, the huge beak made a quick association with my recollection of a southern ground hornbill. I have no regret about the binocular that I bought. As we still had the hope of seeing the rest of the big five, we started to go and wait in potential hunting grounds of lions. Grace to the binocular, I was able to notice brown feline ears, just erected above the grass level which was almost impossible to notice with one's bare eyes. It had been well camouflaged under the cover of high brown grass. Though at a distance, being able to observe the behaviour of a beast that I was dreaming so much to see in reality in its native and natural habitat was a pleasure; I felt human, a civilized human within me while enjoying the way the lioness was enjoying its hunt and I felt dignified and distinct from those who could enjoy a site of a caged animal deprived from its natural habitat and lifestyle, aggressive because of suppression or lethargic because of drugs, shown as a second citizen of the world or a slave. Though I thought she was alone, next to the hunt which was clearly visible via the binocular, a wildebeest opened in the belly as always in hunts of lions, a male was lying down. I cannot recall how long I stayed there as I was spellbound by the scenic beauty of rather the freedom of a wild beast than freedom in the wild. A 'go-away bird' just landed like a paratrooper to the grassland just few metres from me, crossing my telescopic view, dragging my attention to its funny outlook than its beauty. Having lost my focus for an instant from the lions, I was unable to locate them again, they must have found a happier place to rest after a good healthy meal, away from human eyes, into the shade of nature where rules of nature reign, which are threatened by the rule of humans.

In the next couple of hours, we were just stranding to locate a cheetah or an elephant, we had already given up the hopes of seeing rhinos and hippos as we had already crossed the time boundary of seeing them. When every single hope was being melted by the sun that just started to sink behind us, a triple of tuskers appeared from nowhere to our surprise. I remember that my father used to say that one can be desperate or hopeless but no one can be completely desperate or completely hopeless. As I had heard, it was not the aggressive triple of parents and the cub but well-grown adult triple enjoying mouthfuls of acacia as if they were bothered about nothing on earth. As I had already learnt a good lesson from the Cape buffalo, I tried my best to take the maximum use of my telescopic lenses, even though I did not have theoretic knowledge as a professional photographer, I was able to take some close shots which were fairly beyond the average, while my heart was pounding like a rice mill. The giant tusker of Amarula bottle was before my very eyes for a while, indifferent to my repetitive clicks of the DSLR, it slowly walked away to join the rest of the herd.

In Sri Lanka, a country where there is a significant population of Asian elephants, seeing an elephant is not something that takes me to 'Ceptieme ciel', but an African tusker, significantly different from the

Asian elephant, with palmyra leaf-like big ears and relatively brownish and bigger structure along with its tougher skin like a the skin of a Banyan tree, reminded me how hard my father tried to explain when I was asking why African elephants are different from Asian ones, 'So do people,' he replied. Even though I later on discovered the reasons, it was an amazement to see the difference with my very own eyes in real time, but the tuskers did not want to be examined for a long time, they just allowed me to see the diversity of their species as if they are scared of showing that everyone among them has a pair of tusks, unlike their Asian siblings. I felt if every single Asian elephant was a tusker, by this time they would have been added to archaeological and history literature, just like the mammoth. Elephant poaching is not unique to Asia, but with rareness of tuskers, protecting a tusker in Asian wilds can me more challenging than protecting a newborn deer cub from hungry hyenas. In Africa, during the colonial time, just like what happened in Asia during British rule, the elephants were hunted for prestige and a hunted tusker was considered as an act of royalty or bravery and later on transformed to a business engaging the local population of Asia and Africa, because of the high value paid for the tusks. Today, elephants are endangered especially in Asia, but the African elephant is also reaching the red line faster than ever. Probably, our next generations would read about those incredible giants as we are reading about the dinosaurs today; I felt I was lucky to see them alive, ashamed of having been born in a time of the destructive generation of human beings but at the same time proud of those who fight against poaching animals in the wild, even though they are the minority who have left with verbal and written weapons to fight with automatic or semi-automatic rifles.

It was one of the deserted days in Kruger, even though I was able to see four out of the big five, a great proportion of Kruger's animals and birds, including the first-ever ostrich I had ever seen in my life, but I was unable to see the liveliness of the grand game park during the daytime safari. A night-time, the safari was waiting for us for few hours' time and I remained hopeful even though the focus was on nocturnal life in Kruger. We have spotted a hyena den as most of the time hyena comes out in the dark, and we missed a lot of the diurnal life in Kruger. By 19.00 h, our jeep was parked near the hidden den we spotted in the morning, and

I heard my heart beating with impatience. It was not a long time after we arrived that we started hearing a hyena's giggling 'laugh' which was something unique to hyenas to experience on a dark night in the bush. All of a sudden, two little shiny little stars appeared out of the den, moved few steps forward, and disappeared back into the den. It was a grown-up hyena. The full-moon was our guide and I noticed the dots of its skin very well, probably it must have seen us, that was the reason why it changed its path and went back to the den rather for protecting the kids than for its own safety.

There was a program about the animals that had been extinct on earth on Discovery Channel in the late Nineties; I was a teenager and had a keen interest in prehistoric and mythical animals. The Tasmanian tiger was one of my pursuits. I was trying to find out more and more about such animals that look like hybrids, and as a result, I became familiar with the hyena, which shares hybrid features of a dog and a wild cat and I used to read literature on them and observe the opportunistic and aggressive behaviour of this strange animal, which is a universal symbol of the supernatural and an eternal enemy of the superpower of the savannah, the lion. Actually, these two beasts are archenemies. Each will attack and kill the other's cubs or elderly or sick individuals given the slightest opportunity. Seeing a hyena was a dream which remained thousands of miles from me; I did not see the distance getting shorter for decades and all of a sudden a site of this scavenger, despite that it was just a second, was like winning a lottery in an unexpected moment.

The hyena is considered as a symbol of witchcraft and trafficked body parts are sold in fetish markets for super high prices, especially in Benin and Togo. In southern Africa, the hyena is often portrayed as the deliverer of a Sangoma's evil spells, and its body parts command a premium price in the local Muthi markets, pushing this ruthless, bloodthirsty, dirty, and extremely opportunistic predator to be another victim of human beings.

The wild had already become a playground for nocturnal wildlife. All of a sudden, a groaning sound shook the whole area, hindering all different sounds of animals and birds and a silence of less than a few seconds made me a bit alert of danger. I asked the guide in a whispering tone, 'Is it nearby?' instead of asking which animal was that? 'A lion, a male, should be a few hundred metres away,' the guide assured but still believed it was not going to reach us. The fear itself was a constant part of night safari as the wild animals see clearer than us, more sensitive to the wild than strangers, and they feel more confident in their skills at night than in the daytime. Again, the groaning was heard, closer and louder than the last time, which really made me sweat. 'Don't you think it's coming towards us?' My question made them laugh, and he replied with reassurance that it was the wind that made the groaning heard closer. The rational part of me was in accord with the experienced guide who had been doing his job in Kruger for more than twenty-five years whereas my emotional side had already been pumping adrenaline into my bloodstream, making me restless. A mongoose broke the silence running out of a bush and crossed the road, as if to make me forget about the lion. The cold night breeze is not just cold and full of fragrances of nocturne flora but also carries messages to animals, vocally and sensorially, an odour of a prey to a predator, the presence of a waiting predator to a prey, locate a date and locate the food, the wild breeze has its contribution. As a very well-experienced guide, Bongani was once able to tell us not only the presence of an elephant in the bush but also its distance from our jeep, which was proven to be true when I noticed giant bat-like ears moving under the pale moonlight. 'Who who who who where are you?' a persistent call for a mate, from an African wood owl, started being answered; they kept on engaging in duets throughout. By time to time, an echo of a wail started dominating over the duets of wood owls, Verreaux's eagle-owl, the centre of superstition as a messenger of death, was calling in total isolation, converting the whole night safari into a scene from a Halloween movie.

We started moving a bit along a small pathway into the grasslands because our guide anticipated a potential scene as we started hearing a few fast whoops, which is for sure a spotted hyena confronting a lion or another hyena, either for a prey or for mating. As we advanced, the strong head beams caught scavengers in action. The first time ever I was able to capture a scene very often telecasted in Discovery Channel that I never forget, a small party of spotted hyenas had almost captured a hunt from a Lion, which was already being chased away. The carcass of a wildebeest had been already cleaned till the rib-box and still the hyenas were defending what they looted. It seemed they were not afraid of the presence of our jeep with halogen beams; they kept on making mockery faces at each other while whooping and fighting for the last bit of flesh attached to the ribs before starting to eat the bones. It was my first encounter with a real-time game in a wild that I had only seen on TV, a moment of eustress and discovery. I felt that the world is more charming than what we think of, the charm of the wilderness is the ultimate gift of nature, which humans are already too late to realise. I thanked my father for encouragements and his words deposited in me in the form of fantasies, which took me a long way, upon hurdles and avoiding snares while facing enormous challenges in many occasions. At the same time, a sharp sadness pierced through my heart that I would not be able to tell him my experiences while I was following the footages of his stories. As in the wild, life is a cycle, a struggle of survival when one member of the herd is hunted by hungry lions, a time of sorrow comes which is diluted by the fact that the herd has to move on, otherwise another easy meal will cost a life or many lives, cherishing the memories left with loved ones as the earth has no objections for bearing the weight of the bones left by hyenas, vultures, and foxes.

'We are going to go back.' It was our guide. I was at a stage of high expectations being unable to realise that it was not possible to experience all what is shown in a documentary in one day, as documentaries are usually a product of hundreds of clips taken in a length of a couple of months or years, connected chronologically together and presented as an ongoing event. The most unpleasant thing I heard that evening was 'we are going back'; I felt my inner-self reacting as a preschool child who is being forcefully pulled out from a toyshop. 'Kruger did not give enough,' I thought, but it will never be enough. I knew it. As long as one is not satisfied with something, there will always be something else to pursue, till the desired satisfaction is achieved, one will switch from one thing to another and give some goals for life.

In a weekend newspaper called *Silumina*, there used to be an article published every week on the thrilling incidents that a wildlife professional, a retired forest officer of Sri Lanka, had faced during the thirty years of time he held office in different wildlife reserves in the island. 'Mahawanaya Mada,' meaning in the middle of the forest, an article I did not miss. I might have had a rather deep passion to wildlife deposited in my subconscious than just an unconscious liking for the thrilling sensations generated by the incidents. And today as an adult, I strongly believe that despite that passion, nothing would take me here even though the thousands of miles journey seemed not being able to fill the gaps of my imaginary picture of African wild that I was visualising for decades. I decided to change my ticket and reroute it to Kenya.

Two days later, I was on transit in O. R. Tambo International Airport in Johannesburg to go to Kenya with high expectations about Masai Mara. As the transit time was almost seven hours, I did not forget to enjoy a well-done T-bone steak that I ever loved at one of the in-house restaurants in O. R. Tombo and started surfing in the Duty Free zone looking for some souvenir and a book to read. *A Long Way to Freedom* written by Nelson Mandela, even-though it was quite a thick book, I decided to go for it as Mandela was one of the political figures I respected a lot, not only in Africa but also in the entire world. It could be the fact that his nonviolence initiatives though he had to fight later on and to me he was the only African leader who fought for freedom of both oppressor and oppressed whereas his contemporaries such as Robert Mugabe, Julius Nyerere, Kwame Nkuruma, Jummo-Kenyatta, and Patries Lumumba were fighting for black man's freedom against white man, in a quite aggressive approach, without realising the intercontinental interdependency of a forthcoming globalised one human civilisation, being a part of communist movement, unconsciously or consciously dragging many African countries into cold war that leads the way to many military coups and civil conflicts, making the countries insatiable politically and economically for several decades to go. The Democratic Republic of Congo and Zimbabwe are classic examples, whereas Kenya, Tanzania, and Ghana joined timely to non-allied movement which fuelled their economies and concreted the stability in many dimensions. However, all those are great leaders in their times, for their people, and for their territory. I grabbed the book and went to a vacant couch near the departure gate of my flight so that I would be at the safe side.

It was Nairobi that welcomed me to Africa four years ago, and this time, I was going to see Nairobi as a tourist. I was filled with an exciting feeling when the flight landed in Nairobi and the taxi was waiting for me for the transfer to Masai Lodge. I knew what I was expecting in Mara but

I did not have a clue what Mara would have for me in its store. However, I had time of three weeks for my leave days to be vented; therefore, I decided to stay till animal migration starts in fortnight.

It was my first time to get into a hot-air balloon and float in the air over a territory where there are sharp canine teeth and paws full of knife-like nails would grab you alive before you fall to the ground and die, in case something goes wrong in the balloon. I dared not imagine of a scenario where I would fall near a tusker who would trample me to a Chinese chilli paste and add salt by peeing on me. I clenched my teeth and closed my eyes till the balloon stabilised. It was like the experimental Bartolomeu de Gusmão's airship for me. First time ever in my life a trait of acrophobia came into surface; it was a normal response to a new experience associated with incertitude and a real danger. Anyone who loves the life would feel the same and it takes some time to adapt to new experience overcoming the fear. It was the same thing I felt when I was trying paragliding for the first time in Bali islands in Indonesia, and later on paragliding became one of my favourite activities in less than two weeks and I tried skydiving as a result of being able to break the fear barrier. I tried to recall those moments of life as a psychological preparation for the rest of the journey. 'The balloon is safe,' the Kenyan guide said with a tone of confidence.

The aerial view of Mara was just amazing, as amazing as an inbuilt wallpaper of a Mac Os, carefully selected by apple team that no other would do better. The grassland expands to infinity, with giant trees fragmented carelessly even though there are bushy areas, most probably acacia trees had occupied a proportionally a significant area as a food store for giraffes which break the monotony of the panoramic scene of savannah, with their colourful texture, and elephants which are rocks in the grass. The journey of survival had just begun; the most wonderful experience that one would be able to encounter in Masai Mara, probably the most joyful moment ever in one's life. Herds of wildebeests, uncountably numerous, like a Roman army, tirelessly marching giving the camouflage to topis and gazelles from the waiting predators for an easy meal. The zebras in hundreds are in a parade which looked like a funeral parade in the middle of the wild, with both black and white colours together as if they express their condolences to those which lost their lives during the migration due to the attack of wild predators as well as poachers in a multiculturally sensitive way. In sooth, a lot of Zebras become victims of predators along the way and way back of the annual migration from Serengeti to Masai Mara and at return. I wondered why animal rights and environmental activists scream until their vocal chords start bleeding in advocating the government, nongovernmental organization, communities, and the entire world in a larger picture to protect the wild life in African savannah whereas millions of animals still exist. It was such a continuous floor of migrant herds that one would definitely think that they are not endangered or at risk but they are certainly the livestock of the highly endangered predators like lions, leopards. However, I had read, seen, and heard in and through reliable sources that the story of wildlife in African wild is not so breathtaking like the picturesque and panoramic aerial view of animal migration from the hot-air balloon.

In Kruger, I was unable to see even a white rhino, though I managed to see a dozen of them in a rehabilitation centre on the way to Johannesburg from Nelsprit. I did not bother to see a black one as I was convinced that it would not be a possibility. In Masai mara, I was not lucky to see any of them from the air where a greater area can be covered with better visibility. Elephants would follow their path in the near future in case there would not be any strict measures to protect the wild. Nonetheless, a rare moment in real safari life, but a very common moment after being telecasted in many programs related to wildlife 'cheetah hunting antelopes', was caught by my eyes. Thought of an impala gripped by the sprinter in the big cat family, and it was like an advertisement, Cheetahs, I had been seen on television just jumped out of the screen and hunted an impala in the savannah. I was lost among real, unreal, and surreal worlds for an instant.

We reached the camp in the late afternoon. I was delighted to see the animal migration by my very eyes but I was not contented about not having been able to see the rhinos and lions at close distance and enough wild games. I had again a feeling of 'it's not going to be enough'. I told the guide to put my name in the manifest for the safari of the following day and the day after.

The following day at dawn, we were given predeparture briefing and linked with another group of tourists from different countries, most of them were Chinese, probably those who lived in Kenya as they spoke with the guide in quite acceptable Swahili. Unlike in South Africa, we were boarded to a Toyota High Ace minibus, with a opened Sunroofs with a polycarbonate canopy on the top, which was for sure unable to protect the passengers either from sun or from a potential attack of animals; however, with the provided resources, we started moving into Great Masai Mara, a place like nowhere else for African wildlife, a paradise for tourists, and occasionally for the poachers, but having seen the number of safari vehicles on the ground, I had a second thought whether it was any-longer a paradise for wild animals. The engine of the minibus came to life making a loud sound just like an old steam locomotive, everyone started laughing except the guide. It seemed that was a usual thing for him whereas we were worrying about a possible breakdown in the wild. A Chinese guy, turned towards the crowd and told in broken English 'Ask elephant push'. If I was not wrong, he meant that we would ask an elephant to push in case if it broke down in the wild. It should be an ideal scene for an old soviet cartoon but such a horrible nightmare in real life that I would not want to happen. As if everything is quite normal in the vehicle, we started moving into the wild.

I took my 400-mm telescopic lens and fixed my cam as I was expecting a moment when that would be useful, and took my backup camera which was also a Nikon but a pocket digital cam for close shots so that I would not miss anything that would pop up instantly. In less than five minutes, I made my best shot ever in African wilds 'A Neck Fight of Giraffes'. They were engaging in unique neck fight in the middle of the yellowish grassland, under the clear blue sky over Mara and only two of them for the whole horizon. It was rather like a game than a fight, like two wrestlers, harmless, and technical. This would definitely go to my dream exhibition, I thought. I felt that Masai Mara was where I should have come instead going to Kruger but Kruger too fed me with so much of positivity specially a sense of accomplishment that no monetary value could be given, therefore with no regrets, even though Kruger did not reveal all what she had in her hands, I enjoyed the experience.

Athkadhalihini is a mythical bird which is believed to be living in the Himalaya area in India, which is as large as to take two well-grown elephants by its paws and fly with them. That I heard from my grandmother when she was relating me a story about India. The old generation was full of myths but those stories were quite interesting and exciting to hear when you are a child. It was like an imaginary tour in an ancient Disneyland. 'Lions too kill elephants', it was her again, I could recall, when she was telling about the origin of Singhalese ethnicity which I belong to, thought to be having an ancestry from a lion. A mythical reference made to 'lion eating the brain of the elephant,' was widely used in South Asian folkloric literature, but it was just a literal allusion made for highlighting the ferociousness of the lion and its position in the wild 'King', 'the ultimate predator'. When I saw a party of lioness enjoying a decomposing carcass of an elephant, entering into its wide open belly as if it was a big cave, all those childhood folk stories came back to my mid. Slowly with patience our driver drove near them, few meters away from the carcass and lions, we stopped. The smell of the decomposing carcass of this gigantic animal made me feeling nauseous and in few minutes I started suffering from a severe headache. The lionesses seemed not disturbed either by our presence or the terrible smell, but the Hyenas which were trying to penetrate the front defence line of Lioness. Every now and then, one or two lionesses had to chaise the coalition of vultures and hyenas as if the lioness were like Macdow in *Macbeth* who was trying to defend his fortress against Malcolm who was advancing with integrated forces at the end of the day hyenas will conquer the carcass with or without flesh, and they would still eat it till it disappear. After a while, we left the lioness and the carcass, allowing the sky and the grassland to witness the destiny of carcass and I was more than pleased to evident the live games in the wild that I was dreaming to see. It was an incident of a documentary on discovery coming alive.

River Mara, few dozens of meters below the gravel path, flows down across the savanna, making a roaring noise like a hungry lion. There was mysteriousness hidden underneath the aggressive noisy waters in the river that made Mara river looked like a death trap. There used to be man-made canals around the ancient fortresses in Sri Lanka to prevent the enemy forces penetrate the defended area easily, there were stories that there had been hungry crocodiles and carnivorous species of fish in them. My first impression on Mara river was such and of cause I was well aware, under the brownish waters there was jaws of death hidden till the Sun rays heat up the earth, then they will come out and sunbath in rows like in a tourist resort with their wide scary jaws wide open pretending they are fast asleep. During the migration, nile crocodiles in Mara enjoy their annual food festival converting muddy water in to a blood stream.

A group of herd of impala's were drinking water at a far end. I focused my telescopic lens and noticed something that I did not expect. 'A dead hippo' A giant hippo carcass was being decomposed in the middle of the river as if there was no scavenger to feed on it. As we came closer, the whole area was smelling like hell, the swollen colossal body would take at least few weeks to disappear from the site clearing up the air and the water and probably the crocs might finish it before it would ooze into running water.

Herds of Wildebeests and impalas had covered the horizon of the grassland, followed by anxious Cheetahs and Lioness, just like what I used to see in the TV programs. I was more anxious than the hungry Hyenas to see Cheetahs chaise an impala, I was waiting with pounding heart with short breath and just in a second the cats started to chaise an impala which was at the end of the hard, apparently a pregnant female, within seconds they made her isolated from the herd while the others were running for their life. Next moment was the moment of festivity for the Cheetahs while the innocent expecting mother is been caught between sharp feline canine teeth. When her last breath was released while being eaten alive by hungry cats, another unborn life became a soft meal for cheetahs or probably for hyenas which were ready to invade the hunt already, even before seeing a single ray of African sun. That was the most exciting wildlife game I had ever witnessed even-though my excitement turned into sadness seeing how cheetahs were tearing the impala into pieces but it is the nature, its rule and its creations. We human beings do not have control over that, it was just one single incident among hundreds of those which happen in the wild a day. We moved on, and I felt relieved as I wanted to move from the site, I did not want to witness a faetus coming out and an unborn is being eaten. For the first time an urge of leaving the wild came to my mind. Even though I was longing to see a Cheetahs in action in the wild, the fact that witnessing a kill, specially of a harmless life, was painful.

A herd of tuskers took us out of the negativity induced, having seen a bloody hunt. I took a deep breath and zoomed my camera and captured a few shots of the tuskers, they were really the pride of Africa. Beyond the limit of the naked eye, a cluster of vultures occupied a tree top, which was clear communication of a carcass or a fresh hunt yet occupied by the predators. They were waiting for their time and probably the spotted hyenas might be making their witchy faces at the lions or cheetahs, while trying to encroach and grab the hunt. After over ten days in the wild in South Africa and Kenya I had developed some senses to assume the occurrences in the wild to some reasonable extent. I was unable to resist my mouth 'Waaw'. It was very seldom that once could notice a leopard with its hunt on a tree, the neighbouring three where the vultures had gathered, was a Leopard with a freshly killed impala. My previous guess was surprisingly wrong; the hunt was not on the ground. The wild is completely an unpredictable place, especially when you are not a part of it. We reached to a place where there was a piece of rock, a natural one where there were two letters 'T' and 'K', the guide got down from the vehicle and we followed him.

'T' is for Tanzania and 'K' is for Kenya,' he said.

'Now I'm keeping one foot in Kenyan soil and another on the Tanzanian' he smiled showing his rotten teeth which looked like a corroded hand shaw.

One Chinese tourist wanted to go to urinate and he started to move a bit towards Tanzanian territory while zipping off his trouser, the guide told him 'Stop you can't go, you need visa'. The joke made him react instantly without thinking and turned back with the unzipped trouser being the clown of the safari.

'We are now going to see a bit of Serengeti' guide added while going back to the vehicle.

I had heard about the tree-lions one time when my father was relating me a Sinhalese folk story about 'Cat-the teacher'.

'The cat thought the Tiger to climb the trees but he did not want to teach how to descend from the tree. As a result, the tiger was vexed and swore that if he would not be able to eat the cat, would eat at least the faeces of cat. That's why the cat hides it's faeces under the soil once it is done.'

'All the big cats are the same, despite lions in Tanzania,' he said.

When I saw four Lionesses were napping on a tree as if they were on vacations. Uninterrupted by presence of our noisy vehicle with bunch of people and dozens of camera flashers, they kept on napping even disregarding the impalas walking few meters close to the tree. Unlike human beings who kill for joy, recreation and prestige, animals kill only for hunger or in self-defence. They do not exhaust their livestock which is the only source for sustaining their lives, in that sense wild animals are more forethoughtful than human beings who are considered as civilized and developed but still seems not having any idea about his contribution of sustaining the life on earth. By this time, I had roamed in African wild from West to South and South to East but seeing a Rhino in its natural habitat remained still just a dream. We returned to the camp for getting ready for another adventure for two days. To discover the Masai Life, taste their way of life in their own way, I was planning to stay two nights in a Masai hut.

When I was flying with Kenyan Airways to Nairobi from Dubai, four and half years ago, the jumping tall figures in cardinal dresses with neck full of ornaments, handful of multicoloured bracelets and strange ear lobes stretched like the ones of Load Buddha appeared in the personal video screen gave me an impression of a group of comedians who try to imitate a traditional game that had existed hundreds of years ago. And the funny sounds that they made just made me laugh. But before I came to transit Nairobi, I had already learnt those were the people called Maasai that my father told, living in Southern Kenya and Northern Tanzania who drink blood of cows, dare to challenge the lion, and ultimately kill it with no gun or bow and arrow. I was imagining Hercules like people with muscular bodies, breaking the neck of lions, but when I saw the ultra-slim figures like the victims of famine in Somalia and Ethiopia in the Nineties. I instantly judged that my father was wrong.

'It was disinformation indeed', I thought.

'How can these skeletons kill a lion?' It was my monologue and reaffirmation to me but later on I realised that I was wrong.

Showing a wooden stick, quite heavy and strong, with a ball-like end which is really hard like a piece of rock and the other end is the grip. Apparently, the weight and the form of the stick are able to deliver a mortal strike on a human head for sure but I was not sure about a Lion head.

'This looks simple but it is a deadly weapon' our guide told showing the head of the stick which is round.

'And only Maasai are allowed to carry this in public in Kenya' He added.

'What was the basis of the ban or restriction?' I asked. I found it was kind of an irrational idea as it was just a piece of wood that is less harmful than a cricket bat which can be found anywhere in Nairobi even in hands of children.

'It is a heritage and a symbol of Maasai people, it is the traditional weapon of them, and it's not allowed for any other to use'.

I nodded as a gesture of understanding. It was a similar context like the indigenous population of Sri Lanka. 'Veddas' whose traditional weapon is a hand axe called 'Keteriya' which they use for hunting and they are allowed to take it anywhere in the country whereas the axe is considered as a weapon and no one else is allowed to take such sharp utensils to public places. Even when they come to TV interviews they come with 'Keteriya' on shoulder and in traditional attire which is just a piece of cloth which covers their genitals and buts. It was easy for me to comprehend the simple idea of protecting the traditional features that are marketable in modern context, which is behind permission granted by Kenyan legislation for Masai to carry their weapon in public and restricting it exclusively for them.

A circular fence, 'Ekang', built with thorny acacia, guarded the little village, 'Enkaji', which consisted of little huts apparently made out of timber poles and grass. I had a second thought of spending two nights in such an unsecured place in the middle of dangerous wild animals. No one is able to understand the eco-friendly yet and so sophisticated engineering skills of these semi-nomadic population, at a distance. When I entered the fence and got close to the huts, I noticed that there was obviously something concrete and rational behind this basic shelter. The guide started explaining the indigenous technology used to build a Maasai shelter.

'This Kajijik hut is completely made out of the locally available materials such as timber, grass, cattle dung, ash, and human urine'

I could not understand what was the role of human urine in the construction of Kajijik.

'Human urine?' It sounded rather astonishing than questioning but I wanted to know.

'In an environment where the water is treated as it should be, as the most precious resource left on earth, they use human urine for mixing the paste of grass, mud and ash to apply make Kajijik' The guide kept on explaining.

Mara becomes dry and lifeless and dry season, the vibrant game park transforms to a killing ground, a place where a drop of water becomes rarer than finding, a Dodo. The earth cracks as the Sun reigns the sky where clouds belong to the past, and the life begins to spill out. Most often, the nature turns to be so cruel and ruthless that until the last drop of water is evaporated, the rains would not fall. Instead of live animals the skeletons occupy the cracked earth where was the stronger survivors retain with hope of a drop of water, with dried eyes without even being able to cry for the dead. I thought that Masai people are very practical tribe who had pretty well adapted to the habitat.

'Kajijik' is usually made and renovated by the women.' He was pointing at some women who were already on the roofs, repairing them like men do in many parts of the world. During the discussion, I got to know that the roof is completely waterproof, cow dung is used for making it waterproof. With cattle being the major livestock of Maasai people, finding cow-dung is not a challenge, and unlike other tribes who are into partial agriculture who usually uses cow-dung as fertilizer, Masai people do not have such a need, hence they use it otherwise which is science and innovation which is not found in the book.

The Inkajijik are either star-shaped or circular as they were originally designed for semi-nomadic lifestyle even though the moments of Masai people are not encouraged now. The structure is made of timber poles found in the bush fixed directly into the ground and interwoven with a lattice of smaller branches, which is then plastered with a mix of mud, sticks, grass, cow dung, human urine, and ash. The size of the house is pretty small and low in height, around 150 cm, in which the Masai families do all their functions—cooking, eating, sleeping, storing stuff, etc. And within the fence, the cattle belong to each family where their main food comes from.

An existence of a tribe that eats beef, raw beef, drinks both milk and blood of the cow, looks mythical or an utopia Maasai do prevail in the wild, as a healthy tribe whose meal mostly consist of raw meat, blood, and milk of cattle, which is a reality in contemporary human existence on earth. Some would call them uncivilized, but if their food habits have been adopted in a healthier way than what we consume in luxurious restaurants in the cities. Some of our indicators of civilization might not be accurate.

It was an unnerving experience to see slaughtering of cattle early in the morning, especially when you are from a culture of nonviolence in which 'abstaining from killing' is one of the main five precepts that we observe every morning and evening. I was familiar with the bleating of goats and mooing of cows, calling to unknot their ropes every morning when I was small but slaughtering animals was not a part of our life at all. Rituals associated to blood or killing remained far away from our spiritual practices. It was my first morning; I was invited to draw blood from a cow. I hesitated first and then decided to go and see if it was something that I could see or not. First thing I wanted to check was whether the cow was going to be slaughtered. Maasai man who led me there said no. No it was clear that I was not going to witness a killing but still I was having a second thought of magnitude of suffering that the animal would go through.

'This arrow would do it, the animal will still be alive,' he showed an arrow with a sharp point with relatively round and wider head. I was still unable to believe the last part of his statement: 'the animal will still be alive'.

Few other tourists except the Chinese were there, carefully looking at the Maasai men who were tying the neck of the cow with a piece of cloth disregarding its struggle to run away. Two other men held the head immobile while another came with the arrow and bow, and started checking the neck of the beast for locating a vain. Another hurried from a Kajijik with a traditional bottle which was a dried melon shell or something pretty similar to it. The next second, when the man who was with the arrow and bow finished locating the vain, he stepped back and pulled the rope of bow and released the arrow.

'Tik' as if arrow hit a piece of wood, it emitted a sound and less than in a sound, just like from a broken faucet, blood started being plumbed out and the man with the bottle was collecting hot blood. The cow remained calm until a bottleful was collected. Almost two to three litres of blood, I was wondering whether the cow was going to survive. The next moment, they lose the belt piece of rope tightened around the neck and tied it tight right on the place where they made the hole. As if it was a routine activity cow stepped out and went out from the little opening of Ekang. I was still wondering whether the cow would survive or not and did not notice a Man was waiting for me with some blood to offer for me.

'You can stay the whole day without food,' he said. I was awakened in shock from my pensiveness and said 'No' quite loudly though it was not my intention.

The Masai man laughed aloud and a few others among them joined his laughter. And then a brave Chinese came to try the challenge. His face started to tell a story that his mouth was unable to tell. He took the bottle and took one gulp, his semi-open Mongolian eyes closed fully while others clapped and cheered him. After few seconds I saw my hair on hand slowly regaining their positions.

On my request, even-though our guide had concerns, I was allowed to join with four Masai men for one of the most exciting events that only a few outside the tribe might have had the opportunity to join. As we did not have a common language, our guide also joined us. He was a Kenyan who grew up in a village next to Mara, who knew in and out of the villages as much as Masais knew. With Masai men, we started walking into the savannah, their watchful eyes, like ones of eagles, were moving not only left and right but up and down hundred and eighty degrees, with each careful step they advance, which was a bit of difficult exercise for me. My heart started to pound like a base drum and I felt as if it was trying to come out breaking my ribs. They stopped all of a sudden, and signalled us to remain silent. They must have noticed something, I guessed. When I was not able to see the lions in proximate distance, I was not satisfied and I made my trip to Mara in order to make my experience complete. And what I saw astonished me and filled with a feeling on fear and happiness together. It was like a delicious fruit of a poisoned tree, I knew it was a clear danger but it was simply irresistible. A party of lionesses enjoying a hunt, a wild buffalo. Masais were watching like a gang of thieves, fearless but patient. I did not have a clue, but as we were asked to be silent, I was watching what was going to happen. The mild humming sound generated by the breeze blew across dry reeds made me breathless turning my blood into water. I thought it was Lion behind us. It was a moment dominated by intense fear, and I was looking at the Masai men moving slowly forward as if they were going to get a rabbit caught in a snare. My eyes were still and anticipating one among those hungry lions pouncing on those four men who were advancing to grab the hunt. Any animal can be extremely aggressive when they are disturbed while eating or having sex. For lions, being dominant predators by nature and being the most confident carnivore in the wild, the probability of charging was very high and in that case we all will be victims of wild cats. But as Maasai men were advancing with confidence, the lionesses started backing off, one by one, but one stopped and showed all its teeth and sit partially as if she was about to retreat. It was all about the confidence of those brave men, and they intimidated the ferocious lionesses in seconds. I was frozen, simply immobile. Masai people looked not disturbed with the stance of attack of the lioness, and by few other cat faces hidden behind the bushes, as they kept advancing the last heroine among the Lioness moved backwards, still looking at them. Once the Masai people reached the pray, the Lionesses were still looking at the way how the best meat out of their meal was being cut off, and they may have retreated. In a matter of a few seconds, the full back leg was on the shoulders of one Masai, and they started rushing back and in less than a minute they joined us with the best piece of the hunt.

'It was a thrilling robbery,' I told to the guide, 'more thrilling than a bank robbery as you steal in front of the eye of a killer.'

He smiled and said, 'Your life is the bet for the piece of meat you try to steal to feed your hungry children.'

'A slight mistake can result in everyone of us being a victim of a deadly attack, for them six of us is nothing, it is a matter of one being courageous enough to cross the borders and the rest will come for help,' The guide was explaining. I felt numbness in my whole body. It was such a great risk I took to witness a real-time robbery in the wild. Human scavengers in action were a bit weird but it was one of the passive ways of hunting by the Masai people, but it sometimes turns to be confrontational. In such situations, the Masai people usually give up. However, they are a brave and tactful bunch of people who possess a great level of stamina and skill to self-sustain in dry savannahs in East Africa.

We returned to Enkaji after almost one hour of walking through the reeds. Throughout the walk I felt as if I was walking in a minefield, every second was filled with anticipation of a wild animal jumping on me. I went into the Kajijik allocated for me just to have a rest for few minutes. When the hot sun burns down every little thing in the savannah, the interior of the Kajijik remains amazingly cool and moist. It is a masterpiece of eco-friendly and sophisticated engineering of the Masai people who coexisted with the tough climate in East African savannahs. I felt as I was in a heaven and had fallen asleep on the piece of mat, without my knowledge. When I heard the guide calling my name, I woke up and got to know that they did notice that I was fast asleep and did not want to be disturb.

'You were sleeping so sweet, and we felt sorry to disturb you, but these Masai traditional dances, you cannot miss them,' he said. My first flight to Africa came to my mind. The jumping tall mystic figures are going to be real, I thought.

'Eunoto' is the Masai name for the ceremony which is a significant life event for the young Masai warriors, like a passing out of a trained military regiment when they reach the proper age, which is actually not counted in years but measured by one's built as Masai people count the time by number of moons. The most iconic part of 'Eunoto' is 'Adumu, Aigus' which is the famous jumping dance of the Masai people. A circle is formed by the warriors, and one or two at a time will enter the centre to begin jumping while maintaining a narrow posture, never letting their heels touch the ground. Members of the group may raise the pitch of their voices based on the height of the jump. Everyone wants to be the best jumper and tries their best to go higher than the other which made the event looked rather like a competition than a traditional dance. I took my camera and focused from a ground level to capture a warrior going up as if he is up in the skies. The blue sky over Mara made my dream come true. A Masai warrior in bright red traditional attire appeared in the background of the blue sky, just the sky and the Masai warrior—one of the best shots

I had ever taken of humans in action and one among my best captures in Africa which will go to my dream exhibition one day.

While their sons, brothers, and spouses engage in the jumping dance, the ladies sing traditional songs in Maa to encourage the men. I felt, what a harmonious culture and supportive environment that we had already lost centuries ago when the concrete jungles started to appear in our habitat 'cities' where people are extremely individualistic and self-centred.

The festivity mood is radiated with the brightness of Masai ornaments, which were made from clay, shells, ivory, or bone. Black and blue beads were made from iron, charcoal, seeds, clay, or horn. Red beads came from seeds, woods, gourds, bone, ivory, copper, or brass. These bead works date back to hundreds of years, even before they came into contact with Europeans, and still remain not only just as ornaments but also as a strong feature of their traditions and outlook.

Modification of body from genital mutilation in both sexes, which remained a secret to the external world, to modification of ear lobes, which is open to outside, are vital customs of Masai life. Every single woman in Masai community goes through female genital mutilation and every man goes though male circumcision. I noticed a few boys wearing black dresses like sarongs, which I had never seen in any documentary about Masai and could not resist my temptation to ask from one of their leaders who is quite conversant in English.

'Why are boys in black?'

He replied, 'They are just after entering the adulthood.'

As he was not fluent enough to provide me with the descriptions I was longing for, I had to ask the same question from our guide.

'After the male circumcision, the boys wear black for some weeks,.' He was able to convince me.

'You will see not only circumcision but also Masai remove the canine teeth as well.'

I did not really take note on those tiny things but as many other African tribes, Masais do body modification as a ritual, and to be part of the society, everyone has to go through those cultural practices that are executed in the wild, hiding from the rest of world.

I saw a 'yoyo' in a hand of a Masai kid, which made me wonder whether it originated in the middle of the savannahs. I asked my guide to ask the lady with the child from where he got it.

'They had bought it from a toy seller'. He said with a suppressed laughter.

In the middle of the savannah, apparently Masais were amidst a struggle of their own. The devil of modernisation in the skin of the goat of civilisation had already started its journey across the dry grassland, caving out its way faster than the wild dry winds of Mara, demolishing the ecological and cultural sense of the place for this long-prevailed tribe. Day by day, maintaining the traditional pastoral lifestyle of Masais has become increasingly challenging due to the influence of the outside 'modern' world. The policies, laws, and regulations of modernising civilisation beyond the frontiers of the wild had already limited the rangelands of the Masai, imposing new changes in lifestyle that they had never been used to before. Today the reality is that Masais are not as traditional as what I saw in the Masai huts which were open for tourists. When I moved from the so-called Masai Kajijiks and the Enkaji, life in all dimensions was somewhat different.

'We never ate maize before.' It was the direct translation the old man told me while chewing roasted corn.

The semi-nomadic lifestyle has drastically changed and in the process of being transformed to an agricultural lifestyle that was not even in their nightmares decades ago. Especially in Tanzania, Masais have a new subgroup called 'displaced Masais'. To be displaced, they should be victims of either a manmade conflict or a natural disaster. A stylish technical jargon in humanitarian literature, the 'IDP' or 'Internally displaced population', caused by civil conflict or disasters, is reasonable, but a third category had not yet been recognised yet. It sounded like the Masais were IDPs because of forced migration due to the serious concerns of ecologists because of the impact on savannah rangelands and wildlife in East Africa, but still the poachers are free and many of those who make policies enjoy their piece from the poachers, whereas Masais do not have a word for 'bribe' in Maa.

That was my seventh day in Serengeti and Mara running up and down with a hope of making a 'once-in-a-lifetime' experience complete.

One part of me had already given up and the other part was still in denial that it would not be possible to quit the wild without making my journey complete. It was at the peak of the 'tug of war' of my positivity and negativity when I heard a strange whining sound that was heard also by the guide.

'Let's stop here,' he told in a whispering voice.

'It should be a white rhino cub, mother also should be around.' It was the most exciting news I ever heard after getting inside the African wild, from west to south and from south to east. This time, my heart started pounding with impatience, unlike last few times in the wild when I was palpitating at the verge of death.

'Usually they are not aggressive like the black rhino, but they do not like to be disturbed,' the guide was briefing in a very low voice is if he was telling me a secret.

Little pig-like ears started to show up over the bush, and within a second, the horns of the fifth member of the African big five appeared before our eyes. It was like a strip show, except that patience was not in my control and I was waiting with suppressed feelings covered with self-imposed patience till the Rhino uncovered herself. When a long-awaited scene was still demanding us to wait, it became annoying. I asked the guide to move the vehicle forward so that I would be able to see them behind the bush.

'You are going to miss this chance' he said.

'We will wait a bit and they will cross the road for sure,' he was confident.

Almost fifteen minutes after our conversation, the Jurassic-like head appeared out of the bush. The shape of the animal itself was strange, I felt. It looked like a conserved head of an animal from the Palaeozoic era. Even though I know from my whole consciousness that I was witnessing a live animal in the present time, in real life, I was unable to believe the compatibility of this gigantic beast with disproportional features into the present time. Following the mother, the cub appeared as the guide said and they crossed the road, taking their own time, calmly and indifferently. I felt again that we were aliens into the wild and our civilised society is not respected by these wild animals who are civilised in the eyes of nature. They stopped near another bush as if they were searching for their delicacies and ate a bit from every one of them and reserved some for tomorrow, unlike human beings who abuse the natural resources at his disposition. Wild animals, even though they had never been to school even for rain, they are very well oriented on utilising resources with moderation and leaving them for the future, the psychology of wild animals is amazingly preset in accordance with the philosophy of nature. Though the mother and the cub disappeared from my sight, they left so many thoughts in my mind. I heard a gunshot all of a sudden. The guide was silent and I was confused. They had already disappeared and should be safe, I thought.

'There is still a lot of illegal hunting going on, poachers are everywhere,' the guide said, breaking my pensiveness.

I was packing after my dinner on the last night in Kenya, thirty years ago, I heard, twenty years ago I read, and fifteen years ago I saw on television, along three decades of timeline I was seeing in dreams, all of what I saw in Wild Africa during the last four weeks. I was a dreamer, and when the dreams were translating to realities, the dreamer had become a wildlife photographer and a writer because of the hypnotic charm of the wilderness in the continent. And I felt, instead of rib-breaking palpitations provoked by the bush walks with Masai and while taking close shots of buffalos and elephants, a wildlife conservation activist was trying to erupt out of myself. It was the moment I heard about the assassination of Cecil, the lion in Hwange National Park, Zimbabwe, by an American recreational game hunter, Walter Palmer. For what I believe, every life is the same, irrespective of its form. Walter killed not only a father, a brother, and a husband but also deprived his own children's right to see the true beauty of world, as if the so-called civilised world is becoming ignorant or family ties and rules of nature and turning to be 'wild'.

Chapter 14

COLONIAL GOD

With the encounter with 'Muru' in my English textbook of grade 3, it was in 1986, I came to know a country called Nigeria.

'I am Muru, I'm from Nigeria.'

A little introductory phrase written under a photo of a black boy, with curly hair and heavy lips. I can recall that my English teacher gave a brief introduction of Nigeria.

'Nigeria is in Africa, they eat yam.'

Yam being a side dish for us, I was listening to her with surprise. That time, my little head was not ready to accommodate the idea that not everyone on this earth eats rice, though I had heard that white people eat bread. When Portuguese arrived in Sri Lanka, as a result of being caught by a storm, they had been eating bread and drinking tea, at the coast, which was interpreted by the spy men of King Rajasinghe as that they eat marble rock and drink blood. When one is not exposed to other cultures, it is natural that what is seen is interpreted via what is familiar to you. So, Muru eating yams instead rice sounded unbelievable.

Later on, being a student of English literature, I studied Chinua Achebe, Gabriel Okara, and a few other African Anglophone writers who were Nigerians. Oraka was one of my most favourite Nigerian writers and inspired me with his profound analytical ideas and concerns that he brought forward about sociocultural changes in postcolonial Nigeria. *Piano and Drums* is about the cultural conflicts in postcolonial Nigerian society, the culture acquired by the Westernised elites or in general Western influence, and traditional ancient indigenous Nigerian culture which is threatened. And the novel *Once Upon a Time* is like a guiding start for postcolonial Pan-Africanism. Not only world-renowned writers, orators, or politicians I had heard, read, or seen, but also most of the Nigerians that I had interacted with during my five years in Africa somehow managed to give me an impression that they were not easily accommodating the West and its influence on their lives. I tried my best to look behind the lens that I had been given by what I had already seen in Ghana about colonial times in Africa, without being judgmental and avoiding a probable prejudice, but crystal clearly, it was noticed that Nigerians in general were resistant to what comes from the West, irrespective of good or bad, and have an attitude of 'we know better' and 'your time is gone'. I felt it was an unconscious reaction of defence as a result of being threatened along with irrational ego developed with a postcolonial radical mindset.

One of my colleagues always used to say whenever he saw something related to Africa where there is a European or American involvement, 'White man is wicked, he wants Africa to be under him forever.' When he says that, his voice rises uncontrollably, his hands tremble without his knowledge, and he does not forget to add, 'His time is gone,' with a hysteric laughter of a demon. Contrary to his verbal outburst, he used to wear full suit like an English businessman and come to office, smoke cigarettes in Royal Navy style, and drink exclusively Scottish or Irish single-malt whiskey. Not only that, he was married to a British woman once upon a time and divorced with two kids left in England, then remarried to a Nigerian woman who was twenty years younger than him. He was in his full youth in his mind though he had already crossed late fifties, and use to go to church every Sunday, not just as a devotee, but as a pastor. I call him Sam, short form of his name 'Samuel', with whom I used to work in the same office building, on same floor, for the last five years.

Every day we cross paths a few times, and every single time, I heard some verses from Bible. Sometimes, he sings Gospel songs out loud, disturbing everyone in neighbouring offices, instead of using a civic sense to gauge whether what he does is right or wrong; in a diverse environment where everyone has to be respected, he used to take pride in singing 'Gospel' good news, messages from the God, to all of the others who had different faiths, and most of us found it simply ignorant and disrespectful. One rainy day in September, the rain was like an impenetrable curtain, and the way was like a river from heaven to hell, Sam was waiting to go home, near the security cabin, partially wet, when I was arriving to pick up my wife from the office. I stopped the vehicle and asked him to get in. He got in with a naive smile, shivering like a wet chicken, and said 'thank God!' I did not expect any thanks from him, but the perceptual set that he had created in everyone's head, along with what he said in that very moment he got in to the vehicle, set a wildfire-like impulse in me. But later on I realised that it was simply his inability to recognise the help extended by another human being, and he was absolutely blind with the divine lens that his colonial masters had left in their country. Samuel was just another person among millions of Africans who see the world through the ideology imposed once upon a time in history on their ancestors who used to have animalistic beliefs or, in other terms, tribal cults.

One Anne whom I met in the same organisation, from Kenya, a matured woman almost about the age of retirement, married with three children who also have their own separate families, turns into a Charismatic preacher whenever someone comes into her office for any official reason. Irrespective of what religion you belong to, you will verbally be baptised before you leave her office. 'God willing, her checkout will be processed soon.' I was following up the checkout process of one of my colleagues because someone in her office was sitting on the documents because of mere laziness and acquired habit of procrastination. In government-type entities, efficiency is merely a stylish word, and one click of a mouse could have solved the whole problem—there was nothing that needed God to descend from the heavens and interfere. I was stupefied thinking left and right to comprehend the spiritual mess that the woman created when there is a clear practical solution which is within reach of the hand.

Every single meeting of staff union of a widespread organization in Liberia, the president of the local staff association turns the whole meeting in to a service at a church, though 40 per cent of the staff are Muslims, and respecting diversity is one of the core values of the staff. When Samuel starts his hour-long preaching, almost a half of the association members fall fast asleep, adding a hymn of groaning to the prayers of his followers. Later on, everyone got to know that he works as a pastor in one among hundreds of churches in Liberia. One day, he approached my colleague and myself in the elevator, opened an old file with muddy papers that one would assume dating back to a few decades, his eyes looked like the ones of a fox that just killed a chicken in a village farm, his gestures seemed unaware of his already failing attempts of camouflaging his guilty consciousness, and told us, rather in a tone that it was an obligation of us than a kind request from us, to contribute in US$100 each to the humanitarian nongovernmental organisation that he had formed few years ago, aiming at rehabilitating the children who were victims of sexual and gender-based violence. 'It is an affiliated organisation to church as well,' he added. A few weeks later, he was found using office vehicles for personal usage and tried to claim that it was not for personal gain but for his organisation which had a divine motto. At the end of his God-given journey, he ended up finding himself being arrested using a good sum of money donated for his local NGO, for his personal use. Still he was praying to God to win his court case.

One Nigerian peacekeeper had been beaten by members of a remote community, by 22.00 h, on 12 May 2011; his weapon was missing during the mob. Apparently, the cause of the incident was that a Liberian woman had literally trapped him to get some money. Most of the evidence, even though they might not be true at all, stood against the peacekeeper, yet he was trying to justify his action, telling in God whom he trust that he paid her three notes. And the girl demands $100, screaming at him that he tried anal sex and raped her. To be clear, all that the lady was trying to say was that the guy had anal sex against her consent, which was considered rape, and the third truth is that she was a prostitute; unlike in normal circumstances, the benefit of the doubt, too, was added into his file as it is clearly stipulated by the UN secretary general's bulletin on sexual exploitation and abuse that prostitution is a violation of the UN code of conduct as it creates the demand. This time the 'God he trusted in' had not been his saviour, but instead, the US$3 on which what he kept repeating was printed on the backside—'In God we trust'—had become an evidence at a jury conducted by humans, not by a God and ultimately not the 'God he trusted in' but the Americans trust in, made him not only unemployed but also splashed mud on his country as well as on the United Nations. He was not the only one who prayed to the 'Almighty' after having violated the rules and regulations in the country.

One person from a Southern African country, well educated, father of two children left back at home, was living with one of his country women in my neighbouring apartment in Monrovia. It was late 2011, the lady started showing signs and symptoms of something seriously happening to her; by late 2012, the lady passed away due to pneumonia as many of the AIDS patients were coinfected with tuberculosis. Her boyfriend was still in his cupid wings on his back, flying around, with teenager Liberian girls every day and night, even though he was under antiretroviral treatment plan: 'It was not me who decided to give this to me, it was God, who is up there,' he says.

Mauris is a married man with no children with his wife who is also from Sierra Leone, working for a communication company in Liberia. He talked about himself with kind of a suppressed frustration as they did not have children. He believed that she was a witch and that was the reason why she cannot have the god in her womb to get pregnant. To every single such thing, I had become quite indifferent as I had enough; later on, I noticed his behaviour had significantly changed as if he was going through a crisis, very low tolerance, irritability, mood swings, and reporting to work under influence of alcohol became a part of his everyday life. 'Mauris, you got any problem?' I just asked as I noticed his changes. 'One woman in the community say.........' He stopped. 'Says what?' I asked. 'She's got a child for me,' he said hesitantly. 'She got belly,' he added after few seconds of silence and looked up and said, 'Belly is not for me' as if he was calling witnesses. My god knows that 'Belly is not for me'. He came closer to me and whispered, 'You know, women get belly on god's will, no man and woman thing needed.' He was indirectly referring to the birth of Jesus Christ, so did his girlfriend. I felt that God is a real saviour for these people, as any wrongdoing can be neutralised by one word: 'God'. By that time, I had realised that I neither was the right person nor do have the right faith to make an attempt to talk about God, and how he has been abused. I counted him as a classic experimental sample of another prototype among different types of believers of almighty god under the broken roofs of miscellaneous churches in Africa.

I met Ester while working with an intergovernmental agency. She was educated in Ghana and Switzerland, a licensed lawyer who demonstrated such hyper-resistance to topics such as gay and animal rights, whenever we were having friendly chats in the evening. 'God created Adam and Eve, not Eve and an Eve or Adam and an Adam.' She sounds intimidating. These are European conspiracies to eradicate the African population from earth. 'Can you imagine a man on a man?' Her gestures portray feelings of disgust. 'No no no no! No way! God created Adam and Eve.' Finally, she becomes the centre of discussion of all others who are drunk above the level of frontal cortex, and keep us laughing the whole Friday evening. She is an African elite, from Ghana, a lawyer who had European education, who has come to Liberia to advocate the host government on human rights. But the inability of detaching one's profession from faith had brought her many challenges in her professional life that she didn't want to accept. A faith-centric nature is just like a closed cave where one is locked in forever, in the obscurity of unwillingness to admit that others think different, others feel different, and others' values and norms differ from yours.

Those days, in the Eighties, there was not much noise about 'animal rights', but living in a Buddhist society, we were taught that they do have the right to life, freedom, and to their natural habitat, and so on, as we do. Simply as a Buddhist child, I grew up with a compassionate attitude to all sorts of animals rather than having a rights-based point of view. 'They eat every living thing.' When we hear this, my sister used to pull our cat to her lap and start stroking its head and my father reassures her that they are thousands of miles away from us. As human minds never delete anything permanently, though we find it difficult to retrieve the information archived, but as it happens often, when there is a trigger, the latently remaining information comes to surface. When Esther was denying the fact that animals do have the right to life as we do, highlighting biblical references that God had created them for human consumption, my father's very words 'they eat every living thing' popped out like an error massage in a computer. The Bible is used in their favour, my friend winded up the discussion, leaving the victory to Esther who was very proud of having proven that the divine shield was able to stand in their favour. Whereas Africa had already lost a significant number of endemic species and many more have been classified as endangered, vulnerable, critically endangered, or else, some of them are protected in the zoos or conservation centres as are 'extinct in the wild' as a consequence of the enforcement of God's law and order in the wild by human beings.

'They killed the missionaries and ate them.' 'A lot of missionaries became victims of cannibals.' such phrases I had heard a lot during rainy afternoons, sitting in the living room veranda, with my father, while watching the rain. Watching the rain used to be one of my favourite activities during rainy seasons in Sri Lank when heavy rains hinder all the other noises in the environment and take control over the place. I enjoyed the mild cold and monotony of falling waters that took my mind away from everything else. The religious impact of colonial time on Asian countries are very minimal compared to Africa though there is a significant presence of diverse Christian denominations in Asia. Also, there were no brutal bloodsheds or savage attacks in resisting spiritual ideologies of invaders during colonial time in Asia, maybe because deep-rooted religions already existed for thousands of years, and there was no room for a new ideology and the Asian reserved cultures were not hospitable for Christianity to spread even though the coastal communities were mostly converted as they were completely under the Portuguese, Dutch, and British administration whereas the interior of most of the countries in South Asia enjoyed more autonomy with least interference of colonial administration. When my father told about the cannibal attacks on missionaries, all that I could imagine was that 'Mother Theresa was killed by a bond of savages' and taken for their supper. Every sweat gland of my body responded to what I was hearing. 'No, they are good people,' I said to him with heartfelt sympathy. 'You know, savages are not civilised people, they do not know what is good and bad, when they see a stranger, they kill and eat.' The explanation of my father was like a passive intimidation, I wanted to see it for myself. I dreamt that night, I was hiding behind a big tree and looking at some tribal activities in a thick forest, some dark-skinned, bushy-haired people roast something in fire. It should be a human body, I told. I woke up sweaty and panicked, it was 3.00 a.m.; then I realised it was just a dream. It's been almost two decades, and today, I 'm astonished to hear from that the very Africans whose ancestors were the ones who killed and ate those missionaries are preaching in disseminating the Gospels of those who were eaten. A drastic change in ideology, in colonial terms, true transformation from savages to become civilized, or involuntarily being neatly brainwashed, is dreadful. Dreadful in the sense that the expansion of the Christian ideology is in width and length of the continent but not in depth to the minds of the people to truly follow the principles of life in the core teaching of Jesus Christ and to master the discipline of true Christian life in real-life situations.

When Christianity came to Africa, sailing through the Atlantic, unlike the way it spread through the north-east of the continent, it came with a new 'Mask of civilization'. By that time, Christianity was already in the continent, in the North-East, where the present Ethiopia and Eritrea are but those areas, being the early footprints of human civilization, have not been considered in the group of my focus. Yet postcolonial Africa, the territories conquered by European nations during the scramble to Africa, remain today as more God-fearing than those who brought the faith to the continent and simply, the continent have been transformed to a battlefield of two main faiths, Islam and Christianity. Nigeria has the largest population that is composed of the two major religions in Africa with extremism in both poles; on my first visit in search of modern forms of slavery, not under the flags of colonialists but in the name of faith, I decided to start with Nigeria and go to Uganda.

There is no other better suiting metaphor than animal migration from Great Masai Mara to Serengeti, to the arrival terminals of Murtala Muhammed International Airport of Lagos. Each predator will have their share and then the scavengers wait restlessly in the same hunting ground to grab the best part left by the predators. Every single passenger feels like they are wildebeests, wanting to be with the group, taking refuge in the shadow, hiding behind one another, and in a second of isolation, you will simply be a prey, a prey of a human predator which pounces on the wallet, senses the dollars that you carry. It is normal that out of the blue your luggage is missing and no one is there to take responsibility till you pay some bribe, then the lost or missing luggage would appear from the skies and handed over to your very hand with a mouthful of smile, or else till you pay a little something, you might not be able to pass through the immigration or customs, and history holds the witnesses that those who believed in right-doing missed their flights just because they were following the right procedures, having right documents, and having respected the rules and regulations of international travelling. What you will face in the airport and who will decide your destiny are a probability of frequency of activating some weird strategies of finding an illegal living of the who have been posted in the airport. When the immigration officer asked me $10, emphasising that I would not waste time if I do so, indeed a passive threatening, I realised that this place is a place of crows. The channel reporting any injustice or inconvenience caused to passengers is the very same channel where the black money are pumped, therefore they will 'look in to your problem' and they will ensure you will miss your next leg if you decide to wait till they come back with an answer. After paying $10, the immigration officer transformed himself into a priest, with a kind smile, he said 'Thank God you will not miss the flight.'

I was hosted by one of my friends who worked with me in Indonesia nine years ago, an Indian who works with an international organisation based in Lagos, all the logistical requirements for my trips to churches, in the coming few days, had already been planned by him. Next day being a Sunday, I was given a very tight schedule of visits to services of churches that belong to various denominations. I started early morning and stopped at a famous Catholic church in the city limits. As I entered with those who go to the service, along with my friend, no one noticed a stranger had entered. Anyway, I'm not a complete alien, as my mother is a Christian, I had been significantly exposed to rituals and Christian discipline. And in Sri Lanka, everyone does often participate inter-religious activities which give an adequate orientation about the etiquette of every religion.

Service started, like in any other Roman Catholic church, serene and calm, a sense of veneration and tranquillity had filled the room. The high arches and colourful glasses have added a refined air of Roman Catholic structures, and you would forget the visitors hyper-vigilance syndrome that anyone who comes to Nigeria acquires. I felt that I was in a Roman Catholic cathedral somewhere in Belgium or Italy, and nothing much of a difference except Nigerian English that I hardly understood were to be noticed till it comes to the time when the tray is passed for collections, the voice of the priest heightens, sounding as if he is possessed by the god, which I had never heard from any other place, in anywhere else in the world, his serenity turned into a demand till the tray came back full of bank notes. That made me say, 'Oh my God!'. It was not church of elite class; it was mostly attended by very poor people who live in urban ghettos of the densely populated Lagos, those who work as labourers in the market, porters, taxi drivers, housemaids, prostitutes, pick-pockets, pavement shopkeepers, and so on. Those people live in constant desperateness, hopelessness, misery, and despair where the phenomenon of God remains as their only consolation which is constantly abused by the priests, exploiting the poor population of Africa. The fancy Hummer that the priest was driving cannot be something that Vatican has funded, that was the luxury the clergy enjoys, out of the lives of those who do not have enough food in their stomach, no means to buy medication, and no hope for their future yet plead God for a brighter tomorrow. He who is in heaven now has to come down to earth to see how his teachings are being abused.

A church of another denomination in Lagos suburbs, which looked something like a warehouse, was vibrant and musical when I entered the service that has already started. The loud melodious prayers with body movements of devotees, with their hypercolourful dresses, reminded me of a carnival in Rio de Janeiro. Instead of the calming effect that anyone who goes to a church expects, the environment in the house was hyperenergetic and restless. The pastor was young, sounded like a good orator, better suiting for politics than in spiritual leadership. Every word he uttered reached beyond the frontiers of the church, to all directions, probably to the heavens and hells as well, as if he calls God down, waking the sinners in hell who were in deep sleep, praising those who had gone to heaven to get some donations from up there, finally making everyone else in the room pull out everything till the last note from their pockets, just like an involuntary verbal-armed robbery in the name of almighty. To my surprise, it was all about money, survival, and control; the medieval method of using religion for social and political control has been transformed into a weapon of financial control that no one can question as it is the one who is up there who pulls your money out. One's faithfulness to God is judged by the amount of money that is donated for the well-being of the priest, whereas the religious institutions should be the key to the well-being of the society.

'We really need a church,' Shaggy, a Jamaican reggae rap singer winds American slang in a church in Kingston, and I enjoyed the visuals of the song that looked radical in my eyes, but a situation where radicalism was a reality I did not dare to expect; yet a church that belongs to a relatively new denomination, situated in a blind corner offers a blessed orgasm during its services. It was a day club, everyone looked hypnotised by the shaking butts and boobs, and the pastor looks like he is at his climax and going to connect with the lord in the Seventh Heaven, as his prayers exceed the sound-producing threshold of vocal chords, words turn into a creaky sound that human beings cannot easily do, his physical gestures become something completely incomprehensible, looking like a hybrid of a human and an unidentified animal that anyone who notices gets scared to death. The hysterical behaviour of the priest is instantly acquired by the audience and the entire crowd looks psychotic, which reminded me of the Marabou healers in Togo. An observer who has not seen this dramatic approach to prayers would end up with shell shock. The experience is obviously beyond usual for those who are not in their circle. I felt that I was in a red-light district in Amsterdam. When the service is over, the pastor came down from the altar, with kind of a royalty yet his gallant look was popping up when his female followers approach him. Like a peacock which expands its colourful feathers and dance to seduce the females, the winker mirrors of his Mercedes S600 start flashing to signal as if he has empty space for three. As the winker mirror communication seems a habit, three of them run into the car as if they found the shortest way to heaven. The car disappears while the laughter of some guys cracks and they look for those who are left in the holy ground. Later on, I had a chance to interview one of the victims of an attempted sexual assault by the pastor of the same church and my speculation was proven to be true. She had been told that having sex with a pastor who is committed to God brings her divinity.

Unexpectedly yet like a joke of destiny, I met Ebrahim, a Mauritanian who has been converted to their denomination through an Icelandic lady who lived in his homeland a few years ago and presently working as a teacher and visiting house to house to disseminate the religion as a part-time job, for which he says he is paid around $400 a month. As a result of his advocacy campaign in the villages in Islamic Mauritania, he has been expelled from the country, it was according to him. Now he is living in Nigeria as an active member of the specific church. His outlook shows that he is a victim of a chronic decease, and his nerve functions have been affected as his hands and head shake vigorously when he talks. 'Muslims are extremists,' it is his conclusion. 'Every Muslim is an extremist, they will be burnt in the hell.' I did not want to question an apparently brainwashed victim of someone's agenda using his sick and weird look. He asked me, 'You should be a Christian too, otherwise you cannot be successful in life.' I said 'I'm a Buddhist.' His eyes became like goggles with surprise, which reminded me of a baby frog, and told 'You too are an extremist, you should be cheating people, you will go to hell.' My mind went back to a quote from *Macbeth* by William Shakespeare: 'Things without remedy should be left without regard.' It would be complete waste of my psychic energy if I tried to make him understand that we all are human beings who are born equally and we should respect the diversity. I simply said, 'God bless you!' and left the place.

I left Nigeria the next morning and headed back to Liberia, taking Asky Airlines, which is one of the Nigerian-owned aviation companies. The small jetliner took off from Lagos and everyone started praying to their God for a safe flight. As everyone is praying, I thought that God will not play his trick to crash the flight simply because one atheist in the flight doesn't pray. As the flight landed safely, I heard everyone was saying 'Thank God!'. I rushed to the counter as my next jet to Uganda via Kenya was supposed to start shortly.

When television programs were full of stories of abduction of children, in Northern Uganda, especially in Acholi communities, and that was the time I first encountered a visual of a child soldier on television though I had heard about LTTE (Liberation Tigers of Tamil Elam) abduct children in North and East Sri Lanka. My father used to burst out whenever he heard about children being used in the frontline of LTTE even though he didn't have any idea about the 'child soldiers' in African context by that time. However, the quest I started inspired by his free-time stories, at that time via documentaries and literature, today has brought me to the northern part of Uganda, where the Sudanese and Congolese borders meet the one of Uganda, once called Acholi land, a fear-ridden territory almost a decade ago because of Lord's Resistance Army, known by famous acronym LRA, lead by Joseph Kony, who proclaimed himself the spokesperson of God and a spirit medium and had been considered by some as a cult of personality and claimed that he was visited by a multinational host of thirteen spirits, including a Chinese phantom. Ideologically, the group was a syncretic mix of mysticism, Acholi nationalism, and Christian fundamentalism, and claims to be establishing a theocratic state based on the Ten Commandments and local Acholi tradition. In the name of God, in the name of the Holy Spirit, movement of Protestant Christianity, guided by his own interpretation of biblical literature, Kony terrified the Acholi region, in truth his own people, displacing almost two million people, abducting around 66,000 children and using them either as soldiers or sex slaves, for twenty years, from 1989 to 2009. The profound spiritual nature of Ugandan people enabled them not only to follow him but also to carry out his will in unbelievably brutal ways. Those who were old enough to hold an AK47, and young enough to be called children, were abducted from their houses, forced to kill their own parents, stabbing, cutting, or sometimes burning them alive, and then their life in the jungle will start with AK47. A child soldier is born in the name of the Lord who is almighty, his mission will be to kill, rape, loot, and do whatever the Lord says. Rehabilitated child soldiers of LRA have been integrated to the society, living with their lifelong psychological scars, in Northern Uganda and most of their stories still remain unheard, hidden under the blanket of fear and stigmatisation.

The journey from capital Kampala, 450 kilometres of distance, north of Kitgum, is a spine-juddering seven-hour ride down potholed tracks made impassable by rain. During the time of LRA, no living thing survived in this area. We stopped near an old convent where my interviewee for next two hours, a victim of sex slavery and a child soldier, was going to reveal an unheard story about LRA leadership.

At 12 years old, Bongomin should have been playing with his mates in the village, but instead, he was handed a gun. Abducted by LRA in Northern Uganda, he had a simple choice: kill or be killed not simply by being shot but being tortured and cut to death. Like more than 30,000 other children brainwashed by notorious militia leader Joseph Kony, he was transformed into a bloodthirsty assassin eager to commit atrocities.

Bongomin confessed that the crimes were truly grotesque. I was the first one ever in his life he had counted on, not because I was good to him but because he knew that I knew nothing about his identity and I was just a foreigner who would never come back to see him. 'Once, I tied five people together, poured petrol over them, and burned them alive,' he told with trembling heavy lips that looked like bunkers guarding his secrets. Another time, he had cut the head of a man and ate it in front of his family. Again he took the gun and went back to his neighbouring village and raped the mother of the girl whom he dreamt of, simply because she was not at home. Three months later, he managed to abduct her and keep her in the jungle with the help of his commander. But he had to let his commander enjoy the pray before he consumes the leftovers, that was the order. '"Bones will be left for dogs,"' the commander ordered me,' he said with an indifferent gesture. He had to respect the hierarchy and finally he took his chance.

'What did you feel when you saw her being raped by your commander?' I wanted to check his reaction, but he was looking at the infinite sky pensively and did not want to discuss it. Looked like he had realised the gravity of the act and was traumatised.

Just before he became invalid during the Christmas night offensive in 2008, he wiped out ten innocent civilians in a hail of bullets without any provocation.

I met Bongomin, 11 years after his return home, after 12 years of survival in the bush, with rebels as an LRA soldier.

The last time he saw his mum, he was an innocent schoolboy.

Today he is a hardened killer who had taken more than 130 lives, among them most were innocent civilians. A serial rapist, looter, and once a cannibal, that is what his stories reveal, yet he was an abducted child soldier, a damaged personality, with a destroyed life full of traumatic experiences with lifelong psychological scars that may never be forgotten till he dies.

Never letting slip his cold executioner's stare, Bongomin provided a shocking description of the indoctrination rituals child soldiers were forced to go through.

'For training we would raid a village,' he told me. 'Each of us had to shoot two people through the head.'

'It took me too long to kill someone, they said, so I had 150 strikes of the cane right on my naked back.'

'If you show any nervousness or hesitation, you would be shot.' He added. 'We were forced to lick the blood of the people we shot and eat some parts.'

'We had to cut their skulls open to remove some of the brain which we had to eat in front of them.'

'After this indoctrination, our orders were to kill the first person we met as we walked to the next camp. That was the point you are reborn as an LRA member, follower of Joseph Kony, the intermediate between the God and Uganda, the representative that God has selected for Uganda, probably for the whole region. Being like this became normal. We would gouge out the eyes of some people. We cut off their ears if they didn't listen. These were divine punishments and we were delegated with the divine powers to execute anyone who go against us.' His words were powerful with such a vigour that he was still being possessed by Kony's so-called divinity. But his youth has been completely snatched away, as a result of having been forced to take part in East Africa's bloodiest guerrilla group. Now he is an ex-child-soldier, invalid young man, who is also a victim of repetitive and multiple traumas.

'I was a child whose not only childhood has been deprived but also my whole life and future had been brutally usurped by God.' I wanted to know the story of his abduction, so we sat in front of the mud hut where he lives and he started to speak of being force-marched into Sudan after his kidnapping.

'I was badly beaten and threatened with a gun,' he told. 'For days and days, we walked and along the way they abducted other children. They tied us together with rope. We walked day and night with few chances to drink or eat—some children became too weak. One man would point his gun at whoever was complaining and pull the trigger. More than ten children were killed along the way. When we got to Sudan, we met Joseph Kony for the first time. He said everyone there had been kidnapped from Uganda. He said he had been abducted by God and if any of us tried to escape, we would be killed. "I, Joseph Kony, is the God on earth. God talks to you through me."

Right then, he pulled one boy out of the line and told his commander to shoot him dead in front of us and I felt that I was going to faint, but it was for few seconds then he pointed at me, two of them pulled me out of the crowd. He who had killed hundreds, raped innocent child girls, looted poor people, tortured villagers, and ate human flesh broke out with a cry of a little kid.'

'Bongomin!' I held his hand, first time ever in my life, I had chance to practice my profession in the middle of Acholi land, providing psychological support to enable him to create a healthy rapport to enable him to open up.

'He spit on me and pushed his whopper in my anus, I was ashamed.' His cheeks are flooded with tears, like a little boy, and apparently, he had not talked about it ever since because in Uganda, sex among men is a taboo, matter of marginalisation, a subject that will cause stigmatisation. As a result, he had bottled up his traumatic experiences for more than twenty years. It was like an eruption of an volcano, had several spells of crying and then he looked at me and told, 'Please do not tell anyone,' and asked me to use the pseudonym 'Bongomin'.

In 2006, Bongomin was shot in the leg in a battle with Ugandan government forces. Airlifted to the hospital by his captors, he was finally free of Kony. Instead of camouflages and AK47, now he wears a white-coloured t-shirt, ill-fitting cotton shorts, and a pair of red flip-flops and dreams of a simple life back home with his mother.

A few years ago, Kony cut out two of Bongomin's front teeth and upper lip as a public punishment for talking too much.

'Kony said he would teach me a lesson. He grabbed a knife and, before I could react, cut two teeth out of my mouth. The pain was unbelievable, like nothing I have ever felt before. But then he told me to carry on talking. This was a mortification. I accepted guilt for what I did. But I just could not consider escape. If I had disobeyed orders, I would not be just dead, they would torture me to death.'

Kony fooled his young troops by claiming the Holy Spirit entitled him to seize power in Uganda and he justified all his actions and motives as the will of God. The rag-tag LRA looted villages, topping up its numbers by kidnapping new young victims. Children slept rough on the streets of Gulu to escape its roving soldiers. Now 12 years after his rescue, Bongomin seemed to be demilitarised and trying his best to adapt to the life back in Gulu, in the little mud hut with his mother. But rather than being a supportive son to an aging mother, he had just become a weight on her shoulders as a result of several lead particles left in his thigh due to being shot during 2008 Christmas night offensive of LRA, Kony's holy war, as peace talks in Sudan broke down. As a consequence of extreme spirituality and blind faith, hundreds of thousands of Acholi children had become victims of psychological and physical torture and had become permanently disabled, left as least priority of the society. In the name of God, lives were taken away, women were raped, properties were looted not only in Uganda but also in Sudan, Central Africa DRC, and Kony, as if the Lord is still in his favour, remain alive in Central African Republic.

I left Uganda with a weird feeling not about the existence of God, or Christianity, but about the presence of God with wrong people, at a wrong place and at a wrong time. And it looked like colonisation has a modern approach, an ideological slavery, imperialism though faith, finally taking the control over the population and then the resources. Is that because Africa's traditional beliefs remained primitive and underdeveloped to be dominated by the ideology of the invader? It looks rather an acquired ideology that can easily be used in favour of leaders irrespective of whatever they do. But Christianity barely had nothing to do with the 'Colonial God' though he travelled across Atlantic and remained exploitative for the rest of his life which is infinite in Sub-Saharan Africa. Whereas in East Africa, specifically in Ethiopia, between the fifth and thirteenth centuries, the dominant religion was Christianity, though Islam made some inroads on two coastlines. The first one was the Indian Ocean coastline, where Islam became the dominant religion from the eighth to tenth century onwards, on a thin stretch of land ranging from Egypt all the way down to northern Mozambique. Progress inland was very slow, however, and little Islamisation of the interior had occurred by the nineteenth century.

The other 'coastline' was the Sahel, in many ways the shore of the Sahara opposite the Islamic areas of North Africa, ranging from the Senegal to Darfur, and adjacent to 'mainland' Sub-Saharan Africa. Islamisation here started in the tenth century but with a few exceptions (the upper Senegal valley), was rather superficial, limiting itself to the rulers and upper classes. In general, Islam tended to be so mixed with animist religions in these areas, that Muslim travellers such as Ibn-Battutta in the fourteenth century regarded them with horror as pagans. By the nineteenth century, this syncretism and the growing influence of Islam were enough to prompt Islamic fundamentalists to declare a series of jihads over a huge geographical area, from Usman Dan Fodio in Nigeria to Amadou in Senegal. Today, the very Sub-Saharan Africa is a battlefield between the 'Colonial God' and 'Allah', making it a cemetery of Satan, soaked with blood of both religions, that mixed with no difference in the battlefield.

After my visit to Kitgum and Gulu, I called my journey to discover the Colonial God to an end. The destruction brought into the continent, the deterioration which was visible in the social fabric of Africa, the number of lives sacrificed in his name, and the level of exploitation that Africa as a continent went through in his name are immense, countless, never-ending, and devastating, which looks more devastating than two atomic bombs that the friendly allies dropped in Hiroshima and Nagasaki, as the impact is expanding to the fullest width and length and penetrating deep into the continent, thickening its ideological obscurity, keeping it as the continent of darkness for the full life span of the universe.

Chapter 15

SLEEPING SICKNESS

'AFRICAN TRYPANOSOMIASIS, MOSTLY KNOWN as sleeping sickness among the ordinary people, is a vector-borne parasitic disease which is common specially in Sub-Saharan and East Africa,' the facilitator of predeparture training sounded like an announcement of epidemic prevention and his words had rather a technical outlook with a fear-inducing intonation which was quite discouraging for participants who had been dreaming to go to Africa for their first international humanitarian adventure.

'The disease is transmitted to humans by tsetse fly bites which have acquired their infection from human beings or from animals harbouring the human pathogenic parasites,' he added with the same tonality and intonation making our Imaginary Africa look like a paradise for virus, bacteria, fungus, and for parasites and a hell on earth for human beings, especially for those who go there from other parts of the world.

At the end of the predeparture briefing, I was left with a dozen of old Latin medical terms that I was even unable to pronounce correctly, and remembering them was out of my imagination. Beyond that, all sounded similar, specially the ending. Therefore, the best that one could do in such cases is to link each thing with something that can easily be remembered. Trypanosomiasis is sleeping sickness, malaria remained the same whereas schistosomiasis which is caused by a fresh water snail was remembered as snail fever. As there is a great difference and distance between the theory and the practice in many subjects, I did not refer to any of those theoretical literature given during the predeparture briefing. After I came to Africa, 'African trypanosomiasis faded away from my memory even though I remembered the imaginary nightmare that the facilitator verbally created during the briefing but the 'sleeping sickness' remained in usage but for another side of human life in Africa. A life that is not like in any other continent, a life that is acquired in African countries, by expatriates that anyone seldom could stay away from. Even-though it is an individual choice, the choice is an offer that one would not have much resistance as a human born besides that expatriate hotspots use the audacity of the human desires to scrape every single penny they earn on the soils of Africa.

Sajj in Monrovia is like the heart of expatriates in whole Liberia, nucleus of the expatriate night life of the country, the labour room for gossips on the personal life of expatriates, and the best meat shop for those who are carnivores, where one can find his or her pick for Friday night. Every Friday, not only young and energetic crowd, but also from middle- to senior-age expatriates rarely miss Friday night salsa even though most of them are not going there to dance. After a tiresome week, everyone comes to relax and dance with enhanced mood with few pegs of one's preferred liquor or with few club-beers, a Swiss beer which has a production plant in Liberia which within Liberia is advertised as 'Proudly Liberian', while their eagle eyes are fixed at moving bodies as if they are waiting to pounce on the pray of the night that is caught by their sharp eyes. With every sip of alcoholic beverages, the fire of desire conquers judgement and common sense and pushes the desires to the forefront as if they are going to live the last night of their lives. When the time comes when stimulated nerve-ends and inebriated the mind interpret the visual stimulus, every female in the dance floor is seen as a horny slut who is ready to go to bed with anyone who blows a whistle from the crowd irrespective of whether she is your colleague with whom you are obligated to have a healthy working relationship or it is your boss or subordinate with whom you are to be an exemplary professional and age or race does not matter when the darkness falls and African sky is dark and the earth is cold and the values and virtues dissolve in the dirty waters stagnating in roadside drainage systems, just next to Sajj, clogged with anything and everything on earth, from cotton buds, clothes, shoes, used sanitary napkins, food, empty beer and soft drink bottles, loads of mud, sand, human and animal faeces, and sometimes, dead domestic animals like dogs or cats which were fortunate enough to die and start decomposing in cover before they were caught by someone who is hungry among the local population.

The Saturday morning sun comes out of its secret cell with surprise and frustration, which was not probably because of hangover due to alcohol intake but because of seeing the person who is lying naked next to you or who is already up and looking at you as if she wanted to walk back in time and erase what had happened hours ago.

'Take it easy. Its life' is the common philosophical answer that comes out next moment when she goes to the dressing table and starts getting dressed carelessly as if she is living merely because she was born, just like a patient with unipolar depression. But above words, that comes out of his mouth rather with expectation of continuation for some time probably till the next catch than to convince her or in apologies of what was made to happen the previous night. As adults, even though there exist diverse cultures, it is finally an offer that you cannot refuse which they call simply one of the common forms of expatriate life in Africa.

Every evening, despite hyperphobia of mosquitos, I used to spend my writing time at the balcony of my apartment, having tea break when my eyes get tired because of having looked at the screen constantly for a long time. I usually enjoy observing people passing along the street and, from my location, the balconies and main corridor of another apartment building where a lot of expatriates, especially from the international companies, intergovernmental entities, and NGOs reside were visible with crystal clarity. The local girls, dressed in weird flashy clothes, often with deep and wide colours, bright-coloured leggings just like in a fancy dress show, and some in super-short skirts, posing their bodies like cheerleaders in a rugby match with exception of constant calls coming in to their mobiles, wait near the line of small roadside huts made with an umbrella fixed to a rickety table where men, women, and children sell peanuts, roasted meat, spaghetti, small bulbs of mayonnaise, sour milk, coal, and many more, under sharp rechargeable LED lights widely known as Chinese lights, until their regular client or the client referred by someone arrives to his apartment from work. When the first Land Cruiser comes inside the compound though the high blue gate crowned with barbed wires that make anyone think that even a pea crow cannot fly over the place, one girl among those who were waiting creeps in, in front of the very eyes of the serious-looking security officer, with muddy yellow shirt which was once white, black trousers with holes in many places—apparently never been washed—and his boots with no proper sole, who seems having immobilised his baton that was given for a purpose and shut his mouth. A couple of dollars had empowered the teenage girls over the authority of the gatekeeper of the compound who is employed to ensure the security of the tenants. Every time the old metal gate creeks, a humanitarian 4 × 4 goes, followed by a girl waiting in the crowd except in cases where the all-terrain vehicle already carries a female human being. Then my eyes catch couples walk hand in hand along the corridor, as if they are just married.

When my second cup of tea is ready on the little cane coffee table on the balcony, well after two hours, the doors start opening, one by one and the girls rush outside like lemurs coming out from their dens. And sometimes, it is not rare that my first sight in the morning is a girl who is rushing out, cleaning her eyes, from one of the apartments seen from my balcony. During my stay of thirty-six months, two weeks, and five days, despite the rainy days when the balcony becomes nearly a lake and impossible to stay, days I was on vacation, and the days when I got up late or went to bed early, cache-cache of girls in the apartment building where the expatriates working for nongovernmental organisations and intergovernmental agencies live used to be a part of my daily sights.

One morning, as usual, I came to the balcony that overlooks River Doe, which is picturesque at a distance even though it is the common toilet of thousands of urban slum dwellers in Monrovia living in its banks, full of every sort of waste remains in mountains, a paradise for flies and pea crows, sipping my morning coffee with my fruit breakfast along with my daily notebook to plan the rest of the day. When the sun is young and the air is fresh with a water view at a healthy distance, life is not that bad in Liberia. I used to take early morning coffee time for jotting down my daily plan, sitting in the balcony, reflecting in the calmness of the surrounding. A girl hurrying out from an apartment wiping her eyes, or else a woman walking in the street near the building carrying doughnuts or cornbread does not disturb or take my attention away from my imagination of a successful day.

'You, you, you!'

An unexpected scream of a woman, at an unusual hour even though it is a place where witnessing a woman being beaten is quite common, twisted my neck towards the road as if I was caught by the mighty hands of an ape. A naked woman screaming at someone in the next apartment block, even though all doors remained closed, the sun light that hit the windows directly revealed a few faces looking at the road from the building apparently targeted by the nude woman who was in rage on the road. Obviously, those who peep through the curtains of the windows were just audience of the street drama which had for sure started in one of those apartments. Almost everything that the woman was telling was not clear to me except one thing which reassured my doubt that the cause might have been 'man and woman business'—sexual intercourse in Liberian English.

'The man cannot pay me, oh,' she was telling to the people who were on the street. It seems that no one except me or a few other expatriates watching the early morning street drama is disturbed or astonished. Some of the people who were passing by just passed as if it was an issue to ignore with no regard or else it was a kind of common scene on the street like a Nighanta walking nude on a crowded street in India.

'Five dollars? You cannot fuck a monkey for five dollars.' the lady started to scream again when a bra and a few other lady stuff flew down to the street from the apartment building. No one responded to her despite throwing her clothes out and the woman dressed herself right in the middle of the road while curious schoolchildren, street food sellers, and many others were passing near her. Immediately after she put on her last piece of cloth, she waved to a moto which was passing by and got on and disappeared. Next moment, window curtains were closed

271

and no-peeping faces were to be seen, as everyone got back to their own business; the incident had already become probably a part of urban daily rumours, a subject for leisure time discussion of cornbread and peanut sellers and yet another expatriate-local experience which is just a random sample of hundreds of such events happening not only in this post-conflict African capital but also in many cities and villages in Africa. A humanitarian, a diplomat, who had come to serve this nation that has been torn apart by one of the most inhumane civil conflicts in Africa, known as the third world war, instead of doing the expected prime purpose that the organisation hired him for, has been transformed into an exploiter who not only sexually exploits the local population but also harms the perception of locals about his country of origin.

'Five dollars, just five dollars, you can get any of them.'

I think many of the tenants of our apartment complex might have heard what is above, probably not only one time but whenever the security guard has a moment to exchange a word with a tenant. In many places where there are expatriates, the security guard of the compound plays a role of a part-time pimp, and from each deal, they expect at least US$5. Pimping for humanitarians has become a new livelihood in most of the conflict-ridden Sub-Saharan African countries where I had been, such as Sierra Leone, Liberia, Central African Republic, Democratic Republic of Congo, Ivory Coast, and Burundi.

It was one dry season, early February in 2012, the earth was being beaten by the hot sun's rays that had stamina to creep through the curtain of thick sands of Harmattan. With extremely high humidity in the western tip of Africa, the dry season is the most difficult season to survive even though life is limited exclusively to the areas where there are paved road networks in the rainy season. It was natural that anyone who is not used to the combination of heat and high humidity would get allergic reactions, such as rashes, headaches, boils under the armpits, and so on, and no one would give any importance for such stuff appearing on your skin as everyone is aware that is a gift of time. One morning, while I was on my way to the office, I came across one of my friends, a lady working for a famous regional body, who was from a Southern African region, in a supermarket and noticed that she had changed a lot specially in her body mass and there was a rash quite visibly spread on her hands. She used to live pretty close to my apartment block, with one of her countrymen who was also working for an international organisation.

'Hey you have lost quite a lot of weight,' I told informally rather than asking it as a question so that she could choose just to say thank you most of the time. But in her case, it was not losing extra weight; she had almost been transformed to a skeleton from a plump, medium-built Southern African woman.

'No, I was following a diet plan.' She smiled reluctantly and replied spontaneously. Her face was looking a bit disturbed; probably she was offended with what I told.

As we used to have rest and recuperation time off every eight weeks, I was away from my workstation for around two weeks. Upon arrival to Robert's International Airport of Monrovia, I noticed her with one of the medical staff, a nurse, at the boarding area for Kenyan-Airways flight to Accra, Ghana, where there is acceptable level of health facilities in the region.

The face was shrunk, and the fungus had already conquered her face and neck; she was lying on the stretcher looking terribly sick and helpless.

'Hi!' I said.

She looked at me carefully, observed my face as she had never seen a face like mine before.

'This malaria is killing me,' she muttered. I barely heard what she told. I had already seen what was going on with her, and I knew that was killing her even though she was not suffering from malaria. She was stepping to the valley of death through the last stage of HIV/AIDS with a coinfection of drug-resistant tuberculosis and the phenomenon was making her way faster than expected.

'I'm not sure whether she would be able to make her way to the final destination,' the nurse said with a sympathetic glance at her but I felt that she had already decided her final destination which is most probably not what is on her boarding pass. As speculated, the sad news was delivered to the staff that she had passed away in Dar-Aslam on the way to Harare.

Africa is a continent where rumours are more supersonic and than any other part of earth; rumours determine many aspects of human life in Africa. In summary, the African society is completely rumour driven.

'She had that even before she came to Liberia,' one was saying as if the person tested her status.

'No, she got it from her boyfriend who was sleeping around,' the other one defends, being a friend of the deceased.

'Her husband died with the same sickness five years ago,' another comes in to the scene.

'She slept with a white man, he should be the one who gave her the virus.' This common defence wall against HIV in Africa raises its voice.

Finally, someone says that it was the choice of God and everyone keeps quiet as if they all agree upon it.

Amidst of the rumours fabricated by different people, in different ways, based on type of relationship they had with the deceased person and sociocultural background they were from, my team was requested to provide psychosocial support for her close friends as a part of critical incident stress management.

'She used to date my ex-boyfriend,' one of the staff members expressed her intense fears during a personal one-to-one counselling session.

'Have you ever checked your status?' I asked her gently.

'No,' she started crying loud. It is usual in many cultures of Africa to cry aloud to express some human emotions such as sadness, grief, or fear. They cry hysterically, most often roll on the ground or else lean on someone. A funeral without crying is an ill-omen. Crying helps them to vent their emotions and make them feel light and consoled, therefore hysterical crying is a psychosocial coping mechanism that had been practised since generations.

'Have you ever had unprotected sex with your ex-boyfriend?'

Her gesture of looking at the sky with her hands partially up as if she was praying, hinted me something serious but I was not able to think beyond what I felt.

'I have a 2-year-old son for him.'

I was wordless. She was crying, looking down, and tears poured out and dropped on the cement floor just like water dropping from a cracked roofing sheet when its raining. She was clenching her teeth as if she did not want her tongue to say anything anymore even though her mouth was trying to push her tongue out. Her hands looked stiff and rigid. She was gripping the edge of the table like a hawk grips a chick. I wondered whether it was anger, fear, sorrow, frustration, shock, or any other human emotion that I had not experienced yet in my life. May be it was a combination of all sorts of negative emotions just like different ingredients which make a perfect soup with its unique taste depending on the quantity and the time it takes to cook each ingredient, which determines whether it is edible or not.

Finally, she and her child were found positive of HIV type 1, which is a rapidly progressing type of the disease. Her boyfriend is now working in South Sudan upon completion of his assignment in Liberia and he is living with his new girlfriend who is an Ethiopian who recently joined the humanitarian world after completing her education in one of the leading universities in New York City. Her destiny had already taken her to the mouth of the dragon during her very first assignment as a humanitarian. As a result of tracing the contacts of the index case who was deceased, more than eighteen internationally recruited individuals were found, and most of them have their families back home. For sure, the innocent loved ones back home might have been already infected. It was not just contacts, it was a gigantic tree, an African Baobab of sleeping with one another. I remember T.I.A. that my friend from Ghana used to say whenever something unique to Africa happens.

It is always considered as a taboo to be gay in Africa, and most of the Africans are stuck with the perception that the homosexual orientation is relatively less in Africa than any other continent in the world, which is certainly a myth as those who are homosexual are in cover in Africa as they are highly stigmatised and in some places such as in Uganda, gays are killed by aggressive mobs. And in many countries, especially in West and East Africa, there are nationwide organisations that mobilise communities against gay rights. One of Ghanaian female lawyers who was educated in Geneva stated once in front of my very eyes that in Africa there cannot be rights for gays and animals. She was not the only one who voiced against the animal and gay rights being employed at a well-renowned international agency of which core values contain to respect the diversity; many Africans, even though they do try not to be vocal, carry the same rigid attitude towards these two matters. But obviously, as anywhere else, there exist a gay population which is significant but behind the screen. In sooth like many other things in the continent that the Africans do not want to admit the existence or origin, such as Ebola or HIV/AIDS, 'being gay' remains in darkness. However, there are bunches of foreigners who come in to the continent seeking their same-sex dream partner, for an exotic black homosexual adventure under the cover.

I met Jean-Baptise, a French-born pastor from Toulouse from the southern part of France, in the Ugandan city of Kampala when I was on my way back from an extremely risky journey to Gulu to see an ex-member of Lord's Resistance army. As we had a common language, during my long waiting hours in transit, we happened to have a friendly conversation till our boarding time.

'I have my friend here, I came to take my friend to France.'

He was excited that his Ugandan friend has been granted visa for a long stay in France, after a few failed attempts of getting Schengen Visa. A while after we had the first conversation in the waiting area of the airport, a well-built, tall, and quite young black guy came to join us.

'This is John.' 'J O H N, like the British do write,' he added while introducing his friend. In their gestures, except for the way they use an intimate voice, nothing was visible about the kind of relationship they have—maybe because they were in the territory of Uganda. Later on, Jean told me that John was his boyfriend, sexual partner, and he wanted him to be with him in France at least for some time. And after we boarded the flight, I witnessed the first same-sex French kiss between Jean and John even before the flight quitted the aerial frontiers of Uganda where the democratic parliament had passed an act in favour of eradicating gays. Just a few thousand feet above the hyper-conventional country, the colours of rainbows shining high up in the skies enjoy the freedom of nondiscrimination. Jean and John are not exceptions; there are a hundred thousand Jeans I had met, even though Johns are quite hard to trace as their wings are tied by the manacle of culture, but like Kandahar remain as the gay capital of South Asia, even though Taliban and Afghans in general condemn homosexuality, Africa remains somewhat similar to Kandahar.

Marcelo's reason for working in Africa with humanitarian organisations, coming all the way from the Philippines, is pretty similar to the one of Jean but Marcelo is not a committed partner as Jean. He first came to Uganda with a famous nongovernmental organisation that provides emergency medical assistance, as per him, his dream was to contribute in supporting Africa, especially children. Entering to Africa through Uganda with his first mission; he was not in a position to show his sexual orientation publicly but he finally managed to find his partner in Uganda or the time of stay in the country. After one year, he moved to the Democratic Republic of Congo with the same organisation and he was open about his sexual orientation as a gay. His yellow shoes, lipsticks, contrast clothes, earrings, and different nail polish enjoyed their freedom in Congo and he managed to make his Congolese dream come true by finding his local partner. Every weekend when he was free, he used to take his local partner somewhere in the field to stay away from others. One day, I met both of them in the south-eastern capital of the Democratic Republic of Congo, Katanga, with a boy who was not more than 10 years, going shopping. The boy had some shopping bags full of stuff, apparently bought by one of them. At first I assumed that the boy was someone related to the local guy, but as Marcelo introduced the boy as their friend, my assumption proved to be wrong, and instead, a doubtful thought came to my mind. I asked myself many times why these guys were buying so many stuff for the boy. I tried to recall the details of the meeting, such as the body language of the boy and so on. Every time I tried to recall, a shy little face appeared in my mind.

'Are they . . . paedophiles?' I asked myself. Maybe it was just a doubt but it made me observe his behaviour closely. However, as I did not have much time in the Democratic Republic of Congo, I left them behind. With the time and my busy work schedule, my memories and suspicions about Marcelo disappeared from my thoughts.

Surprisingly, one day, during my temporary consultancy in the Philippines, one of my friends started talking about an incident of termination of contract of an expatriate in her organization as he was found taking naked photos of local children in one of the Central Asian countries.

'A Filipino who came from Congo. . .' as she kept on describing, something familiar hit my head.

'His name is Marcelo?' I asked.

'Oh my God, you know him, too?' She confirmed with a laughter.

'You know the guy had been in Sri Lanka as well and he was repatriated due to a case of child abuse,' she added.

One evening, when I was with my wife, taking dinner in one of the few star hotels in Monrovia, located at the banks of the Atlantic, I noticed someone that I had seen before. He was in his laser-pink Adidas sports T-shirt, a black shorts, and in purple sneakers, and there was an earring in his left ear. Unmistakably, it should be Marcelo, I thought.

'Hey how are you? You are here now?' I asked without verifying whether he was the same person or not.

'Hi!' His melodious hi was quite sufficient for me to identify that was him.

'I am here for the Ebola emergency response.' With his response, I started wondering why some organisations always go for the choice with predispositions of conflicts of interest and traits that are against the ethics of the organisation. As history is not disconnected from the present and continue to the future, we started seeing him with Liberian boys here and there in Monrovia; even though no one noticed, he found another African paradise for his fantasies to become realities whereas his misconduct is conflicting with his organisation's strict policy of zero tolerance to sexual exploitation and abuse with regards not only to the workplace but also to host communities. His presence left me with a serious thought about the repetitive mistakes that most organisations do in terms of recruiting wrong individuals for the humanitarian field that often end up with more eternal black marks on the organisation than on the individual who will just leave the country.

'It is a fantasy in the white world to have a sexual adventure with a black.' It was an American female colleague of mine with a Barbarian ancestry who repeated many times during one of our discussions about one expatriate who was disgraced in front of everyone present by a Ghanaian prostitute at the lobby of the hotel where we stayed, for not having her paid what she demanded. Apparently, the lady who came in, knowing that he was a foreigner, had demanded more money than what they discussed prior to the visit. It is undeniable that humankind has a desire to experience diversity, but it is not easy to give a racially bias interpretation to what had happened as it was just the gap of financial resources that has led the way to exploitation, which is two way. At the same time, each race looks at the issue with their racially-preset lenses and the issue is seen though their perceptual set. However, whatever whoever says, two-way sexual exploitation continues in most of the places of Africa, which has been extended to the level of human trafficking within the region or zone based on the demands created by the sexually determined stereotypes.

Lebanese communities in many African countries, especially in the western part of the continent, have a significant control over the retail and wholesale market of many commodities. In brief, a lot of businesses are owned by the Lebanese and the prices of most of the important commodities are controlled by them at their free will with no internal control by host governments. In absolute freedom and impunity, Lebanese are widely engaged in drug and human trafficking inside Africa.

'Bossman told me that I will get a job in a hotel as a room girl, and I was sent to a hotel in Beruit.'

'And then besides the room-girl job, I was sold to guests and there were couple of other girls from Ivory Coast and Guinea,' a Liberian girl who was undergoing a rehabilitation program after returning home from forced prostitution in Lebanon mentioned. And there were several of them who have been rehabilitated in the same institute financially and technically supported by an international nongovernmental organisation. While a dozen of girls who managed to escape from the captivity are being rehabilitated back in their home country, hundreds or many be thousands of others are being forcefully engaged in prostitution in Lebanon.

Lebanese in African soil do not only set their own rates to the goods that they import but also for the girls and again they seemed to have gone further than just being traffickers or brothel owners, to an extent that their existence had torn the social fabric of many Sub-Saharan African nations.

The Lebanese business community in Sub-Saharan Africa have left a considerable population as their offspring as a consequence of their sexual adventures with locals. The hybrids, who are known as Mulatoo, have a high demand in the society, and many of them do live at least a little higher than the standard of life of the indigenous population and they do take pride in having a lighter skin than their co-Africans, which says a lot about their attitude towards the blacks and collective mentality as a cross-breed.

'I'm a Mulatoo, surely my rates are higher,' a mixed-looking girl in a Burmese short sitting just behind me in the bar areas of Déjà-vue told the white guy who had already lost not only his equilibrium but also his sense of hearing.

He looked like a Latino, his voice was not clear at all; leaning on the girl's back already, he was bargaining.

'I will give you ten more dollars, right?' His voice supersedes the loud music in the club. Dozens of faces from the crowd of moving silhouette suddenly look at the guy, through the mystic smoke of tobacco and marijuana, coloured by twinkling disco lights. A mad laughter cracked among the dancing figures.

The woman drank the whiskey left in the glass in one gulp and dragged the guy next to her just like a leopard taking its pray to a treetop, to consume it without being disturbed.

'God bless his wallet,' I heard a spell of the same mad laughter following what the barman just said.

Déjà-vue is the wildest nightclub in town where one would see the dirtiest and hidden part of expatriate nightlife in Liberia. Most of the international organisations, especially United Nations, have declared Déjà-vue as 'off-limits' to their employers just due to the fact that the is club involved in prostitution and the level of security for the expatriates is not at the desired level. But most of the outgoing male aid-workers, merely driven by human desires fuelled by alchohol, do always find themselves dancing behind bulky butts of local girls on Friday late nights, after their ritualistic Saaj time where they try their weekly hunt of international ladies.

Most of the time, the Lebanese-African hybrid girls are sold at a higher rate in the flesh market in Monrovia nightlife. Not only expatriates, these girls have a high demand among the Liberian elite population as the lighter the skin the higher the demand is among men in Liberia.

'She is fine fine woman, light-skinned,' they would always notice hybrids and give them the first preference unlike in Southern African or Eastern areas where the mixed breeds are given the treatment of mother-in-law. But when it comes to sexual preferences, the Africans look for the difference, a light-skinned.

Most of the restaurants and the pubs in many of the Sub-Saharan African cities are in the flesh business for expatriates. Even though it is not visible to the outside, the most reliable way of transmission of messages in Africa, the oral tradition, guides the expatriates at their arrival about where to go for their different needs, which is the induction for social life of an expatriate in Africa. Irrespective of your gender, country of origin, religion, or colour, you have a series of adventures waiting for you in case you cannot suppress the bubbles of desires induced by the expatriate trends that catch many of those who come in, like the killer currents in the Atlantic.

Selena, a blond, attractive young lady who was from one of the new republics, emerged from ex-Yugoslavia, once beaten by the bloodiest war in recent history in Europe. She landed in the continent through Roberts International Airport as a volunteer, a first missioner, with an international nongovernmental organisation which was based in Gbarnga, a small township located around 200 kilometres away from capital Monrovia. Even though it was not a significant distance and the road conditions were quite acceptable compared to most of the places in the country, the access to many necessary commodities including drinking water is a challenge for an expatriate, especially a female. She was quite happy of having been chosen for the job, but immediately after she was sent to her county of assignment, she started struggling with the poor conditions of life, safety, as well as the health issues which started stealing her sleep and peace of mind. The first time I met her in the lobby of Royal Grand Hotel, one among three-star class hotels in Monrovia, she demonstrated an immense confidence in her.

'We also went through a tough time with war, we were refugees at one point,' she told.

'I'm used to these conditions and I can understand these people,' she added with a voice full of confidence but my mind, for some unidentified reason, translated her statement as unconsciously uttered words of overconfidence.

The next day after her arrival was a Friday, she appeared on the dance floor of one of the famous expatriate hotspots, with a couple of her colleagues. Probably they wanted to entertain her before she goes to her place of assignment where the night outs would remain merely a daydream.

'A new chick in town,' somebody among those who were drinking in the table next to me said.

As vultures notice a hunt from high skies even before the hunt is dead, many of the men who were there had noticed the new face, new prey.

When the dance floor is heating up with Latino music, the drunken girls are rather making the moves of destruction than dancing, and the alcohol starts interpreting the environment before the messages go to the brain, the eyes of vultures see every single woman who dances as a piece of hunted meat. And every single advance taken then on is merely sexually motivated. Especially when someone new comes to town, she will be known as fresh meat and everyone set themselves in a cold war to get to her first. As a result, the first few months of a female expatriate in many places of Africa is absolutely like a life of a newborn impala in the African wild full of predators and scavengers.

After our first meeting, I did not see her for almost six months till we crossed paths accidentally in John F Kennedy Hospital in Monrovia, which is the largest and the only general hospital for the whole nation of a population around four million. I was going to visit my local colleague who was critically ill with a renal infection.

'Hey, what's up?' I asked.

'Hi, I'm okay,' she replied as if she was just okay and wanted to slip away from further conversations. I did not reply but something somewhere inside me hinted that she was not okay at all.

As we do acquire a greater proportion of our habits via constant interaction with the environment where we do live most of the time, most of the expatriates apparently acquire the culture of rumours after a stay for some time in Africa. I met Senala in the morning, and by evening, I was sitting in Jamal-Cafe, another expatriates' hub in Sinkor, watching a football game. By coincidence, one of my old colleagues with whom I worked in Indonesia met me in the cafe and invited me to his table where there were a few other guys who were working for different entities such as oil companies, humanitarians, and diplomats.

'Your chick is back in town, I saw her this morning,' one guy told to another with a sarcastic tone.

I did not have a clue of whom they were talking about, they kept on describing a girl with their sexually explicit diction with almost abusive metaphors.

'Senala, she has one long gray one, among her pubic hair,' one confirmed his discovery before everyone else, while others were listening to him as if someone was pouring honey into their ears.

'Did you count she had only one gray hair down there?' another asked

When the conversation turned to be extremely sarcastic and vulgar while everyone at the table was trying to defend their word, the right to a life with dignity of a girl who had become a victim of a bunch of hungry predators seemed completely deprived.

'Not a long time ago, she had an abortion,' another gave his contribution to the ongoing assassination of character of a fresher. But the fact that I met her in the hospital in the morning and her peculiar mood had something to do with what this guy says? I questioned myself. However it was amazing how strong the expatriate networks are and the way the women are being traced just like world renowned spying or intelligent entities such as FSB, CIA, ASIS, Mossad, or RAW. And their covert activities are constantly launched to hunt down the new arrivals wherever they are based in. It is just like a herd of wild goats, the stronger mates with the females first, followed by the others and they make sure that the last male, too, have a chance. I did not pay much attention to the further discussion and moved to another table as I needed to watch the game in tranquillity, and eventually the stories of Senala were forgotten with not much emphasis as I had been hearing so many stories and rumours about different expatriates arriving in the country.

Even though the rumours have their wings and spread faster than the truth, the life of a rumour is no way longer than the truth. It is an added advantage that the expatriates community of Monrovia is compact and well connected, for truth to be revealed faster. We used to say that every rumour is chased by the true story in the next second.

'You know we had to evacuate that young girl because of a health issue, it was pathetic that she went through all these in Liberia where there is no single reliable health facility,' one of her countrywoman, her second-level supervisor, who felt really bad about what she went through, said with a tone of sympathy.

'She had tried a abort a child here in Liberia and ended up with an infection.' Her forehead had wrinkled like a skin of an African tusker. She was concerned about the life of the young lady. And she mentioned that the father was an aid-worker from a neighbouring country, working for another organisation based in Gbarnga, and he had a family back at home and did not want a child from a stranger, especially from the womb of a white woman, whereas sleeping with a white woman is a privilege or a dream for them. As a result, a life which was about to come to see the world is dead and those who were partially responsible remain insensitive. Thinking about the sad ending of the mission of a colleague whom I met only a few times during my tenure, I started packing my luggage for my next vacation.

The sky was pregnant with heavy gray clouds by midday, it was not still enough for heavy monsoons, even though the earth is soaked with water just like a paddy field. The sun seems forgotten the last day it had seen the earth through the thick curtain of clouds, and pouring started like a cow that pisses. In this part of the earth, a shower cap is enough for a local to walk under pouring rain, and they walk as if it's not raining. I was on my balcony with a hot cup of green tea, looking at the locals passing in the road under the rain, reflecting whether I need to go a bit early to the airport as anything can happen on the way when it rains without cease. Darkness in the daytime, thunders that crack the gray sky into pieces of fireballs, lightning that are like devilish lights that spot you before thunder falls on your head just in front of your very eyes, seen through the window frames like an ekphrasis, done by a schizophrenic painter just before he committed suicide. My thoughts were still with the incident of the young lady who was evacuated, just like the rain seen through the window frame, my journey has become nearly uncertain, just like her life, caught by the sickening rain and the next second is not in my hands, but walking in obscurity, leaving footprints for others to follow, not knowing whether the journey would be possible in current circumstances.

Many people come with sanity in their minds without knowing insanity waits for them hidden in the darkness and would infect them for the rest of their lives. Having accessibility of locals for sex, lack of gender balance in the working environment, and financial affluence as an expatriate along with sensations and persuasions, their transformation is irresistible and the consequences are unavoidable. At the end of the day, instead of African trypanosomiasis, a biologically known sleeping sickness which everyone knows irrespective of whether they have come to Africa or not, psychosocially transmittable sleeping sickness which becomes a lifestyle that has no cure and opens doors for many other diseases not only for the carrier but also for loved ones, infect many expatriates who come to the continent.

A sudden cascade of water started falling right in the middle of the corridor of the apartment building, making a loud noise which broke my pensiveness. In a culturally diverse environment, I did not know how to interpret a broken roof—a Russian would say that I would have a safe journey, whereas for my grandmother, I should not leave the house as it is an ill omen, but for a Liberian, it is usual and life goes on even without the roof. I called a colleague to drop me to the airport for the break that I was longing for.

Chapter 16

DRAGONS VS YOGIS

Eк 788 TO DUBAI is about to board in Kotoka International Airport in Accra, Ghana, which usually goes to Ivory Coast before departing to Dubai from Accra, as usually scheduled at 17.35h every day. Whenever I travel home or towards any European or Asian destination, I used to take an Emirates flight from Accra and fly via Dubai as it is reliable in terms of safety as well as punctuality compared to the other airlines flying in to western part of Africa where a limited number of airlines come especially after the Ebola crisis. The flight was twenty minutes late even though I was already at the boarding gate before the prescheduled time of boarding. In such situations where I had to wait, I usually open my MacBook Air, which I always take with me, and write something related to my office work or else personal leisure writing. That day, for some reason, I forgot to bring my charger for Mac and I had already exhausted the battery during my first leg of the journey. As I was left without my usual activity while waiting, I just lifted my eyes up and observed the crowd who were coming to the boarding area. It was just a random thought that emerged all of a sudden to break the boredom. Two African men in full suits were walking in, greeting a few others who were already seated in the boarding area and to the ladies who were at the boarding gate as if they knew each other, looking like Ghanaians who were quite known to people here, probably frequently flying businessmen or diplomats, I assumed. Some passengers were carrying typical shopping bags with hard shell overloaded and apparently heavy as they were coming home after weekly shopping, which reminded me my first flight to Africa via Nairobi in which the ground handling staff tried his best to throw my hand luggage which contained money, certificates, and other belongings into the checked-in cabin as all the overhead lockers were already occupied with shopping bags of those who were travelling to Ghana and Liberia via Nairobi. A group of Indians, apparently two families, were having their heavy snacks wrapped in old newspapers just like a group of crows gathered around a packet of food left on the road. One white couple, looking like tourists with heavy backpacks, shoes, and sleeping bags hanging in the bags, in African tops with Ghanaian colours, probably with the excitement for their vacations still with them, came to the line of seats where the Indians had their food fiesta and made their faces with expressions of irritation and disgust as if they had found a dead rat on the seat and started wiping it with some tissues. Indians were looking at them from a distance smiling at each other as they expect someone else to come and clean the seats where they ate. I felt as if I was in a classroom where a practical session on cultural differences is taught.

After a while when everyone was in the room, the number of Africans were the minority even though we were in an African country. Hundreds of Chinese who were waiting to board into the flight surprised me. Later on, whenever I took a flight to Africa either from Dubai or Qatar, a significant number of Chinese were to be noticed at the boarding gate, which reminded everyone not only that China is the country with the highest population on earth but also of how far China has spread its limbs, penetrating other continents on earth, especially Africa. It is impossible that no one goes without noticing how many Chinese are heading to Africa, and we say in South Asia, 'Chinese would come only to take something from you.'

My first interaction with Chinese was in my childhood. In the small township where I was born, there was one Chinese family who had a small shop where they used to fix artificial tooth. A Chinese in my childhood was always a tooth maker. I still remember my uncle had gotten a tooth made by them, and he used to keep it in a small glass of water when not in use. Every day after his tea shop is closed, he comes to his room, annexed to the living room of my parental house, and take his tooth out and put in the glass. One day, after months of waiting in curiosity, I took my chance to explore the mythical gadget made by Chinese and ended up breaking it into two. The rosy-coloured piece of plastic and the white tooth in artificial material separated. I put two pieces back inside the glass of water as if nothing happened. Next day morning, I heard that my uncle was telling my grandma that his tooth was broken and have to visit the Chinese again. In the Eighties, the Chinese were known only for communism and teeth in my part of the world despite that we knew that they had eyes like Japanese. Koreans were not in our common usage, unlike nowadays. Chinese crept in to Sri Lanka bunches with development projects funded by the Chinese government; Japan and Korea remained dream heavens for blue collars in Sri Lanka. But when I look at the number of Chinese popping up in each and every corner of Africa, the number of Chinese I had seen in other Asian countries is just negligible.

The influx of Chinese, like an army of red ants, retrieved instantly all my archived memories in Kenya and many other places of Africa where they suddenly appear in front of my eyes triggering the thought, 'What the hell are the Chinese doing here?' In Nairobi, in 2011, it was almost a decade after China made its aggressive advance in conquering the continent, via Kenya as the entry point, taking the maximum advantage of short-sighted African leaders who were thrilled at having a deep-pocketed partner willing to make big investments and start new huge projects that they rarely paused to consider whether they were getting a sound deal. And no one except China knew that those investments were just an injection of paralysing saliva of an octopus which was going to take the whole continent into its grip and dismember Africa in the long run.

When long-retained fantasies of some of the African leaders were promised to become realities, they became completely blind with the pompous pride of having some modern stadiums, highways, airports, or hydro-dams in their territories just to show their neighbour or the

Western world that they were ending the era of being dependent on Western powers without realising that those projects would leave their nations saddled with heavy debts and other problems, from environmental conflict to labour strife, but the African leaders, except few such as from Ghana, even though thousands of Chinese businesses worth billions of dollars are still running at the fullest interest of China, welcome Chinese investment irrespective of the visible consequences not only in debt-laden economies but also in social and environmental aspects. The Western powers play their aid-trick against the Chinese grip in Africa, warning African governments about the long-retaining consequences of embracing the Chinese hand, even though it has apparently turned out to be an act of playing violin for a deaf elephant.

However, jumping over the hurdles and avoiding the snares set by the west, China has dug African soil deep enough to the nucleus of the continent in such a way that every single activity in Africa has a Chinese touch.

$13.8-billion-dollar worth of Chinese investment on a new railway connecting Mombassa and Nairobi, which is the replacement of famous Lunatic express that remained as an eternal colonial icon of Kenya is the simplest example for Chinese control in the continent over long-existed Western powers. The railway cuts through Nairobi national park, creating another environmental catastrophe of noise pollution in the middle of a wildlife conservation site, and connect to Uganda expanding its length beyond the frontiers of Kenya, ensuring the Chinese influence and visibility regional. With the large-scale development projects, China sticks into their policy in creating employment opportunities to Chinese beyond the borders of China. Along with the fund that comes in as a loan, a greater proportion of the granted loan which is for the labour cost is directly pumping back to China. Not only that; along with the diplomatic ties, individual investors make their way and lean on local business partners first and then create their own space. We used to say in the 1990s that there are more Chinese restaurants in Sri Lanka than in China, just because during the Nineties, Chinese restaurants started popping up like seasonal mushrooms after April rains and most of them disappeared in less than half a decade, same as the destiny of mushrooms, drying out under the sun. During my stay in Nairobi, I had seen more than twenty

Chinese restaurants, either owned by Chinese or where Chinese work and I'm sure that I might have missed a greater number of Chinese shops and restaurants than what I had noticed. On busy streets, on a manic Monday, after office hours when everyone rushes home, in the capital of an East African country, I came across more than a few dozens of Chinese in less than two hours. I would never forget the old short Chinese woman who knocked her head against my elbow at the exit of Nairobi mall and yelled at me on the road in Chinese. According to her facial expressions and body language, I assume that all her words could not be words of pain but certainly of filth even though I did not understand a single word of her yelling but felt that she had not given a single chance for her mouth to be touched either by toothpaste or mouthwash for her whole life. And not a long time after the encounter with the old lady, I saw, in Jumo Kenyatta International Airport, a Chinese guy caught at the security check with a tea bottle in his hand luggage; he kept on talking to airport security personnel in Mandarin as if all of them were Chinese. Instead of getting pissed off, the security officers started looking around as if they needed the help of an interpreter. A miracle happened in less than few seconds; a lady, with a full-size backpack, which was only a few inches shorter than her, on her back came running towards the gate. Her motivation was quite visible to everyone. She was rushing to help her countryman who was unable to explain a thing in English. Chinese solidarity is amazing and unique and they are like opposite poles of a magnet, wherever they are, they stay attached as a community, like a little China which brought Chinatowns in many parts of the world, into my imagination.

Not very far from Kenya, just beyond the frontiers where there is not even a fence like in many countries, Chinese president Xi Jinping landed to enter to the resource-rich continent, as a part of his first foreign trip, immediately after having given the oath as president of People's Republic of China in 2013. Entering Tanzania with his ready-made papers of trade, development, and cultural accords, he made his way to the richest nation in natural resources in the continent, the Democratic Republic of Congo, where the prolonging conflict and political and economic instability is caused by its enormous quantity of resources. Being the second largest investor in Tanzania, China is tightening its grip in the agriculture, coal, and iron industries in the territory while assisting the infrastructure of the country that would facilitate the Chinese to link Chinese-run mines in Congo with Tanzania. When diplomatic and political ties grow stronger, it is easier for the small-scale businessmen to creep into Africa and conquer the continent in no time, and on the other side, local markets get overwhelmed with Chinese products in such a way that one would get an impression that China makes everything for Africa.

Lesotho is a landlocked country located within South Africa where there is not much external influence except from the Southern African Region. During my stay in Morija, quite an interior small township in Lesotho, I visited one of our friends a few dozens of miles away from the little town which is almost a remote village where there was only one retail shop where illiterate villagers go to buy the necessary stuff for daily living. When you enter the shop, a wonder, a Chinese girl who barely speaks English is at the cashier despite two Basotho men who work there as shop assistants, no one else is apparently there for assistance. Even though there are significant linguistic barriers between the cashier and the customers, the girl seems managing the shop pretty well using the maximum out of the available resources. From household appliances, food items, clothes, construction material, tools, to cosmetics, all the necessities for life have been made available under one roof for villagers, which prevent a demand being created for other shops in the area.

At first sight, I was shocked to see a Chinese girl in the middle of barren mountains where inhabitants talk only Sutu, not even a word in English, but later, I realized that she was not an isolated case; in many areas of Lesotho, including the capital, Maseru, Many Chinese shops can be seen. None of the cashiers, who are Chinese nationals, who are also the owners of the shops, speak English and Sutu but they make their business run better than other shops owned by locals. They have established their chains of shops and referral system even though the Chinese network has not yet reached a level of trade monopoly in Lesotho. In addition, the involvement of Chinese in stable economies in Southern Africa like Botswana and Namibia have been criticised, over issues like the taking over of local construction industries, or the proper execution of building projects, working conditions, and the proliferation of Chinese newcomers, many of them illegal migrants who have begun to dominate low-level commerce in a number of countries in the Zone. However, as the days, weeks, months, and years roll, it will not be impossible that in every little corner, there will be a Chinese face, and Ocean Basket or Pick and Pay will probably be written in Chinese in many Southern African countries like Lesotho, Swaziland, Namibia, Botswana, or Zimbabwe.

Besides the fact that The Great Wall of China is the only construction on earth made by humans that is visible from space, the Chinese have used the reputation of The Great Wall in penetrating Africa along with the famous yet mythical dragon. Great Wall hotel in Liberia is the centre of all sorts of activities in the Chinese community in Liberia. Every single Chinese in Liberia knows The Great Wall in Monrovia. Ranging from the labourer to the diplomat including, nongovernmental workers, UN personals, construction workers, businessmen, and others who do not belong to the categories mentioned above gather to The Great Wall Restaurant and Hotel, in the evenings where they can dine and wine as if they are in China, and all the other agendas and discussions among them follow. Besides that, prior to arrival to Liberia, every single Chinese who come in is aware of where they have to go to re-establish themselves with cultural, demographical, linguistic, and gastronomic sense of place. Coming from different places in the country with the world's largest population which is nearly 1.3 billion and 9.5 million square kilometres in size where it is impossible to know each other back home, the Chinese businessmen who come to Liberia, meet each other at The Great Wall. But The Great Wall is not the only Chinese restaurant or hotel in Liberia; conquering slowly but steadily, the Chinese grip in this conflict-ridden nation has been tightened up with development projects, especially the roads which are vital for the mining industry for Chinese, and infrastructures such as buildings for governmental offices as projects based on low-interest loans granted by the government of the People's Republic of China. In reality, in the West African zone, especially in countries like Liberia, Sierra Leone, Ivory Coast and Guinea, the political leadership is not concerned about the long-term consequences, in many cases even the immediate consequences of certain projects that extract the resources of the countries, as long as the foreign investors give them 'something'. The level of corruption in many African nations has created an easy gateway for Chinese. Like termites that come out from the earth from a small fragile space on a concrete left by mistake and create a colony in minutes, the Chinese take the systemic and ethical gaps in African governance systems and steer not only the whole system but also the whole continent towards their interest.

It was one evening. I was on transit to South Africa and had to stay overnight in Accra. Though I am usually not a fan of television, I switched on the television in the hotel room just to break the boredom. Surprisingly, my first sight was a Chinese man surrounded by Ghanaian policemen and I could not resist my desire to know more.

'A Chinese again,' I said to myself, a bit loud, as my mind immediately connected to one of the incidents I witnessed in Robert's International Airport. A Chinese woman was trying to carry a sum of money which was much greater than the amount which is legally allowed through any port of Liberia, which is $7,500. And she was screaming at everyone like a rabid dog and resisting the custom officers in checking her luggages further. It was apparent that she was afraid to lose her money but simultaneously she had already dared to violate the law of the country. As foreigners living in a zone where life does not have much value, usually we do think not only twice but many times about our conduct as any expatriate who lives in post-conflict zones of Africa has an added risk than locals. But these little creature seems not fearing the fact that being unlawful or violation of regulations can cause even losing one's life.

The highlight of the news was telecasted again with the same photo of the Chinese surrounded by the policemen. This time with the title: 'A Chinese national trafficking cocaine arrested.'

The next day, during the transit, there were dogs and special teams at the security check counters as if they tightened the security just because of this isolated case. As predicted, the checking was just a show, to please people. Authorities seemed to already know who was behind it, as the drug business is always sheltered by a big local fish whom no one dares to go against. Aside the drug business in Ghana, an estimated 50,000 new migrants, most of who are said to have hailed from a single county in southern China, showed up a few years ago to conduct environmentally devastating gold mining. This set off a popular outcry that forced the Ghanaian government to react, resulting in arrests of miners, many of whom are being expelled to China.

When I was around 8, I came across the word 'prostitute'. It could be bit late but in a significantly reserved society like that in Sri Lanka, it is natural that certain realities of life are usually kept away from children as much as possible.

'Street prostitution in Bombay—currently known as Mumbai' was the title of a column article that appeared in a hebdomadaire called *Daily News*. The common reasons why most girls and women choose prostitution in India and how it has developed to an extent of a social tragedy in some cities of India had been widely and profoundly discussed in the article. In a restrictive environment, naturally, a child who was about to reach his early adolescence would become extremely curious about what is not discussed publicly. As a result of my curiosity, I happened to read literature about prostitution in Eastern Europe after the fall of Soviet Union, human trafficking for sex slavery, sex industry in Thailand, and the rising prevalence of HIV in Manila caused by prostitution, and so on, but the first time in front of my very eyes, all that I read about prostitution in different contexts were compressed in one single Chinese phoceene plateau and offered in Africa by Chinese clubs. It looks like a plate of sushi where different kinds of sushi, with different tastes, different colours for those who have a different level of appetite, Chinese girls in all varieties are employed as dual-purpose waitresses. After the restaurant is closed, their role changes to strippers and then to quench the long-cherished dreams of many Africans that came into the peak of their mind after seeing faking Asians in interracial porno clips. Probably, the hard-earned few hundred dollars of an African farther lost in an Asian fantasy disappear into the mouth of the dragon, while a virgin imported from China, who is made a virgin each twelve week, weeps, mourns, and screams as if she is been attacked by a tiger and a black man judges himself as the strongest on earth before another fake made in China brand. As prostitutes and low-level business communities, who are mostly involved in illegal businesses, more than a million of Chinese have crept through the ports in Africa as illegal migrants, which is another rising concern and a growing wing of Chinese presence in Africa that made it look like Africa is going to be an extended part of People's Republic of China in the near future.

It was a coincidence that I happened to go to one of the famous local markets in Abuja, Nigeria, where anything on earth can be bought as in many of the African local open-bazaars. Finding a snake, alive or dead, in a basket for few hundred Niras is not a challenge here, and most often, snakes and any other unspecified bushmeat, ranging from rodents to monkeys, are quickly sold more than chicken, beef, or mutton. But among all back faces, it is certainly a wonder to see a Chinese woman selling fried termites, roasted tiny woodworms, and snakes in the crowded market. It is not a secret that in many parts of Africa, termites are eaten either fried or raw. I remember the kids of my colleague who hosted me celebrated one night when the termites flew into the house attracted by the light. I was looking at those little faces radiant with happiness of finding a seasonal delicacy, and only mongooses could be happier than them back in my country at times when flying termites get attracted by lamp posts on roads. Seeing street food of fried and roasted insects is unique to East Asian countries such as Mongolia, China, Cambodia, Thailand, Vietnam, and Laos. Though it is not an African thing, I witnessed that she is well established in the market, and people pick up something while passing by her, for a few Niras. Looking at her success, the day someone among those Nigerians would start frying all flying and crawling creatures and sell them at the roadside or at the bazaar will not be so far.

For the last decade, China's passive invasion in Africa has resulted in the exploitation of resources of the continent, nations laden with debts that cannot be paid back for centuries in the name of commercial loans, illegal immigration, illegal business, encouraging corruption and a market flooded with cheap and low-quality Chinese products, leaving no space for the locally produced or imports from other countries, creating a Chinese monopoly in the African market. As a consequence, China's relationship with the continent is entering a new and much more sceptical phase. The doubts do not come from any soured feelings from African leaders themselves, most of whom still welcome and profit from China's embrace. The new scepticism has a lot to do with the hectoring of Western governments, the traditional source of Africa's foreign aid and investment and interference. The United States and European powers have been warning the African leadership for the last few years about the advance of China, without investing much in helping to strengthen African civil society and, thereby, governance. However, China seems to be in an extreme hurry and is so often seen to be looking out for itself, the potential downsides for many Africans have begun more and more to stand out: accelerated environmental destruction by mining and other activities, disregard for labour rights, the hollowing out of the local industry, and even the stalling of the continent's democratisation. As a result, there is a fast-growing scepticism about China from Africa's own increasingly vibrant civil society, which is demanding to know what China's billions of dollars in infrastructure building, mineral extraction, and land acquisition mean for the daily lives and political rights of ordinary Africans.

Well after a decade or a bit more than that, China seemed to have realised that there are some 'growing pains' in the relationship between China and African states, and there are always Europe and the United States to scratch the wounds which are already there as a gesture of acknowledging that it needs to improve both the style and substance of its push into Africa.

'Assure our African friends in all seriousness that China will never pursue a colonialist path like some countries did, or allow colonialism, which belongs to the past, to reappear in Africa,' Li Keqiang, prime minister of the People's Republic of China, mentioned in one of his official visits to a couple of African countries.

When closely considering the pattern of intervention of China in Africa, setting up huge mining operations, building infrastructure to facilitate the industries set up by them, taking primary resources and selling manufactured ones back to Africans, the essence of colonialism is clearly visible with an additional element unique to Chinese. Unlike European colonialists, they use equipment and labour imported from home, without transferring skills to local communities, which ensures that every single penny goes back to China and prevents the development of host territories. But still, China offers potentially extraordinary upsides to Africa. Without question, the continent is badly in need of more and better infrastructure.

In the end, though, what will minimise any downsides of China's involvement in Africa is the deepening of African democracy. Grass-roots activism and vibrant independent media are, everywhere, the ultimate check on corrupt legislators and on foreigners who get lucrative but unsound deals by handing over bags of cash.

However, in the form of investment and development, China has already taken the continent of darkness into the darker dragon's mouth from where greedy and short-sighted African leaders see the lights of the external world through the sharp teeth, transforming Africa into China's second continent where Chinese migrants are building a new Dragon Empire.

When hundreds of thousands of Africans were being pushed through the gates of no return in the coastal belt of Africa, a significant number of Indians sailed in ships of the colonialists in 1860 and set themselves somewhere between the black locals and white rulers in South Africa. As a result of colonisation and slave industry which came along with it, the gates of Africa wide opened for Indians. Since that time, Indians are pushing themselves into Africa in many paths even though the Western powers and the United States seem not worrying much about Indian advance in Africa as they do with China. However, since well over a century, Indians started to spread seeds of Indian occupation in Africa.

When Chinese were entering the continent via Kenya, Kenyans were eating pilau as a part of their daily meal and a few Indians were already in their parliament. But this is not an isolated scenario in Kenya; a long before Chinese thought of penetrating African frontiers, Indians remained as an integral part of African society, especially when it comes to the southern part of the continent, particularly South Africa, Indians played a vital role in the anti-apartheid defiance campaign.

'Mandela was supported not only by blacks, in African National Congress; Indians had a significant contribution, especially committed activists like Mac Maharaj, Ahmad Katrada,' my father added while watching the inauguration speech of Nelson Mandela in 1994. I was 15 years old and had acquired a sound knowledge not only in the dynamics of world politics but also a good knowledge in constitutions and governance, grace to my father's private tuition classes he used to conduct on a daily basis, in a small room annexed to my bedroom. More than five hours a day, I used to hear lectures he was giving to the students which not only created kind of an interest in me about politics but also encouraged me to take political science as a major subject in my advanced level studies and at the university for bachelors. The stories of freedom fights of many countries including South Africa, Sri Lanka, India, United States, Ghana,

Tanzania, along with the names key actors involved, I had repetitively heard from him. His mentioning about Indians having a key role in anti-apartheid in South Africa completely turned me upside down.

'Indians in South Africa?' I asked with surprise not because I was unable to believe that there were Indians at the leadership level in the South African freedom movement but simply because I was not in a position to realise that there were Indians living in the continent of Africa. Africa was always associated with the imaginary picture of blacks, cocoa, wild animals, poverty, conflicts, and cannibals, not at all with Indians. After nineteen years, I realised that there was another India in South Africa when I visited Durban in 2013. It is impossible to find another city with such deeply rooted Indian traits in the African continent. A vibrant city along the coastline of the Indian Ocean, where different cultures merge like nowhere else on earth, without a doubt, Durban is the most African among South African cities—it has an African soul, an African history, and African realities like no other African cities; it has a unique cultural blend that would not work anywhere else in the world. You would see the mosque and a Catholic church side by side in one street where an Indian market is just at the end of the same street. The city of cultural coexistence where every single culture has added colours, fragrance, textures, and melodies into the collective culture of the city called Durban, where the most dominant culture is Zulu, the culture of the largest ethnic group in South Africa, the mighty warrior nation united by King Shaka; the warriors fearlessly fought with the British army giving them the worst-ever defeat in 1879. I was fascinated by the level of tolerance for diversity presence in the city and I have not come across a place, out of more than 100 cities around the world, where Indian culture has been absorbed and integrated into a pre-existing culture which is still strong. If one wants to experience this wonder in Durban, Victoria street market is the best place to be. It is simply a passageway to India, one would feel that it is Chandeni-Chor in old Delhi where elements of all subcultures are found and sold under one open market. Victoria market was built in 1980 replacing the old Indian market which dated back to 1910 and destroyed by a fire in 1973. I was walking down along the Queen Street of Durban, without my backpack, just in a casual bottom and a shirt and I was pretty sure that everyone saw me as of native

Indian-descent South African which made my life easier, especially in markets where bargaining is the most important part of shopping. When we reached the intersection where Queen Street meets Victoria Street, I already started feeling the aroma of the Orient, the place where barrels of Indian spices and incense infuse to the air of the flea market where a new culture called Afro-Oriental culture is born. Every single essence for religious rituals representing almost every single religion in India ranging from dominant Hinduism to Jainism, every single spice to make curries of any ethnic dish in India, and every single latest ethnic fashion found in India are found here. It was just like an expansion of a typical Indian open bazaar in Africa. Unlike the Chinese who always stick into their own labour force, in some Indian shops, the blacks were working hand in hand with them, and it was not difficult to see Indian youth with African youth and married couples. My Durban experience ended with a very positive note on what is called cultural coexistence and rise as a nation. I called my sister who was in Swaziland and told, 'Here I'm like a native, free like a bird, great that I look like an Indian.'

Since their ancestors touched the sands of Durban coast, in 16 November 1860, Indians have been a part of South African society enriching the rainbow over the port of Natal. They came not only as labourers but also as passengers looking for fortune in a land that held great promise. Even though they found themselves in the wrong side of the racial divide in South Africa, apartheid in South Africa fuelled the freedom fight in India. Apartheid hit Mohandas Karamchand Ghandi in South Africa when he came as barrister for fighting a court case against a wealthy Indian family in South Africa. After he was thrown out of the first-class train compartment in Pietermaritzburg, his transformation to Mahatma Ghandi, the leader of nonviolence freedom movement in India, from Mohandas Karamchand Ghandi, happened in South Africa and thereafter the inspiration for fighting against the apartheid came from Indians and they are an integral part of what is called South Africa today.

IT companies like TATA consultancies, NIIT, have come into place pumping knowledge into the youth while the diplomatic relations between India and South Africa remain stable since 1994. And today, Indian investments are found in every sector of South Africa and it looks like two growing economies are well aligned and move together like nowhere else on earth.

They are South Africans in all means but they have not lost their identity from where they came and merged into the existing system and added their colours into the colourful culture of South Africa for 150 years and many centuries to come.

My next destination was Mombassa, another vibrant city along the coast of the Indian Ocean, which is the second largest city in Kenya and the regional cultural and economic hub of Mombassa country, earlier known as Coastal Province. Mombassa, being a coastal city in Eastern Africa, possesses a rich history in trading with different nations especially with Arabs and Indians. Today, besides the Swahili and Mijikenda, people who are majority, there is an Indian community which is significant, who have historical roots as well as recent migrations. Through one of my Indian friends, I booked Maharaja in Babburi in Mombassa where the Indian spirit of Kenya is live, vivid, and touchable and with South Asian hospitality and warmth, I was welcomed by the hotel staff with the cold breeze coming across the Indian Ocean, as if to say that it was the breeze that took them to this coast from India. I was waiting for a special couple whom my colleague introduced to me a couple of weeks ago via mails, having my tea with milk looking at the waves that break at the coast. It is the same water that hit the coastline of India, and my motherland Sri Lanka, and it looks like the immense water that runs to infinity has made a bound between these continents. My imagination had run longer than the distance of naval miles from the Horn of Africa to Palk Strait when a slender fair-skinned lady with a long black hair appeared with her tall and well-built Kenyan husband and greeted me in Hindi, then her husband greeted me in English. Once by accident I happened to watch a documentary on YouTube about one Indian lady married to a Kenyan man who was even below middle income level and went to his mud hut as his second wife. She had accepted the polygamous union and descended from her palace to come to live in the hut with him, working every day with mud, dust, and smoke, going to dirty markets every day to buy necessary stuff for making sure food is on the table on time, preparing Ugali, Irio, Wali Wa Nazi not only for her and her husband but also for the extended family. That I found hard to believe. I was unable to treat it as an isolated case as I found another couple, an Indian woman married to a Kenyan shoemaker. I was persuaded to meet the friends of my colleague who have the same racial composition in the family to understand what collate the Kenyan and Indians together.

I did not know where to start with them; therefore, I asked them to place an order for them. While the lady I would call Laxmi, which is a pseudonym for her, places the order of drinks for them, I took the slight gap of time to pose a question to her husband.

'How did you meet her?'

'I worked in his father's shop, and then I made friends with her,' he replied with a humble tone.

I did not say 'Waaaw' intentionally but his reply surprised me. As I could imagine the reaction of her parents once they got to know about their relationship. I immediately felt that my reaction was not appropriate and sounded quite judgmental. While apologising for what I said, even though Laxmi's husband, Musa, not his real name, did not feel offended by my gesture, I asked them about the reaction of their families when they came to know about their relationship.

'Laxmi's family was against the relationship,' Musa added, bringing a smile in Laxmi's face.

'My father said that he would rather cut me and give me to lions than allowing me to go with a black man,' she said with a smile.

'What was the opinion of your family?' I looked into the eyes of Musa who was also smiling as if the tough time had gone long ago.

'They were quite helpful to us but they were afraid of our future.'

'Inter-racial marriages are not common in my society,' he added.

As per Musa, there were some concerns about their relationship, from the side of their relatives and especially when it comes to a marriage with a daughter of a wealthy Indian family. They anticipated that their son would be in danger and wanted him to give up and they did not want him to be hurt. On the other hand, they had respected the choice of their son and helped Laxmi to deal with new situations in her new life, as it was another story of descending from a palace to the life of an ordinary Kenyan, though she did not end up in a mud hut. Being a courageous man with adequate level of education for doing an executive job in a private firm, by this time, Musa and his family had reached a level that the parents of Laxmi cannot reject them any longer. But it is not the usual destiny of other Indians married to Kenyans in villages.

However, as a result of changes that occurred in the space of time that passed by, which is almost a decade, the old wooden rickety chair of the shop that the father used to sit in for last five decades, has become her seat, and the father had left millions worth of properties in Kenya in her hand along with her aging mother to take care of. And the gates of the palace are also left open not only for Musa but also for his parents. And the extended family of eight members, four Kenyans, two Indians, and two mixed children, are living in the palace-like mansion built by Laxmi's father. Over the death of her father, her family had recovered their fortune. And Laxmi and Musa had opened a new shop in Nairobi as an extension of their main shop in Mombassa. As per what they told me, they are one of the success stories among the Kenyan-Indian couples. Before they left me, Laxmi gave me a bunch of business cards of different Indian restaurants and shops in Mombassa and Nairobi where I would be able to get things for cheaper prices if I mention their names. There were more than fifty cards. I was unable to realise that fifty Indian shops are located in these two cities. Then I got to know that there are even parliamentarians with Indian descent in Kenya. I realised that Indians are not just businessmen in Kenya—they are a part of the Kenyan society in all dimensions, even though some Kenyans look at them with detest.

'One comes first, and then next day, you will see a whole village full of Indians,' one Kenyan Nurse who worked with me in Liberia told me.

'I worked in an Indian hospital in Kenya; it was not easy to work with them,' she explained that the extent of work that the management expected were not imaginable and the way they treat locals were rude.

'They are born to micromanage,' she added with a gesture of disgust.

However, since 1896, when Indian labour was taken in by British for the Uganda railway project, Indians have landed in the soils of Kenya for many reasons, especially for business. Even though they are even less than 1 per cent of the total population of Kenya, they are playing a significant role in Kenyan economy. From little retail shops in open markets to giant industries in Kenya under names of Indians, among whom majority are Hindus, some of them are Muslims and Sikhs who have not left their core beliefs when they migrated to the land of endless savannahs. As everywhere else where Indians live, Hindu and Sikh temples are found in many places of the country, slowly merging into the society as an integral part of the general outlook of the country.

In every single city in Africa where I had been, from Cape Town to Casablanca, Accra to Nairobi, almost every ingredient required for a complete Indian meal is present. Aata flour, lentils, Indian masala, and so on, can be found in any place in the continent of Africa, just like the Indian faces and the retail shops on the streets of Africa. Every African city has at least ten shops belonging to Indians and at least a couple of Indian restaurants as if being an Indian, one would never stay hungry or stop seeing their countrymen wherever they go in Africa.

Most of iron mines in Africa are supplying the materials for the famous steel company Mittal, which is 88 per cent owned by a Lakshmi Mittal. In real sense, the iron mining and steel industry in Africa is completely under Indian monopoly. Unlike Chinese, Indian companies operating in the continent hire local labour but for extremely low rates using maximum advantage of unemployment in the continent. While Chinese exploit the fossilised resources in the continent, the Indian business community is involved in both human and fossilised resources.

Arthur worked first in a famous Indian restaurant in Sinkor, Monrovia, where he helped the chef at the kitchen for two years and then left the restaurant because of the salary which was low even for his basic needs. Finally, he ended up being a domestic worker in compounds where UN employees reside in Monrovia, especially in Sinkor, and happened to be my houseboy for almost eighteen months, and even after we left Liberia, his stories about Indians prevailed.

'Bossman, you look like Indian but you do not behave like them,' one day he burst my wife with laughter until she came to the point where tears came out of her eyes. I was listening to him trying to resist the laughter that forces my fence of teeth just like a raging Tsunami on a wave breaker.

'I say no lie oooo,' he looked at me.

'What is the difference between me and an Indian?' I asked as I was curious of what he has to say.

'You treat me good, not mean. Bossman, they do not pay you anything extra, but they want you to work extra for nothing.' Liberians are born lazy. It is like the chance of a blind turtle would see the full moon through an air bubble in water that a Liberian demonstrates willingness to work overtime, as a consequence of that, it is natural that there will be work style clashes with Indians who are naturally hardworking and result oriented, which are usually perceived as interracial issues and generalised easily. However, the employer and employee relationship between Indians and local Africans are not so healthy. Coming from a society where caste has predetermined how one will be treated and looked at in society, even before he or she is born, and again with the class gap which is like earth to sky, Indian employers' attitude to African employees can be obviously perceived harassing and inhumane. Trying to extract every single drop of energy of their employees at the lowest cost possible is the common relationship model between Indian 'bossman' and African 'workers'.

'The man beat me one day left and right.'

'For what?' I asked as Arthur is a very careful and honest person with a positive attitude and relatively a hardworking person.

'An egg fell down, it was my mistake, and he beat me for that with the hot spoon till I run away from the kitchen.'

The way he kept on telling me the story made me feel the pain he went through being beaten with a hot spoon which was in oil.

'Look Bossman still I have the scar, that was my last day in the restaurant, with Indian bossman.'

He showed me a scar on his right shoulder, a clear burnt mark which has popped up as usual in black skin, like a snail on his shoulder. I, in truth, did not have a word to say as saying sorry was not enough. And I felt that it is reasonable that most of the time Africans show hateful attitude to all the South Asians based on the fact that we all look alike and they cannot demarcate an Indian from a Sri Lankan or a Bangladeshi from our external appearance.

It was an evening in December in 2012. I just landed in Keneth Kaunda International Airport in Lukasa, Zambia, from Johannesburg. It looked like those who were working in South Africa were coming back home for Christmas with bags full of gifts for their loved ones back in their homes. With hundreds, maybe thousands, of passengers with trolleys full of luggages and shopping bags like donkey caravans of gypsies were lined in the customs and I was only with my small hand luggage and a checked-in luggage which is even less than ten kilograms with my clothes and shoes. As everyone passes, my chance came. The customs officers who were not even paying attention to the bags like cement packs thronged around me as a group of crows attracted by a dead rat.

'Open your bag,' one said with an authoritative voice as if I was already in custody for trafficking drugs, gold, or illegal bank notes or else as if they caught a listed internationally recognised criminal. Their tonality rather made me furious than scared. I opened the bag; there was no illegal items or things to be declared. One guy took out one of two new shirts that I had in my checked-in luggage.

'These are dutiable, you know?' The custom officer looked at my face as if he was expecting any sign of being intimidated. This kind of interactions I had been having since the first day I entered Africa, in Ghana, Nigeria, Ivory Coast, and in Liberia, in most of the airports, especially in the West Africa region, asking for bribes, creating situations where you feel like there is no other way, have become a livelihood which is accepted by the government authorities.

'Open your hand luggage,' the next one comes in adding some weight to the group of custom officers. I had my liquid money around $5,000, cards, my MacBook, and DSLR in the hand luggage; aside from those, I had nothing expensive. I opened while keeping my eye on my checked-in luggage which remained already open.

'Count your money,' the other one said, looking at the envelope I had in my travel organiser. The customs officers who were trying to persuade me to give them something and avoid their harassment crossed my level of tolerance. I knew that I had not violated any of the regulations of customs or immigration, and I had my UN credentials which I did not show them yet, and I had enough time at the airport as my final destination was Lukasa. On top of everything, the colour of my passport was maroon, not black, which they did not see yet which also pumped some confidence.

'Okay, now I counted money and I do not have which is considered to be declared, not even the illegal software application which are illegal everywhere, except in Africa and what else you are waiting for?' I asked the guy who was still having one of my new shirts in his hand.

'Your law of immigration and immigration or customs do not allow a person to have two new shirts in his possession when entering the country?'

'Or else it that your personal regulations imposed looking at the face of passengers?'

I raised my voice and kept on asking them questions after questions.

'Do you think I am an Indian to pay you five or ten dollars as bribe and slip away from your harassing behaviour,' I said finally and felt relieved. It was a release of an impulse, releasing a feeling accumulated for years due to being harassed at many African airports and border posts based on the assumption that I was an Indian who would pay some bribe and slip away from any situation without confronting or standing against the injustice. Besides that, many of them take things to trade which are taxable, and as they are in the weak side when it came to arguing back with the immigration crows waiting for bribes, as they have violated the regulations and the only solution left for them is to give something and slip away. This is a common feature of the Indian-African relationship in entry points in Africa, which has now been generalised in such a way that whoever who looks Indian is immediately surrounded by the customs officers like greedy crows. An Indian is always seen as a person who would rather like to give some bribe to avoid following procedures and respect regulations. As a result, consciously or unconsciously, Indian presence in Africa had enormously contributed to the growth of the existing culture of corruption in Africa.

Once upon a time, Africa used to be the dump land of European and American vehicles. Starting from the Hunter bicycle to Mack heavy-duty truck, every single European and American marks can be found on African roads still, but mostly in very old conditions. Those were already used enough when they had reached Africa, and it is like their insurrection in Africa, serving the underprivileged continent with their second life with lot of complications, with extreme air and noise pollution, breaking down on the roads, and causing mortal accidents, killing innocent lives, unnoticed to Western eyes where those killing machines have been sent from. It is a usual site in downtown Monrovia, a few American trucks either broke down or completely turned upside-down right in the middle of the road, blocking completely the circulation on roads and the recovery can even take more than a day. It is just one example. And one day, a UN vehicle along with a few other private cars was pushed and sandwiched by a huge truck with a heavy load as a result of a break failure in a hilly intersection in central Monrovia. Despite all hassles and messes in the towns like Freetown, Conakry, and Monrovia where old European and American second-hand vehicles play their demon games, flying elements made in India take a considerable number of lives every year. Bajaj, TVS, and Hero-honda motorbikes are widely used as a public transport which is mostly rode by the youngsters who are uneducated and victims of civil conflicts in West African countries. Their foresight is usually hindered by the thrill of speed and forget the value of not only their life but also the life of the passenger who has nothing to do with their sensations. However, so long as the moto-taxi culture remains in many African nations, the Indian bike market remains stable within the continent. Usually hardware shops owned by Indians operate as bike dealers in case there is no direct dealer. However, they make sure that the constant flow of bikes and spare parts can meet the demand. Despite sons of Lebanese businessmen or locals from very rich families ride Japanese or European bikes, mostly those who have speed fever, who are fans of either trailer bikes or flat-road models, all the others' bikes are made in India. Even though the Chinese started importing their bikes, their attempts were completely knocked down by the Indian bike companies because of their well-established reliability in terms of fuel consumption, durability, availability of spare parts, and mechanical simplicity. That was one domain where the raged invasion of dragons was silently defeated by the nonviolent Yogis in Africa. By now, the culture of moto-taxi is being slowly fading away from many African cities, and Asian tuck-tuck, in other words the three-wheeler taxis, has come into being. Before Indians brought their three-wheelers such as Bajaj and TVS into the continent, there were very poor-quality Chinese ones seen randomly in busy African streets, but by today, China had been effortlessly pushed away by better-quality Indian marks such as Bajaj and TVS with their long history in Asian public transport as well as reliability in service and repair-related customer care.

During my road trip to Gulu in Uganda, in the trip to Bunia in DRC from Goma, from Conakry to the Liberian border and in many other places, I was reminded over and over again about Marshrutka, the shuttle bus I often take in Ukraine whenever we visit the mother of my wife. Unlike the ex-soviet Marshrutka, a passenger minibus which is quite comfortable with a limited number of passengers and acceptable interior and good running condition, the African version is a delivery van without glasses or proper ventilation, converted to a passenger mobile prison with small holes in both sides of the van for light and ventilation and packed with passengers like goats or cows taken to butchery. And a yawning or a fart besides the constant smells of sweat and food can make anyone unconscious in the room. In the worst scenario, one may end up having a shower of vomit from one of the attached neighbours on the journey who is travel-sick. Then you have to wait till the next stop of the minibus, with all sorts of particles of food and gastro acids and enzymes of your African brother, sister, mother, or father, who may even have one or more infectious diseases, not to wash but to wipe out those stuff from your head. Sometimes, you can be fortunate to have some water to wash your head and face and to get rid of the remains of vomit, but not the disgusting smell of it. You, after, do not have the luxury to wash till you reach your final destination. Sometimes, chickens can wake you up in the minibus during your semi-fainted status of mind that you may attain due to suffocation and tiredness. When you open your eyes, you might take some time to understand what is right on your head or face, on which you had been sleeping comfortably for the last few hours of the journey. It can either be a butt, tummy, or breast or anywhere else of anyone travelling in the packed meat bus. This is a typical African reality which is facing a gradual but a slow-changing process with the diplomatic ties of many African countries with India. Ashok-Leland buses started appearing in some West African countries as donations by the government of India as a result of state-to-state relationships that is also a silent pursuit of the way of the dragon. Especially, Eastern Africa and some parts of the South have already given up the minibus culture grace to affordable Indian buses which are pretty good with African road conditions making a new shift in the culture of public transport in Africa.

In many poor townships in Africa where ordinary life is many nautical miles below the line of poverty, life is still in a constant struggle of remaining colourful, despite all sufferings. China's cheap and very low-quality electronics and other gadgets had always been the sunshine for their life. Fancy cellular phones with touchscreen, high-resolution cameras and polyphonic sounds, headphone sets, or ear pods almost looking like original Beats, Apple, or any other top brands and watches like Rolex or

Swatch with similar emblems and outlook but made in PRC, lifted the beaten mentality of the poor population of urban ghettos in Africa to a certain level within their minds. But there was not really a lifting up of anything despite scraping the wealth of the poorer among the poorest, to the marrow bones by selling them things which stop working after the second day of purchase and there is no warranty for the products and not even a brand name to check for spares. As a result, Chinese electronics start fuelling the growing pains of Chinese-African relationships during the last couple of years opening a gateway from silently waiting Yogis to console broken hearts and bring back the happiness to Africans through the union between Indian and Africa.

In recent years, instead of unreadable Chinese names on phones, or mostly the mobile phones without brand names, brands like Micromax have invaded the mobile phone market in Africa. With a limited warranty and at a reasonable price, and besides all with service support provided at any Indian electronic or mobile shops which are like popping up mushrooms after spring, the Indians have pumped fresh blood into Africa with some trustfulness in their relationship with Africa while giving a nonviolent slap to their rival for years not only in Africa but also in Asia extending the border conflict between China and India to the continent of darkness. They are engaging themselves in a silent combat in obscurity, the long-lasting relationship between Africa and India that has a colonial history and beyond seems not affected by the empire of dragons with millions of migrants in Africa. Dragons are still moving in and Yogis prevail.

Chapter 17

STOLEN PETALS

UNLIKE THE TURNING OF the year 1998–1999, which was full of debates about the common currency in eurozone, since the beginning of the second fortnight of the month of December 1999, everyone was obsessed with an imposed preoccupation about the millennium by the media in every single country, who were engaged in a ruthless campaign of filling their accounts sufficient for the next thousand years. When snow was melting with the heat of millennium fever in Paris, and traditional serenity of peacefulness of Christmas seemed hindered by the heat and rush of millennium, my mind had already been taken away by an article I found in *Elle*, a French monthly magazine, to a nomad land in the Horn of Africa where Christmas had never been celebrated and the chilling nights and burning sands will remain for next millennium exactly as it remained so far. Life has no preoccupations about so-called celebrations provoked by media campaigns or any other artificial factors except the fact that the real festivity comes in with the arrival of long-awaited rain clouds which is like the millennium celebration for those who battle with life there, and everyone forgets their worries and hardships and enjoy a natural shower, a blessing from the Holy Spirit, almighty Allah. Month-long prayers and unbroken faith under the hot sun and on burning sands seem to have been answered.

An upperbody-nude woman, in the front page, whom one can at first perceive as a South Indian if the person does not have exposure to the features of Northeast Africans like Ethiopians, Somalians, or Eritreans, with a pleasant smile, under the heading 'FGM'. That was my first exposure not only to the abbreviation 'FGM' but also to the existence of female gender mutilation and the name 'Waris Dirie'. That point, there was not a single sign in me that I would be affiliated to the same organisation she was affiliated with as a diplomat in advocating the campaign against female gender mutilation and would come in to the continent where she went through every single bit of trauma as told by the author of *Desert Flower*. As my father used to say, motives that remain deep in your mind can take you to the places where you visualise.

After having read the article, I was persuaded to buy the book *Desert Flower*, which I bought in less than two weeks and ended up reading the book more than three times, probably because of the information thirst about the newly discovered African reality which was a brand new horizon that had never appeared in my life of twenty years spent in Sri Lanka where the horizon is open to the whole world, being an island. I was aware of circumcision of males in Islamic countries and even we used to make fun out of our Muslim friends, calling them 'Three-quarters', but the practice of circumcision among females was kind of an eighth wonder to me. And I was unable to imagine how it affected them and how it looked like.

'My father should have at least a clue about this . . . but. . .' my monologues remained monologues as so-called barriers imposed by culture stood between me and my father as it is not usual in Sri Lanka to discuss about sexual matters between parents and children. Grace to the Internet, I was able to search for detailed information about female genital mutilation in different counties in Africa and I kept on surfing for more information which opened my paths to read the other two books about Waris, *Desert Dawn and Desert Children*, which intensified my curiosity to explore dark ends and corners of life in Africa. Days, weeks, and months passed by, I had gathered a lot of information and accumulated within me about GFM, just like in an advanced data management system, demographically disaggregated information, geographical distribution of FGM, different forms of the practice, cultural and religious affiliations to FGM, methods and tools used for FGM in different regions, myths about the practice and that encourage the practice, fight against FGM, and the social, psychological, and biological impact of FGM. And I had gathered magazines, books, documentaries, and articles about the practice representing different points of view, represented by different cultural, religious, and social groups by the end of 2004. I was interested in discovering what were the latent factors, if there is any, that made people deeply plunged in believing in such brutal practices in modern time. I did not know whether fighting against FGM had ever been a part of my African dream but I knew it is a well-established African reality, like a cancer in the lungs, that existed since the time we know with its slow but sure progress in silence hiding behind the darkness of the continent that has to be cut off one day. Along with the killer tides of tsunami that hit Sri Lanka along with few other countries in Indian Ocean, I woke up in the middle of another episode of my African dream and had to face the reality of time in my motherland. As a result of the calamity, I started working with American Red Cross, Psychosocial Support Program, which was the initial step of the ladder which was the gateway for the realisation of my African dream in pragmatic and real world reminding me of a unique proverb probably invented by my father, which he used to tell to one of his friends who used to visit him often in the evenings to chat with him. He was a man who was merely a dreamer and he was a man full of words and we used to call him the lazy man.

'You have to wake up in the middle of the dreams and look whether you are in place where you can reach them.'

Whenever my father tells this as if he wants to remind him every now and then that his friend is just lost in dreams that are surreal and he had to move his butt and work for what he dreams to have in his life, his face becomes like the sky in a stormy evening and he stands up slowly as if he is an osteoporosis patient and touches his belly followed by a yawning just like a ritual and he leaves our place. Even though father never encouraged our acts of making fun of his friend, everything happened to him under our roof. I do still remember like a series of common cartoons we watched in our childhood, but along with the quotes of my father just like the one above. Sometimes, when he left, being quite angry with my father, my father goes directly to the kitchen and makes a cup of tea, comes and sits on the step of entrance of house. While sipping his black tea, licking sugar in his palm after each sip, he used to say, 'Crazy dreams can come true, all that is needed is just an opportunity.' He asked me to bring the Catapult left on his old book rack and next moment is a moment of excitement and joy. We shoot mangos, bunches of ripe Mangos start falling down one after the other, from a huge mango tree in the public school compound in front of our house. My grandmother said once that it was a dream of the first head-mistress of the school. She wanted to see fruit trees in the school compound for children to eat. After almost half a century or probably more than that, the tree stands right in the middle of the school just like the centre of the institution.

Till the end of my humanitarian missions in Asia, Waris and her books were far away from me even though they were in my library at home where there are more than 500 books about diverse themes of Africa collected from different sources. When I saw the dawn of my dreams coming true, by the end of 2010 with my possible deployment to Africa, all elements of my African dream, including FGM, got out from the cells of the prison of archives in my brain and formed a full map of Africa visually in front of the eyes of my imagination but it was momentary sensation that came to the surface like a blue whale in immense waters on the ocean yet visible and real but disappears in an instant and reappears at any point of time, as my deployment contract was not offered by that time. After one month, it was certain that I would land to the soil that had witnessed millions of cries of small girls who had been brutally cut, sewn, and absolutely deprive from the gifts of nature of their womanhood. I wrote down in my notebook, 'Stolen Petals', which came to my mind after I saw some graphics of female genital mutilation years ago, which had been haunting my mind for years. Another secret corner to discover at the horizons of darkness and I did not know how to initiate as my instincts warned me being a foreigner, especially looking like an Indian, and being a male, I would not be able to break cultural, religious, and gender barriers in discovering a top secret ritual executed behind the curtain of culture but I was determined at least to meet a victim of female genital mutilation one day during my parkours in Africa.

Almost two years after I entered the continent, I met Yatta, a Fula woman from Kankan while I was on a road trip to Mali, via Guinea. She was a very close friend of my colleague who guided me throughout the journey till Timbuktu which I dreamt to visit since 2000 after having read an article published in *Geo Magazine* French edition. She joined us from Kankan and left us in Bamako on her way for an official meeting of the international organisation with which she was affiliated to, at that time. Grace to the time of year, in April, when the roads are easier to pass, especially the road between Kankan and Bamako, was the best part of the whole journey; we had time to talk instead of worrying about pushing the minivan, getting down every now and then and being obsessed with backaches which are the usual preoccupation while on road trips in many parts of Sub-Saharan Africa; we had some time to talk and be acquainted with each other. Before we ended the first leg of our journey, I had already sensed that Yatta is a quite open and unconventional lady forcefully wrapped with a black phantom-like dress that had suppressed her radiant life prisoned inside the dusty black attire that falls from head to toe. The moment I saw Yatta, some itchiness in my subconsciousness was trying to trigger something that was deposited like coffee tar in a brewer. Female genital mutilation, she should have undergone this for sure as per the literature I had been reading for years. Fulas who are distributed in West Africa practice FGM. An irresistible urge came from deep inside of me to ask my friend Seydo to ask whether it would be possible for him to make us meet again and from the other end of my conscious mind my urge of making a move to ask him was kept suppressed as I thought he might misunderstand me. However, even before we reach Timbuktu, just like a raged water stream that runs out from a broken flood-gate, my tongue superseded the speed of my thinking.

'Seydo, do you have the contact number of Yatta?' My question wrinkled his head with a slight smile of sarcasm, but I did not see what was the dominant thought hidden inside of him.

'He he, you like the woman ?' He asked me, well after a few seconds.

His response was quite flat and lack emotions despite his smile, and I thought not to disclose the reason why I wanted to meet her again but to divert the reason to another.

'My brother, how can I say whether I like her or not even without seeing a millimetre of her?' I told with laughter, which was followed by a face of surprise from Seydo's end.

'Then what you what from her?' He looked completely confused and kept looking at me as if he was expecting an answer which he cannot expect from a man.

'As she was working in an international organisation, she must know a lot of developmental challenges and social issues existing at community level?' I added, just to give a professional outlook to the conversation and to eliminate the probable suspicions caused by misdirected speculations.

'Of course, the woman is very experienced and worked in many countries in the region,' he said with a tone of reaffirmation.

'I just want to know about developmental challenges and psychosocial issues in Guinea, Mali, and other areas where she had been working, if I was given a chance to talk to her again,' I knew being a part of the same society and same faith, he would not allow me to have a chance to meet Yatta, in case I talked about female circumcision, but for developmental and other issues could be an easy path to follow and after I cross the first hurdle, the success or failure will be determined by my skills of negotiation and convincing, which is completely within my control and my responsibility.

He gave me her business card, which was with her contacts in Guinea, and we stopped talking about her for the rest of the journey as we were stopped by military to not proceed as they cannot assure the safety and security of foreigners because of the rising number of incidents of kidnapping foreigners in Northern Mali by Touareg militia groups.

'Sir, you cannot be allowed to go beyond this point,' a captain of Armée Malienne told me politely in such a way that I would not have anything else to question. The direct and simple yet respectful approach of the military man prevented me from being reactive to what I heard from him. The first time in my life I saw Timbuktu in French education of *Geo Magazine*. It was around the same time I learnt about FGM and Rokia Taore who is one of my favourite African singers who sing in

French. Learning that they were the tallest mud buildings in the world and about the marvellous engineering of desert people, the first seed of my dream to see Timbuktu was planted, but when I heard that my dream of seeing those colossal mud buildings would just be a dream, just like seeds planted in burning sands of the Sahara that will never ever turn into plants, I heard a sound of a collapsing building inside of me for years.

'Dreams can be shattered but there is always a way out,' it was my father who used to raise his voice at his lazy friend. Those were one of the rare moments where we had heard him raise his voice, which we never forgot.

We got down from the minibus, then crossed the road to catch another bus going back to Bamako. Almost after two hours, a minibus full of plastic barrels, bags, trunk boxes, and many more stuff appeared shining in the mirage like a donkey caravan of gypsies. Old enough to be out of service, yet serving more than what it is made for, moved faster than its physical ability yet limping due to overload, it stopped near us with an irritating creaking sound of its brakes, and lucky me, a huge metal barrel rolled out from the overhead rack and fell right behind me, just touching my hair, making a terrifying noise.

'Allons, grouille toi!' It was Seydo, pushing me, who is terrified with very the first experience with the bus we were about to get in.

It was just like a goat mesh, people were packed inside without leaving a single centimetre between one another, and the heat makes everyone perspire, creating an unbearably unhealthy environment inside the shuttle bus. Frustrated not only because of unexpected conditions in the shuttle bus but also having been unable to complete my journey to the destination of my dreams, I was thinking left and right about alternatives to do in Bamako or else to go to another destination where I do not require visa. Breathing barely sufficient quantity of air filtered through dozens of armpits carrying all kinds of smells of sweat, with growing back leg and neck pains by trying to stay alive inside of the shuttle bus adapting to the dynamic shapes of space, my ability to think had just disappeared in frustration and burnt in pains. I was unable to think what we were going to do except to head back to Guinea and then to go to Ivory Coast or Burkina Faso as I had already a valid visa for those two countries. But having nothing planned properly ahead of time, it is often impossible to make things happen smoothly in many Sub-Saharan African countries and often such attempts will end up spending twice or thrice more than the usual price for accommodation, transportation, and often having been unable to do many things as pre-planned. Therefore, with the second thought of not trying that option but keeping it as last resort, I got down from Bamako with a sigh of relief of coming out of shuttle bus and the immediate sight at the bus stop surprised me.

'There is a chronology of everything in life, so do the dreams,' I wanted to be a bus driver at one point of my life when I was around 5 or 6 years old. Whenever I travel in public transport with my father, I used to go and sit near the driver and observe the cockpit closely. Upon returning home, I used to draw the cockpit of each bus I travel. My irresistible passion for motor vehicles and driving came to a point where my father had to warn me as I started neglecting homework given in the school. He might have been afraid that his only male child was going to detach himself from the common dream of Sri Lankan parents, seeing their child becoming a doctor, proctor, or an engineer, not a bus or a truck driver. He might have wanted to show me the practical side of life in a way that a kid would understand. However, later on in many circumstances of my life, 'there is a chronology of everything in life, so do the dreams' stood behind me being my only encouragement, sometimes being my backbone keeping me standing on my feet, sometimes helping me to cope with failures and so do this time.

'Yatta, you are here? What happened to your meeting?' Seeing Yatta waiting in the bus stop, I rather felt a feeling of mission accomplished than surprised, even though my pre-planned visit to Timbuktu had already become a daydream.

'My meeting was cancelled due to security reasons as one of our internationally recruited personnel had been kidnapped in the north,' she said with a frustrated tone.

'Same here, security reasons sent us back to Bamako,' I said.

It was already late and it was impossible to cross the border to Guinea if we took the shuttle bus by that time, so we decided stay in Bamako for one night and to start the trip back to Kankan early next morning.

'If you guys are okay, I can talk to my office here for arranging our guest house for you two as well,' she asked Seydo.

'Of course that would be great,' I said before Seydo opened his mouth as I knew that would be a golden opportunity for me to have a chat with her about the topic I was longing to know about since years. My head was preoccupied with forming a sensitive questionnaire amidst of loud French hip-hop music played in the old Mercedes taxi heading to Hippodamaire where I had been one year ago on an official reason and the familiar smell of garbage from the mountain of garbage brought by the wind that comes across Niger river whispered to me that many things still remain the same since the last couple of years though Bamako is ranked as the fastest growing city in Africa and the sixth in the entire world. Bamako is a busy typical Sub-Saharan African city that had acquired a lot from the Arabic world, not just being an Islam country but being a country with a long-rooted trading culture with Arabs but certain African realities do remain unchanged. Dirty busy markets; garbage sites in the city limits that are breeding and feeding places for flies, rodents, and many other species living in unhygienic environments; busy roads full of traffic and highly increasing urban population who choose or are compelled to live in poor and insufficient infrastructure. Driving through some familiar parts of the city and my memories affiliated to them, we finally reached the guesthouse. A quite poche huge house with modern appliances and a small swimming pool near Hippodomaire in Bamako.

'You guys can go and check in, I already have my room booked here, I will come in one hour,' Yatta told us while calling the caretaker of the guest house. They talked for a while and he came to us and helped with the baggage. The rooms were nice, spacious, and fully equipped, but rather than enjoying the room and bath after a long tiring trip, my head was in a long battle strategising how to start and go about asking Yatta about FGM.

'Now that you have been given the chance, one and only chance, do not hesitate.' Dialogues between my plus pole and minus pole started being auditory within my ears. Next one hour time, I should be in the restaurant area waiting for my next friend hoping for an untold story to unfold but it could be a probability of one out of ten thousand. I decided to try my luck.

It was 8.30 p.m. GMT, when a silhouette of an African woman, who is almost 172 cm, entered the blanket hall, cutting through the colourful dimmed-lights of the restaurant, I tried to control the lub-dub sound of my palpitating heart, not to be heard by anyone outside. That was a moment in my life, I felt how scary and challenging to break the barriers imposed by cultures.

'Hi!' Unlike before, her 'lil' was like a hammer shot on my forehead. I said 'Hi' as if I was already guilty for something.

We ordered herbal tea as none of us wanted to have supper as tiredness had suppressed the appetite and hunger. For the first time, she appeared without covered face, even though her head was covered and she was always in the black long dress like the robe that is put on those who are condemned to death, just before they are hung. Her face rather reminded me a face of audacious worrier than a typical woman, which gave me some sort of a confidence to start with casual stuff related to work and direct the conversation to where I wanted. But still I felt just like what I felt when I was about to ask out the first girl in my life when I was 15 years old.

'How long you have been working in the humanitarian sector?' I asked indifferently.

'Well' said she, with a serious tone of start, just like a head master of a school. 'It's been over twelve years now, and I worked in different projects in aid work.'

'You must be having experience in many typical social and developmental issues in the region?' I said adding some confidence and a credit to her words.

'Yeah I was actively involved in the activities such as SGBV, hygiene promotions, and community-based health activities in a few countries in the region.' Her reply made my way easier than anticipated, SGBV, sexual gender-based violence matters have direct liaison with FGM, therefore, I suddenly felt that this is the right time to drag her into my track.

'Have you ever worked in programs that fight against female gender mutilation?' She looked at me and said, 'Impressive, I cannot believe that you know about it', her answer placed me in a place which is between two assumptions. The first one—Asians or anyone from the external world is not supposed to know about it. Second one—it is amazing that the message had crossed the borders of the continent. I tried to be positive and picked the second assumption and went ahead explaining how I got to know about FGM and also a bit of my African dream.

319

'You mean you have read a lot about FGM and you are against it?' Her voice was firm, as firm as a rock. Her suppressed reaction was my gate way to the subject matter I was trying to direct the whole conversation. I was happy that she was quire reactive than being reserved, so that we would have something to discuss, argue, agree, or disagree.

'Yes, I do believe that it is not right, it had a lot of consequences, psychological and physiological,' she was listening, looking at me from time to time, but very attentively, as I explained her every single bit of what I had learnt, heard, and seen about female genital mutilation in Africa.

'Pramudith, I cannot understand why a man is so interested in this subject, what you really want to know? What are you going to do if you get to know more about this issue? You knowing about circumcision would bring us what?' A chain of questions that one could easily perceive offensive or rule, to which direct answered expected, were thrown at me like a thunder strike.

Before I think of an answer, she added, 'Would you think women here will talk about those things with a stranger? They do not even talk about those within themselves'. Nothing but a multibarrel rocket launcher came to my mind, before one falls into enemy zone a dozen is already launched within seconds. I was under a shower of direct questions and a verbal defence.

'I was born in a country where gender mutilation is nonexistent, despite that male circumcision exists among the minority Muslims, in a family where all most of my siblings are female. I was raised in an environment where toture is not a part of life and in a culture which is extremely sensitive to human suffering, a culture of nonviolence. For us, imagining of cutting off someone's flesh, wherever it is, despite a medical intervention to save one's life, is not at all acceptable. And we are traditional, reserved in many aspects, but we are taught not to harm anyone. Would you think someone who had grown up in such an environment would ever tolerate such a brutal act like female gender mutilation? It is traumatising to hear. Forget about seeing and no-question about being a victim, being forced to undergo that inhuman crime. Do you think that men should not speak out of this? To raise their voice against that? Don't you think that your God Almighty Allah created females with additional pieces of flesh to cut off? I want to engage myself to make a voice against this at least by a narrating a story of an unfortunate victim, to make an unheard story be heard to the whole world. To wake up those who were sleeping, pinch those who were indifferent. Finally, to document a true story of eternal deprivation of the glory of womanhood in the name of a culture or faith, even before a girl discovers that her pleasure is centred in the little piece of flesh which is stolen at childhood, and future generation to refrain from this practice.'

I told all what came to my mouth at one stretch, without giving Yatta a breathing space.

'May be I was fantasizing to change the world with a story of two pages' I added.

Just like one drop of water always falls on earth before a pouring rain falls, a drop of tear had already fallen on her notebook, blotting the ink right on her name 'Yatta' and with her face that was looking down seems laden with many unsaid for decades. After a while of silence, she looked at me with eyes full of tears. Her fingers in both hands were shaking with tremors and then she tightened her fists.

'I will break it, I am going to break it,' she said, probably to herself even-though the words came out of her mouth.

'Break? what?' It was me with confusion.

'S . . . i . . . l . . . e . . . n . . . c . . . e.'

'It was the day after my 7th birthday, end of the school year, very beginning of the school vacation, when I was taken to Baradjeli, in Fulani, which stands for the woman who traditionally perform excision. It was my aunt who took me there. I do still remember, I was playing with my friends in our neighbourhood, just behind my uncle's house. She told me that she was going to visit a friend to the village and to accompany her daughter to visit another friend whom both of them knew from childhood. She used to take me for walks across the village many times so I did not have any doubts ad I did not know about the excision at that age even though I knew my elder sister died couple of months ago, few days after returning home from a long walk, she went with my aunty. She was on the bed after returning from a walk, mourning and crying, her legs were tightened with a piece of old cloth and she had a large belly before she died. When my mother started crying when she got to know that my sister Aminatta is dead, my grand-mother said she was a witch that's why she is dead. That was the only bad memory associated to my aunt but I did not think that she had done anything for Aminatta to die because everyone said that she was a witch. She was a witch and a bad spirit therefore she left us for our good. The same evening they carry them out, and I stopped seeing her at home again. She is gone forever, the witch my grandmother said one day while we were cutting wild Almonds. I no-longer heard my mum's screams in the morning, 'Aminatta . . . get up! get up!' just like a ritual which wakes everyone up, specially my father who does not want to wake up till the food is ready at home. Instead, she started yelling at me every single morning, 'Yatta . . . Yatta . . . up up! Go fetch water for me!' I never knew that meant something, till the day I was taken to Baradjeli, it was me who was next, right After Aminatta.

We reached the little mud hut of the friend of my aunt and she was already waiting for us with her daughter who was little bit bigger than me. She joined us without talking a single word as if they already knew where they were going and what they were going to do. And we walked in pairs to next house where my friend in the community school lives, and she joined us along with her grandmother. a few other girls accompanied by an adult female joined us silently. I can recall, that was a terrifying silence, no one talked, I was looking around nervous to hear a human voice among anyone of us but everyone were like deaf-mute and was in a march of mystery. But I was with my favourite aunt, I felt secure, but after a long time, Aminatta came to my mind for no reason. If she was with me, I could have walked in the village with her while talking about many things that we liked in common, plucking mangos from trees on the roadside, she used to be my partner in crime. We followed the path along a stream where we used to swim, and stopped at the hut of one of the old ladies who used to come always to see my grandmother. We used to call her red-old woman, as she wore a red-coloured robe often. Whenever she came to our place, grandma used to treat her with respect mixed with a bit of fear and always made sure she gives her something. The day Aminatta was taken to the graveyard, she came in the evening and told, "I knew she was a witch, she screamed unlike human." I did not understand a thing but I heard it. I never forgot those words as Aminatta used to scream at me too. Her words mixed with my personal experience with my elder sister who always screamed to control my foolish acts, made me think that she was right. At the age of six, I strongly believed that she was a witch, evil spirit who brought curse to the family.

One quiet old woman, grandmother of one of the girls who came with us, went and talked to the woman in red robe and then we were taken down to the stream where no one could see, we were given bath. I was absolutely lost of what was happening and still the silence that reigned around us despite the sound of water. One thing that constantly bothered me was why my own aunty who used to speak like a parrot often keeps quiet. That alarmed me that something which is not good was going to happen. After the bath, I was given a towel to wrap around my body, as all the other girls did. And suddenly, my aunt advanced her feet and held my head and wrapped a piece of cloth around my head, completely blindfolding me. Aminatta's face just before her death suddenly appeared in front of my eyes, and I started hearing she was calling me. I tried to scream but the voice did not come out. I was like frozen with fear and confused with uncertainty of what was about to happen. The first time the voice of my aunt rised bit higher than a whisper, let's go inside the house. Her voice was like never before, I had never heard a voice of a witch, despite small Aminatta, I thought an adult witch should sound like my aunty's voice of now. It was raw and rough like I had never heard before.

I couldn't see a thing to identify where I was led to, it was a close environment where I could hear echoes of screams and sobs out of pain of other girls who went with us. My aunty's devilish grip right around my right wrist had already made my hand numb and I was listening to horrifying and terrifying mourns, screams, and wails like the goats of my father which were looking at the goat that my uncle and father slaughtered for last Eid. They looked frightened but they were fenced and some of them were tied. They might have known that their turn would come one day, but except wait for their turn, nothing else is left for them. The screams of girls reminded me of bleating of goats when they were being hung on a branch by their back legs. I could not imagine anything else, there should be bloodshed like what happened to goat last Eid. Though I was blindfolded, an imaginary picture of my school friend in a pool of blood started appearing when I started hearing her voice laden with pain.

When my aunt's hand was released from my wrist and laid upon my shoulders with a rather sympathetic touch than an empathetic one, just like an undertaker who always have a sentiment of sympathy immediately before hanging someone, I felt that my turn had arrived. I was taken inside the room from where I heard screams and sobs. A lady asked me to lie down on a bench. I did not know how many of them were there exactly, but there were few women, probably four of them including my aunt who gripped me like a rabbit trapped in a coil of a python while one of them removed and lifted my towel. Then they stretched my legs wide open and held tight as I was unable to move an inch. I did not remember whether I had been tied with ropes or cloths or they had just held me completely immobile.

The moment I felt my towel was lifted, I realised that they were going to do something with my female body parts but I did not know that it involved blood shedding. I assumed that they were going to check something in it, as I remember my mum was telling every time not to sit in a way that my female parts are to be exposed to others, especially to men and it will cause a lot of pain. I thought there was a man that's why the girls were screaming and sobbing. I heard the voice of my grandmother's friend, the red-robed lady approaching me, and it should be her hands that reached my private area. She held my clitoris between her rough fingers and pulled mercilessly causing a pain that I had never gone through. I thought that was the moment of pain, that was why girls were loud but it was proven fault when something cold touched my clitoris and then next second I could not support but scream loud with the darting pain that conquered my body, mind, and soul at the same time, I remember my spine cured up, tears jumped out from my eyes as I was unable to move to absorb the pain, they were holding me pressed to the bench in a manner that the lady who cut me, the red-robed old one, can perform her duty with no interruption. The next time the cold hands of the woman touched me I went blank, just blank like an empty sky. And when I started seeing, blinking starts inside of my eyes and burning pain between my legs, I could not get away from the grasp of the old women. I had already been taken out of the room. My legs were still lifeless and my head was spinning. She had used a sticky substance to glue me together so that I would heal closed. I dared not to look at anyone who was around, I knew my life had already changed. It is no longer as it used to be. I had fainted and they had taken me back home, I did not know how, but when

I gained my consciousness, pain swallowed me completely from head to toe. I felt wetness in areas around my upper thighs and private area, my instinct said that was nothing else but blood. Aminatta in a pool of blood came to my mind over and over again. A sharp pain started paralysing my movements, whenever I try to move. I screamed, cried, and wept but no one seems empathetic to me. Instead, my mother came smiling as if she is extremely delighted to see her only female child left alive, among three of them she gave birth to, in a process to become a witch, being taken to the graveyard and vanish in the air eternally from the memories of others. I could not connect her body language with what I went through and the worse part of it was, she came and told me that I brought dignity to the family, to the community, and for what they believe in. She added proudly that I had become an eligible lady in the community. There was no more strength left with me to listen to her and understand what she says but I felt they must have told all these stories to Aminatta as well a few days before her death. I started feeling that sooner I will be called a witch, but I won't be there to hear it.

The first night I was gathering my energy from every single cell of my body to battle with the sharp, constant, and unbearable pain. I could not sleep a single moment. Whenever I close my eyes, I started seeing all that happened to me at Baradjeli's, as if it was happening again and again, I felt the smell of blood, heard the scream of girls, and suppressive voices of elderly women. Besides all, I started to hear Aminatta was calling me. I was afraid to close my eyes. Whenever I tried to sleep, I started shivering with heat followed by vigorous palpitations and sweating. Next moment I found myself crying with fear of death. After some time I had nightmares and I often woke up frightened. No one in the family was sensitive to what I was going through, even my own mum, who had gone through this in her childhood, she used to come on and off, noticing me crying, would tell not to cry but how could I bear an intense constant pain of a wound in the most sensitive part of my body and a deeper and a lasting wound in my mind?'

In most of the countries in the zone where FGM is highly prevalent, seeking external emotional support for anything that causes psychological or physical pain is considered a taboo, a weakness, or an act of cowardice which brings disgrace to the family or the clan. Every one of those girls suffers from intense emotional shock, acute stress syndrome, acute stress disorder, and a significant number of them develop posttraumatic stress disorder, also known as PTSD. In many villages in rural Guinea, for those girls who experience mental health problems during the aftermath of the extremely traumatising traditional practice of female genital mutilation, it is very simple for the community to label her as a witch or a mad woman and push her to a corner of the society thinking she is no use for anyone anymore. Every single mental disorder irrespective of curability and severity is subjected to the socially imposed perception of 'madness' which is equal to 'invalid'. The traditional healers with their fetish, or voodoo tricks and magic come into play to remove the evil spirit that posses the girl victimised by human acts. Sometimes, the girls go through double or multiple traumatic victimisations due to some painful procedures contained in the traditional voodoo rituals. Instead of hearing the individual who is already traumatised, traditional interventions provoke the anxiety of the victim, triggering the traumatic memories of the victim. At the end of the day, the procedures that were done intending to heal the psychological wounds of the girl aggravate the condition that she already goes through, making her life almost impaired.

Yatta carried her childhood trauma throughout her life. During the time she was going through the period of intense physiological and psychological response to the trauma, her family saw it as a very normal reaction as every female in her family tree had gone through it once in their life, and some survived even though they were not lucky to have a usual and healthy human life. Therefore, dynamics in response syndrome of a female child to FGM since the time of cutting till complete healing of the wounds or death due to infections are nothing new to the people who live in the zone where FGM is widely practiced. Most of those culturally blind, ignorant populations in Sub-Saharan Africa who almost lost their way forward in the fog of faith do not look at the issue in victim-centred point of view but rather with a cultural and faith-based attitude. Therefore, most of the girls who underwent FGM carry their unresolved psychological trauma in every single step taken along the passage of life.

'By the fourth day, I was already started feeling a numbness in my private areas and kind of pain that was not constant but spread along my back and tummy. Following day my tummy became like a balloon, swollen and shiny, and I felt strange wetness in my private areas and a foul smell that took me back to the times when we found out a rotten rat inside the old trunk box of my grandmother. That evening, I could not eat, I felt weak and started shivering with fever, it was worse than the times I got malaria. My father had left home to call the healer, and old ladies were around me, my mum was crying looking at my dry lips and pale eyes which were half-closed. After a couple of hours, my aunt who took me to the place of the red-robed woman, Baradjeli, appeared in front of me, making me shocked again. When Aminatta was about to die, she appeared and told she was a witch. 'An evil spirit for sure,' she said to my uncle, I heard it so clearly. I felt that I was passing the last few moments of my life on earth, I prayed to Almighty Allah to grant me Zannat. I looked at my mum, speechlessly, said bye to her in silence. I did not know whether I love her or not anymore, but for sure I felt she loved me before I was cut. The day I was cut, I held everyone of my family responsible for the death of my loving sister Aminatta. I discovered what they had done to her. I felt the pain she went through and I suffered the same way she did. But grace to the Almighty Allah, I was allowed to live. The herbal treatment that the traditional healer gave me to drink as well as applied in my wounds worked. Otherwise, you would not hear this story today.'

She paused and remained pensive in silence for a while. I allowed Yatta to take her time. It was almost eleven thirty and the lady in the restaurant was already making her faces at the cashier which I quickly translated and responded to them that we will order something more. I walked to the cashier, and put a $50 note on her palm. 'Let us stay for a while and I will order a snack, probably two portions of French fries.' He looked contented with the note fell into his pocket, the order was not what he was interested in. The waitress interrupted her silence and pensiveness. 'Merci beaucoup.' Yatta threw a sympathetic look at the waitress as if they both shared the same experience and said with a very low voice.

Guinea has the world's highest prevalence rates of FGM among women aged 15–49. At 99 per cent, the practice is almost universal across regional, ethnic, or religious groups. For women aged 19 and younger, FGM prevalence rates are slightly lower, at 97 per cent. FGM has long been common in Guinea. Irrespective of religion, almost everyone practices circumcision, both male and female, but male circumcision is not fatal and life-threatening as what is practiced on females. The women of the Guerze group have the lowest prevalence rate, around 88 per cent, which is also high compared to many other countries in Africa.

Most of the time, the traditional Baradjeli is not a person who has been trained to perform a medically safe surgical procedure during circumcision. Razor blades, curved locally made small knives, or else any sharp object that can slice flesh out, are used during the procedure, besides that, often the Baradjeli takes as much as twenty to twenty-five girls at a time without sterilising the equipments. And on top of everything, the herbal substances that are applied on the open wound are usually already contaminated with bacteria and viruses as the process of preparation is not usually hygienic. And again, the tragic part of the traditional practice is that the girls are forced to bear a pain which is probably worse than what a woman may go through during the delivery of a child. Aside from the extreme physical torture and trauma the girls encounter, most of them get various infections during the process of influbation, which leads to the death of many victims. Even though most of the circumcisions in the rural are still being done by the traditional practitioners, there is an increasing number of circumcisions done by a trained nurse, midwife, or a medical doctor, which is life saving, but it is just one line of light in an immense dark cloud. Involvement of a medical practitioner and following safe surgical methodologies to get a girl circumcised do not address the consequences of the act, or do not reverse the impact of the act on womanhood. It assures only safety in the surgical intervention.

'May I ask you a question? But you are free to choose to answer or not to.' I broke the silence that was growing between us.

'Yes, please.' She lifted her head and looked at my forehead, as if she did not want to maintain eye contact. I did not know whether it was because of shyness or guilt of revealing the untold about her culture and life to a stranger.

'Did you have any complications after the wounds have been cured?' I gently posed a question to break the growing silence between us.

'Later on I realised that my whole external genitalia had been mercilessly cut off and sewed, leaving a small space for me to pass urine and menstrual blood, but every time I used to have periods, I went though severe pains and complications, sometimes postmenstrual infections as the small space is not enough for freeing everything that comes out during menstruation. Whenever we complain, my mother used to tell that it was a part of the life of a woman, pain is inherited by women since the moment they are born which I never agreed.'

'Yatta,' I disturbed. 'If you do not mind, would you tell me a bit about your marriage? How you adapted to a married life with all those brutal modifications that were imposed to you?'

As Yatta being a middle-aged and educated woman who demonstrated an open attitude to life and to the world, I did not hesitate to ask her details about her marital life which cannot be questioned usually from a woman from social setup where Yatta was from. Despite her exposure, education, and openness, my question seemed to startle her a bit as if she did not expect such a direct question demanding details.

'That was the second death of me. To be honest it was not a nuptial, it was a funeral. They made me eligible for marriage when I was seven, cutting off the gift of god as a woman, and sewed me like a torn linen with zero sensitivity and sold me to a 50-year-old man as his second wife when I was just completing my fifteenth year.'

She paused and held the glass of soft drink in such a manner that she was going to squeeze it to pieces. Then, she shook her head as if she was trying to vent her frustration that lasted for decades in one single gesture and released a long sigh as she wanted to release the loads of pains and anguishes accumulated over many years in one single moment.

'I had already told you a lot, a lot more than what I had ever shared with anyone else, maybe because you are a complete stranger and you are not from my society.' Her words were firm and clear.

'He was a local businessman, and he already had a wife and kids when he came to ask my family to marry me. He would never be my choice if I had been ever given one. My father had given him the word, long ago, since he was one of the best friends of my father, and he had wealth. He had cattle, he had goats, he had even a motorcycle. Those days, having a motorcycle was a big thing in my village. Everything had been decided between my parents and himself without my knowledge as it happens often in my society which is normal to everyone in my community. I was not scared to be his wife because I did not know what was happening between a man and a woman by that time. But I was hesitant to go with his as he had a lot of cattle and I knew for sure I would be going after them all day. I was a teenager of 15 years, few full moons after my first menstruation started which even scared me at first day, as it reminded me of the pool of blood where Aminatta was lying and which certainly I went through as well. During periods, I used to have nightmares of the red-robed Baradjeli and Aminatta and I used to wake up in the middle of the night screaming and frightened. I did not have a clue of sexual intercourse between man and woman, and if I ever known that there was something again involving my genitals, I would run away into the bush and die.'

Yatta emptied her glass of soft drink in few gulps. A few minutes of pensiveness followed by a silence and then she started to explain again. It looked like she was feeling an anxiety response even when she talked about what she went through during the nuptials.

'I was taken to his mud house, which was relatively the biggest in the village where I sat on a mattress for the first time in my life but I did not have a clue that I would hate that mattress for rest of my life. I did not have an idea what was in store the following couple of hours to happen on that mattress. He was a strict Muslim; he went to pray, and before sleeping, he came to the mattress with a small gas lamp. My house had never been that full of life at night as we used kerosene lamps or sometimes candles. He asked me weather I was tired or afraid. I said nothing as I had never sat with a man before in darkness. My heart started beating hard and my hands became cold like the dew on the grass in some mornings. I was of course afraid of what will happen to me as he was a complete stranger and I was supposed to live under his shelter for the rest of my life. Other than that thing came to my child mind. He said he will bring Atae for us and left the mattress. My father used to drink Atae in the evening, one or two cups, but when he drank a lot, he used to call my mum behind the grain store and starts groaning like a wild cat. He prohibited us to come to that side in the evening, especially after the dark and we never went there, but I remember my brothers used to laugh whenever they hear that sound. That was one of the mysteries of my father and mother that I did not discover till I was taken out from home as a wife.

He returned with Atae in a metal cup and he was sipping it looking at me, his eyes were shining like fire that was going to burn me. He was silent unusually. Except from the noise he made while he was sipping Atae, nothing else was there to disturb him that night. It was mysteriously silent as if no one is there to hear anything. I felt that I had been taken far away from human habitat, I felt lonely and afraid. Without my knowledge, tears had already started coming down along my cheeks and a blunt sound of sobbing came out of my mouth which instantly took his attention and allowed him to come closer to me. He put his hands upon my shoulders and rather squeezed me with greed than hugging me or comforting me. That intensified my fears. Then he started to kiss my face and touch me in a way that no one ever had done to me before. I tried to move but his grip was harder than the grip of the women who were holding me while I was being cut. And the moment that I never wanted to experience happened as if history repeats. He touched my genitals and he showed his few yellow teeth through his bushy beard, I guessed he was smiling. Smile of my aunt came to my mind and I started sweating and shaking with fear but I did not have strength to scream or I forgot to scream out of shock. After my encounter with the Baradjeli when I was 7, I did not want anyone to touch me. He said not to worry and he pushed me to the mattress and I did not dare to sit again and pulled my robe and again touched my genitals with something which was cold. History repeated again. I felt a similar sharp pain in my genitals. I screamed loud but not for a long time as his iron hands covered my mouth. And he fell on my body and while keeping his hand on me and pushed something hard into me, irrespective of the severe pain I went through down there. He pushed and pulled, ground and mounted and while keeping one hand on my mouth, preventing me scream. I tried to roll and escape from his grip but nothing proved successful. Then after a while, he stopped and wrapped his cloths around him, looked at me indifferently, emptied the Atae left in the cup in one gulp, and left the room. That was my first night with my husband. When I was a child I was cut and sewed, and he cut me and opened. Nothing but pain and anger is left in my mind about my womanhood. And I would call it partial womanhood as I learnt a couple of years later that women can feel pleasure during sex, which I never felt. I had never got an orgasm in my life and I know my womanhood is partially impaired for eternity.'

If, as per the key beliefs existing in Africa, man and woman are created by the Almighty God, who is considered superior to everyone, there should be a reason for creating a woman with clitoris, inner and outer labia. There is a reason why pleasure is used as the key driving factor in sexual activity to keep the process of reproduction at the desired level. If mutilation of a female based on the belief that depriving the ability of feeling pleasure in sexual activity keeps her faithful to her husband, it is just a myth as 82 per cent of broken marriages are due to other factors. As per the societies where FGM is widely practiced, the fundamental eligibility of a woman to get married is being unable to feel the pleasure in sexual intercourse, which is, in other words, being able to be a passive silicone vegina for a man who is not confident on this manhood, who is lost in the myths, and who is not taught to see a human female as a human being but just like a donkey who carries his weight, without complaining, everywhere he goes. Men do not talk about it openly, hiding behind the curtain of culture, they make the demand. If a girl is not circumcised, no man will take her. That demand is the main factor of continuation of FGM in many countries in modern days.

I had seen a lot of nongovernmental and intergovernmental organisations working with communities to fight with the war called FGM against women in many countries I had visited in Sub-Saharan Africa, such as Mali, Niger, Guinea, Uganda, Kenya, and Chad. And I had spoken to many activists as well as the victims of FGM in all of those countries who had undergone different forms of mutilation. As a result of all discussions and observations, I strictly believe that there should be more weight focusing on creating demand in men for women who are not mutilated, through sensitising them on consensual sexual life with mutual pleasure. But still, men in the zones where FGM is highly prevalent are so far behind when their alacrity for such learning and in accepting a woman who is natural as their Almighty God has created. Hence, as a result, even though many nongovernmental organisations and UN agencies had reached many landmarks such as minimising the practice by the traditional Baradjeli but with involvement of midwives, nurses, and the doctors, still GFM is practiced in medical facilities which means that FGM has not been rejected but there is a significant number of people who have understood the risk of traditional practice. Despite the deprivation of sexual pleasure, nature's gift of womanhood still remains the same and continues even though most women who have opinions favouring the abandonment of FGM cited 'painful experience' as a reason for their opposition. Some thought the practice led to medical complications. Other reasons mentioned by women for opposing the practice included that it decreased sexual pleasure both for women and that it was against the religion but still many women do not want their daughters to be deprived from their right to be married specially in the rural areas and among less educated women whereas there is a significant change of attitude favoured to the abandonment of FGM among women living in urban areas and with higher educational attainment.

'Yatta you said you have a daughter?' I asked.

'Yes.'

'How old is she?' my question did not please her. Her facial expressions showed kind of an irritation.

'Sixteen years old,' she said with a low tone.

'I believe you did not allow your child to go through the same pain and torture you went through in your childhood.'

She started sobbing and another drop of tear fell down on the same place where her name was written on the note book.

Chapter 18

NORMS OF SATURN

CERTAIN LESSONS, ONE LEARNS in childhood, are retained for life and often develop into key characteristics of one's personality or character. Probably, the lesson might have been taught by adults, often by parents and grandparents, for one reason, and interpreted in the child's mind in many different ways and applied to various situations in life and ultimately becomes a personality trait which can probably be transferred to the immediate surroundings of the individual, and sometimes depending on the position, the person is placed in the society and the fame or authority thronged around the individual, one's childhood lesson could become a slogan for social mobilisation or even the key driving factor for a revolution that dismantles existing social systems and transforms the societies. The abovementioned thoughts were triggered, many times, when I was reading biographies or autobiographies of many people. What parents and grandparents first push into the fresh minds of children can hardly be unlearnt, and often are retained at least till the age that the individual develops a rational thinking pattern when many of the learnt lessons in childhood are challenged and start to be unlearnt. In the meantime, society does a greater duty in the process of unlearning, when the individual is pressurised to unlearn the 'heard' against what is known as 'first-hand experience'. On one hand, the society helps in unlearning, and on the other hand, the social system itself can enhance, sharpen, or widen already learnt things during the process of social interaction.

In exceptional circumstances such as complex emergencies or natural disasters, by which the integrity of a society is highly threatened in all aspects of life, such as culturally, environmentally, economically, and politically, the social system can demonstrate a sudden shift or else a complete or at least a significant change.

When disasters strike, especially the ones that can be categorised as mass calamities, most of the population who lived in the affected area, who were placed in different layers of society, rich and poor, educated and illiterate, low caste and high caste, everyone else, are placed in the same position where they have to be helped and who will have the right to help and who are in need of help. During the South Asian Tsunami, which is the largest natural disaster ever known to the world so far, many people who lived with dignity, who did not ask for help even when they were in need in daily life situations, were pushed to the position of 'complete losers' in terms of many aspects of life, loved ones, wealth, and subsequently, mental and physical health. When you are left with one choice, which is to go on with what is left with you, which is your life, surviving on what is given to you, which is given to everyone else irrespective of what you used to do and how you used to live, at one point, you have to let your shame and pride vanish in the air for survival. The days you were a 'provider' has already gone behind the mist of debris of collapsed buildings that stood proud at skyline, and you have become merely a 'dependent' under the temporary tents given for you which is your home for an unknown future. The days you said 'no thanks' for something offered to you, the days you were selective or choosy in your food, had passed behind the rainbow of past and instead a gloomy sky has not given many choices except to survive on what is given or simply die. Hence, it is normal that abnormal events that break down the social structure tear the social fabric, obviously threaten the value systems established in the societies that had remained for ages, sometimes as key determinants of stereotypes of certain communities and societies.

It is normal that affected individuals, the population in a larger picture, feel that they are helpless, 'feeling of helplessness' even though they are resourceful in many ways. But the pattern of humanitarian aid management, the role of politics in humanitarian interventions, the kind of interventions delivered to the populations play a key role in supporting the affected population to overcome the psychological impact of disaster, which is mostly manifested as 'helplessness'. But in many occasions, the kindness of strangers, in other words 'humanitarianism' which is merely based on irrational sympathy, allows 'helplessness' to escalate to 'dependency' which had become a way of survival in many parts of the developing world, especially in the areas where mass calamities or complex emergencies are highly prevalent. The Africa version of dependency learnt from the complex emergencies and natural disasters seems gone beyond a way of survival and evolved into a 'lifestyle' which has already become an integral feature of cultures of some countries.

Though there is a reasonable story behind every human behaviour, when you look at it non-judgmentally, as a human being, being judgmental is helpful always for you to decide what's right, choose the right thing, and to do the right thing. Otherwise, you may end up helping a person not to overcome his or her helplessness but to plunge into it. Even though your decision of not saying yes for what is asked is often perceived as rudeness, ruthlessness, or insensitivity, it is not necessary to take an effort to make the receiver's end understand something that the he or she is not ready to understand. Hence as long as your motive is for a long-term positive change, it is always good to be the bad boy or bad girl from others' view point, still stand for what you believe in. Sometimes your act of foresight may be translated in to an act of disrespectfulness to cultural diversity or insensitivity to human suffering. Or in extreme cases, you can be held responsible for not keeping your word or as a lier or a criminal whereas there is nothing you had promised and nothing you are bound to give or do.

It was a Sunday morning, I was in my balcony facing 'Doe' river, reading a book while sipping my morning coffee whereas my house mate who was a Ghanaian, a strict Catholic, was ironing his cloths for going to morning service. That is the time, we often have freedom to talk, even if we stayed in the same house, we had busy schedules which prevented us staying at home at the same time. That is the only day we both meet the cleaner of apartment Albert who was a Liberian, a young man at his early twenties. As a habit that we had developed over the last few months, we used to discuss issues and assign him different works, every Sunday morning, I heard the voice of Albert with his usual 'good morning' which did not contain any energetic feeling that should have been in a greeting, especially in the morning. He repeated 'good morning' again right behind me as if he wanted my attention which was not usual.

'Good morning!, how are you?'

I asked him as I felt that he was not sounding well.

'Trying, small small,' which is a common expression of Liberians, meaning that they are struggling and not well. But it mostly referred to financial difficulties than from physical or psychological issues.

'My holiday is on you, Bossman.' His response completely confused me. Even though I was still struggling to understand Liberian English which is quite an underdeveloped and limited dialect with similar traits of Pidgin English in Nigeria and Ghana, I heard what he said clearly but I was unable to interpret it with a reasonable sense as it was the first time I had heard such a thing.

My housemate who was fully concentrating on his pressing turned to me and asked what Albert was saying. As he knew that I was quite new to the context and always had some difficulties understanding what Liberians were saying. Hearing my housemate was asking what he was asking, he repeated the same to him.

'Oh, he was asking for some help for his holiday' he started laughing.

'Sure, you should not come to work tomorrow.' I was happy to give him a free day. But it looked like my answer did not satisfy him. Instead of being happy of getting a free day, his face was covered with an expression of unhappiness, just like the skies laden with dark clouds in an autumn morning. I was quite confused and a bit pissed with his behaviour which was contradictory to what I expected and what one usually can see in a similar context in many parts of the world. I ended up asking him whether he still wanted to come to work instead of getting a free day.

'Bossman, give me small small please.'

It took some time for me to realise that the help he was asking was merely financial support.

We used to give him $100 a month which was far beyond the average salary of a cleaning boy who worked with expatriates in Monrovia by that time, early 2011. On top of that, he used to come only five days and nothing much was there for him to do. And during the initial discussion, before he was taken to work with us, we agreed upon that was the comprehensive salary including everything, which was still higher than what others around you get. He expressed his contentment and joined us. However, in reality, he had even lesser quantity of work than we agreed upon and in many months he used to work for one person as either I or my house mate was away from duty station. Considering all these real-time situations, Albert was well paid and he was given some privileges than other workers, such as he was able to have lunch in our place, he was given clothes, and I was personally paying for his school fee which is around $400 a year. If he had had at least the gratefulness for what we did, he would not have shown his bitter face to me when I was more than happy to give him a free day. However, as most of the aid workers and diplomats are seen with a tattoo of a dollar sign on the forehead, it had become a normal phenomenon that the locals tried to extract money whenever possible. Treating the case of Albert as an isolated case, I pulled out US$10 which I thought quite enough for him to enjoy his holiday, and gave him with pleasure, apologising for not being able to understand what he asked.

'Bossman gave me twenty,' he said as if he belittles what I gave him while pulling US$10 bank note from my hand. Even though I did not expect a gesture of gratitude, he could have simply thanked me, but the attitude of courtesy is apparently inexistent. That was the last day and last time that I gave someone something which is not deserved by the person. I determined that I would not give any penny to anyone again when there is no real need and if the person is not taking real efforts in finding a living. Albert's holiday did not change the way I felt about the people who were living in desperateness and poverty, or the people who are affected by conflicts, natural disasters, or complex emergencies but my action towards them changed a lot. Rather than acting on mere sympathy, induced by witnessing or hearing human suffering, I started not to give any easy bread to anyone as I strongly believed that discouraged begging.

Not a long time after the first encounter, on Albert's holiday, Liberia having the highest number of holidays in the world, Albert approached me after a couple of weeks. By that time, I had already made my mind to tell him that he should have either work more to earn more for holidays or else plan better to save some money for holidays and not to ask money from others when he is agreed upon a fixed salary. His first reaction was as if I was joking, but later on he left and started washing my jeep which I usually do not ask him to do. Finally, it made me give him US$5 which is standard amount that one would pay for a boy who gives a car wash. He could not but be content with the little extra money he made and it was the last time Albert came to ask money for free instead the quality of work started dropping drastically to an extent that I had to stop him working with us.

Albert was replaced by a lady called Tracy, whose father was from Sierra Leone and mother from Guinea. She had been living in Liberia since she was small with her grandmother and later got married to a man from the Fula tribe from Lofa, in Liberia. She had been working for one of my colleagues for last seven years, and she recommended us Tracy. As she was recommended by a reliable person and as she was not really from the very piece of earth Albert was from, I decided to give her the work. The first week on we noticed a very significant change in our apartment and things started turning proper and organised as never before. Irrespective of the existing salary differences between men and women in the country, even if they perform the same duty, she was paid the same amount given to Albert, of which she was happy about. I and my housemate were quite satisfied with the work of Tracy and recommended her to another friend of us for part-time household work.

One day when I returned home, there was a piece of paper with a small note on my table.

'Bossman, tomorrow my son's birthday.'

It was a situation of repeating history for me, even though the event was different, the expectation and the latent attitude were the same. This time, I knew that it was something monetary she was expecting than a mere gift for the son. Instead of clarifying, I decided to confront the hidden motive of her. I bought a couple of exercise books and some pens and left them on the table with a note 'Many Happy Returns of the Day' so that she would find it when she arrived the following day.

I thought that she would take them home but instead I received a call to my mobile when I was at office.

'Bossman, my son had enough books.'

A feeling beyond shock just went across myself, making me almost numb and left nothing to talk about. I just said 'Okay, just leave them on the table, I will give them to someone else who can use them.' But when I returned home, they had disappeared and probably they had already been sold to someone else or exchanged for a new hair or some second-hand fancy clothes or shoes coming from the United States. Or in the most reasonable case, the money made out of books might have been used for buying some food for home that the birthday child would at least have a share of it.

When experiences which are similar are being piled one upon the other, it is inevitable that a perceptual set which would later on lead for stereotyping is established in oneself. I believe that was not just another event for me but it was for sure another seed in the yard of generalisation which I tried my best to avoid, but in next couple of years, my perception was cemented and concreted by the actions of locals and stoned as a conclusion that it was a trait in this part of the world.

There is not much supermarkets in Monrovia, it's been a little township than a city, though it is the capital and the only township for the whole nation, there is less than ten supermarkets where most of the expatriates do their shopping either after work or on weekends. By five in the evening, on every weekday, the ex-rebels who had been mutilated throng in the parking plots of supershops waiting for expatriates. The moment you get out of the vehicle, they follow you till the entry of the shop and wait till you come out as if they were waiting to get something that you owe. Most often, you are surrounded by a few of them and the security guards of the shops do almost nothing to prevent the invasion whereas you are forced to give a couple of dollars to each person. Sometimes, after getting US$1, they show you the middle finger to show their dissatisfaction, which makes you more embarrassed and vexed.

I always used to say no whenever the guys on the clutches come near the jeep even though my colleague used to sympathise them and give 'small small' whenever they approach. Often she will end up venting more than $20 at a time when she finishes with the security or the guy at the park, who is the last man to pay. And I was always the bad man for them and they always used filth words whenever they see me. One evening, I finished chopping with my wife and reached the car with the stuff we bought from a budget shopping centre in Sinkor, called Era. There were three guys on clutches and started shouting at me showing their famous gesture of middle finger to me using very abusive words. That was one of the rarest moments of my life that I discovered the demon in me. They were showing me to everyone who was passing, and yelling, 'This man do not want white woman to give us money.'

It is not a unique thing to Liberia; beggars are everywhere on earth and there were worse things I had witnessed in Asia, in places like Delhi and Kolkata, but the behaviour of making you obligated to give them what they demand I had not seen anywhere on earth. It is as if they have the right to claim an amount that they decide from your income and get it anytime they want, which had an outlook of rather a criminal act than just begging. If you do not give money, you are a cheap and bad man who deserves to see impolite gestures.

When you finished giving money for the boys on the clutches and trying to get in to the jeep to escape from forced drain of your wallet, the security guards, who did not do anything to prevent you being robbed strategically, come running to your door, push it as if your door was not properly closed, and keep looking at you like zombies with no movements till you give them 'small small' which is not the last point where you need to pay. After you are done with the security, the boy who just run behind your jeep when you are reversing, as if he was controlling the traffic for you to occupy the road, stands in front of your door. The moment you throw some Liberian dollars to his hand you can release a sigh of relief till the next time you come to the shop. This is the repeating reality of every shopping experience in Monrovia whatever your nationality is, whatever your skin colour is and everyone is trying to make you feel obligated to give them some money.

When the rainy season arrives, many roads in the city turn into lakes, making most of the roads impassable for small cars. And it becomes a very common scene that the 'yellow machines' are broken on the road, most often in the middle of the road causing terrible traffic, caused by attempting in passing water pools on the road. After the first few days, when everything on the road had turned into a complete mess just like a hell on earth, a few men appear in luminous aprons and white helmets and fill some holes on the road. They just partially fill the mud puddles, put a read corn on the road to stop the vehicles that pass, and start collecting 'something' which is at least one dollar from everyone. It has become a seasonal livelihood but obviously a passive yet forceful collection of money that police and all the other responsible government entities have their blind eye on. Sometimes, one tends to be paranoid to an extent that the same people might dig the holes in the streets so that they would be able to make some living.

After crossing mudholes and paying money to those who fill the holes, or for clear understanding those who pretend to fill the holes, you might be trapped again at one or more signal lights by those who come with a dirty wet towel and wipe less than one square feet of your windshield and stand at the side of the driver expecting some money. If you do not pay a good hard shot from their fists would land on your car, probably followed by showing middle finger. They appear every single day, and if you give them something today, they will thank you and smile at you and they come back to you tomorrow as if you are obligated to give their daily share. In case you failed to give what they expect, all the good you had been doing to them disappears in the air in less than a second. Probably the one who sits next to you will also be disgraced showing the whole world that in Liberia there is not help which is remembered for more than sixty seconds, which is obviously the differences of values in different social setups that everyone of us who work as expatriates understand but as humans there should be a bottom line for human values which make us special.

Besides all roadside activities, all the access to beaches where the expatriates are often interested in going is blocked by villagers. Everyone who wants to go to the beach have to pay something which is also another easy way of finding a living on the expatriate population in the country.

Duco palace is one of the most famous war monuments in central Monrovia, which is a ruined hotel which was Monrovia Hilton before the war and as a result of the war, today's Duco palace is an abundant building that everyone who comes from outside would like to have a look at because of its iconic importance and location from where a panoramic view of the whole of Monrovia is offered. Anyone who reaches Duco palace will be followed by some boys and kids who pretend to be guides and try to get something out of you. Seldom, there had been cases where the expatriates had been robbed by those who come as guides. They just follow you, even though you do not want them to come, and when you are about to go, they surround you and demand money for the service they had offered whereas there was nothing but embarrassment. The same scenario is very common in Hotel Africa, which is also an icon of war in Liberia that rest in peace under deterioration in Northern suburbs of Monrovia. Hotel Africa was built during the time of Tolbert, for African Union summit held in Liberia in 1979 which faced its pathetic destiny as ruins of war during the civil conflict of Liberia. Today, just like Duco palace, many people who come to Liberia would like to go see Hotel Africa and they do face similar situations like those who do to Duco Palace. Hotel Africa, being a quite remote place in the suburbs, the locals tend to be more hash to the visitors, making the best use of the pre-existing fear and vigilance in visitors who come to post-conflict countries.

As a result of constant interaction of dependency syndrome, many of us had developed such an inhumane insensitivity, along with unbelievable level of distrust and resent towards the abovementioned type of people who were common in Liberian society. And most often, I avoided saying 'good morning' in the morning as I was aware of the kind of reply I would receive—'trying small small', which is obviously a formulated answer to get something 'small small' early in the morning.

One day, I was driving to pick my colleague who lived within less than one kilometre from my apartment, and we met the gardener on our way. She just winded the shutter down and said good morning, as it is a gentle and polite gesture to say 'good morning' to someone you see in the compound, especially to a person you know.

'Gerry, almost died,' he replied, making me crack with laughter.

'You almost died? With what?' I asked, suppressing vague of laughter.

'I was dead yesterday,' he told again.

'You are resurrected now?' He threw a look of a mongoose at me as if I was a snake.

343

'I'm feeling bad,' Gerry said with his full voice with full of energy which is completely different from his mood that manifested a while ago.

'You have malaria?' I asked.

'No, just headache.'

I accelerated the vehicle so that my friend did not have much time to be melt by the manipulation of Gerry. As we passed, I was looking at him through the centre mirror. He threw the shovel aside and looked at the jeep that was passing just like a monitor which just missed its easy prey.

Despite all components of dependency syndrome found in people who have been pushed to live far beyond the level of poverty, that one would easily reacted to with sympathy unless it does not cross your limits, the attitude of dependency and learnt helplessness has spread wide across the society and rooted deep into each layer of society. It does not really matter whether you are rich or poor, your are working or not, but the whole intention is to get something from someone for free, and most often to make others feel like they are bound to give you what you ask which is typical and unique to this little nation of 4.3 million population.

One day, by accident, not within the territory of Liberia, but in Dubai International Airport, I met Mr Massaquoi, who was around 80 years old, a retired government servant of Liberia, who is now living in Houston, Texas, with his son's family. Both of us were on transit for the same destination, 'Liberia'. I was coming from France and he was from the United States. As there was a couple of hours left for boarding, we happened to have a chat in which I could not resist my urge to ask him about the root causes of the dependency syndrome that most of the people see in Liberians. It was kind of a situation where his response would be either a reasonable answer that is based on facts and realities with no judgments and defence or an aggressive and defensive reaction charged with emotions of nationalism and Africanism against an Indian man who tries to let the Africans, then Liberians, down. Either A or B, there will be an answer anyway, and I just asked him politely that I had noticed that there is a lot of dependency not only among the commoners but also in the institutions across the country. Surprising me with his maturity and truthfulness, along with his knowledge, Mr Massaquoi told:

'This country is a country based on charity, which was the foundation of present Liberia. The day the settlers, freed slaves landed in the coast of

Liberia, the country turned to be a part of Saturn not of Earth.' He was serious.

'They came and marked their land along the sea coast, so that they have the access without any consultation of anyone among the indigenous population in the country who lived on that piece of land for centuries, probably for thousands of years. Those people who lived in Pepper Coast were farmers, hunters, herdsmen who had their centuries-old livelihood, they felt the vibrations of the piece of land where they lived with harmony with the nature, according to the rules of nature. Their belief systems were primitive, some of them practised cannibalism, extreme rituals, they did not wear what was known as clothes to the Western world, dialects were not developed and they did not have much interactions with the external world but they lived in their own way till the settlers known in different names such as Congo people, Americo-Liberians, came in. The very first interaction between the indigenous and the Americo-Liberians was that they looked down at the indigenous as if they were a bunch of savages and that was the very first mistake that was made in our history which hindered all our potentials into weakness. It was colonisation even though people say that Liberia has never been colonised. When and external power comes and try to control or take control of the indigenous population, their resources, what else do you use for that action? It was a colonial approach. Liberia was founded, colonised, established, and controlled by the American colonisation society.

And then besides all wars and frictions between settlers and the indigenous, the declaration of Republic of Liberia on 26 July 1847, the gap between us, settlers as the superior beings who decide for us and rulers, and we as indigenous as the ruled, helpless uncivilised and inferior beings. That point on we grew up in two major camps, the provider and the consumer, rulers and ruled, superior and inferior, so on. Two completely different environments were created in one country which is as small as 111 square kilometers and our thoughts, attitudes, values, and behaviours developed within the imposed frame. The ruling class, settlers who were 5 per cent of the total population, decided what 95 per cent of indigenous ruled should do, what we should not. They were the ones who decided what to provide us with and what not to provide us with. During the process of that governing structure, the pre-existing social systems collapsed and disappeared in no time, leaving us completely dependent on the rulers. It was their strategy to take the control over the majority of the population. We were strategically taught. All of these happened freely and easily as the ruling class was supported by America, since the very beginning.

As a consequence of the strategy of ruling of Americo-Liberians, or in other words Congo people, dependency syndrome started growing in Liberia. The indigenous who already had a productive system had gradually been transformed into mere consumers who were waiting to be fed. Later on the political direction of the country took a different route with military coup by sergeant Samuel Doe who was the first to be president among the oppressed but as he did not have proper direction and vision, the society started to follow the same norms and mores came into being during rule of Congo men, and probably faster than in their time. Today, we kneel down before anyone and everyone and ask for help but most of us do not even know, not only how to pay gratitude but also that helpers cannot help forever. They have completely forgotten that we have to help ourselves rather than seek help from strangers. Knowing very well that the fatal mistake that we did as Liberians was seeking help from unknown, we keep on doing the same. That is a fate chosen by this African nation who is a creation of an outsider, at their interest disregarding the interest of the soil where their feet was on. Today, our dreams do not match with the ground reality; we are still governed and judged by the norms of Saturn whereas we are right on this rough earth.'

Massaquoi was emotional but he was pretty reasonable as per what he believes in. How a state is established, especially when there is a lot of diversity in terms of ethnicities or religions or in any other social dimensions, is the foundation of its society and its values. Liberia looked liked a sick baby even before it was born and sick with a persistent chronic dysfunction that no remedy on earth can cure. Massaquoi anyway hit some points which were apparently realities in Liberian context and reminded me of a few encounters I had experienced with some colleagues with whom I worked directly or indirectly at the workplace or beyond.

In a country where the roadside universities, which are smaller than primary schools of many countries, and those who teach do not have a basic degree in some cases, quality of education is a question. And on top of it, many people simply buy their bachelors or masters from the university without stepping into it even for a rain. They are the ones who later become 'the working class' without any knowledge beyond what they acquired during their primary or secondary schools that they attended randomly as the series of wars deprived the opportunity for systematic education. Knowledge-wise or at level of attitude, there is not much impact that education had done in the population in Liberia which is even projected through its 85 per cent illiteracy which is one of the lowest in the world. In such a system of growth, they, instead of unlearning the dependency that they learnt in the family, tend to master it more, the more they interact with the external society as their ambitions are higher than others and they tend to see the outsiders as pools of resources freely available for them. In rare cases, those who had been educated from foreign universities work within the territory of Liberia even though the majority of that class live outside the country making their fortune in safe havens in Europe and the United States. Hence, the working class is the debris left within the country after the cyclone of brain drain since the conflict broke out and constant unsuitability became the only stable element in society. Therefore, the working class left in the country mostly possess the same personality characteristics and traits which have not been impacted from formal education. Besides that in educational institutions, whether they belong to public or private sector paying 'small small' to every layer of workers from administrators, teachers till the cleaner is the only way to get you through the intentional hurdles created as bribe points which encourage that one who can pay, even though you do not want to attend for the classes, a certificate can be obtained. In addition, assuming that the student participated in the classes regularly, but as a result of prolonged interactions with people who are corrupt instead of being exemplary, the students tend to acquire the attitudinal and behavioural traits of their seniors and teachers and tend to practice them in a social system where there is no resistance or enforced litigation against such acts. In brief, the undeniable reality of Liberian working class is that before they come to the workplace, they have already become a link of the chain of corruption that rolls on dependency.

Liberian national police, the prime civil law-enforcement entity of the country, formed and trained by multidisciplinary experts from diverse countries, investing millions of dollars on capacity and facility enhancements, today remains as one of the most corrupt and dependent entities in the country which is a vivid symbol of the level of dependency and corruption which are 'norms of Saturn' as per Massaquoi. From the very top to the very bottom of the Liberian National Police, one common thing is asking 'small small', other than that, no uniformity that should be a part of police exists.

It was a rainy Monday in June 2014; I went to the National Headquarters of the Liberian National Police, known as LNP, to see one of my friends who worked as an advisor to LNP. Coming from a country where there are relatively high standards at work even though we were from the same continent, he used to complain most of the time that even though the kind of work he does is directly improving the standards of personal and professional life of police in Liberia, they do not want to cooperate with him unless he gives them some money or sometimes gifts. The kind of attitude demonstrated to the facilitators who have come to help their own institution is discouraging and frustrating not only for those who work as advisors but also those who hear such stories. When a mentor comes to give them some expertise, instead of appreciating and acquiring it at its best, a culture of demanding money or favours along with the knowledge he or she is there to deliver has come into being.

The day I walked in to the office of Joseph, he was quite pissed with his counterparts. His face was not the cheerful face that everyone always talks about. We always see him with his smile with wide open mouth till the ears, showing his pearl white teeth which become crystal clear on his jet black background of his face.

'You know, to contact their officers in the counties, they want me to give them money for their mobiles.'

'I suggested them to use my official mobile but they do not want to use it either, they want money.'

He kept of saying even without greeting me which is a very rare situation when Joseph is concerned.

I just did not tell anything and waited till he calmed down. Then I asked what really had happened. According to Joseph, every time he goes to office in the police headquarters, his counterparts ask him money for their mobile phones, saying that they have to call their colleagues to get the project work done properly and on time. Whenever he offers his phone which is an official one paid by his office, they do not want to use that, which means they need money for some other purpose. That particular day, a delegation from his country had visited the office and one had tried to ask money from one of the delegates and later from him to call the county offices for coordinating their field visit which had made Joseph burst out.

Even though I was a third person who was just witnessing what was happening, my visit to Joseph strengthened my pre-existing perceptions about deep-rooted dependency which exists in the surface of Liberian society visible to anyone who comes in. The helpless kindly ask for help, Liberians demand for help even when support is already given which is very much unique to them and it has already become one of the dominant features of Liberian identity. It has come to a certain extent that, when we meet a Liberian who expresses willingness to work more than what is asked, or who is willing to give something without expecting a bigger return, or someone who does not want to accept anything freely, we are surprised even though in many developing countries in Asia or Eastern Europe, people hesitate to ask or take things freely. We treat it as an exception if we found a Liberian who is reluctant to demand money. This attitude is demonstrated not only for foreign nationals but also for affluent Liberians, which is recognised as bottom to top 'horizontal dependency', and also, there is another version which is 'vertical dependency', which stands for demands and expectations within the same social and economic layers. This multidirectional nature of Liberian dependency is unique even though its horizontal version especially from bottom to top is very common everywhere in the globe.

The incredibly invading skills of imposing the thoughts of being obligated to cater their demand are a very Liberian feature that I have never encountered anywhere else. When someone unknown calls you 'my brother', its time for you to know that there will be a financial part at the end of the sentence. Or sometimes, the conversation is debuted 'my good friend, you have to help me with 'small small or with food', and it might continue until your hand reaches back pocket. And in the most probable case, you might not see your 'friend' again as he/she does not want to pay it back. If you try to remind them, they would either pretend that you gave nothing and raise their voice before everyone as if you had committed a crime or in the best case you would hear 'Ooo sorry ooo, next time'. But that next time never comes.

Just a few days after the incident at the police headquarters, my time had come again without my knowledge. I was walking into my office on an early Monday morning, one of my local staff colleagues who was on leave had come to the office even before seven. She usually comes to work even after nine thirty, almost one hour after the reporting time to work. I greeted her as usual and asked why she was in the office during the vacations.

'Tomorrow, my birthday, just came to remind you all.' First time after good 31 years I lived on this earth I met someone who had come to remind her colleagues about her birthday. I could not resist my laughter, which obviously sounded sarcastic, but it was the natural reaction to an abnormal stimuli.

'You came to remind us, your birthday?' I thought it was how they pass an invitation across.

'Did you invite us before? Sorry I cannot recall' My response was honest but I usually do not forget, specially events.

'No no, I say, I came to remind you guys that my birthday is on you.'

I had heard that part many times. My housemaid had put their birthdays, funerals, holidays, and even service of the church on me. It was kind of an 'enough is enough' situation and on top of that, we had already planned something for her in the office as we do to anyone else in the office, irrespective of whether they were nationals or internationals. And she knew it but apparently she had come to the office to collect some money from everyone in the office for her party at home. Rather than asking help in a gentle way, her fashion of attempting to make you bounded or obligated to cater her demand and beyond that, on my birthday, she was one of the first few Liberians in the office who came and asked for a party, just a month ago, that I had not forgotten yet.

'Both your and my birthdays on me? What is that rule? From where it came?' I asked in the form of a joke, expecting an answer, but I did not hear anything.

These traits and behavioural patterns with unchanging attitudes of dependency blended with dishonesty govern every single interaction in Liberian society. From family to school, school to the workplace, workplace to society in relationships at all levels, those abovementioned traits that Massaquoi called 'from Saturn' have become the essence of this tiny nation blocked in illiteracy, extreme poverty, one of the lowest life expectancy, and unemployment.

My father used to go to an astrology class when he was around his mid-forties. I do still remember that he had old dusty exercise books in which there were quadrates with partitioned areas within with different zodiac signs. I used to peep at them when my father was studying and he used to describe the impact of different planets on human behaviour, body, and mind. Saturn does nothing but keep you straying and having no goal in life. Jupiter stands for intelligence and calmness, and so on. Massaquoi's symbolism through my father's astrological classification suits exceptionally well to the very nature of the present reality in Liberia, which has probably developed during the foundation of the country as Massaquoi says, and heightened over and over again with chain of civil conflicts broke out in the territory and Ebola crisis of West Africa.

The day I was preparing to leave Liberia after spending a greater proportion of my half decade spent in Africa, a deep sad feeling conquered my whole self than never before in nowhere on earth where I had been working before as an aid worker, peacekeeper, or diplomat. A feeling that held me guilty for not being able to do what you dreamt of or intended to do. I knew it was because of a disabling environment that existed in Liberian society in each layer, especially in the working class. Nonetheless, when I looked at their society where nothing much have significantly changed even one good decade after the civil war, there is no sign of the dream that suddenly embraced my mind when I was passing infinite landscapes of green and waters while coming from Roberts International Airport in 15 February 2011, coming true for even next two decades' time. Today, Liberia is a nation that sells everything to the outside world in raw form and import almost everything from outside while the majority of them are still living far below the poverty line and still do not want to sweat but to beg. The norms and mores of Saturn that first germinated in Bushrod island in Doe River by the freed slaves who were brought by so-called 'dream of liberty' have stolen their human dignity.

Chapter 19

IN TIME OF EBOLA

It WAS JUST LIKE yesterday, one evening during summer vacations, we used to call it 'kite flying vacation' as we didn't have significant seasonal changes being a tropical country, we were sitting in the open veranda of our ancestral house, with my grandmother, counting the mongooses, palm-civets, and flying giant fruit bats, as we used to do every vacation time while listening to the thriller stories about ghosts, wild animals, and about Second World War events. Those moments were a few of the most memorable times with my grandmother who passed away in 1998 when I was 17 years old. That particular day was a holiday, my parents were free and they joined us with a pot of hot black tea and jaggery, a traditional sweetener for tea widely used in South Asia. As long as there is hot tea in the pot, the conversations can drag hours after hours and the subject matters can range from simple day-to-day life events to complex cosmic or spiritual matters and the discussions shift their themes instantly from one to another like a relay system of a Pandle. It was such a moment, my father was denying the idea of the existence of ghosts, brought in to discussion by my grandma, and a giant bat that was hanging on the mango tree in front of the veranda, defecated right on the edge of the concrete steps; it reminded me the Dhal curry bowl that once slipped from my hands and fell in the middle of the dining room. 'Oh nasty bat, it had shitted on my white shirts left on the rope last night.' He stepped out blasting at the bat. He was able to walk only a few steps and the second load was released on his back and we heard its creaking sound like a mouse along with the clapping-like noise of its wings. He was at the climax of his fury, numb and nothing left to say but rushed to have a wash. At his return, back to his calm state of mind, laughing, he started talking about a strange disease that spread vigorously in some areas in Congo Basin, due to the fact that the people down there eat fruit bats. 'Ebola'—the word itself was like 'vampires' to us, such a virus that can penetrate human skin in seconds and make a living being deteriorate and dead within days, was like a story of black fairies to us.

'Mostly in Congo Basin, people die with Ebola often'

I was imagining that a situation like 'Black Death' in Europe, or 'Small Pox' in India, where thousands of people die like cattle in times of the plague, and bodies were decomposing all over public spaces. The vultures, crows, dogs, and foxes enjoy the feast and eventually they themselves die adding, more food for other scavengers.

'There is no cure, and it's a hemorrhagic fever, like dengue but more dangerous than that.'

Dengue, being the only deadly hemorrhagic fever in Sri Lanka, was the only comparison which would have been understood by children. As a result of extensive sensitisation programs on media, along with the very strict surveillance and monitoring strategies implemented throughout the country, every single citizen had knowledge about the disease. Despite dengue, seasonal flues and common cold are the only rapidly transmittable diseases found in Sri Lanka, as malaria remains locked in history.

Bleeding zombies started haunting my mind; it was like a Halloween show, and Ebola remained embedded with Africa like black people. It was just like HIV/AIDS, Ebola and Africa became inseparable in my imagination. Since that day, whenever I talked about Africa, I talked about Ebola and its tongue twisting 'haemorrhagic' part that I was unable to pronounce properly during my childhood. However, knowing about Ebola was a something to feel superior and knowledgeable as a kid in school, and most of the time even the class teachers of primary school did not have a clue about what I was talking about.

'Nurses and doctors are dying in Congo caused by an unknown fever.'

It was a chapeau of a short article published in a tiny column reserved for international news in a weekend newspaper and that was my first-ever piece of literature about Ebola I read when I was a child. It was about the Ebola virus outbreak in Zaire, presently known as Democratic Republic of Congo, in 1995, killing 254 infected persons. There was a blurred photo, in black and white, of a patient lying on a hospital bed, looking better than weird photos that the media used to publish about HIV/AIDS, but those who were near him looked obviously strange to me, in fully covered space gears which reminded me Neil Armstrong's photo on surface of the moon, but instead of being in the glamour of human achievement in Neil's case, it was instant woe and fear that crept into my nerves, with a thought that human is not still top of everything. A couple of years later, I got in contact with an French epidemiologist in Marseille, who had done researches on infectious diseases in Sub-Saharan Africa, and one day, we sat at a roadside coffee shop and started talk about our whereabouts. It was a pretty casual one and I did not expect that 'Ebola' would come back into the show for the second time of my life. He had been in Congo in the 1970s when the first known Ebola outbreak occurred introducing the new haemorrhagic fever caused by an extremely virulent virus to the world.

'It was an accidental but an unforgettable time of life, summer 1976, I went to Lisle the capital of Mongala district of Zaire for field survey of rural tropical diseases in Congo river basin. Actually, why I went to Lisala was because my uncle, who was a missionary, was based there. I used to go to every little clinic and missionary hospitals, there were not many of them, two or three times a week to collect data about the patients and prevailing diseases and trends. One Sunday, after the service at the church, my uncle told me that there was a rumour about an unknown fever that kills people faster than witchcraft. People become completely bloody and ugly before they die as if it was a curse of a demon. The headmaster of the school was the centre of attention; he was doing a great job to the communities and some people hated him as he was a foreigner who was respected by villagers. He was talking about the index case of Ebola outbreak in Zaire, Mabalo Lokela. He sounded shaken and frustrated, as he had been a constant victim of malaria and couple of times he was nearly dead and nothing but by the grace of God he came back to life. Next morning, with my colleague who was a Congolese, a nurse by profession, headed to Yambuku missionary hospital where the first case of Ebola was reported. Actually, by that time, no one called it 'Ebola' and even the first case was clinically misdiagnosed and had been treated as malaria, but later on the patient had been reported again to the hospital in a critical condition with profuse bleeding from all orifices, vomiting, acute diarrhoea, chest pains, headache, fever, and in an agitated and confused state. After a few days, he passed away. The case had been ignored even though a few months ago there was an outbreak of a fever with similar symptoms reported in a nearby village in South Sudan killing more than 150 people; however, the two outbreaks remained unrelated as per the records. When we reached there, there was another patient reported with same clinical manifestations. Later on, cases started popping up one after the other, proving that the disease is highly infectious and deadly, taking the attention of the Centre for Disease Control (CDC), World Health Organization (WHO), and other parties involved in and found out that those cases either received injections at the hospital or had had close contact with another case. Shortly after family members prepared his body for burial, in accordance with local customs, twenty-one of Lokela's friends and relatives fell seriously ill and eighteen later died. However, it was concluded that the lack of capacity of Yambuku mission hospital in terms of equipment, human resources, and expertise to handle such a disease with a high individual and a community risk. The microbiologist Peter Piot highlighted that continuous use of unsterile needles had largely contributed to the growth of the epidemic. Even though it was contained after quarantining all the villagers, but the human cost of the outbreak was over 280 out of 300 plus affected individuals. The survival rate during that time was below 10 per cent.'

He released a long sigh, looked at me who was silent like deep waters, asked me whether I still wanted to go to Congo.

'It is full of risks and a hard place to survive and now there is a never-ending conflict on top of already prevailing risks.'

I smiled while ordering another pot of coffee, as I felt that it was not horrifying enough to shatter a childhood dream that had pierced deep into oneself like an arrow. If I tried to pull out my dreams, that would do a greater damage to myself than risking life in the middle of nowhere, where I had been dreaming to go since I was a child. Risk is the first stage of development, where there is no risk, no way forward. That was my last discussion about Ebola.

On and off the media brought Ebola into public attention: the outbreak in 2007 in Democratic Republic of Congo, then 2010 in Gulu in Uganda, where I went to meet ex-child soldiers of Lord Resistance Army of Joseph Kony. Despite those outbreaks of Ebola that were easily contained, the bleeding zombies remained as a minor concern of my travel plan to Africa, even though Ebola, Marburg fever, Lassa, and malaria were like mantra in my mum's mouth when I was preparing to go to Africa.

It was new year morning, over the ring of thick and obscure Hamattan dust, the sun was struggling to give a new hope to a zone, of peace, stability, and prosperity that they were longing for since the beginning of the last decade, after being torn apart into pieces by devastating civil conflicts, but it looked like the 31 night prayers had not been heard. An awaking alarm, instead pleasant New Year wishes were passed in the form of a rumour: 'Ebola outbreak in Guinea, in a village at close proximity to Liberia and Sierra Leone.' I was in Liberia, in Unicef office having a friendly chat with one of my friends, who was a in a senior managerial position, he was the one who whispered into my very ears. It was a wakeup call of all hallucinatory bleeding zombies who were sleeping since the 1990s, since I first heard about Ebola that I never thought of being present in anywhere I live. 'Are you sure?' I asked him, trying to convince myself that it could be a lie, as lying for making people confuse and panicked has become a part of Liberian life.

'Wait a minute, I will show you the official correspondence.' He turned his screen towards visitor's chair. It was from WHO—World Health Organization—and was sufficient enough to convince the rational part of me, but the emotional part of me was still in denial and trying to reframe the whole thing in a scenario of a Lassa fever outbreak which is very common in Sierra Leone and Guinea and of which the symptoms are not significantly different at initial stages. The hot news was the dominant discussion among everyone in the mission and was wandering almost everywhere on the tip of everyone's tongue, at the smoking balcony, lobby, shuttles, offices, and finally came out as an official circular by the medical section of United Nations Mission in Liberia, convincing everyone that there is an outbreak of a haematologic fever like Ebola in the southern part of Guinea, along with travel restrictions to Guinea for United Nations Staff. But a lot of staff from Africa, especially from Guinea and Liberia, denied the existence of Ebola in Guinea, probably as an emotional reaction to the fear of being stigmatised and being subjected to possible movement restrictions. And again the activation of the African defence wall against the rest of world could be another reason for denying the fact that Ebola has penetrated the frontiers of West Africa, which was not its usual ground. The heat of the topic cooled down in few days and life turned to normal despite some extremely vigilant people who talked about it, on and off. Nonetheless, the expatriate community was very alert and vigilant about the fact that a virus to cross a fragile border is not a big deal and we would probably hear the cases in Liberia in the near future.

It was in late February 2014. I was on the way to Conakry from Liberia by road and I met Nicola who was working in Conakry, the capital city of Guinea, with a nongovernmental organisation, supporting the government of Guinea to fight against the outbreak. We were packed in one taxi wagon, almost seven of us like cows taken to the butcher's place and the smell of sweat and smoked meaty food make the two of us, not the others, suffocated as if we were under a poisonous gas attack. And the stories of Ebola were running upwards with every pulse making the journey more fearful than a disgusting experience. Nicola had visited the affected villages to see her local counterparts who were involved in the water and sanitation program especially focusing on preventive methods of further spread of Ebola virus disease and on her way to Conakry.

'With indigenous belief system, it is hard to control,' she said. However, the world's experience about Ebola outbreaks was that it can erupt like a volcano all of a sudden, take some lives away, and go back to sleep in some time. That was the assumption of Nicola but she looked tired of the continuously failing attempts of sensitising the rural communities on cultural and communal rituals in terms of death and burial, which increase the spread of Ebola. Traditions dominate any society, but in Africa and some part of Asia, traditions stand rigid as if they are the prime purpose of human life and when it comes to a birth, marriage, or death, in major life events, they take the upper hand on everything. A funeral is a long process especially in West Africa, and it takes relatively a longer time, like almost two to four weeks, and then a series of rituals that involve handling the body, by touching and washing, by the close relatives of the deceased which is vital for a dignified burial of a loved one who has passed away. It is necessary for those who are left behind by the deceased. It is vital for those who watch from outside, how the burial and whole funeral process is being handled; its a matter of dignity of the family rather than the dignity of the dead.

'One of our volunteers was seriously beaten in a rural community in Guéckédou while he was conducting a focus group meeting in the process of sensitising the village leadership in isolation of contacts of second cycle of infection from the index case, who is Emile Ouamouno, a 2-year-old boy who lived in the village of Meliandou, Guéckédou,' she added

The people in the surrounding areas of the index case believed that the health workers purposely spread the disease and they are paid by international organisations, while others believe that the disease doesn't exist and keep complaining on the community mobilisers that they are spying on the villagers. Therefore, the infected people are hidden either by themselves or by their loved ones and that way many of them evaded surveillance and infected many others. Last week of February 2014, riots broke out in the regional capital, Nzérékoré, when rumours were spread that people were being contaminated when health workers were spraying a market area to decontaminate it. Afterwards, it became usual that the villagers attacked the health workers and burial teams. 'It was a situation where when your family members are taken away for isolation camps and they never return and on top of the grievance that the family goes through that the various rumours such as international organisations taking organs of people and so on provoke violence and promote the increase of the disease not the message of prevention.' Even though we had a common language, 'French', for security reasons, we talked about sensitive things in English, using as much as technical jargons so that the villagers in the taxi did not have a clue of what we were talking about, as our journey would be more than nine good hours, a long constantly changing road from gravel to paved, about 690 kilometres through the isolated countryside of Guinea. 'One time, a mother had been taken into an isolation centre, in the regional hospital, as we did not have Ebola-specific isolated treatment units built here, leaving the child along, which was not ethical, and villagers were afraid to take care of the child. Such ethical barriers sometimes become challenges to health staff as well as fuel latent anger of communities.' No mother on earth would leave a child alone, well knowing that she would never return and there is no one to take care of the child, she would prefer to die with the child, which is the understanding of the commoner whose emotions are dominant over the knowledge. But with emotions being the governing factors of human life in most of the situations, people do take risks even though their actions are catastrophic. I was not trying to justify the actions of those ignorant villagers who are on a verge of a biological calamity, keep on continuing traditional rituals that promote further spread of Ebola, but outsiders' inability or unwillingness to be empathetic also cannot be justified. For them, it is their father, mother, daughter, or son who is dead, he or she will never return, and on top of grieving, they try their best to ensure a dignified burial to say goodbye or reconnect with the person in the next life by executing every tiny bit of rituals that their traditions lasted for generations pronounce. It is all about the norms and mores of the society, their belief and value system. My consciousness squeezed between two hemispheres, one that is dominated by human emotions and the one which is rational and recognised as pragmatic in modern terms. However, while we were on the route to Conakry, that took almost nine hours, the cases had been increased by eighteen, which means at least two new suspected cases per hour, that looked like a beginning of a disaster—a disaster that had firmly gripped the easy land where everything would support for its spread like a wildfire.

With terrifying information that flows like a fallen damn, from Nicola's mouth, I did not have enough time to analyse and understand the situation; they just kept on accumulating in me in such an overwhelming pace and bleeding zombies started haunting in my mind again, every single person in the taxi was bleeding from every little opening visible to the outside, that is how Nicola should also feel, though she does not show, I thought. I said bye bye to Nicolas, in the suburbs of Conakry where she lives, and headed to the hotel I booked for the next three days as soon as possible with minimum contacts with people. Next day morning, I had to visit the Honorary Consulate of Morocco for processing my visa for the next holiday but things remain uncertain under the same sky of West Africa where I lived for nearly four years. After my personal experience of malaria, a feeling of withdrawal from my prime purpose of staying in this continent came to pop up in my mind for the second time. Has the time arrived to leave the continent with the book written halfway? A population of 8.7 million is under a high risk of an outbreak of one of the deadliest diseases on earth, and 4.3 million from Liberia and 6.1 million from Sierra Leone might join sooner or later; why should I escape like a coward when the land that accommodated me for the last four years is under threat, irrespective of what they are, who they are, as fellow human beings, we have to be there for them. I decided to come back to Liberia the next day, leaving my visa application forms to Morocco on the dressing table of the hotel. Heroic traits usually come to surface as a reaction to intense fear or threat, but the heroism would not last long; I crossed the border of Liberia exactly five minutes before the border closed and decided to stay in the United Nations Regional Field Office of Vonjama, in Lofa county that shares its borders with Sierra Leone and Guinea, the whole night my mind was like a parliament, a debate between fear and terror party caused by bleeding zombies and my unmet desires conceived by free-time stories to discover the continent, pulling and pushing me, trying to tear me in two.

The Liberians were in complete denial of existence of Ebola outbreak in neighbouring Guinea, instead they complained the usual white man for conspiring to eliminate the black population, and kept on living their usual lives attending funerals of their relatives and friends in neighbouring Guinea whereas the expatriate community in Liberia became more and more vigilant as the numbers increased from the other side of the border, an epidemic of Ebola virus disease EVD is being officially declared by WHO and the ministry of health of Guinea on 25 March 2014.

While rumours about Ebola was heating up, a simultaneous outbreak of Lassa fever was reported in Magibi County in Liberia. Lassa fever, being a highly contagious viral haemorrhagic fever which is endemic to West Africa, specially to Sierra Leone and Guinea, and sometimes penetrates the borders of Liberia on and off. Rumours are supersonic in this part of the earth and started spreading in different versions; as always, everyone in the chain adds their own part to each rumour, that it was Lassa fever, not Ebola which is in Guinea, just like the contained outbreak in Kakata, in Magibi. They thanked God for it being Lassa fever not Ebola and kept on enjoying the last bit of time left for them to realise that they are already in the jaws of a shark, and on 28 March 2014, suspected cases of Ebola were reported in Lofa county and Nimba county that share borders with Guinea. Both of the suspected cases in Liberia were contacts of cases in Guinea as they had gone to attend the funerals of their relatives who died in Guinea. The ignorance and inefficient border control added another 4.3 million population in to 6.1 million who were already under high risk of EVD. Liberia welcomed Ebola in March and still people in Monrovia, around 2 million out of 4.3, concentrated in Monrovia in urban ghettos were telling, 'Thank God it's in Lofa not in Monrovia' and continued their usual way of life with close social contacts and meals rich in bushmeat ranging from fruit bats to monkeys.

Simultaneously, United Nations Mission in Liberia had announced its scaling down and exit from the country in the coming years, transiting its roles and responsibilities to the government of Liberia. And also a lot of nongovernmental organisations had wrapped up their recovery and reconstruction programs and taken their programs into the route for community ownership and transition to locally operating, community-owned entities in Liberia. Once the presence of Ebola was announced in Liberia, most of the local staff were happy due to the expectation that their job will be secured assuming that UN would stay for a few more years. Such an opportunistic approach to life, and self-centredness I had never seen any of the countries I had visited so far in anywhere in the world. And those who were not part of the local staff converted their denial into a doubt that those cases were fake and it was just an attempt of international organisations and United Nations for staying a few more years in Liberia. When paranoia is the platform of living where lies and rumours are the most reliable media for the public, there is no space for a healthy media culture to grow, simply all the newspapers in Liberia followed what was marketable 'rumours', that are sold like hot cornbread on Monrovia's streets. Behind the shadow of rumours that flew up and down, left and right of the country, Ebola was progressing its way towards the capital Monrovia, by Mid-June, the first confirmed case was reported in Liberian capital. It was a red light to all of us who were expatriates even though the local community believed in the power of witchcrafts and might of God rather than admitting the civic responsibility that every single citizen had to prevent further spread of the deadly virus. The government of Liberia too showed a passivity to the matter as if it was a responsibility of international community to fight with it and dense Monrovia once affected by a bloody civil conflict once again in the hands of death, the numbers kept on multiplying while the neighbouring Sierra Leone, another nation ground into dust by a cruel civil war, has become a part of the regional crisis by 26 May 2014, just one month after the index case of Liberia was reported, and six months after the index case in Guinea, which is considered to be the index case for the West African Ebola outbreak. Finally, after several dozens of lives were gone, and several hundreds of contacts are being established, the president of Liberia, Ms Ellen Johnson Sirleaf, declared that most of the borders of Liberia were closed except commercial shipping ports and airports where there were screening facilities, on 27 July 2014, and we, as expatriates, started feeling a new kind of life was about be unfolded, whereas locals were still praying in darkness.

While Ebola remained as the main concern of expatriates and another reason for praying for locals, the frequency of hearing about cases abruptly increased, and instead of the sirens of presidential escort that goes up and down few times a day, along the Tubman boulevard, only main street in Monrovia, the sirens of Ambulances started being heard several times a day and as days and weeks passed, every five minutes was followed by ambulance sirens and the roads were busy with the ambulances and burial teams escorted by the relatives or parents of the dead. Hand washing was shifted from a hygienic practice to a compulsory ritual not only in everyday life but also in every single moment of life. At the entry of every single building, a barrel with a faucet, full of overtly chlorinated water, came into being a standard—before you enter you have to wash your hands, as Ebola is transmitted through a noninfected person coming into direct contact with the blood or body fluids of an infected person. The virus in blood and body fluids can enter the body through broken skin or mucous membranes in the eyes, nose, or mouth. Hence, as a preventive measure, everyone was obligated to wash the hands frequently with either alcohol or chlorine solutions. For the first time ever in Monrovia, plastic buckets with plastic faucets fixed to them were to be seen opening a new short-term livelihood in the region, but unfortunately, the Indian and Lebanese monopoly of trade in Liberia brought the cheap Chinese products in kicking the belly of the locals who were trying to make a living in the sudden opportunity that erupted out of Ebola. Later on, personal sanitizers, along with a little metal hook that could be used for hanging on a backpack, waist belt, or on trousers came into being with 'Made in China' label, adding a special corner in every super shop for Ebola-related hygiene materials. A devastatingly growing biological catastrophe was slowly creating new trade trends in the region with the changing lifestyle.

While hand washing becomes a ritual, sanitizer and chlorine become essentials; a watchman near the hand-washing point was there to ensure that everyone washes their hands while another person was standing next to the entry with a gun-type infrared thermometer to measure temperature of everyone before entering. Later on, the chlorinated sponge rugs came into use in most of the supermarkets and offices to clean the shoes before entering, besides all the other procedures. It was a challenge to adapt to a new lifestyle, things that we had not done before in daily life, but the persistent fear of being infected and the latest job in the region, the bucket keeper's position made it sure that everyone washes their hands before they pass the entrance which sometimes became irritating. When things were adding up to the daily life in time of Ebola, the social interaction was affected in diverse ways in the three affected countries, especially in traditional greetings, way of eating and community functions.

One of the things the people of West Africa are very good at is greeting each other. In most of the region's countries, it is often perceived rude to great merely with an American-style 'Hi, how are you?' and walk on. In West Africa, the normal thing to do would be to stop, reach out one hand, or even two, shake warmly, and then embrace. This is followed by much backslapping, more handshaking on points of agreement; 'but now that Ebola is in town and no shaking hands!', posters with Ebola prevention messages highlighted 'No handshaking', 'No hugging' or any form of close contact with people. Liberian handshake, called 'Liberian finger snap', that involves clasping hands in the normal way, then—as the hands are released—each partner clicks the fingers of the other which produces two loud snapping sounds, was the most affected gesture in whole region. The iconic finger snap that had been seen and heard over centuries in Paper Coast observed silence till an unforeseen day in the future as if the whole nation had become extinct in no time, behind the dark clouds of Ebola. To my surprise, everyone seemed to follow the rules in elite residential areas like Sinkor where influential and affluent Liberians live, within expatriate community who were very concerned and hyper-vigilant, and in all the establishments like supermarkets, companies, and other governmental and nongovernmental buildings, but Liberia remained as the worst affected country with the highest number of deaths in the region.

As the first responder to the epidemic, MSF, Medicines Sans Frontiers, doctors without borders, came to the affected countries, first in Guinea followed by Liberia and Sierra Leone, adding a new set of technical jargons to our daily life. First Ebola Treatment Units, widely known as ETUs, in all three affected countries were established by MSF giving a sense of hope to the region. The red-belted zones that were used to demarcate the safe zone from danger zone, the PPE, personal protection equipment worn by the staff in the ETU, and by the burial teams, just like scientists working in Kennedy Space Centre became the latest additions to common usage. A man who is in PPE working in an ETU appeared to be the symbol of deadliness of the disease and later on a group of men who were carrying a dead body bag even became normal and I personally became indifferent to that as everyone else says. Despite all that, the infection rates were still ascending and death rate, as if sooner or later everyone will be eradicated from the country.

While everything is apparently ready and on the ground in Liberia, response and prevention programs had already widely spread in Guinea, though it was a constant challenge for health workers to access the villagers, do surveillance, and implement the community sensitisation programs in most of rural areas in Guinea due to deep-rooted traditional beliefs and mistrust. The burial teams were often attacked, suspected patients and contacts reported fleeing from surveillance teams and besides the loads of information disseminated, regulations imposed and resources invested in all possible means of containing the outbreak in Guinea, centuries-lasted trust in traditional healers reduced the impact of response programs at a great level.

Liberia's capital Monrovia is the only town in the country, though there are little areas where there is only one brick building that Liberians would call a town, are remote villages that are completely disconnected from the capital, especially in the rainy season when all gravel roads are transformed to swampy lakes. The openness or accessibility to the remote villages in Liberia is very limited during the rainy season, despite that there are United Nations helicopters and small flights covering some main counties. The traditional beliefs and mistrust in health workers existed to a significant magnitude in rural Liberia where the literacy is less than 5 per cent despite all those factors, the spread of the disease somehow was slower than in urban Montserrado County where the capital of Monrovia is, though Monrovia has changed a lot in its social life and its outlook was considered. The wild, shaky nightlife had come to an end with imposed curfew, supermarkets and shops closed their businesses not later than seven, the roads of central city once full of traffic, left solely for ambulances after seven in the evening, the expatriate hotspots like Saajj House, Level One, and Fusion d'Afrique became almost empty, most of the nonmedical organisations started quitting the country, leaving their programs partially implemented, and in little groups as expatriates, we tried our best to maintain our social life in our apartments by inviting friends exclusively internationals, even though our gestures and greetings were restricted to nonphysical contact policy. Shaking hands was perceived as having unprotected sex with a stranger. And the hyper-vigilance and rumours had already crept into the relationship of the expatriate community with the local Liberians, creating an iron wall that was growing wider and longer every single day such as walking pillar walls in Gaza and the West Bank constructed by Israelites. In welcoming, instead of trying the usual handshake that most of us could not do properly, meeting a Liberian for any reason became a moment of fear followed by somatic reactions. When things were turning gray in terms of expatriate and local relationships, on 20 July 2014, a Liberian-American, Patrick Sawyer, flew from Monrovia to Lagos. He had severe symptoms of Ebola upon arrival to Nigeria and died after a few days. As it happens always, rumours started spreading about Patrick Sawyer, that he came to Liberia to attend to his sister who was sick with Ebola in John F Kennedy Hospital in Monrovia, where there was an isolated ward for EVD patients, and then knowing that he was infected with EVD, left to Nigeria. Apparently, on 9 July 2014, he had informed the management that he had been exposed to the Ebola virus. They had referred his case to the Liberian Ministry of Health for observation. They had requested that he not return to the offices for twenty-eight days. However, Sawyer had utilised an upcoming conference in Calabar, Nigeria, to petition the Liberian Finance Ministry to attend as an 'ambassador'. His departure had been approved even-though he had been enlisted as an EVD contact. The Liberian government apologised for the lack of communication between offices and for not listing Sawyer's name at the airport; nonetheless, the Sawyer's case concreted the prejudice of the international community in Liberia about the dishonesty of Liberians. Rumours flew to all directions, faster than lightening, that Sawyer threw $100 notes with his blood on them, to the crowd, in order to infect the others, and it was common to hear expatriates cursing Liberians as a result of fear of being infected. 'They want others to go with them, they do not want to die alone,' was one of the hundreds of things I heard about them. On 6 of August, the first confirmed Ebola case was reported from Nigeria, a Nigerian national, the nurse who attended Sawyer, and a few more cases followed, intensifying the detestation that everyone was mastering towards Liberians. On 30 September 2014, the United States Centers for Disease Control and Prevention declared its first case of Ebola virus disease. Another Liberian, Thomas Eric Duncan, became infected in Liberia and travelled to Texas on 20 September. On 26 September, he fell ill and sought medical treatment but was sent home with antibiotics. He returned to the hospital by ambulance on 28 September and was placed in isolation and tested for Ebola. Thomas Duncan passed away on 8 October. Two additional cases stemmed from Thomas Eric Duncan, when two nurses that had treated him tested positive for Ebola on October, persuading a number of states to impose travel bans to those who were coming from West Africa.

A country that was not familiar to many people from other parts of world quickly attracted the attention of the rest of the world with cases of Ebola. 'Le mot clé' for all media channels like BBC, CNN, Al Jazeera remained Ebola followed by names 'Liberia, Sierra Leone, Guinea', along with scary photos of health workers in personal protection gears, dead bodies left alone along the roads, burial teams in PPEs carrying sealed dead bodies as if people are dying on the roads every five minutes. The local media of many countries with no much profound understanding of what really the outbreak looked like often selected the scariest and most dreadful clips or photos with exaggerated stories as if Ebola would eradicate the total population from West Africa, creating a perceptual set for the rest of world that West Africans are viruses, not human beings, while some media linked the epidemic with the end of the world, giving it a spiritual outlook.

It was a Saturday, 16 August 2014, I was driving from Hotel Africa, towards the mission headquarters, which is around a twenty-five-kilometre drive but due to unpredictable traffic conditions, no one on earth can give a time of return, as most of the time, old American-made prime movers which are not fit for running on roads either broke down in the middle of the road or fall upside down with container boxes blocking the circulation of the road, which would take hours to be removed, or else a slight rain can make some parts of the road nearly impassable on top of which broken yellow machines slow down the traffic as the rest of the vehicles have to wait till they are pushed aside from the road. The moment I reached the area called Bushrod Island, which is near the famous bridge on river Doe that was a landmark of the Liberian civil war where a lot of fighting broke out which connects the so-called industrial suburbs and the main city, the circulation had already become immobile, which is usual often, but the presence of United Nations Formed Police Unit from Jordan and Liberian National Police Riot Control Units made me think otherwise, but I did not expect the news which was waiting for us with the dusk: 'An angry mob had attacked the Ebola quarantine centre in West Point and patients have escaped.' What I heard reminded me of a local proverb in Sri Lanka: 'As the bull attacked the man who fell down from the tree.' At the very peak of the outbreak that had already claimed over 700 lives, infecting more than another 1,300, the attack of the Ebola isolation centre in West Point community was a clear sign that the epidemic will soon turn into an unprecedented epidemic. Some predicted that there is a probability for a civil unrest to breakout in following days.

'All patients who ran away had Ebola,' Sam Collins, Liberian National Police spokesman, said to the media.

'It was an attack from people afraid of Ebola,' Collins added. 'Everybody is afraid of Ebola.'

But later on, I learnt different versions about the motivation behind the attack on West Point assault in local media yet the reliable sources confirmed that the assault was followed by looting of commodities in the isolation centre established in West Point. If the mob is caused by perceived fear of existence of an Ebola isolation centre, in a densely populated sum, what on earth made them think of looting the mattresses, clothes, and equipment used by and for the EVD suspected cases in the centre, knowing that it was an act of suicide.

By late October, the epidemic in Sierra Leone turned to worse instead of improving the situation; the forced quarantine efforts of the government of Sierra Leone using their military capacity worsened the situation, and unlike other countries affected by the deadly epidemic, from every single administrative district of Sierra Leone, cases were reported while the index cases of Ebola in Mali, and then Senegal were reported followed by one case in Spain and another in the United States, a medical doctor who worked in Liberia, not a contact of Sawyers case, breaking regional frontiers and was in a process of invading the whole world. On 8 August 2014, the World Health Organization declared the outbreak a public health emergency of international concern and many more countries imposed travel restrictions and bans to those who come from West Africa. Some countries like the Philippines called all their citizens employed in West Africa to return on immediate effect, and those who returned were kept in a quarantined island for twenty-one days before granting entry to the country; as a result, over 200 uniformed personnel from the Philippines, deployed in United Nations Mission in Liberia, were pulled out abruptly, creating a significant vacuum in security in the mission area. Even though there was a parallel nonconnected outbreak going on in the Democratic Republic of Congo, those who came from West Africa were quarantined for three weeks, and Kenya followed more restricted rules, banning anyone, except Kenyans, to travel to Kenya from affected territories. Only Brussels Airline and United Nations Charter Flight were flying out of Monrovia, and many flights including Air France, Delta

Airline British Air lines, Kenyan Air Ways, stopped completely their regular flight to affected territories, transforming the whole region to a quarantined zone. Even if one travels with any of the available flights, even though making a reservation was almost impossible as everyone was fighting for a few available flights, one had to go through a process of screening, first obtaining the Ebola clearance certificate from the United Nations Clinic, forty eight hours before the departure and a series of temperature checking at the entrance to the airport, before departure, at arrival in Ghana, and so on. In case of a slight fever and cold, the whole plan of travelling will be messed and end up in a quarantine centre for twenty-one days in an unknown country, instead of travelling. My plan to travel to Casablanca and Marrakech for my rest and recuperation was messed up with cancellation of flights; I was just one among thousands of people who got stuck in the snare of Ebola in Liberia, Sierra Leone, and Guinea.

'A dead body is left on the road for two days,' I heard in the parking lot, someone was telling, though it was the kind of news that we started hearing from time to time, after the outbreak aggravated. Even though free hotline numbers were designated by every single cellular service provider in the country, the time to reach out to some destination can vary from hours to days, hence it was common to hear that bodies were found decomposing in the communities, sometimes by roadside. The dreadful image of dead bodies that are infected with the virulent, highly contagious deadly Ebola virus, being decomposed in open places when pouring rain falls throughout the day washing the dead bodies and flooding the town where a great majority of urban population live in urban ghettos or slums that are directly affected by flash floods caused by rains on a daily basis. With every little incident, a dark cloud of rumours covered the whole country, provoking people to violent acts and creating an environment of hostility and mistrust. 'People use body parts of Ebola patients to avenge their enemies' was one of the hottest gossips of the month, probably of the week as even before the rumours cooled down, another one followed—that was the trend. As the information flow was not always efficient and the information is not always complete, there were so much of gaps to be filled with the people who were in the chain of rumours; as a result, when they reach the international community, they were miles away from reality. However, Liberian, Guinean, and Leonean local newspapers repetitively scrambled to grab the hottest news which could be the most marketable, irrespective of what was the probable consequence of the release of nonclarified information, whereas from one hand, the governments and the humanitarian community, along with the UN and the international community, tried their best to disseminate the message of prevention through all available media at their reach. It was like the fight between evil and good spirit, in African understanding, that sensations and thriller induced by rumours retained more marketable than the message of fighting the epidemic, although, as time passed, the public acquired the behavioural changes that were repetitively disseminated to fight the further spread, which later on contributed to contain the outbreak.

Liberia had only seventy doctors for its 4.3 million population, with poor health infrastructure; Sierra Leone and Guinea, too, did not have any better conditions. With the progress of the outbreak, many health practitioners became the initial victims, among whom, many were nurses and doctors, which enormously had a negative impact on the battle against Ebola as most of the medical facilities were closed, and whoever had symptoms similar to Ebola, shared by most of the viral and parasitic fevers in the region, were sent to isolation facilities. Many people died with easily curable diseases like malaria or any other illness as they chose to self-medicate due to the fear of being sent to an isolation facility, stigma, or else unable to access necessary medical aid. Ebola had taken the local population into its grip tightly in all affected areas and was creeping into international community, especially those who work in developmental agencies and humanitarian organisations. A 33-year-old American medical doctor contracted Ebola in Liberia, while he was working in one of the few ETUs that Liberia had at the beginning of the outbreak. Dr Rick Sacra was the first international humanitarian to be infected in Liberia, whereas there were two cases reported from Guinea, including a volunteer. After the bad news for the expatriate community was delivered, that Dr Rick had been medically evacuated to the USA, following up on his condition, whether it was a progress or deterioration, became a daily ritual of expatriates. The place where they used to talk about their sexual adventures or thematic discussions with complicated humanitarian technical jargons while sipping some alcohol transformed to a dining table of hospital workers; they talked only about Ebola, the condition of Rick, and finally, about the prevention and thoughts of leaving the country. But one part of most of us was with the affected population because of our consciousness as human beings to support others when in need; nonetheless, dealing with fear and paranoia was never easy.

My position in the United Nations mission as a staff counsellor and my temporary affiliation with Unicef for psychosocial support to the Ministry of Health and the staff became overwhelmingly demanding like never before, which made me nearly burnt out, as while dealing with my own fears and concerns, while living in the affected area with the affected people, working with them directly on a daily basis, my job demand on providing psychosocial support for UN and the affiliated staff who go through the same situation in diverse levels, starting from local staff who were probable contacts, who lost their loved ones because of Ebola, and international staff who undergo intense reactions of fear, paranoia, and phobia, deprived my peacefulness from me. Instead of being empathetic, as it should have been, I started losing my tolerance. 'I dreamt to come to Africa, I wanted to follow the footsteps of the free-time stories but I did not dream of living in isolation, stuck in a zone where a highly contagious, deadly disease attacks everyone as a rabid dog,' I told my sister on Skype as she was the only one who would look at the situation pragmatically without immature emotional response, but I never thought the moment I never expected would come to me in two days after the Skype call made to my sister.

Everyone considered Pan-African Plaza, eleven-storied building owned by family members of late Mohoman Gadafi, which is the headquarters of United Nations Mission in Liberia, as the Malbork Castle in West Africa and there is no chance of Ebola to creep under the security gates with laser detectors or jump over the high walls with barbaed wires. But within the mission, in silence and obscurity, there were a few cases kept as classified information, among those one was a Nigerian peacekeeper and others were locals. All cases were kept top secrets for some time; not too long, not even forty-eight hours passed, the local newspapers started a firework show with the incidents, adding their own colours to each case. 'UN is no longer safe in Liberia,' a heading was about one case of a Liberian national staff who died after contracting Ebola. The interaction between nationals and internationals kept on detaching significantly. It was a shame to mention that many times I was hesitating to give a lift to my national colleagues as I did not know with whom they have contacts and I knew that they were not truthful too therefore the national staff were seen as biological weapons. When the red lines were being drawn between national staff and international staff within the UN, my neighbour in the office, who was the lab technician for the level 2 clinic in the mission, believed to have been contracted Ebola by an attempt in drawing blood from a national staff who a suspected case who was a national staff.

Abu-Fadel and I shared the same working space, in the level 2 clinic of the United Nations Logistical base of Liberia for almost two years and we used to spend our free time together chatting about different topics as they pop up. The day before he was hospitalised, I saw him in the cafeteria and offered him a double espresso as he loved it, being a Sudanese. We talked about his French classes and he wanted to review some lessons with me. 'Probably next weekend,' I told him. Next day morning, my mobile set brought me the worst news I had heard after my father's passing. It was chief-medical who rang me in by six thirty, that Abu-Fadel had manifested signs and symptoms of EVD and was just admitted to the Ebola Treatment Unit of Doctors without borders MSF. Before feeling anything about him, I felt the next would be me but my job was to prepare him psychologically for his treatments in the local treatment centre till he would be sent on medical evacuation to Germany. But I remained clueless for a moment that I was unable to recall how long, when I came back to reality I heard still he was talking from the other end, the phone was on call all this time. I quickly hung up the phone and decided to call 9000, the emergency number that I had contacts with him so that I would be monitored. As per their assessment as I did not have any physical contact, I was not in the quarantine list. But around seven traced contacts were quarantined. It was the time my emotions entirely controlled my whole life.

It was around 8.30 a.m., just after two hours of his hospitalisation, on the same day I rang his number. Instead of his usual try in speaking in French with me that he always used to do, he said, 'Hello, good morning.' One thing in life that we cannot hide is the changes of our voice that mirror our emotions. He tried his best to sound positive, being a health professional, but the human being within him did not hide at all to demonstrate what he was going through. 'I'm doing fine, day after tomorrow I will be medically evacuated to Germany, Inshallah, everything will be okay,' he told me, trying to hide his distortions burning him like a wildfire within him. After a couple of minutes of silence, his voice suddenly turned to be normal, which is a tone of a weep, a normal reaction to the abnormal situation that he was living in. It was, however, good that he sounded a bit hopeful as it would help him to hold on till he reaches Germany for better care and treatment. He sounded that he had not given up. But my sense of empathy clued me that there were intense emotions suppressed in this man.

'I do not know what to say to my children, there are eight of them, do not know who will feed those mouths.' He melted.

'My boss is responsible for this, I was not ready to draw blood from that lady, but I was forced.'

He did not sound angry or complaining, those were purely words composed out of hopelessness and helplessness, but it was obvious that he did not expect to be sympathised.

Abu-Fadel's last day in MSF Ebola Treatment Centre, he was about to fly to Germany in two hours, I rang in. 'How are you? Are you all set?' He replied with a short reply, 'Okay,' as if he did not have much time in life. And I dared not say 'Aurevoir' as I used to every afternoon.

Abu-Fadel was a volunteer, a very soft personality, respectful, very tolerant, and bit weak in putting his ideas across the table or to confront the wrong, and as a result, one of his supervisors asked him to draw blood from the female national staff whose symptoms were evidently EVD, which sounded not ethical as there were no single staff by that time who was specialised in handling EVD patients. As a result of someone's autocratic behaviour mixed with his weakness, thousands of dreams he brought from the burning sands from Sudan were shattered into dust and diluted into the ruthless waters in Western Africa, when we learnt from CNN: 'The UN personnel under EVD treatment in Germany died.' Prior to official correspondences announcing his tragic untimely, autocracy-induced death, most of us learnt in and out about it via global media and the e-mails started flying up and down coping to everyone, expressing their anger against the organisation and the individuals, grievances, and fear. To the expat community outside of UN, it was a hot and dreadful news as the illusion was that UN's internationals would remain magically untouched by Ebola.

Today, he has become history, remaining in the statistics of the 2014 Ebola outbreak in West Africa; maybe in narrative parts of some reports, his name 'Abu-Fadel' and country 'Sudan' have appeared, but the family had lost his warmth and care for the rest of time. The death is a death caused by Ebola and some would consider it as an occupational hazard, but I would call it homicide as no one has right to force someone to do something that the individual refuses because of risk to life associated with the action. However, after some time, the heat of the event cooled down, fading the memories of Abu-Fadel from everyone's minds, and everyone started focusing on themselves and work, while hand-washing and temperature-taking were going on, reminding me of the famous poem 'Out Out' by Robert Frost:

'No more to build on there, And they, since they,

Were not the one dead, turned to their affairs'

That was the third moment the thought of urging me to quit the continent started to push me. Nonetheless, my wife arrived to Liberia with another wing of United Nations, who gave me some stamina to continue till my mission is over, but every second was charged with intense fear which impaired my daily functioning in my job and social life.

The outbreak started taking its grip on new counties in Liberia, and generally all over Sierra Leone while the disease was still dominating over Guinea. Though UN was late as always, United Nations Mission for Emergency Ebola Response, UNMEER, had already been operational from Ghana with its sub-offices in Sierra Leone, Liberia, and Guinea, which increased the momentum of the ongoing EVD control and prevention operations. Over 3,000 American troops came to Liberia, with their logistical and medical support, establishing a huge military logistical base near Robert's International Airport with the heavy-duty helicopters and trucks. But there were no significant development in the government-owned health infrastructure; instead, the respective governments became more and more dependent on the international community. MSF, USAID, and Red Cross enormously contributed fighting Ebola out of the region, and despite all the challenges from top governmental level to grassroots level, there was a significant progress, but the outbreak remained unprecedented. While things were calming down slowly 'small small' as Liberians do say, another case was reported in the mission; it was in Pan-African Plaza where every big shot of the mission was based. Flomo, a national staff who worked with 'internal-courrier' service, by nature of his job, he used to visit every single office of the mission. Rumours started breaking the silence, like a battle, the most disastrous weapon ensures one's length of survival; everyone was busy in concocting the hottest version of Flomo's story. 'He had come to the clinic, collapsed bleeding and he had brought his passport with him expecting him to be medically evacuated.' That remained at the number one position of the rumour hit list in Monrovia. Even though the Liberian's credibility and truthfulness are always questionable, and they had already created a well-known identity in being extremely opportunistic, the likelihood of a seriously ill person planning his medical evacuation at such a stage is hard to imagine, but people by their nature enjoy the thrill of rumours and eventually ended up circulating disinformation. Flomo was admitted to a local ETU, and he won the battle at last being the only Ebola survivor among those who were infected in UNMIL. He got it at right time, rather than saying he was luckier than the others, as he came on time and referred to the ETU on time, but after coming back from ETU, his time turned to be tougher than he ever imagined. The post-Ebola life of Flomo demanded a lot of adaptation in physical, psychological, and social aspects of life. His own family members were scared of his return; his neighbours and relatives behaved as if they did not want him to return; his colleagues did not want to share the bathroom in the office with him. He decided to change his residence and rented a room in the other end of town, but he was still a subject of fear in the office. The stigma remained the main challenge for Ebola survivors, especially in the process of reintegrating them into the society. Taking the scientifically proven facts into consideration, that the Ebola virus remains in semen for seven to twelve weeks, probably more in some cases, there is always a possibility that one can contract Ebola through a survivor; however, when the certain behaviour of people cannot be controlled by the public law, and people are not trustworthy, or honest, the release a survivor can be considered a risk. Due to the fear of death, it is natural that people fear the returnees of ETUs. In addition, there were cases that contracted Ebola through sexual intercourse with survivors, hence to fight with stigma and its impact on social reintegration of survivors. However, the efforts of the international nongovernmental organisation and the government of Liberia, along with UN, were able to over-sensitize Liberia's urban population at a significant extent even though the rural population remained stuck to their traditional beliefs, as a consequence, the outbreak diverted its spreading path from the capital Monrovia to isolated communities in counties like River Cess and Grand Gedeh, whereas in Sierra Leone and Guinea, traditional barriers minimised the impact of flight against the disease.

Like in times of war, the curfew and woe rained on the Christmas day, 24–25th night's services we held but according to Ebola rules, first time in their lives, these three nations celebrated a chlorinated Christmas, the mass was not about the usual God business for prosperity, happiness, and so on as pastors, priests, fathers, and brothers used to preach for last decade; this time, all prayers were pronounced loud and gospels and carols were sung aloud to reach the very end of the heavens, until the all -mighty wake up from the holly sleep he had been fallen for last nine months but no one understood that they had created an open space of the disease to spread by gathering thousands of people in condensed church halls. They believed that their prayers would be answered one day, but they did not know when and how and they did not realise the human potential in preventing disease, rather they waited till God comes down with his magical weapon against Ebola.

After tens of thousands of deaths, and over 10,600 cases, the outbreak was contained in Liberia as in 30 April 2015, Liberia was about to be declared Ebola free, not by the grace of God but by the immense efforts of the international community along with some realistic and committed Liberians who had the genuine attitude of helping the nation, and after almost thirty-nine days, a new case was repeated, it was suspected as a sexually transmitted case, and then again another case, a female, most probably another victim of a male survivor whose uncontrollable urge and opportunistic attitude sent the woman a few feet down under the earth. Sierra Leone and Guinea still remained red lighted.

On 9 May 2015, Liberia was declared as Ebola free, and I remember I felt a great consolation, I was with my wife near the ocean after a long walk in the beach, once a busy place with locals, now haunted and isolated due to Ebola, and told her that the beach will be again dirty and noisy as if the time of Ebola had brought tranquillity to the surrounding, but it was indeed not calmness, it was the sign of death, fear, and isolation. Tomorrow on music, dances, and club beer will be on the beach, girls will roam around again in search for their hunt for the night, and most probably the suppressed lives of international colleagues will come to an end. And they will forget that Ebola can be sexually transmitted till some time after recovery. I heard that people were thanking God for making Liberia Ebola free—not MSF, UNMEER, Samaritan Purse, Red Cross, American Troops, or thousands of other organisations and individuals who risked their lives to bring hope to this God-fearing nation. I started thinking whether there is no space for human persons in Liberian hearts; it was fully conquered by the God.

Life became normal, most of the Ebola treatment units, ETUs, were winded down and many operations pulled out, including UNMEER, assuming that the country had built its capacity to respond effectively and contain another wave in case. Shops started to open as they used to, people started going to restaurants, expatriate hotspots started being vibrant especially on Friday and Saturday nights, and people started their usual jigi-jigi (*Liberian term for making love*) business. Yet some people assumed, and also rumours started spreading, that there were still cases though the government of Liberia did not want to disclose, which kept some people away from risk-taking behaviours. Sometimes rumours do have a positive impact on society.

In most of the places, the chlorine bucket was removed and the watchman and the guy with thermo-gun had apparently lost their jobs. The fauceted-bucket sellers had either returned home with the leftovers or might have gone for some other products, as often the street vendors change the type of things they sell as per the demand or else as per availability. But in most of the Lebanese-owned supermarkets, the procedures had not been eliminated; the bucket and the guys were still there even though their life became tougher as customers started resisting hand washing and being exposed to infrared thermo-gun, insisting that there was no more Ebola. The transformation that was taking place for over one year was facing its reverse effect; it seemed that in the whole society, every individual had gone through a complete change in life and the process of reversing would also take some time, a lot of effort, and energy.

The monsoon rains in West Africa started a bit late in 2015; by mid-June, the rains started falling at night, over the galvanised roofing sheets as if the skies were falling on the head. Many people tried to make associations with the rain as the main cause of the second wave of Ebola in 2014, predicting that there would be a third wave in 2015. One or two rumours about new cases in capital Monrovia started flying around but they did not last long as there was no confirmed information. Everyone had a second thought but we all were positive and content that Liberia had at last overcome the most challenging hurdle that they encountered after the brutal civil war. I was happy that I did not escape during the time when the people were in need, and looking back to my Ebola psychosocial interventions with UNMIL, UNMEER, and Unicef, I was wrapped with a feeling of satisfaction, inner reward, that no words would be able to explain. But unfortunately, the neighbouring countries were still in struggle in which the end remained in obscurity, but there would be a bright ray of hope at the end of darkness. It was a hope and a wish that everyone, all over the world had.

Ebola conquered every single piece of life in affected countries—economic, social, political, and educational—growing beyond the frontiers of an unprecedented epidemic, ending up being a global humanitarian crisis that was beyond the collective capacity of humanitarian organisations, UN agencies, especially WHO, and contributing and host governments. The epidemic first stroke the health system, eradicating several doctors and nurses from already poor health care systems, affected by poverty, conflicts, and corruption in addition to lack of human resources. At one point, most of the hospitals and clinics became totally dysfunctional and inaccessible to the patients just because of usability of handling Ebola cases, and due to that fact many people died with easily curable diseases as they were deprived from medication. Today, Liberia itself has lost more than fifty nurses and twenty doctors among a total fifty doctors that they had for the whole nation. Only one foreign doctor is left in John F Kennedy

Hospital which is the central hospital of the country, who is a 73-year-old Sri Lankan called Dr Kanagasami, who was recently decorated by Ellen Johnson Sirleaf, the president of the Republic of Liberia for his service especially during the time of Ebola. But logistically and technically, the capacity of the local heath care system has been built grace to foreign interventions during the time of Ebola.

Though it was unusual in many parts of the world, it was a common site to see men and women, who were around twenty years, sometimes forty years, to go to primary school in Liberia and Sierra Leone due to the fact that decades-long civil conflicts usurped their school life at right age. It should be appreciated and recognised their efforts of getting some sort of education to be able to overcome the challenges that they face as a nation. Sometimes, I had met a father, mother, and children in the same class, which might be a shocking site for someone who doesn't have a clue of what they had gone through, but indeed, they just started to make their best efforts to bounce back to normal life. They did not have the luxury of getting systematic education parallel to their chronological age but they were more than happy to go to school, day and night, to learn something that would bring their living standards a bit up. But the happiness did not remain for a long time. A nation with 85 per cent illiteracy was just about to see a light of hope at the horizon to overcome its main challenge and an eclipse of Ebola swallowed the light in no time for a time that no one knows. Schools were closed and teachers lost their jobs; some searched for alternative employment and the luckiest found places in nongovernmental organisations as social mobilisers, which gave them an opportunity to use their skills in another domain while earning something and contributing to the fight with Ebola. Though the schools were open in the second quarter of 2015 after the epidemic was contained, a lot of children had been dropped out either because of finances or being orphans as both parents had died of Ebola or they themselves had left this world, and the teachers had got better options with better salaries with NGOs or some of them had been taken by the burial teams, the schools were never like before; the enthusiasm for education had escaped from the back door and disappeared somewhere in the horizon. Many classes had empty chairs and desks where the same name will never be written again and some familiar letters on the blackboards of some classes will never be seen again, the most loved or hated teacher would never return to class.

A lot of airlines pulled out from the zone followed by closing down of their country offices, then many companies shut down their operations and pulled their investments from the region; as a result, hundreds of thousands of the poor population not only lost their jobs but also lost their only means of survival. We were hinted by many sources about a potential price increase of all necessary commodities as the stocks of food and other stuff got stuck in the ports. The opening time for shops was restricted due to imposed curfew to minimise the interaction of people; the economy of affected countries struggled like a fish taken out of water, taking especially Liberia and Sierra Leone back to their times of civil conflicts. It was visible that life will never be the same for next few years; three nations had been left with Ebola orphans instead child soldiers left with them during time of war. Today, instead of physical scars of mutilation that everyone could see either in Freetown or in Monrovia, there are thousands of mental scars to heal, it is a collective responsibility that has to be initiated by host countries and supported by the international community. Scars of Ebola would remain for decades, maybe for centuries, as a part of history not only of West Africa but also of the whole world.

When you ask an old person in most of the places in West Africa, they would reply, 'it was in time of famine' or 'in time of white man' or refer to any other significant event in history that they are able to make an association with time. One day, the descendants of our generations would hear, 'It was in the time of Ebola', as it had become a significant part of Liberian history today, but for Guinea and Sierra Leone, it was their future. Nonetheless, the authorities of Liberia decided to open borders with their neighbours under strict measures and conditions in order to cushion up the economy, but it was seen by many of us as lack of foresight. We unconsciously anticipated a bad news soon, though it was not our expectation.

It was a fresh Tuesday morning, 30 June 2015, the sun had appeared after a couple of rainy days; I did not know that a bad news was about to be unfolded in my inbox. 'A new Ebola case is reported in Liberia' the theme of the mail just dragged the cursor towards it without my knowledge. After a few minutes, the cycle of rumours started circulating with hundred different background stories but many of us were positive about the remaining international interventions that are quite sufficient to stop the new case to be the beginning of the third waver, that would usurp parents from children and children from parents, husbands from wives, wives from husbands, sisters from bothers, and brothers from sisters, eradicating a few more thousands from the nation.

I took my old notebook, searched for the old drawing of an African map, which I did decades ago, and spotted the Ebola region and marked 4,808 in Liberia, 2,507 in Guinea, and 3,947 Sierra Leone, Nigeria 08, Mali 06, as at 1 July 2015, over 11,000 lives have been sent to the hands of death by an unseen devil even African voodoo cannot control, like never before, and there is no guarantee that the devil would not return; the future has become more uncertain than ever. Life will not be the same as it used to be for centuries. A mango or an almond fruit left by a bat in the compound of Palawa huts will be a prohibited fruit; the taste of a piece of unspecified bushmeat would be merely a memory, a memory just as those who had gone with Ebola, time will never walk backwards.

While packing my luggage for my vacations, I recollected the very moment that I heard about Ebola, it was a thrilling story, as thrilling as it is real and I witnessed the imaginary bleeding zombies in reality even though I did not think that story would ever be a part of my real-time experience in Africa.

Chapter 20

THE JOURNEY OF NO RETURN

THE DAY I WAS travelling to Africa, I updated my Facebook status. 'Here I come, my beloved continent of Obscurity,' on one hand, I guess it was rather out of excitement induced by the feeling of achievement than calling it 'continent of Obscurity' consciously. It was a long-lived dream that had come true, through constant struggles of getting there over decades. On the other hand, I had already been fed with various information that had already created a perceptual set of 'Obscurity' about Africa, which was just like my reading glasses through which I saw the continent before my foot hit the red soil and burning sands of Africa. Continent of 'Obscurity' in terms of racial classification, isolation, or disconnectedness with the part of world where I lived, development and social issues that Africa was experiencing or in clearer language that the media often talked about had a significant portion with what I initially visualised as 'continent of darkness or obscurity'. Nonetheless, the day I landed in Nairobi, Kenya, on 18 February 2011, my preset perception was challenged at the very entry to the continent and many more times during my journeys across the continent, from East to West and North to South.

As a result, I gradually unlearnt the old learning and attitudes acquired prior to my arrival and tried my best to look neutrally at the part of the world where I spent half a decade while travelling, working, meeting people, discovering cultures and lifestyles, feeling the touch of untouched nature, and living in conflicts and humanitarian crisis that the population lived in, which is a considerable proportion of my life not only dedicated to peace and development of the continent but also principally to follow the paths of 'free-time stories' of my father that were my primary and very first contact with Africa and motivational factor to visit Africa one day. It was an act of trying to look behind the lens of 'Obscurity' which was 'perceptual set' or 'prejudice' and overcome deep-rooted attitudes developed over decades and make an attempt to comprehend the reality in its own form. The transformation that the time brought was inevitable with no exception to my case, shaping my core beliefs, attitudes, and behaviours, with each interaction with humans and the environment in the continent, sometimes erasing pre-existing stereotypes, perceptual sets, and attitudes; sometimes enforcing and reinforcing them; and sometimes replacing them with new ones. When I reached Addis Ababa, which was my gateway to exit, on a sunny Saturday, in March, I was no longer the same person who entered the 'continent of obscurity' five years ago, just like Africa itself that had transformed into a different world for the last semi-decade, while once peaceful Mali turned to be a battlefield, long-existing Timbuktu fell on barren lands just leaving valueless pieces of clay debris, Gadhafi's dream of United Africa was buried alive brutally by dream of western type of democracy which could not breath dry air in north Africa. For the second time, United Nations came to Bangui shortly after ending its first mission leaving a question before the world whether the peace had ever been built, M23 invaded Goma and disappeared in the air after a few months, reminding United Nations and the Western World that The Great Lakes conflict has not yet ended, the Nobel laureate, anti-apartheid, South African icon Nelson Mandela leaves the living and xenophobic terror lifts its head in South Africa, leaving a doubt about sustainability of political solutions for conflict resolution. Expected positivity by the division of Sudan into two vanished in the dry air across Sahara, leaving another newly formed national state in absolute impunity. Once safe, Kenya became a playground of Al-Shahab, reminding me of

LTTE attacks in border villages in Sri Lanka during thirty years of ethnic conflict; Burundi, a part of the story of Rwandan genocide in 1994, seems to have forgotten its bleeding history; Tunisia, once a safe and cheap heaven at soul-calming Mediterranean sea, has already turned to a death trap for tourists, while Muslim brotherhood burning down the churches in Egypt, one would doubt that the next generation would be able to see a pyramid; Islamic State extremism has already conquered the Sahel and penetrating the deep rainforests of Sub-Saharan Africa with its different faces like Boku-Haram in Nigeria, Death of Cecil, a Lion in Hwange national park in Zimbabwe which was hunted down by Walter James Palmer, an American leisure hunter, a dentist made the whole world forget not only about millions of animal poachers in Africa but also the Syrian crisis for a few weeks, and the Ebola epidemic in West Africa, once limited to minor outbreaks in Central African region, especially in Democratic Republic of Congo formerly known as Zaire, penetrated West Africa where it had never been found among humans ended up as a global humanitarian crisis with its unprecedented epidemic in 2014 devouring more than 10,000 lives within less than twelve months, and I had been following the footsteps of my father's 'free-time stories' in the mist of the dynamics that occur in utter 'obscurity', I had already developed my own ways of looking at Africa, ready to take them out of the continent from Addis, where I was supposed to fly away from the continent, which looked like a 'gate of no return' in Cape Coast for me because of the fact that I had witnessed a rapidly changing Africa that was not heading nowhere in a positive direction which rather pushed me through a Gate of No Return than trying in vain for making a change of which there was not a clue at its horizons.

Infested with thousands of nongovernmental organisations, known as 'Humanitarian Vultures' who rather focus on implementing programs merely to satisfy the donors' interests than addressing the real needs on the ground, which leads the ways to changing of regimes, power shifts, and also for sustaining the conflicts such as in the Great Lakes region and many more complexities such as creating dependency syndrome, further divisions in communities or groups, and so on, have significantly hindered the possibilities and probabilities of development in many places in Africa. Especially when it comes to access to aid, which should be based on nondiscrimination as per the basic humanitarian principles and standards, it is openly violated by many aid organisations converting the recovery into secondary catastrophes. On top of that, some African leaders are rather aggressive towards the West than investing their knowledge and time in filtering what they really want to get from the other side of the world to push their countries towards sustainable development. They prefer short-term and immediate personal gains to the national interests and long-term developmental goals and projects which do not have a 'piece of cake' for their family, even though there are sustaining impacts on growth of country's economy. Another group of so-called African leaders have embraced the West tighter than the healthy proximity and have just become the puppets who dance according to the beats that the West plays which is also not what Africa needs but the leaders want. As a result, Pan-Africanism seems a superficial blanket that the leadership of member countries wear to protect themselves from the general public who suffer from the policies and the deals that their leaders make and the level of corruption that they do for maintaining their luxurious life. In such an extremely hypocrite and controversial environment I could not take the 'common typical African explanation' that the west creates complexities in the continent to exploit the enormous deposits of fossilised resources. Nonetheless, it is obvious that the West has its interests and reaches them via the local leadership and sometimes interfering with existing rebel groups for overthrowing regimes that deny their cooperation or even direct intervention like in Libya, Central Africa, and Ivory Coast. But the bottom line is that there should be a considerable number of people from the ruling end or opposite end who embrace the strangers against their own people who most probably are motivated by direct or indirect personal gains or secondary gains. Therefore, I simply did not digest the idea of 'West' that creates problems in Africa in its raw sense, but it's Africans who cater the Western interests against their own kind, which is pretty similar to slavery, 'Obscure history' in Africa, a journey that is through absolute 'obscurity', from 'obscurity' towards 'obscurity'.

While the 'West' is having its own interests in Africa, the dependency syndrome, lack of willingness to work towards collective growth rather than individual gains, and embracing anything without analysing the long-term impact on the continent and its people, have created an enormous space for the 'West' to play their geopolitical games and exploit not only the resources but also decide the direction where the continent is heading, which could be seen as a form of an 'acquired imperialism' which is diplomatically and politically embraced and there is no logic or probably a right for complaining that the 'West' is exploiting Africa. In 'free-time stories', I heard many times the 'colonies' in Africa, 'African slaves' to which I reacted 'poor Africans', 'innocent people' as per what I understood as a child, decades ago. The day I saw the Pulitzer prize winning photo taken by South African photographer Kevin Carter in Darfur, Sudan, 'The Vulture and the Child', I simply broke into tears, by human sympathy and sensitivity to human suffering, but without really looking at the causes and the complexity of the crisis and the underlying political, economic, and social realities involved in front line diplomacy. But today, I have to admit that the ground realities I have witnessed in Africa transformed my pre-existing hypersensitivity to suffering in Africa which I had before I had my feet on the soil of Africa, into a rational-seeking attitude even though my human compassion was not transformed into indifference, but it rather made me discover the veracity than being merely caught in waves of instant emotions and react based on a widely visible superficial content without examining the invisible underlying game playing on political interests amidst mass suffering, which I consider an eye-opening 'walking out of obscurity'.

A place of undeniable bitter truths which are typical of contemporary African realities, mostly unique to the continent, common in many parts of it, that might be rarely found in other parts on earth, such as purposely impaired human lives, mutilations of legs, arms, genitals, sexual and gender-based violence including rape followed by extremely inhumane torture, almost irreversible psychological and social impairments that last for generations such as forced prostitution, abducted children as child soldiers, that one would notice often in many parts of Africa exceed the threshold of human cruelty which in many ways traumatise not only those who encounter them as first-hand experiences but also those who witness them as a third party. I remember I was often avoiding the places where mutilated ex-rebels run after the expatriates to get some 'small-small' money in Liberia. And once in Shire, in northern Ethiopia, I visited a centre where victims of torture were held for rehabilitation, which allowed me to realise that 'devils' live nowhere else but within human beings. Stories that the victims of sexual violence in the Democratic Republic of Congo add some good weight on what I was always carrying on my head about the extent of inhumanity that was present in many parts of the continent that, one would not even believe unless seen. And finally, the rebel stories of Liberia, Sierra Leone. and ex-child soldier of Lord's Resistance Army, from Gulu, Uganda, related their stories of multiple victimisation, continuation of cycle of victimisation which is a rare story outside the continent in the contemporary world even though in the history of every single continent, there are pages written in blood, but many countries in other parts of the earth seemed to have learnt from the kind of atrocities committed in the past and take pragmatic measures to prevent repetition of such things in their territories. Germany, after the inhumane chapter of Nazism, is a classic example, which is not the only one on earth. And one would argue that Rwanda is a country which can be recognised as a country that had learnt from the 1994 genocide. But the pathetic truth is that what happened in Rwanda had spread beyond its frontiers into DRC, and Burundi with the support of the invisible hand of Rwanda. Ethnically motivated killings in Burundi in 1995 and 2015 and series of conflicts triggered in Great Lakes area, especially in DRC, are directly or indirectly supported by Rwanda based on its ethnic interests. Series of attacks on foreigners in South Africa triggered by xenophobia sent a strong message to the world audience that the lives lost and the extreme suppression and violence South Africans lived in during its fight against apartheid are limited to the pages in the history books. The value of human life in Africa has gone below the value of 'cattle' and 'goats' with which they at least pay a bride-price and the human values have gone buried in profound 'Obscurity' by either extreme competition for basic needs, endless greed for wealth, or else hunger for power, or a combination of the three of them? Or simply an immense reserve of precious resources which transform humans into bloodthirsty devils who are absolutely insensitive of the suffering of fellow human beings? If not a common racist viewpoint which emphasise that the potential for finding peaceful resolutions for human problems which is even found among Bona-boos 'we make love instead of fighting' is still far away even though the so-called process of civilisation was brought to the continent by sailing ships of colonial powers since early the fifteenth century till late nineteenth century? At one point, I came to believe that conflicts of Africa have more to do with the attitudes of its people than imposed colonial borders of present national states, or else often pronounced Western agendas to exploit resources in Africa.

I entered Africa with my own perceptions acquired and fed by external views which either grew high or melt down with my first-hand experiences, just like a journey in 'obscurity', many times without enough light on the way, uncertain about the destination, I walked through the memories of his 'free-time' stories, on burning sands, under ruthless sun, muddy paths under pouring rains, through the battlefields which reminded me of tribal wars across the lands of total impunity, passing thick impenetrable rainforests where sharp thrones plucked out my flesh, through savannahs where the theory of 'survival of the fittest' is the only rule, living in times of epidemics killing thousands of people in no time, living in social systems where the values do not match or are completely different from the value systems of the rest of world and learnt the diversity in its very sense and learnt tolerance to the fact that we all do things differently and we all have our own standards based on our own reasons as per the realities we live in. Realisation of what true African realities are made my stay easier in the continent. In most of the occasions, I truly and humbly spoke out the 'obscure' side of Africa and Africans to the their face, even though some of them followed the common reactive response of hiding behind the defence wall whereas there are many Africans who are open to experience who at least take feedbacks constructively, which hints that there will be a day that comes over to Africa, even though it might take some decades or a century, that long-persisted 'obscurity' would disappear with progressive evolution of human society.

At the end of an era of my life, a semi-decade which was dedicated to follow the traces of the 'free-time stories' of my beloved father who was the inspiration for many key achievements of my life, who was the main architect of what I am today, came to an end discovering a continent which remained closer in my dreams since the day I heard the first word about it, but many cosmic cycles far from my reality before getting my international job, I had seen the reality by my very eyes against the common stories about Africa. And I smelled, tasted, and touched the enormous potential that Africa had in store in the future even though the population in the continent who are the true owners of this land do not think beyond the horizon which is limited to its oceanic frontiers. The day my dreams have come true, the day I finished the last sentence of this book on 2 December 2015, after having visited from North to South and East to West of the continent, I realised that since the time of 'free-time stories', Africa had been transformed enormously, whether it is positive or negative, constructive or destructive, time had not given up its constant and dynamic influence on every single thing in Africa, just like I who resisted my negative thoughts that discouraged me over the decades due to the fact that I did not have sufficient means to go on my journey of dreams and finally embraced the transformation of driving a long-lived dream come true. Sometimes avoiding hurdles and sometimes confronting them, I had to make it through following either the 'dog' or the 'lion' approach, suiting to the situation, using wit at its climax as a slight mistake could have taken my life and hid it under burning sands in deserts, or in thick deep tropical forests. Just like how my dreams about the 'Continent of Obscurity' were driven true, the day that a maiden sun peeps at Africa, at its horizon, clearing the 'Obscurity', will come over. The day blindness caused by imposed religions, opportunism, greed, and corruption fell into the trench of 'Obscurity', maiden rays of light will appear in African sky, penetrating thick dense tropical forests that the rest of world believed to be 'obscure forever' and a true African smile will embrace the future. On that day on, African children would carry school bags instead of Kalashnikovs; unnerving cries of victims of sexual violence emitting to the empty air in remote villages infested by rebel groups in the Great Lakes region, bush-checkpoints where innocent people's legs and arms were cut off just like cassava roots, the stories of mutilated women whose womanhood and right to sexual pleasure are deprived, inhumane stories of torture, and endless conflicts and crises will be added to what we call 'history' that should never be repeated. And that day is the day that Africa realises that 'Obscurity' is not the skin but the attitude that determines the direction to light or darkness.

As we all live in an interconnected and interdependent globalised world where the equilibrium of our life depends on everyone else, it's us, our desires, our ambitions, interests, and actions that have brought us to the currently existing system of coexistence, competition, and concurrence where one's action has a reaction aiming at everyone, a consequence of one's action should be paid off by all, and power and the wealth shifts from one to another, changing the world's political, economic, and military concentrations and have changed the directions of the world, making global dynamics more interesting and faster than ever before. As a result of that, our pleasure has become a pain to another living in another end of the world or vice versa. One pole of the world produces weapons and the other pole uses them to kill its own people, while from the same very pole where the weapons came from, humanitarian assistance arrives under a pure white flag to the cardinal soil soaked with hot blood of the dead. The media does not count the number of dead but highlight the humanitarian assistance over and over again as if the host government is doing nothing. This is a common scenario in many conflicts, especially in Africa where local media culture has not evolved enough to fight actively against fabricated news as part of media propagandas support underlying political, economic, and other interests of third parties. For-example, the level of aggression manifested in the speech by 'ex-first lady, ex-secretary of state of the United States, democratic presidential candidate, Hilary Clinton, in Dakar, Senegal, against the Chinese who come to Africa reflects that Africa has become a battlefield of third parties, not of Africans. Africa just hosts both cold and hot battles of others at the cost of its future in all dimensions. Taking the history that every one of us is involved in building an African history which is not built at their interest or consent even though their so-called leaders had a share, the time to look at Africa differently had come. The attitudinal change should come not only from within the continent but also from the outside world. So long as we carry our obscure attitude to it, we will not help Africa to come out of its 'Obscurity'.

Nonetheless, time is the governing factor not only in our lives but also in every single thing in the universe that runs faster than anything else. Just like the day I completed my navigation through his 'free-time stories' in reality, I realised that he had disappeared in 'eternal obscurity' when I wanted to tell him about my 'footsteps in obscurity' during my journey in Africa.

At the end of the journey, when the captain announces, 'Ladies and gentlemen, we will be taking off shortly', I had come to the realisation that a childhood dream had made a life live in it for more than three decades, changing the direction of my life in all its aspects, and brought a transformation which is enormous and unbelievable.

'Please tighten your seatbelt, Sir!' It was a flight attendant who brought me back to surface of the world from the profound pensiveness where I had plunged in. I was conquered by some mixed feelings that I did not have enough psychic energy to analyse at that very moment dominated by emotions. A place where one lived for a considerable time of one's lifespan, whether it was full of pleasant, unpleasant, or mixed memories, would not allow a human being to leave without natural human feelings. I felt sad for some reason, I felt happy for some reason, I was already missing Africa for some reason, I felt hopeful for some reason, I felt uncertain for some reason, but the reason behind each feeling I did not understand. It could be natural human fear for change or I was experiencing a reverse cultural shock even before I landed in Sri Lanka. Nonetheless, 'slaves' came to my mind. They would have felt the same. When they were brutally pushed through the 'Gates of No Return' despite the fact that I knew how my destination of return looked like. It looked like a journey of no return.